Imperial Entanglements

EARLY AMERICAN STUDIES

Series editors
Daniel K. Richter, Kathleen M. Brown, Max Cavitch,
and David Waldstreicher

Exploring neglected aspects of our colonial, revolutionary,
and early national history and culture, Early American
Studies reinterprets familiar themes and events in fresh ways.
Interdisciplinary in character, and with a special emphasis
on the period from about 1600 to 1850, the series is published in
partnership with the McNeil Center for Early American Studies.

A complete list of books in the series
is available from the publisher.

Imperial Entanglements

Iroquois Change and Persistence
on the Frontiers of Empire

Gail D. MacLeitch

PENN

UNIVERSITY OF PENNSYLVANIA PRESS

PHILADELPHIA

Published by
University of Pennsylvania Press
Philadelphia, Pennsylvania 19104-4112

Printed in the United States of America
on acid-free paper

10 9 8 7 6 5 4 3 2 1

Library of Congress Cataloging-in-Publication Data
MacLeitch, Gail D.
    Imperial entanglements : Iroquois change and persistence on the frontiers of empire /
Gail D. MacLeitch.
        p. cm. — (Early American studies)
    Includes bibliographical references and index.
    ISBN 978-0-8122-4281-2 (hardcover : alk. paper)
        1. Iroquois Indians—History—18th century. 2. Iroquois Indians—Government
relations. 3. Seven Years' War, 1756–1763. 4. Indians of North America—History—
Colonial period, ca. 1600–1775. 5. British—North America—History—18th century. 6.
United States—History—Colonial period, ca. 1600–1775. I. Title.
E99.I7M24 2011
973.2—dc22

2010021151

For Nate, Daniel, and Joshua

Contents

Illustrations

Maps

Introduction

During an Anglo-Iroquois conference an Iroquois headman approached the British superintendent for Indian affairs, William Johnson, with a special request. The headman relayed to him a dream he had had in which Johnson had given him "a fine laced coat" much like the one that Johnson now wore. Johnson asked the headman if he had really dreamed this, to which the latter affirmed that he had. "Well then," the superintendent remarked, "you must have it." Understanding the significance of dreaming and appreciative of Indian etiquette, Johnson removed his coat and presented it as a gift. Delighted, the Iroquois chief left the council "crying out, who-ah! which is an expression of great satisfaction." At the next council held with the Six Nations, however, it was Johnson who approached the headman. He informed him that although "he was not accustomed to dream," since he had last met the headman in council "he had dreamed a very surprising dream." The headman was keen to learn more. "Sir William, with some hesitation, told him he had dreamed that he had given him a track of land on the Mohawk River to build a house on, and make a settlement, extending about nine miles in length along the banks." The headman had little choice but to reply to Johnson that "if he really dreamed it he should have it." But noting the discrepancy in gifts, "for he had only got a laced coat, whereas Sir William was now entitled to a large bed, on which his ancestors had frequently slept," the headman told Johnson that "he would never dream again with him."[1]

Although there is no evidential basis to this tale, which was recorded in the journal of Indian interpreter John Lang in the 1790s, it nonetheless has much to tell us about the nature of British-Iroquois relations in the late colonial period. There are in fact several versions of this story, in some of which Johnson is replaced by other colonial figures. But even if this specific exchange between an Iroquois headman and imperial officer did not occur, the type of interaction it represents certainly did. During the eighteenth century, the Iroquois Indians and British Empire converged and collaborated, and in the process one side enriched themselves at the expense of the other.

Asymmetrical forms of cultural borrowing and exchange facilitated the aggrandizement of British imperial and colonial forces in North America at the same time that they weakened the position of the Iroquois. How and why this happened is a central theme of this book.

But the story this book tells is much more complex than a straightforward narrative of European triumph over native peoples. Throughout the colonial period, the Iroquois—also known as the Haudenosaunee or Six Nations—who inhabited what is now New York State were critical actors in an imperial drama unfolding in North America. As colonists and empires fought over the land and resources of the continent, they had to contend with the impressive Iroquois Confederacy. As trading partners, military allies, physical neighbors, and claimants of much-desired western lands, the Iroquois were simply too important to be ignored. Consequently, the Haudenosaunee enjoyed substantial room to ensure that their cultural preferences informed imperial-Iroquois relations. Building on recent scholarship that demonstrates that empire was not a rigid structure imposed from above but a series of processes and negotiations shaped by various interest groups, *Imperial Entanglements* demonstrates how native peoples participated in the construction of empire.[2] Europeans adopted Iroquois diplomatic protocol, employed native methods of warfare, and engaged in the costly Indian custom of gift-giving. As a sovereign people, the Haudenosaunee refused to acquiesce to imperial directives and instead found ways to chart their own path even as their options diminished. Although Euro-Americans would eventually dominate British North America, this result should not influence how we recount the history of Anglo-Iroquois relations. For much of the century, imperial forms emanating from the core were renegotiated on the frontiers of empire with the Iroquois playing a deciding role.[3]

Given their powerful standing for much of the eighteenth century, how and why the Iroquois became entangled in progressively unequal forms of exchange becomes even more intriguing. The Haudenosaunee are already the subject of a large and impressive literature, but it is one that has been dominated by such traditional themes as politics, diplomacy, and military history. These topics are certainly of considerable interest because the original five nations of the Iroquois were a mighty political and military presence in North America. During the seventeenth century, they engaged in a series of deadly wars with their Indian neighbors, earning a reputation as a fierce, warlike people.[4] Jockeying themselves to the center of colonial Indian affairs, in the eighteenth century they participated in a succession of treaty conferences with the French and British. Loosely organized in a political confederacy, they possessed a set of diplomatic rituals and forms that impressed contemporary Europeans and modern-day scholars alike.[5] Yet to view the Iroquois in strictly political and military terms obscures other arguably more important dimensions and veils significant shifts in their historical experience.

Imperial Entanglements reconceptualizes the Iroquois experience in economic and cultural terms and highlights the Seven Years' War (1756–63) as a crucial period in their history. During the mid-eighteenth century, the Haudenosaunee became entangled within a burgeoning mercantile British Empire intent on securing commodities, markets, and territories in North America. A commercially expansive empire generated considerable demands on Iroquois land, labor, and resources, hastening their enmeshment within a market economy. Furthermore, British efforts to enlarge their economic empire gave rise to new and revised understandings of gender, race, and ethnicity. The Seven Years' War, which epitomized Britain's new commitment to a territorial empire, intensified the attunement of Iroquois economies along commercial lines. Shifting material conditions generated new pressures on Iroquois gender roles and relations and encouraged them to experiment with new and revised ethnic and racial identities. Their loss of status following the war exposed them as never before to strong ideological currents as colonial settlers, traders, soldiers, and imperial officials reformulated gendered and racial discourses of difference to legitimize their acts of conquest and expropriation. Although Iroquois ability to mediate the material and ideological structures of empire waned as the eighteenth century progressed, they continued to develop economic practices and cultural identities that preserved a degree of power. While remaining mindful of the larger imperial world that increasingly shaped the contours of Iroquois existence, this study explores the imaginative ways in which Iroquois men and women adapted to the forces of imperial and colonial expansion.

John Lang's sketch at the beginning of the chapter hints at the importance of economic themes underlying Iroquois eighteenth-century experience. Although the Indian headman in this story received a much-desired coat, he was disgruntled by his dreaming exchange with Johnson because he understood that he had lost something far more precious. Whereas the value of a coat would diminish over time, the price of land would continue to rise. Therefore the dreaming exchange had been inherently unequal. Land provided the bedrock of indigenous economic and cultural autonomy and un-

derpinned the Iroquois' status as a sovereign people. Yet a defining theme of
the eighteenth century was the steady erosion of the Iroquois land base and
the growing absorption of their labor and resources into a market economy.
Dispersed across a large region of southern, central, and western New York
and located at varying distances from colonial centers of commerce, the five
Iroquois nations confronted differing degrees of market orientation and land
loss, but for all of them economic processes and phenomena, just as much as
political events and relationships, defined their historical experience.[6]

Iroquois men and women were co-collaborators in the creation of a new
economic order in the New York hinterland. Prior to European contact, the
Iroquois subsistence economy revolved around agriculture and hunting. The
production, exchange, and consumption of goods occurred primarily within
the extended lineage, and small-scale trade took place in the noncommercial
context of gift-giving. The arrival of Europeans provoked colossal economic
change, which the Iroquois could not circumvent but could at least arbitrate.
By their own volition they adapted preexisting hunting patterns to join in a
transatlantic fur trade. They also made choices about loaning, renting, and
selling land to colonists, and they took advantage of new opportunities in
paid forms of labor. The Iroquois proved resourceful, finding ways to maintain and modify indigenous economic practices as they met the demands of
a developing commercial world.

But economic adjustment was not without cost or compromise. The partial commercial reorganization of village economies induced tangible benefits in the lives of the Iroquois, but it also enhanced their dependence on
foreign markets. European wares offered luxury and convenience, but when
the fur market declined the Iroquois had to find alternative means to access
trade networks. By selling martial skills, physical toil, and handicrafts, the
Iroquois entered a cash economy, but growing exposure to cash drew them
more deeply into a commercial marketplace. Many Indians prospered, enjoying new forms of status and wealth, but economic stratification emerged
in some communities by the 1770s. Thus, the story of Iroquois involvement
in a market economy is a complex one that involves both loss and gain. The
Iroquois were not unwitting victims of a new economic order, nor were they
absolute agents of their own destiny. Rather, they were ordinary and resilient
human beings who made the best of trying situations.[7]

Furthermore, economic transition did not signify cultural degeneration
or a loss of an "authentic" indigenous culture. Rather, as Iroquois Indians
adjusted to commercial pressures they shared important parallels with their

colonial neighbors, who also pursued a mishmash of "traditional" and "modern" economic practices.[8] The rise of Atlantic capitalism transformed the lives of *all* early Americans whether they were bound, free, black, white, or Indian. In the Mohawk Valley of colonial New York, local Indians and colonial settlers produced crops, furs, and other goods for home consumption, local exchange, and overseas export. By purchasing textiles, crockery, and ironware, they tapped into a burgeoning transatlantic consumer revolution and in the process became "dependent" on foreign-made goods. Both groups progressively relied on cash as a form of currency to obtain desired articles; thus their economic existence became partially monetized. The Iroquois and their colonial neighbors maintained a foothold in both the commercial and noncommercial worlds.[9]

But if common economic forces shaped the lives of the inhabitants of early America, they also led to striking differences. The contest over natural resources—principally land—brought the Iroquois and their colonial neighbors into mounting conflict with one another. In 1768 the Iroquois Confederacy ceded thousands of acres of western and southern hunting grounds to the British, much to the chagrin of the Indian groups who inhabited these territories. By doing so they had hoped to stem the tide of settlers and violence on the frontier, but in reality they relinquished a valuable bargaining tool and brought Europeans closer to their own hunting grounds and settlements. The eastern Iroquois nations sustained the greatest incursions onto their territory. By the mid-1770s, surrounded on all sides by colonial settlements, the situation of the Mohawks—the easternmost nation—was akin to that of reservation dwellers. Land loss not only eroded economic autonomy but also had political consequences. No longer sole owners of the New York hinterland or lorded overseers of vast western hunting grounds, the Iroquois Confederacy experienced a diminished status and power vis-à-vis the British. While never becoming fully subjugated or dispossessed, entanglement in an imperial system underpinned their transformation from a sovereign people to de facto clients of the British Empire.

Entanglement with an expansive British Empire had profound cultural consequences for the Iroquois as much as it did economic. The British Empire, although economic at root, was also an ideological construct. As Eric Hinderaker has observed, "Empire is a cultural artifact as well as a geopolitical entity; it belongs to a geography of the mind, as well as a geography of power." Material needs conditioned the ideological content of empire. The

British desire to extract the labor of Indians as hunters and warriors or to win their political allegiance encouraged them to compose cultural identities that emphasized themes of commonality and parity; Indians were "esteemed allies," "noble savages," and "kings." Alternatively, the act of expropriating land and of instituting relations based on hierarchy and domination required the British to articulate cultural discourses that insisted on difference and inferiority.[10] However, constructing an ideological empire was a messy and uneven process over which the British never held a monopoly. As Philip Morgan asserts, "identities are, above all, invented and imagined in a complex and ever changing process of interaction." Indians refused, altered, and subverted gendered and racialized categories imposed upon them as they engaged in their own efforts to construct cultural discourses of difference. The formation of multiethnic refugee communities, familiarity with the teachings of Christian missionaries and Indian prophets, and protracted participation in a market economy that gave rise to commercialized outlooks led Indians to reformulate cultural identities in quite diverse and ingenious ways.[11] They also created and imposed identities onto Europeans.

Imperial Entanglements explores how the Iroquois and British interacted along a "gender frontier."[12] "Gender" refers to socially constructed ideas about appropriate roles and behaviors for men and women, ideas that vary across cultures and time. "Gender" is also a relational concept that denotes the allocation of power between, but not exclusive to, men and women.[13] The Iroquois and British embraced overlapping—but nonetheless distinct—gender systems. Both recognized warfare as an intrinsically masculine vocation premised on assumed sexual differences. In both cultures as well men monopolized positions of political leadership. But there were also notable differences. Iroquois women dominated agriculture, and clan matrons exercised a level of political influence unheard of for ordinary contemporary English women. Iroquois culture was matrilineal, and relations between men and women, although not free from friction, were generally egalitarian. Hierarchy was structured along generational rather than gendered lines, but still, elder men could not impose their rule on younger males. Power remained diffused and based on skills of persuasion rather than coercion. By contrast, in early modern England, the meaning of gender was embedded within a patriarchal ideology, which, supported by biblical doctrine and political theory, upheld male dominance over women and younger men. Through the judicious exercise of power, political theorists contended, men in their roles as fathers, husbands, and masters were responsible for ensuring orderly households and, by extension, contributing to the social and political stability of the state. Power relations were gendered not just between men and women but between older and younger men as well.

Gender provided a powerful lens through which the Iroquois and British made sense of one another. At times gendered identities provided the basis for cooperation and comradeship: rangers and warriors bonded through a common language of martial masculinity, borrowing and enacting each other's masculine codes of conduct and martial rituals to fight the French. But gender constructs could also reinforce a sense of difference or be used to justify unequal power relations. British officials sought to place the Haudenosaunee within a gendered hierarchy by assigning them the status of submissive dependents. William Johnson was particularly keen to assume the role of patriarch supreme by attempting to control the labor and behavior of his Indian neighbors.[14]

But the Iroquois engaged in their own careful manipulation of gendered practices and identities. At times they played up to Johnson's self-appointed role as generous father as a means to secure protection, presents, and provisions. At other times they complained to him of Britain's "unmanly" performance in battle in order to justify their own refusal to lend martial support. Iroquois women, largely absent in the historical literature, greatly influenced imperial-Iroquois relations.[15] They interacted with an expanding British imperial presence as they traded at forts, accompanied male kin to army camps, attended conferences, and acted as hosts and consorts to traders, army deserters, captives, and deputy Indian agents residing in their villages. Women's vital activities on the imperial frontier forced colonial men, including Johnson, to contend with them, often on their terms. But involvement in a market economy and imperial wars occasioned difficulties in addition to opportunities for both men and women. Although they found ways to ensure that their gendered practices and values continued to influence martial, diplomatic, and social exchanges with the British, in the long run, relations with a patriarchal empire generated constraints on their gender system.

Along with gender, Iroquois involvement with the British Empire inevitably involved the renegotiation of ethnic and racial identities. Historically the Haudenosaunee had embraced a fluid concept of ethnicity that allowed them to adopt and assimilate outsiders. But extensive contact with Europeans and Euro-Americans who cheated them in trade and defrauded them of their land caused them to reassess their definition of group membership. Yet their attempts to redefine the other were more than matched by the uncompromising colonial project of racializing Native Americans. In the eighteenth century, Europeans were busily involved in efforts to articulate and apply a new concept of race in their relations with non-Europeans. Like gender, race is not a biological fact but a social and historical construct. Although there might be real physical differences between groups, the meanings attached to these differences are determined by specific socioeconomic contexts.[16]

The evolution of race as a cultural ideology was uneven and haphazard. The antecedents of racialized thinking were evident in the seventeenth century when Virginian and Puritan colonists emphasized Indian savagery to justify their brutal wars against local tribes. But harsh language and physical violence did not demonstrate the existence of a crystallized racial doctrine. Violence was occasional and situational and not yet tied together by a broadly conceived model of race. As one astute scholar has observed, "the English gestured toward racial identification of the body without providing, yet, a theory that explained generational transmission of bodily variants; this was racial idiom, not a coherent ideology." By the mid-eighteenth century a new idea of race emerged that perceived human differences to be grounded in the body and not, as previously thought, as a product of the environment. Human difference, and by extension inferiority, was no longer deemed mutable and reversible but fixed and hereditary. This construction of race was a peculiarly Atlantic creation, intimately connected to the flourishing Atlantic slave trade. Race gained power as a concept because it served as an ideological justification for the enslavement of Africans. Lifelong servitude and brutal exploitation were legitimized and naturalized on the grounds that Africans were biologically and thus permanently inferior to Europeans.[17]

In contrast to the experience of Africans, the racialization of Native Americans was far more protracted and inconsistent. The importance of the Iroquois to the British Empire as trading partners and military allies retarded the evolution of racist sentiment on the New York frontier. Daily and intimate contact between the eastern Iroquois and neighboring colonial settlers who prayed, traded, and killed together allowed for a sense of commonality rather than difference to dominate relations. Although pejorative attitudes were evident from the start, they existed alongside genuine amicable feelings. During this period, ethnicity rather than race provided the dominant prism through which both sides made sense of the other. If racial models defined differences as biological, permanent, and hereditary, ethnic models viewed human differences as cultural, temporary, and inconstant. By altering external factors, it was possible to alter the individual. Ethnic models of understanding meant both positive and negative representations of the other could coexist. The Seven Years' War heightened this twin discourse. Enemy Indians waging war on the frontiers of Pennsylvania and New England incited virulent denunciations of Indian savagery, while New York colonists, for the most part, continued to refer to the Iroquois as allies. But the tendency to emphasize themes of similarity and friendship declined in the postwar era. As colonists came to value land more than furs and to deem the absence of the Iroquois preferable to their labor, they began to formulate and assign racial categories with greater zeal.[18]

By foregrounding economic and cultural themes, *Imperial Entanglements* brings the era of the Seven Years' War into sharper focus. Often sidelined, if not ignored, in Iroquois studies, this imperial conflict was a considerable catalyst of change, precipitating forces that would undercut the situation of the Iroquois in the late colonial period.[19] The Seven Years' War was a significant event in its own right and not just as a prelude to the American Revolution. The war marked the emergence of a new British empire, one that demonstrated a novel commitment to overseas expansion, a willingness to employ military force on an unprecedented scale, and a readiness to administer and martially police overseas interests in the aftermath of battle.[20]

The Great War for Empire signified Britain's new devotion to a territorial empire. In the seventeenth century, England's imperial designs had been limited to trade. Guided by the mercantilist belief that there was a finite amount of wealth in the world, early imperial initiatives were directed at establishing control of New World commodities suitable for transatlantic commerce. Military activities were confined to defending shipping lanes along the Atlantic, constituting what was essentially "an empire of the seas."[21] Largely as a consequence of the natural maturation of capitalist forces and spurred on by the entrepreneurial efforts of her own colonists, Britain's interest in an increasingly territorial empire soared. More specifically, with the Earl of Halifax assuming control of the Board of Trade in the 1740s, Britain began to place greater emphasis on an "empire of land." Halifax and others of his generation came to see territorial expansion as crucial to mercantilist interests.[22] By midcentury, economic ambition focused on the Ohio country, a region valued for its fertile lands, profitable fur trade, and potential new markets. When the French threatened British interests by constructing a series of forts along the upper Ohio Valley, Whitehall demonstrated new resolve to preserve and extend her American empire. The Seven Years' War was, according to one scholar, "the fulfillment and ultimate expression of mercantilist imperial aspirations." The war not only promoted the growth of Britain's transatlantic trade but also greatly distended its territorial base, fueling ambitions for colonial settlement.[23]

The war proved a double-edged sword for the Iroquois. On the one hand it enhanced their importance on the imperial stage, granting them political purchasing power, creating new economic opportunities, enabling men to augment their cherished role as virile warriors, and reinforcing their nonracialized status as prized allies. On the other hand, the war disrupted village economies, destabilized gendered power relations, began to harden racial attitudes, and ultimately gave rise to a more aggressively expansionist British Empire, which would have major material and cultural consequences for the Iroquois in the postwar period.

More specifically, the Seven Years' War marked an imperialization of British-Iroquois relations. Up until the 1740s, Whitehall remained aloof to matters related to Native Americans. The limited nature of imperial forms on the colonial frontier ensured vital maneuvering space for the Iroquois. But the Crown's widening concern in overseas land and resources instigated new exertions to transform the Six Nations from independent sovereign allies to integrated and subject members of the British Empire. As dependent subjects Iroquois people and their lands, including the Ohio country, came under British rule. Removing the management of Indian affairs from the separate colonial governments, Whitehall established a new centralized office under direct Crown supervision. Through the appointment of William Johnson as superintendent for the northern colonies, the Crown exerted new pressure on the Iroquois for their lands, labor, and resources, threatening to undermine their sovereignty.

But the Johnson-Iroquois alliance reveals much about how the empire worked on the periphery and not as conceived at the metropolis. Serving as the critical conduit between the British Empire and Iroquois Confederacy, Johnson was an extremely adept cultural mediator. As a Crown official with a Mohawk wife, an Irish immigrant who dressed in native clothing while hosting Iroquois guests at his Georgian-style manor house, Johnson moved comfortably between Indian and colonial worlds. Well versed in their political etiquette, approving of their martial rituals, and knowledgeable of their religious customs, he was extremely adroit at facilitating the exchange of cultural forms and values. An investigation of Johnson helps add to a burgeoning literature on cultural brokers in early America. Yet this study also revises that literature.[24] Far from operating as an innocuous mediator, Johnson was first and foremost an agent of empire. He was proficient at employing intercultural skills to advance imperial needs, often blending European, Euro-American, and Native American forms in ways that were ultimately detrimental to the Iroquois. His home, which served as the center point for Indian-colonial diplomacy, was no equitable middle ground.[25] Johnson's apparent cultural hybridity was his most effective political and economic tool for incorporating the Iroquois into the empire on British terms. But Johnson never wielded absolute power. The commercial and martial importance of the Iroquois required him to engage in substantial imperial accommodation. By their close proximity and familial ties, the neighboring Mohawks felt the full weight of Johnson's patriarchal pretensions, but the other nations continued to maintain some distance and by doing so were able—some more than others—to eschew the worst effects of imperial entanglements.

By the late colonial period, the Iroquois were not scattered, impoverished, or demoralized, nor were they wholly triumphant. Extended contact with an expansive British Empire precipitated significant material and cultural change, which through skillful mediation the Iroquois had been able to ameliorate but not evade. *Imperial Entanglements* posits the Haudenosaunee as dynamic participants in a story of empire building in mid-eighteenth-century North America while exploring the causes and consequences of their diminishing status. Although they never became entirely subjugated—as they continued to maintain a level of economic and thus political autonomy—the extent and potential of their power must be seen in relation to the rising strength of Euro-Americans. Despite their inventive efforts to carve out and preserve an economic and cultural space for themselves in British North America, the Iroquois confronted a colonial populace more and more committed to a racially exclusive vision of empire.

Chapter 1

Maintaining Their Ground

In the spring of 1710, after an arduous journey across the Atlantic Ocean, a middle-aged Mohawk man named Tejonihokarawa arrived in the bustling London metropolis. He was part of a delegation of "four Indian kings" brought to London by two prominent colonists (fig. 1).[1] Treated as exotic dignitaries throughout their two-week stay, Tejonihokarawa and his peers enjoyed a bewildering array of sights. They held court with Queen Anne, sat for formal portraits, dined with dukes and admiralty, attended the theater, met with leading scientists and politicians, toured poorhouses and mental asylums, and attracted sizable crowds wherever they went.[2] The absence of native written or oral testimony means that we are left to imagine how Tejonihokarawa experienced his trip. Very likely it reaffirmed a belief that friendship with the English was worth pursuing. Born around 1660, Tejonihokarawa had grown up accustomed to Europeans. A history of violent encounters with the French and their Indian allies encouraged Tejonihokarawa, like other Mohawks, to look to the English for security and military support. In 1701 he was one of a number of headmen who signed a deed assigning western hunting lands to the protection of the English Crown. By this time he had converted to Christianity and had begun preaching to other Indians to dissuade them from joining the French. In 1709 he recruited warriors for a joint English-Iroquois invasion of Canada. The invasion was aborted, but in 1710 he traveled to England with the other delegates to lobby the ministry for support of a second attempt. While in London he took the opportunity to request a missionary for his people, as well as agreeing to sell land to settlers on his return. By his actions Tejonihokarawa demonstrated his conviction that there were genuine advantages to be had by cultivating an alliance with the nascent English Empire.[3]

This brief glimpse of the life of one Mohawk Indian provides an alterna-

Figure 1. *Tee Yee Neen Ho Ga Row, Emperour of the Six Nations,* portrait by
John Verelst (1710). William L. Clements Library, University of Michigan.
This portrait of Tejonihokarawa was made during his 1710 visit to London.
The belt of wampum indicates his role as a man of diplomacy. The presence
of a wolf marks his membership in the Wolf clan.

tive narrative to the older but still dominant story of the wholly destructive impact of colonization. The arrival of Europeans to North America wrought radical changes in the lives of the Haudenosaunee, but it did not signify their immediate or inevitable demise. Indians like Tejonihokarawa secured tangible benefits through forging relations with newcomers. In fact, despite a traumatic century of demographic loss through disease and warfare, the Iroquois emerged in the early eighteenth century as a viable force in North America. Still occupying their lands, controlling vital resources, and preserving their cultural autonomy, the Iroquois maintained their ground in both a literal and figurative sense. Having conquered and dispersed many western Indians, they widened their geographic orbit of influence and cemented a reputation among the English and non-Iroquois Indians alike as a martially powerful and politically unified people. In addition to important geographical and cultural resources, Iroquois success at withstanding the injurious forces of colonization owed much to the restricted nature of colonial and imperial incursions they encountered in New York. The early English Empire in New York was a limited empire in which trade, not territorial gain, served as the principal focus. Consequently, penetration of the interior, with Europeans' subsequent demands on native lands, labor, and resources, occurred in a drawn-out, piecemeal fashion. Within this trading empire colonial officials generally preferred to keep the Iroquois at arm's length. For men like Tejonihokarawa, courted and patronized in London, there was reason to feel hopeful in 1710. Although their world had altered dramatically by this date, it was still a world in which they exercised considerable mastery.

By the time the New York Iroquois first encountered Europeans, they had already undergone centuries of transformation. The Haudenosaunee embodied a rich and dynamic culture. Like most other native peoples, migration, warfare, ecological strain, and economic needs had been a mainstay of their existence, recontouring their material and cultural worlds. Historically they were part of a much larger linguistic group of Iroquoian-speaking Indians. By the 1500s they had located to lands south of the lower Great Lakes and St. Lawrence River, nestled between Schoharie Creek (near present-day Schenectady) in the east and the Genesee River in the west. Although distinguished by their separate abodes and distinct dialects, the original Five Nations of Mohawks, Oneidas, Onondagas, Cayugas, and Senecas were united under a cultural organization known as the Great League of Peace, probably formed sometime in the fifteenth century. They shared in common a complex set of cultural practices and values that governed relations between themselves and outsiders.[4]

Central to Iroquois culture was the concept of kinship, which provided the fundamental means for organizing society. The smallest kinship unit in Iroquoia was the "fireside family" comprising wife, husband, and children. Although this was a bilateral unit, it was largely submerged within the extended matrilineal household composed of mothers, daughters, sisters, and their male spouses and unmarried brothers and sons. Two or three maternal families—an ohwachira—lived together in a large bark-covered structure known as a longhouse. Each fireside family was allocated their own separate compartment complete with an individual hearth, but up to fifty people might live in a single longhouse, which could measure as much as forty-two meters in length. Collectively a group of maternal families made up a clan, distinguished by an animal insignia. Families from each of the three main clans—the Bear, Turtle, and Wolf—resided in most villages. Clan membership, a key element of individual identity, was traced through the mother's line.

The kinship system contained rules governing relations between individuals, the most important of which was reciprocity. The mutual exchange of goods and services bound members of familial groups together. Most notably, clans served important reciprocal duties in the religious life that dominated villages by taking turns to condole and bury each other's dead. Reciprocal ties also meant that individuals could expect food and lodging from members of the same clan residing in another village or nation. The clans were divided into two sets or sides, each responsible for performing duties for the other. The Great League of Peace drew its fifty hereditary chiefs from each of the clans precisely so that different clan chiefs could carry out symbolic functions for the other. But kinship and reciprocity did not always entail parity, and pre-contact Iroquoia was never strictly egalitarian. While reciprocity suggests a mutual give-and-take, in reality it served as a mechanism for creating hierarchy by generating a set of roles, duties, and expectations between individuals and groups. Resting on ideas about social obligation and mutual ties, kinship regulated economic practices, structured gender roles and relations, and provided the basis for group identity.

The Iroquois were a subsistence-oriented society based on farming, hunting, and small-scale trade. Land and its resources underpinned the Iroquois economy. The Iroquois cleared parcels of woodland to plant substantial crops of maize, beans, and squash, which formed the bulk of their diet. They supplemented this activity by hunting wild game and fowl and fishing in the numerous lakes and creeks. The Iroquois also gleaned the forested terrain for its natural harvest of nuts, fruits, and roots. They extracted maple syrup from trees and used timber for longhouses, canoes, tools, and firewood. As local resources diminished over time, communities relocated. The rich bounties of the natural environment ensured Iroquois economic autonomy.[5]

Despite the immense value of land to their way of life, the Iroquois disclaimed private ownership. Land was not an object or commodity that could be privately possessed, transferred through inheritance, or sold for profit. Land was a gift from their maker, the Great Spirit. The Iroquois still practiced an ownership of sorts, however, but it was one based on need, use, and occupation. Collectively, the Iroquois recognized the right of each nation to inhabit a specific region and respected each other's hunting grounds and fishing camps. At a village level, although land was technically held in common, clan matrons determined what land was to be farmed and by whom. Allocation of land rights at the nation, village, and clan level served a practical purpose by ensuring fair and broad access. Even if an individual or family enjoyed special rights to a particular piece of land, they still had no right to sell it or give it away. The very fact that any Indian could assert a right to the land simply by making use of it guaranteed a substantial level of economic equality.[6]

"The Indian tribes have traded with each other from time immemorial," missionary Joseph François Lafitau observed of the Iroquois in the early 1700s. Trade served a critical cultural function as a means to maintain alliances and promote relations of social and political obligation. Consequently, the exchange of goods frequently occurred within the context of diplomatic missions. Western Indians desiring to traverse through Seneca country used red pipestone as a diplomatic gift to ensure their safe passage. Families wishing to make amends for murder or injury sent diplomatic embassies loaded with presents to other communities. Iroquois practices make it extremely difficult to disentangle the political from the economic. Lafitau noted that "Their ways of engaging in trade is by an exchange of gifts. There are some gifts presented to the chief and others given wholesale to the body of the tribe with which they are trading." Upon receipt of a gift, an individual or family was obliged to offer something in exchange. If a recipient disliked the gift he would return it and retrieve the original item. In this noncommercial form of exchange, the value of goods was not market dictated but "regulated only by the buyer's evaluation and wants." By giving and receiving, individuals, villages, and entire nations engaged in symbolic acts of alliance making. The

Iroquois valued the act of exchange as much as the article they traded. The exchange of goods not only signified friendship but could also serve as an acknowledgment of unequal power relations. Tributary nations of the Iroquois in Pennsylvania acknowledged their social and political deference through their annual "gifts" of wampum, small marine shells of white or dark purple coloring.[7]

Small-scale trade satisfied basic material needs and wants by allowing villagers to obtain articles otherwise unavailable to them. Certain minerals and stones, such as jasper, white quartz, chalcedony, and red pipestone, used in the manufacture of arrowheads or believed to be endowed with spiritual energy and thus valued for their use in burial rites were obtained through trade with foreign Indians. Wampum beads were immensely valued because shell was thought to embody life-enhancing energy. Produced by coastal Algonquian Indians, wampum was only available via trade networks. Trade also occurred among the Five Nations: when one community had a surplus of goods they traded for something they lacked. Exchange took place within a bartering system in which individuals swapped one type of good for another.[8]

Labor was performed by all members of the community, but gender, age, and rank determined who performed what. Women tended crops, gathered wild produce, trapped small animals, performed household chores, and took care of children. Men hunted, fished, traded, and engaged in heavy village labor, such as clearing land and constructing homes. Children and the elderly performed labor that was age appropriate. The sexual and age division of labor was not unequal or hierarchical but complementary and reciprocal. Labor was performed through the extended lineage. Through appeals to consanguinity and marriage, kinship determined the division of labor and distribution of resources. Members of an ohwachira contributed to a household economy, sharing and swapping skills and goods. Familial ties ensured that each individual could expect to benefit from the labor of others at the same time that it placed an obligation on them to offer something in return. In this context, the value of sharing lay less in the resources shared than in the actual act of sharing: by its occurrence, it certified recurrence. Ties of mutuality united men and women, young and old, as each contributed valuable skills and resources to the village economy.[9]

Despite pervasive patterns of sharing and reciprocity, Iroquoia was not devoid of hierarchy. In fact, Iroquois society was a ranked society that comprised a social, political, and economic elite. Certain lineages that held titles for the hereditary League chieftains formed an elite stratum of society. The men who claimed these titles, the female heads of households who elected them, and their closest relations who acted as advisors formed the nobility known as agoïander.[10] They enjoyed both social and political status. Jesuit missionaries who lived among the Iroquois in the seventeenth century frequently encountered people of "noble birth" "who managed the affairs of the country." The social situation of the nobility stood in stark contrast to war captives held in servitude. One Seneca woman informed a Jesuit priest how her daughter's noble ranking relieved her from performing domestic chores: "She was Mistress here and commanded more than twenty slaves . . . she knew not what it was to go to the forest to get wood, or to the River to draw water; she could not take upon herself the care of all that has to do with domestic duties." But there were graduations even among the nobility, as Lafitau found that "although the chiefs appear to have equal authority . . . some of them preeminent over the others; and these are, as nearly as I can judge, either the one whose household [lineage] has founded the village, or the one whose clan is most numerous or the one who is ablest."[11]

Paradoxically, the redistribution of wealth reinforced inequality based on kinship. The status of the hereditary chief and his family may have been derived from his affiliation to a particular lineage, but his influence depended greatly on his ability to dispense gifts among his followers. Early Europeans remarked that "The chiefs are generally the poorest among them, for instead of their receiving from the common people as among Christians, they are obliged to give to the mob." However, their generous distribution of wealth was only possible because they enjoyed the greatest access to wealth. Principally this came in the form of prestige goods, items obtained through trade with foreign Indians and whose rarity enhanced their value. It was customary for diplomatic embassies and trade groups to bestow gifts on leaders as a mark of friendship or social deference. By redistributing these gifts to their followers, leaders solidified their power base and, ironically, improved their ability to attain more wealth. Lafitau remarked that gifts flowed in both directions, as hereditary chiefs not only played "a considerable role in feasts and community distributions" but were also "often given presents." Yet gift-giving was not a purely benevolent act. Through gifting, leaders set up certain expectations of rights and duties by placing the recipient in a position of debt; the more gifts given, the greater the debt. As headmen augmented their status as leaders through dispensing their property they simultaneously augmented their right to obtain more wealth, thus perpetuating a cycle of giving and receiving. Through redistributive economics, social, political, and economic hierarchy was possible. Nonetheless, while pre-contact Iroquois society may not have been a haven of egalitarian relations, reciprocal duties of family members and the communal ownership of land and tools prevented extremes of inequality from developing.[12]

In the seventeenth century, a Dutch settler named Johannes Megapolensis was bemused to learn about the Iroquois origins myth. "They have a droll theory of the Creation," he remarked, "for they think that a pregnant woman fell down from heaven, and that a tortoise . . . took this pregnant woman on its back, because every place was covered with water; and that the woman sat upon the tortoise, groped with her hands in the water, and scraped together some of the earth, whence it finally happened that the earth was raised above the water." This woman was Sky Woman, a celestial being who resided in the Sky World, a physical realm that existed among the stars. While heavily pregnant she fell through a hole in the Sky World and descended through the clouds until she was caught on the back of a turtle. With the help of a muskrat, she covered the turtle's back with soil, thus creating the North American continent. Sky Woman eventually gave birth to a daughter, known as Beloved Daughter or the Lynx. In time, Sky Woman and Beloved Daughter traveled all across the turtle's back, exploring the country, naming creatures, and sowing seeds.[13]

The Iroquois origins myth reveals much about the role and high status assigned to women. The story positively emphasizes their crucial roles as life-givers and sustainers. The Iroquois believed themselves to be the common heirs of Sky Woman. In his investigation of Iroquois lore, Megapolensis noted that the Mohawk Turtle clan enjoyed the most status because "they boast that they are the oldest descendents of the woman before mentioned." The second epoch of the creation story, which focuses on the relationship between Sky Woman and her daughter, and which was largely glossed over by nineteenth-century (male) anthropologists, lays the foundation of the matrilineal orientation of Iroquois society and highlights the significance attached to the mother-daughter relationship. Women derived much of their autonomy and power through the extended matrilineal household. Unlike men, who found themselves displaced after marriage between the homes of their wife and mother, women experienced the matrilineal household as a source of strength and sustenance. Living and working together in close-knit networks of female kin provided women with security and support and lessened their dependence on men. Their relative power and autonomy were reflected in the general freedom they enjoyed in pursuing premarital sexual relations, select-ing marriage partners, and initiating divorce.[14]

The creation story also points to women's important relationship to agri-culture. Sky Woman and Beloved Daughter are intimately linked with intro-ducing agriculture to Earth. As she fell through the Sky World, Sky Woman carried with her the seeds of the "Three Sisters" of Corn, Beans, and Squash and their Brother Tobacco. At the time of Beloved Daughter's death, while she was giving birth to twin boys, domestic plants sprang from her grave. According to one version, stalks of corn grew from each breast, signifying her role as producer.[15] Women were the farmers of their community. Lafitau described how women worked in "numerous different bands according to the different quarters where they have their fields and pass from one field to the other helping each other." These gangs planted, tended, and harvested crops. Far from regarding agriculture as menial or degrading, Iroquois society con-ferred considerable prestige onto women's roles as producers and celebrated this role in religion and ritual. Furthermore, their produce and control of valuable economic resources augmented their social status. Men understood the economic value of having a wife, believing they would be "reduced to a wretched life" without one.[16]

If women's roles in society were conceptualized largely in terms of life-giving activities—pro-creation and producing crops—then men's roles were defined predominantly in terms of life-taking endeavors. The role of the hunter-warrior was central to the Iroquois construction of male gender roles. Both pursuits encouraged men to develop valued "masculine" traits of physi-cal prowess, endurance, and bravery. For long periods of the year men left their villages to go on hunting and fishing expeditions. Lafitau recorded that these pursuits were of paramount importance, providing men with "the meats with which he nourishes himself, the clothing with which he covers himself, the oils with which he greases himself and the furs with which he trades." So distinct was the sexual division of labor that boys from a young age refused to do "girls' work." Men who demonstrated adeptness in hunting improved their prospects in marriage. Their manly demeanor was enhanced by their ability to successfully fulfill their side of a reciprocal bond: in exchange for the meat and fish they offered up to female kin, men could expect to be fed, clothed, and sheltered. Early missionaries to the Iroquois noted that men were obliged to offer the fruits of their hunt to their mother-in-law.[17]

The cultivation of a martial spirit was fundamental to Iroquois masculin-ity. Male warriors derived immense social prestige within their communities owing to the key service they provided. They engaged in war primarily to obtain prisoners to replace recently deceased kin. It was believed that through the adoption or torture of prisoners, the social, spiritual, and emotional equilibrium of the community could be maintained. From a young age boys were encouraged to cultivate the virtues of the warrior ethic, including stoicism, valor, and fortitude. Warfare provided the ultimate test of their manhood. The number of captives and scalps obtained was an important hallmark of a warrior's skill and courage. Successful demonstration of the warrior ethic gained them considerable social standing, improved their attractiveness as potential mates, and enabled them to rise up the ranks as non-hereditary political leaders. Warriors avoided all contact with women on the warpath, in particular abstaining from sexual intercourse, believing that female life-giving energy would contaminate and sap their own warrior life-taking energy.[18]

But the world of the Iroquois was not neatly divided into two distinct male and female spheres. The rules of kinship permitted overlap and generated sources of friction. Among women, clan matrons—the female heads of households—enjoyed special privileges. They were deemed the rightful proprietors of the longhouse and all of its material content. They were responsible for organizing female members of their household into work gangs and supervised their labor. They allocated land use and controlled the produce of the harvest, preserving, storing, and distributing crops among family members. By this means they exerted influence over male warriors from their lineage. If matrons opposed a proposed military campaign they could attempt to prohibit it by withholding provisions from men. Alternatively, when faced with the death of a relation, matrons could appeal to these warriors to assuage their grief by obtaining prisoners and scalps. Lafitau recalled how "the women weep, each one exaggerating her sufferings, making an effort to stimulate the courage of their youth by their complaints and words, to excite the young people to march boldly to combat and there to give proofs of their valour and love for the fellow countrymen whose deaths they are avenging." Thus war was not a strictly male affair. Women also partook in decisions regarding the fate of captives, choosing whether to adopt them into their clan or put them to death.[19]

The existence of the Iroquois agoïander composed of elite maternal families who held titles to hereditary offices comprised another form of hierarchy among women. Women did not enjoy equal access to the political decision-making process; instead influence was concentrated among the elder matrons who enjoyed special elective powers. When a hereditary chief died, his office was passed down to another man of the same clan. Matrons were responsible for his selection. Lafitau observed, "The matriarch, after conferring with her household, confers again with those of her clan to whom she makes acceptable the one chosen for the succession." Rather than enjoying unlimited choice, her decision was conditioned by family sentiment. Indicating their important social status, clan matrons took a major role in the ceremonial rite in which the new chief was installed. If he proved inept, matrons could petition to have him removed. Matrons also selected the chiefs' advisors. The communal nature of village politics, in which the Iroquois reached decisions by consensus, also allowed for female involvement. Clan matrons discussed village matters in their own private meetings and appointed speakers to represent their views at village councils.[20]

But Iroquois culture was no matriarchy and women's political influence—even that of clan matrons of the agoïander—was finite. Like European society, Iroquois men dominated leadership roles and diplomatic exchanges with outsiders. Despite the communal nature of village politics, consensus in decision making could be fragile and was sometimes achieved by silencing dissent through peer pressure or ostracism. Furthermore, men had far greater access to positions of leadership. In theory, any man could become a Pine Tree Chief by demonstrating his bravery in warfare, political adroitness, and ability to access and dispense wealth among followers. Non-elected by female kin, these men enjoyed an independent source of authority.[21]

Gender was crucial for defining roles and responsibilities within Iroquois society but not necessarily for determining relationships of power; this was achieved through age and clan affiliation. The Iroquois gender system allowed for a rough egalitarianism between men and women. The economic sufficiency of women coupled with the matrilineal basis of their society buttressed their independent status. But women's ability to elect hereditary chieftains and influence warriors, coupled with men's ability to obtain positions of leadership outside the elective powers of women, created points of tension between the sexes.[22]

Kinship formed the basis for group identity with clan membership serving as a main determinant. Familial ties that connected people across a wide geography provided a means to collectively identify with one another. However, up until the fifteenth century the Haudenosaunee were a people characterized by chronic ethnic conflict. A potent sense of "them" and "us" governed their relations not only with non-Iroquoians but also among themselves as archaeological evidence points to a history of incessant and brutal warfare among the Five Nations. Iroquois mythology, based on the Deganawidah epic, further records a period of unrelenting intratribal bloodshed. According to this epic, Hiawatha, an Iroquois man who had lost his daughters to warfare, was driven to the verge of insanity. Roving in the woods he met the supernatural figure of Deganawidah, the Peacemaker, who taught him a new set of peacemaking rituals including the condolence ceremony and gift-giving. The Great League of Peace, a religious organization founded in large part to bring an end to this ethnic strife, was based on the teachings of Deganawidah. The League helped foster a new sense of ethnic cohesion, one that was reinforced by a shared mythology and set of cultural practices. As one Moravian missionary noted, "The Iroquois call themselves Aquanoschioni, which means united people, having united for the purpose of always reminding each other that their safety and power consists in a mutual and strict adherence to their alliance."[23] Yet Iroquois identity was multilayered and situational; the League, the nation, the village, and the clan all laid claims to an individual's sense of group membership. For the most part Iroquois group identity remained localized and familial.

Although race was a wholly alien concept among the pre-contact Iroquois, a history of brutal warfare demonstrates that they still constructed meaningful categories for acknowledging and marking difference between people. While intratribal bloodshed ended, the Iroquois continued to wage wars against other foreign tribes. They had a longstanding war with southern Indian nations, who by the eighteenth century were called the Catawbas and the Cherokees. Yet Iroquois conceptions of difference remained fluid and malleable. The Iroquois operated out of the mourning-war complex, whereby they conducted warfare not simply to obliterate enemies but to assimilate outsiders. Although warriors often killed or enslaved war captives, it was also common practice to obtain captives for the purpose of adoption. The captive's assimilation into a lineage represented a physical replacement of the deceased, as well as a symbolic restoration. "When they spare the life of any slave, they usually receive him into some family in the place of some dead kinsman, whom the slave is said to bring to life again, by taking the name and the same degree of relationship; so that they call him, like the dead man, 'father,' 'brother,' 'son,' etc.," a Jesuit missionary observed. The captive literally assumed the identity and role of the one he had replaced. Thus, on the eve of colonization, the rules governing kinship were flexible and not based solely on blood ties and marriage. The Iroquois embraced a cultural worldview that deterred them from seeing outsiders as permanently separate from themselves. Through their long-held practice of symbolic and literal adoption they could incorporate outsiders into their extended polity and kinship networks. Through the rituals of condolence and gift-giving they could foster a sense of commonality and mutual obligation.[24]

The arrival of Europeans to North America initiated major disruptions to the material and cultural worlds of the Iroquois, but it did not induce their instant or wholesale downfall. Exposure to mercantile trade and Christian religions generated cultural conflict and anxiety, while the spread of European diseases and rise of intertribal warfare made more deadly by the introduction of guns were physically devastating. Change was profound and pervasive, but it was not altogether destructive. Sustained interaction with the English Empire began in 1664, when the English supplanted the Dutch and established Albany on the banks of the Hudson River. For the next fifty years the Iroquois engaged in a widening array of relations with these newcomers, including trade, diplomatic, and military alliances, Christian conversion, and social and sexual fraternizing. But this was not yet a period of imperial entanglement when colonists absorbed Indians into asymmetrical forms of exchange. Instead the Iroquois enjoyed significant success at incorporating new people, practices, and products into their own lifestyle and mental worldview. In this initial period of colonization, traders, settlers, and officials often found that they had to deal with the Iroquois on Iroquois terms.

The Iroquois enjoyed certain geographical advantages and cultural resources that buttressed their stronghold position: they occupied lands that granted them control of the major waterways of northeastern America; being cushioned between two emerging rival European empires granted them considerable political leverage; operating as middlemen, they secured a central role in a profitable fur trade; their practice of adoption enabled them to bolster decimated tribal numbers; and their religious social organization, the Great League of Peace, provided them with tools for forming alliances with outsiders while also serving as a basis for presenting a politically united front against European intruders.[25]

However, Haudenosaunee success at maintaining power in this period also had much to do with the restrictive nature of the colonial and imperial forces they encountered on the New York frontier. The seventeenth-century English Empire was restricted in size and scope. Although mercantile trade quickly flourished in the new English colony, it was the trade itself and not the actual territory that imperial officials esteemed. Imperial concern lay in protecting trade routes and trading posts rather than in enlarging territorial holdings. Furthermore, the London metropolis took a hands-off approach to the management of internal colonial affairs. By 1696 the Board of Trade— an independent body for managing colonial affairs—had been reorganized, but for the next fifty years of its existence, it demonstrated little initiative or drive in executing a dynamic colonial policy. Power was decentralized in the colonies, resting with each of the provincial governments. Within this rubric of empire, Whitehall devoted little time or attention to matters pertaining to Indians. There was no Crown-appointed officer to oversee Indian affairs, no special funds allocated for Indian conferences, and no imperial effort to regulate the fur trade or land sales.[26]

The Haudenosaunee experienced firsthand the drawbacks and benefits of Whitehall's laissez-faire approach to North America. Iroquois headmen were affronted by the failure of governors to enact appropriate diplomatic etiquette. Many Mohawks were aggrieved by the English refusal to lend military support during the devastating intertribal conflicts of the 1680s–90s.[27] Whitehall's policy of benign neglect granted New York officials involved in Indian affairs significant autonomy and meant that by the 1710s a number had personally enriched themselves through illegal purchases of Mohawk lands.[28] Yet if the lack of imperial interest in Indian affairs worked to the disadvantage of the Iroquois, it also conferred real benefits. Decentralized power in the hands of local representatives awarded a level of intimacy to Indian-colonial relations, allowing the Iroquois some purchase to play off various parties against one another.[29] Whitehall's lack of involvement meant that local custom rather than imperial dictate shaped frontier economic exchange. Although Albany traders made efforts to push the trading frontier further west, the insignificant number of settlers meant that desires for a western trade were not matched by demands for western lands.[30] Furthermore, Whitehall had little desire to promote the settlement of its overseas empire or to extend its borders. As New York officials quickly discovered, Whitehall was averse to lending martial or financial support during colonial conflicts. When New York officials lobbied their home government for an invasion of Canada during Queen Anne's War (1702–13), they met with resistance. Whitehall ministers considered this a burdensome and unnecessary expense and instead diverted the royal fleet meant for Canada to Portugal. Following the visit of the "four Indian kings" in 1710, the Crown agreed to send another fleet to support an invasion of Canada. The fleet again failed to reach its destination after getting lost in fog. Over eight hundred men lost their lives while the undamaged vessels sailed back to England.[31]

Although the Iroquois did not have to contend with a restless body of settlers or an invasive imperial manifesto, other forces threatened to erode their ties to the land. During the first hundred years of colonization, Old World microbes and frontier warfare resulted in a massive reduction and dispersal of Iroquois peoples. Epidemics of influenza, measles, and smallpox played havoc with population figures. Estimates are staggering. With a population of roughly 21,000 at the beginning of the seventeenth century, at least half had perished by the 1650s. The numbers are perhaps even more startling when specific communities are examined. According to one estimate, the Mohawk population decreased from 7,740 in 1630 to just 620 by 1700.[32] Warfare also decimated populations and undermined the security of homelands. On at least four occasions the French with their allied Indians invaded Iroquoia, systematically burning homes, cornfields, and stocks of food, and causing entire communities to flee. By 1700, two-thirds of the Mohawks had removed to Canada.[33]

Yet despite decades of demographic stress and social chaos, colonial pressures did not displace the Iroquois from their homelands. On the contrary, by the 1700s the Iroquois were actively replenishing their communities, rebuilding settlements, and thereby reaffirming their occupation and ownership of their lands. Historically the Iroquois had always relocated on a periodical basis as local resources expired. The exigencies of the seventeenth century simply intensified a preexisting pattern. While a sizable number left Iroquoia, many more chose to remain, moving to new locations that provided for their interests. The fur trade encouraged some Indians to move closer to hunting grounds or places of commerce, while others preferred to geographically distance themselves from Europeans. Reflecting a new confidence they felt in their safety, they abandoned their previous practice of building single large towns on hilltops surrounded by palisades and established instead a new dispersed style of settlement consisting of clusters of small hamlets spread along a one- or two-mile stretch.[34]

Settlements changed not only in physicality but also in ethnic composition. The large-scale adoption of war captives in addition to the policy of inviting and cajoling remnant tribes from the south to settle in Iroquoia shored up population figures, enhancing the spiritual power of the community and, most important, tightening their hold on tribal lands. Thousands of Huron and Algonquian war captives were incorporated into Iroquois villages. Many

were adopted into lineages, some were kept as slaves, and others were permitted to establish their own communities. A Jesuit missionary noted how
one fortunate Huron village "threw itself upon the mercy" of the Senecas and
was "well received by them,—having since then preserved its identity, in the
form of a Village apart from those of the Iroquois." Through mass adoption
the Senecas were able to sustain their population of roughly four thousand
throughout the century. Jesuits estimated that in some Iroquois villages "Foreigners" outnumbered "natives of the country" by as much as two-thirds. In
the 1670s the Onondagas and Cayugas adopted the Susquehannocks from
Maryland displaced by Bacon's Rebellion. By the 1710s, the Iroquois had
absorbed other disbanded and dispossessed Indian groups including the
Conoys, Nanticokes, Tutelos, Mahicans, Shawnees, Delawares, and Tuscaroras. Such large-scale adoption came at a cost, as it took years if not generations for communities to cohere. But by maintaining population numbers,
the Iroquois continued to physically occupy and make use of the land, the
very basis of Iroquois ownership.[35]

Although the size and composition of Iroquois communities had radically
altered by the 1710s, the territorial integrity of the Haudenosaunee people remained largely intact. The Iroquois maintained access over substantial hunting grounds that extended from north of the lakes in present-day Ontario to
the Adirondack Mountains in the northeast, to the Susquehanna Valley to the
south, and to the Ohio Valley in the west. In addition to their hunting lands
they physically occupied a substantial geography. The Five Nations spread
throughout central and western New York, each with their own domain (map
1). Furthest west were the Senecas, the most populous nation of the Iroquois.
By 1700, still far removed from Europeans, their villages were located primarily between the Seneca and Canandaigua lakes. During the first two decades
of the 1700s, while many remained at Seneca Lake, others drifted westward,
establishing hamlets near the Genesee River. Close by but more easterly were
the Cayugas, living in the vicinity of the Cayuga and Owasco lakes. They
were the only community to escape French attacks during the seventeenth
century, although an accidental fire destroyed one of their villages in 1709.
At the midpoint of Iroquoia, Onondaga served as the meeting place for the
Iroquois League. The French had destroyed the Onondagas' principal town,
just southeast of present-day Syracuse, in 1696. Some efforts were made to rebuild this community, but by the 1720s a new town was located on the banks
of Onondaga Creek. Also by this date, the Oneidas had a main settlement,
Old Oneida, located just southeast of Lake Oneida near Oneida Creek.[36]

The easternmost nation of Mohawks resided in two key communities by the 1710s. The village of Tiononderoge—also known as the Lower Castle—was on the south bank of the Mohawk River at the confluence with Schoharie Creek. By 1713 Tiononderoge contained approximately 360 Mohawks residing in 40 to 50 houses. About twenty miles further west was the Upper Castle of Canajoharie. This village, consisting of 20 to 30 houses, extended along the southern bank of the Mohawk River for at least two miles. In addition there were a number of much smaller villages, including the community of Schoharie Mohawks twenty miles south of Tiononderoge on the Schoharie Creek.[37]

While the Iroquois managed to recoup some of their losses of the seventeenth century by rebuilding their villages and holding onto their lands, they still had to accommodate to a new European presence. But the number of migrants on the New York frontier remained small and their penetration of the interior was retarded. Frontier assaults by Frenchmen and their Indian allies made western and northern New York an unattractive prospect to would-be settlers. Furthermore, the distinct landholding pattern that emerged in the colony acted as another deterrent. Large manorial estates dominated the eastern New York landscape, on which landlords rented out tracts to tenants. The fierce desire to be freeholders channeled settlers to alternative colonies. The first substantial group of Europeans, east of the Hudson, was Dutch traders interested in securing furs rather than farmlands.[38]

Nonetheless, by the 1710s, three groups of settlers had made inroads into the outer edges of Iroquoia. In 1661 a Dutch settlement began at present-day Schenectady after the Mohawks sold a small parcel of land to fifteen proprietors. By 1690 the community had grown to 130 residents, and by the 1710s, according to one missionary, it was inhabited by around one hundred Dutch families, sixteen English families, and a forty-man garrison. Also in the 1710s, the English government sponsored the migration of impoverished Palatine Germans, an initiative done foremost out of a concern for trade. The government intended for the Germans to participate in a naval stores project, whereby they would transform the natural resources of the New York hinterland into materials required for the British shipping industry. The project failed but the Germans remained. In 1712 about 150 families settled on the east side of Schoharie Creek or else wintered at Schenectady. The English also established a foothold in the valley with the building of a fort and chapel near the eastern Mohawk town of Tiononderoge in 1712. Named after the governor of the time, Fort Hunter housed a garrison of twenty men and gradually attracted a small number of colonial families.[39]

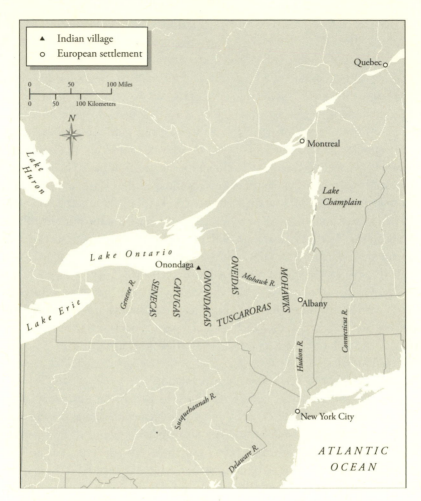

Map 1. Iroquoia, ca. 1720.

The eastern Iroquois confronted new settlers with a mixture of deep suspicion, sympathy, and a sense of opportunism. The Mohawks were unsure
about Fort Hunter. In the context of Queen Anne's War they had initially
requested a fort for their defense. But during its construction, they and the
wider Iroquois community became uneasy. Rumors soon spread of an impending English attack, and the Mohawks prepared for battle. Through careful politicking, colonial officials assuaged Mohawk anxiety, but the Iroquois
would not permit the building of a second intended fort at Onondaga. Local

Indians soon adapted to their English neighbors. A number of Mohawks migrated to the village of Tiononderoge because they wished to take advantage of trade, religious instruction, and other social benefits available from living close to Fort Hunter.[40]

When the eastern Iroquois first encountered Dutch and German immigrants, they incorporated them within fictive kinship networks, establishing ties of social obligation. In their encounters with these newcomers, they transferred land from a position of strength and in accordance with their rituals of reciprocity. For their gifts they expected certain benefits in return. In the 1690s, the Mohawks "lent" a plot of land to the Dutch community of Schenectady "for a Range for their Cattle," accepting in return a small cash payment as a gift. They still maintained ownership of this land, but as Schenectady was becoming a prosperous community, with whom the Iroquois traded, loaning grazing lands was a way of strengthening socioeconomic connections. Indeed there was a high degree of fraternizing between these two communities. The colony had employed its Dutch inhabitants to build Fort Hunter and its chapel. Dutchmen also loaned their services as smiths, they plowed Mohawk lands, and a small number had Mohawk wives. The Mohawks demonstrated their favor for this community when they helped rebuild the town after it was destroyed by a French assault in 1691.[41] Similarly, the Mohawks dealt with German immigrants as potential allies. The Palatines arrived in the Schoharie Valley hungry and destitute and entirely dependent on the goodwill of the local Indians. The eastern Iroquois loaned land as an act of charity. An eighteenth-century headman would recall how the Mohawks had desired to grant the "Poor Germans" land "because we always pity the poor, and they are our Neighbors." Loaning land did not constitute a conveyance in ownership, however. The Mohawks permitted the Palatines to occupy and utilize these lands as long as they needed but expected economic and social benefits in return.[42]

Iroquois headmen soon discovered that ownership of lands, or at the very least *claims* to land, carried with it substantial political advantages in addition to socioeconomic gains. By the early 1700s, the Iroquois had promoted a belief that through the wars of the previous century they had conquered distant tribes and become "sole masters" of great expanses of land beyond their immediate homeland of Iroquoia. To their northwest, the Iroquois assumed rights over a vast territory north of Lake Erie, up to Lake Huron, and stretching west from the east side of Lake Erie to the southern tip of Lake Michigan.

Although the land was originally inhabited by Hurons and other Indians, Iroquois headmen asserted that their "predecessors did . . . totally conquer and subdue and drove them out of that country." The Iroquois also claimed special rights over the lands southwest of Lake Erie, known as the Ohio country. This far-flung region encompassed the upper Ohio Valley, from the Allegheny River west to the Muskingum and Scioto valleys. Through military victory over the Susquehannocks, Iroquois headmen also asserted that they had "wonn with the sword" southern lands in the Susquehanna Valley. These claims were flimsy and belied the reality of the diverse Indian groups who resided in these regions. Nonetheless, these proprietary pretensions were compelling, bolstering Iroquois status in an emerging Anglo-Indian political arena.[43]

By allocating parts of their territory to the English, Iroquois headmen sought to emphasize their power and importance while simultaneously compelling the English to serve as a counterweight against the French. In 1684, fearful of a French attack, a spokesman for the Onondagas and Cayugas granted the upper Susquehanna Valley to the New York governor, affirming as he did that "wee have putt all our land and our selfs under the Protection of the great Duke of York." This act was a means of reinforcing ties of mutual obligation; in exchange for this transfer they expected military protection. Equally it was meant as a show of power; they granted land because they had the sovereign power to do so. The speaker contended that because they were "a free people uniting them selues to the English," it was "in their power to give their land to what Sachim they please." In 1701 they deeded their northwestern "Beaver Hunting Ground" to the king of England. In a practical sense, the deed was meaningless. Despite their grand claims, the Iroquois could not control or dominate distant lands that were occupied by other Indian groups. The French further challenged Iroquois ownership by constructing a series of forts in this region. Exhausted from years of war and having recently entered a peace treaty with New France, the Iroquois were unable to challenge their rival claims to this territory. The purpose of the deed seemed twofold: to remind the English of their substantial—albeit imagined—land base and to make the English accountable for its protection. "Wee have not power to resist such a Christian enemy," they acknowledged. The deed was not a declaration to relinquish their rights to the land but a call to the king of England to fulfill his reciprocal duty to be their "protector and defender." For their own political reasons the English supported Iroquois land claims, and this mutually beneficial arrangement would, for the next half century, serve as a crucial resource for the Haudenosaunee by assuring their centrality in colonial-Indian affairs.[44]

Iroquois access to land and its resources may have buttressed their subsistence economy, but a defining feature of their seventeenth-century experience was their increased involvement in the transatlantic fur trade. Indeed the fur trade soon became the principal arena of contact between natives and newcomers. Animal fur, used in the production of hats and other outer garments, was a lucrative commodity in Europe. For their skill and labor in procuring and preparing this product Indians enjoyed access to a wide bevy of European goods including textiles, utensils, guns, farming tools, and alcohol. The Iroquois first traded with the Dutch at their post, Fort Orange, on the banks of the Hudson River in the 1610s. Displacing the Dutch, the English constructed their own post, Fort Albany, in the town of Albany, which served as the center point of Iroquois-English commerce for the next sixty years.

Older images of the fur trade as an exploitative system of capitalist relations foisted upon a naïve premodern people and guilty of instigating intertribal wars and cycles of dependency have been revised.[45] The fur trade undeniably aggravated preexisting tensions between Indian groups with devastating consequences, but it also resulted in real benefits. Never simply an alien system imposed by Europeans, the fur trade was a New World creation that involved the exchange and blending of Indian and European objects, values, and practices.[46] Although accounts of the untoward behavior of traders are well documented, the Iroquois were never just hapless victims. Their importance as procurers of commercially valuable furs and as middlemen between western Indians and Albany merchants made them indispensable and, by extension, permitted them to draw on a range of resources to shape forms of exchange according to their own predilections.[47]

The Iroquois incorporated trade and trade goods into preexisting economic and cultural patterns. Procuring furs for a transatlantic marketplace did not require them to radically reorganize their usual economic pursuits. Before the arrival of the Dutch and English, it was customary for Iroquois men to spend the winter months away from villages hunting wild game for home consumption. Although beaver had never been a main staple, it did not take much effort for men to redirect their hunting energies. Satisfying the demands of a new consumer economy (both in Europe and in Iroquoia) did, however, require Iroquois hunters to intensify the mode of production. Harvesting, processing, transporting, and exchanging furs was arduous work that drew on the labor of both men and women. Iroquois hunting parties were most active during the winter season when animal furs were at their thickest. While they concentrated their efforts on beaver, they also hunted bear, deer, muskrat, and cat. Women accompanied male hunting parties. Confined to the temporary hunting camps, they collected firewood, prepared meals, and performed the laborious task of processing furs. From May to late autumn—the official hunting season—Iroquois men and to a lesser extent women transported their bounty via foot and canoe to Albany.[48]

The consumption of foreign goods altered the material world of the Iroquois, but it did not cause a radical overhaul of their cultural values. To be sure, the penetration of foreign products into Iroquois homes occurred at an astonishing rate. Archaeological evidence demonstrates that while in the early seventeenth century European materials comprised "10 to 15 percent of the total artifact assemblage," by midcentury "they comprise[d] 75 percent or more."[49] But the Iroquois absorbed European products in ways that tapered the impact of change. While the material of articles altered, the form and function of articles generally remained the same: metal knives and copper kettles substituted stone utensils and ceramic pots; woolen stockings, cotton shirts, and petticoats replaced animal skins. In this respect, foreign goods brought greater ease and comfort into the lives of the Iroquois.

Rather than marking a disruptive intrusion of foreign objects, the fur trade in reality involved Europeans producing "Indian goods" for an Indian clientele. The Iroquois influenced the trading environment by their insistence that Europeans manufacture goods expressly for their needs and wants. Vermilion, a pigment made of mercury sulfide and desired by Indians for face and body paint, was manufactured in China, exported to England, and then shipped to North America. Specially crafted jewelry in the form of armbands and gorgets were made with an eye to the Indian market. Also high on the list of Indian demands was "duffels"—a thick woolen cloth that became an integral part of Indian fashion. "It is usually worn over the right shoulder and tied in a knot around the waist and from there hangs down to the feet," one Dutchman observed. The English replaced duffels with the equally popular "strouds," made in the English town of the same name. They too became, according to Dutch officials, "universally in fashion among the Indians," particularly in the darkest shades of blue and red.[50]

Moreover, Indians put European products to distinctly Indian uses, drilling holes through coins to wear as decorative ornaments, incorporating European clothing in a distinctly Indian fashion (shirts were worn as outer garments, for example), and interring trade goods with the dead because of the spiritual value attached to them.[51] Even alcohol, a trade good that generated many social ills, was used in culturally familiar ways. Unlike Europeans, Indians did not drink moderately. They instead drank for the sole purpose of inebriation. Consequently, their use of alcohol led to violent outbursts, often between family and friends. But repeatedly Europeans observed that Indians did not receive any punishment for their misconduct. After a drunken foray one Dutchman observed, "instead of seeking revenge, they come to one another begging forgiveness, saying, 'We were drunk; the wine or rum did it.'" Similarly French Jesuits noted how sobered individuals evaded retribution by claiming to the injured party, "What wouldst thou have me do? I had no sense; I was Drunk." Alcohol use may have been akin to an older cultural practice associated with the Iroquois medicine society, known as the False Faces Society. When members of this society donned a False Face mask, they were allowed to perform ordinarily unacceptable behavior. In much the same way, intoxication provided a communally sanctioned means to act out aggressive pent-up emotions without being held accountable for such conduct. At a time when the Iroquois were experiencing immense change and upheaval, alcohol provided a valuable tool for redefining standards of socially agreeable behavior.[52]

As Indians absorbed European goods into their own native lifestyle, they also compelled Europeans to utilize articles of indigenous origin. Wampum offers an illuminating example of a syncretic article imbibing native and European intermixture. Long valued among the Iroquois for its spiritual qualities and comprising an integral part of their ceremonial life, particularly the condolence ceremony, wampum changed in both form and function as a consequence of the fur trade. The introduction of metal tools caused Algonquian manufacturers to produce tubular rather than discoidal beads. Wishing to promote trade and recognizing how much the Iroquois desired wampum, the Dutch greatly enhanced its availability by importing larger quantities from New England as well as manufacturing their own. What was once a scarce and sacred object became, almost overnight, hugely abundant and increasingly monetized. In exchange for furs and other goods, wampum served as a quasi-currency. "In the areas which the Christians frequent, the Indians use a kind of currency they call zeewant [wampum]," Dutchman Adriaen Cornelissen Van der Donck observed. "This is the only money circulating among the Indians and in which one trades with them." Because of a shortage of coinage in New York, wampum became the prevailing currency among Europeans as well. "Among our people, too," Van der Donck noted, "it is in general use for buying everything one needs."[53]

Foreign trade introduced the Iroquois to the concept of currency, but throughout the seventeenth century it remained just that, a concept rather than an actual phenomenon. The Iroquois resisted the total monetization of wampum and remained largely indifferent to the monetary use of foreign coins as well. Megapolensis noted the noncommercial value the Mohawks ascribed to wampum, which he mistakenly identified as bone: "They value these little bones as highly as many Christians do gold, silver and pearls; but they do not like our money, and esteem it no better than iron." He recalled an incident in which he presented a Dutch coin to a Mohawk chief: "he asked how much it was worth among the Christians; and when I told him, he laughed exceedingly at us, saying we were fools to value a piece of iron so highly." The Iroquois continued to use wampum as an important decorative article. Van der Donck noted the practice of "wealthier women" who "wear such skirts wholly embroidered with wampum, often worth between one and three hundred guilders." Just as important, they continued to value it for its ritual value. In fact its increased availability enhanced its ceremonial and diplomatic uses. As beads were now available in the thousands, much larger and more elaborate wampum belts could be produced. As an intercultural "forest diplomacy" developed between the Five Nations and the English, wampum belts constituted an essential tool of diplomacy, one that English officials could not afford to ignore. Belts confirmed the veracity of spoken words and symbolically recorded messages and agreements. In this two-way exchange, Europeans were also obliged to acknowledge and incorporate Indian objects and values into their cultural world.[54]

As Indians and Europeans bargained and bartered with one another over goods and resources, they engaged in relations characterized from the beginning by a messy combination of cooperation and contention. While there were frequent examples of misconduct, especially before English rule when it was not uncommon for Dutch traders to kidnap or beat Mohawk hunters, mutual need for one another encouraged the creation of workable, if not always conflict-free, relations. The sheer market value of furs bolstered the importance of the Iroquois as trading partners. Whatever feelings of cultural disdain Dutchmen harbored about them, they depended on the skills and labor of Iroquois hunters. Practical difficulties in language could heighten tensions, although most colonists involved in commerce developed "a kind of jargon just sufficient to carry on trade with it." Unsteady relations were probably more a consequence of Dutchmen needing the Iroquois but not necessarily liking them. The Mohawks understood this view of trade relations as a marriage of convenience. "The Dutch say we are brothers and that we are joined together with chains," a Mohawk man told an Albany official in 1659, "but that lasts only as we have beavers. After that we are no longer thought of."[55]

The arrival of the English prompted fresh efforts to reform the trade. From the 1670s onward, Albany officials imposed a series of regulations, restricting commerce within the confines of their town walls and passing ordinances to minimize social contact between Indians and traders. They also formed a new body, which came to be known as the Commissioners for Indian Affairs, to manage relations with Native Americans. Although violence and deceit continued to punctuate the trade, Indians and Europeans also established a peaceable alliance based on mutual need and cooperation. Albany merchant Evert Wendell held accounts with a number of Indians that lasted for many years, signifying genuine long-term friendships.[56] Despite official attempts to minimize Indian-colonial intercourse, trade continued to take place within a wider web of socioeconomic exchange. Albany magistrates admitted that they were unable to prevent Anglo-Iroquois fraternizing. The fur trade had "produced . . . too much familiarity with the Indians," complained one official. "For, not satisfied with merely taking [the Indians] into their houses in the customary manner, they attracted them by extraordinary attention, such as admitting them to Table, laying napkins before them, presenting Wine to them." Furthermore, officials were also unable to confine trade to Albany. Schenectady became an important venue for Iroquois Indians on their way to trade at Albany, and many Indian hunters preferred exchanging goods with colonists with whom they had already established socioeconomic ties.[57]

The seventeenth-century fur trade resulted in a mixed outcome for the Iroquois, including both upheaval and lasting benefits. Ultimately, involvement in the fur trade caused the Iroquois to become dependent on foreign goods and markets. By the 1700s, English products had replaced most indigenous forms. Most significantly, the Iroquois had stopped producing their own tools of production. Women substituted European ironware for homemade wooden farming implements European ironware, while warriors abandoned bows and arrows for guns and powder. Their lives and livelihoods were now intimately bound up with commercial trade networks. While they would not perish without these goods their circumstances would be dramatically impaired without them. But their dependence was not akin to being in a state of dependency. The New York Iroquois still maintained control over valuable economic resources well into the eighteenth century that granted them important autonomy. Most significantly, a healthy land base promoted self-sufficiency, providing a buffer against expanding market forces. As long as they continued to hunt and farm, their participation in an external market economy could be casual and partial.[58]

Changing material conditions wrought by colonialism had important implications for the Iroquois gender system, both reinforcing long-held gendered practices as well as precipitating change. The new emphasis on trade and warfare worked to accentuate the role of the warrior-hunter. The international fur trade intensified what was already a highly esteemed masculine vocation. As their communities faced demographic stress young men also had ample opportunity to demonstrate their manly prowess and valor by participating in mourning wars. Men's masculine role as warriors made a considerable impression on Europeans who considered them a "formidable" people. Their apparent expertise in warfare aroused both admiration and concern. "They attack furiously, are merciless in victory, and cunning in planning an assault," one colonist insisted. Mohawk warriors, in particular, gained a reputation for their ferocious nature. Their name is a derivative of an Algonquian term for "man-eaters." Defeating the Mahicans in the late 1620s and acquiring their lands around Fort Orange and Saratoga Lake helped establish their virile reputation. Megapolensis observed of them: "They have also naturally a very high opinion of themselves; they say, *Ihy Othkon* ('I am the Devil') by which they mean that they are superior folks."[59]

While enhancing the role of the warrior-hunter, the onset of colonization also set in process a subtle shift in gendered relations between men. At midcentury, family connections continued to play a predominant role in determining allocations of power. As Van der Donck observed in 1653, "No chief has the power to confer rank; authority and chieftainship are hereditary and continue as long as the chief's family produces persons suited to that rank." But the endless succession of wars that dominated this century and the growing need to engage in diplomatic relations with emerging European powers encouraged a larger number of men to achieve positions of "commissioned rank" based "on merit without regard to family or standing." To meet the challenges of colonization, the Iroquois developed a different kind of political entity, known now as the Iroquois Confederacy. Although it borrowed many of its diplomatic tools and personnel from the Iroquois League, it was a distinct body. The evolution of the Confederacy generated enlarged opportunities for men to obtain stations of political headship by demonstrations of bravery in warfare or diplomatic astuteness. Hereditary chiefs still occupied ritually important and politically consequential offices, but as the seventeenth century progressed a growing number of Pine Tree Chiefs began to dominate village politics, thereby challenging their once taken-for-granted authority.[60]

The intensification of hunting and war had a notable impact on the lives of women. The unprecedented number of captives brought back to villages augmented the longstanding role of clan matrons to decide their fate. Furthermore, the prolonged absence of men from villages created more autonomy and responsibility for women. As men devoted a greater part of their productive labor to hunting and warfare, the importance of women's roles as farmers was enhanced. "The women are obliged to prepare the land, to mow, to plant, and do everything," Megapolensis noted. But women had never been confined to cornfields. Their control of food staples meant that they also were involved in trade, traveling to other villages to swap and exchange surplus goods. In the mid-1630s, a Dutch colonist noted the arrival of a small group of women at a Mohawk village who sold salmon and tobacco for some Dutch currency and wampum. Their willingness to accept Dutch money reveals their readiness to adapt older trading patterns to European influences. Women were also receptive to new economic opportunities opening up for them in the fur trade. Mohawk women regularly went "among the Christians to trade and make purchases." At least 20 percent of Wendell's trading customers were native women, who purchased goods with furs and wampum. Some obtained large supplies from the Albany merchant for the purpose of selling them to Indian customers. One noted female trader was Schadseeaaei, daughter of a "chief sachem of the Seneca country." She procured goods to sell to other Indians in addition to peddling wares on Wendell's behalf.[61]

The presence of European men provided other means for women to obtain economic benefits and social status. As wives or consorts to traders, women could secure their families with access to European goods.[62] Women also engaged in more casual relationships by exchanging sexual favors for goods and money. "The women are exceedingly addicted to whoring; they will lie with a man for the value of one, two, or three *schillings*, and our Dutchmen run after them very much," Megapolensis claimed. The cultural background of men like Megapolensis explains their readiness to view women's sexual behavior as a form of commercial prostitution or indicative of their lascivious nature. The Iroquois, however, had a different cultural explanation based on their concepts of gift-giving and hospitality. Sources indicate a tradition of providing female companions to visiting male guests. "Some of their prettiest Girls are . . . presented to the Stranger, for his Choice," an English colonist recorded in one of the first histories written on the Iroquois. "The young Lady, who has the Honour to be preferred on these Occasions, performs all the Duties of a fond Wife, during the Stranger's Stay." Offering female companionship was a gesture of goodwill and friendship and in expectation of a reciprocal response, perhaps a gift in cash or a fair price in trade. The failure of male colonists to understand the cultural meaning of women's sexual overtures may account for why this custom expired in the seventeenth century.[63] This conflicting interpretation of women's sexual behavior demonstrates how differing gender ideals influenced cross-cultural encounters.

In their political relations with one another, both the Iroquois and English utilized a gendered language to define and naturalize power relations. The Iroquois had long employed kinship terms to make sense of their relations with other Indian groups. Kin metaphors encapsulated their ideas about social obligations. Referring to a tributary nation as "Nephew" was a way of defining a bond that was reciprocal but not necessarily equal. By asserting their status as "Elder Brother" or "Uncle," the Iroquois claimed the right to supervise their *younger* relations. During the 1600s they designated the title of "women" to the Delaware Indians of Pennsylvania. This was not a derogative term but used to specify a particular role the Delawares were expected to play. As "women" the Delawares were removed from the arena of warfare and assigned the role of peace advocate. At the same time it placed the Iroquois in a position of social obligation to protect them. The Iroquois sought to mold the Covenant Chain of Friendship—the formal name given to the Iroquois-English alliance—in accordance with their gendered ideals. By acknowledging the king of England as their "Father," the Iroquois did not assume a subordinate role but rather made the king accountable to their needs. They could now demand of him, as their "Father," protection and provisions. The Iroquois referred to the English generally as "Brethren," a kinship term denoting equality and mutual respect.[64]

English attempts to construct a paternalistic rendering of social relations met with a hostile response. Early New York governors sought to integrate the Iroquois into their extended polity as submissive and dutiful subjects.[65] At political conferences with the Five Nations, they assigned the label "Children," thereby affirming their dependent status as "subjects" of the king. But the Iroquois refused to be assigned these less-than-equal designators. When

Governor Edmund Andros addressed the Mohawks as "Children" in 1688, they reminded him that in former times their ancestors had been called "Brethren" and urged, "lett the old Covenant that was made with our ancestors be kept firme . . . let that of Brethren continue without alteration." The Mohawks refused to be infantilized. In much the same way, Onondaga orator Otreouti (Grangula) told the French governor in 1684, "We are born Freemen, and have no dependance either upon the Onnontio or the Corlar," referring, respectively, to the French and New York governors. "We have a power to go where we please, to conduct who we will to the places we resort to, and to buy and sell where we think fit. If your Allies are your Slaves or Children, you may e'en treat 'em as such, and rob 'em of the liberty of entertaining any other Nation but your own." To be labeled a child was akin to being labeled a slave, as both were deemed impotent vis-à-vis the English. Otreouti made clear the Iroquois were neither. On occasion they accepted the term "subject" but not its inference. As one Seneca chief told Governor Thomas Dongan in 1687, "we being the King of England's Subjects though ourselves no ways obliged to harken to him." Some were even inclined to dispute the king's status as their "Father." In dialogue with the New York provincial interpreter, an Iroquois orator asserted, "You say we are Subjects to the King of England and Duke of York, but we say, we are Brethren." Through Iroquois insistence, native kinship terms came to dominate Anglo-Iroquois political discourse. The very fact that the English were obliged to adopt Iroquois protocol highlights the weakness of imperial authority on the fringes of empire.[66]

The arrival of Europeans posed ideological challenges for the Haudenosaunee, as they were obliged to account for who these foreigners were and where they had come from. Just as they had done with European trade goods, the Iroquois incorporated European people into preexisting cultural frameworks without initially having to radically alter them. Whether they adjusted their origins myth or whether it already allowed for a polygenesis view of creation, the Iroquois found ways of explaining the existence of Europeans. "They think that there are more worlds than one, and that we came from another world," Megapolensis recorded in 1644. Although the Iroquois made some reference to Europeans being "of one skinn," physical bodily markers did not appear that significant in encapsulating human differences. Iroquois willingness to apply kinship terms to outsiders and to adopt European captives as family members demonstrates the permeable border that existed between notions of *them* and *us*. Instead of skin color, there were other more potent markers of difference. Notably, the novel iron tools and blacksmithing skills of Dutch traders encouraged the Iroquois to initially employ the generic label of "Asseroni," which meant "makers of knives."[67]

Colonization not only resulted in the Iroquois having to make sense of Europeans, it also had a tremendous impact on Iroquois self-definition, notably by fracturing Iroquois ethnic identity. Never a monolithic entity, the Iroquois became even less so as a century of warfare, disease, mass adoption, Christian conversion, and outward migration altered, fragmented, and diversified formulations of ethnic consciousness. Missionary influence undercut a consistent group identity. The influence of French Jesuits in Iroquois villages in the 1660s and beyond precipitated social division and upheaval. Many Catholic converts chose to resettle in Canada, thus giving rise to new ethnic groups such as the Kahnawake Mohawks, while other Mohawks, under the tutelage of Dutch missionaries, converted to Protestantism.[68] The seventeenth-century ethnic makeup of the Iroquois further transformed when they assimilated thousands of Huron and Algonquian war captives into their lineages. Historically the Iroquois had three clans; by the 1700s the western Iroquois nations had up to seven or eight. Some of these clans were very likely the product of Iroquois wholesale adoption of groups.[69] If large-scale adoption points to the fragile and fragmentary nature of "Iroquois" ethnic identity, it also equally demonstrates a people's determination and skill for survival. The mixed ethnic makeup of the Iroquois and the new pattern of dispersed settlements meant that identity remained extremely localized.

While particular forces splintered Iroquois identity, an expanding European presence also encouraged collective ways for articulating group identity. To enhance their stature and political importance in the eyes of Europeans, Iroquois headmen promoted the impression of unity, particularly as they reorganized under the Iroquois Confederacy. By ritualistically recounting their seventeenth-century wars and referring to lands they had "wonn by the sword," Iroquois headmen carefully constructed an image of martial potency and ethnic cohesion. They "think themselves by Nature superior to the rest of Mankind, and call themselves Ongue-honwe; that is, Men surpassing all others," one colonist observed.[70]

Although the English generally preferred to identify the Iroquois as dependents or subjects of the Crown, they were equally receptive to embracing Iroquois self-definitions as potent sovereign allies, as and when it served political needs. Bewildered by a confusing array of Indian communities and languages, English officials sought out a single unified "nation" that could represent and speak for others. Given the Haudenosaunee's strong martial reputation and their success at cultivating such an image, the English seized upon them as potentially useful partners. Keen to secure Iroquois allegiance, the English looked for and underscored signs of commonality. Early English commentators described how each of the Five Nations comprised an "independent Republick," yet "joined together by a League or Confederacy." Applying a common vocabulary to the Iroquois lessened their otherness. In the context of imperial struggles with New France, emphasizing the sovereign and noble status of Iroquois allies served a political purpose. When plans were afoot for an Iroquois-English invasion of Canada during Queen Anne's War, colonial officials hoped that stressing their allegiance with Mohawk "kings" would add credence to their imperial ventures against the French. The excitement and flurry generated by the visit of the Indian delegation to London demonstrates the ability and ease with which the English incorporated native peoples (or at least their "royalty") into the imagery of the early empire. Tejonihokarawa and his peers played up to this image because they hoped to secure attention, gifts, and religious instruction in return.[71]

While early Dutch, German, and English colonists residing on the New York frontier were far less celebratory of their Iroquois neighbors, the nature of close living, the omnipotent threat of the French, and the all-consuming importance of trade encouraged them to form genuine ties of cooperation. Socioeconomic ties bound these communities together. Cross-cultural sex gave rise to a number of biracial individuals who served as important cultural brokers on this early frontier. Hilletie van Olinda, daughter of a Dutch trader and a Mohawk mother, used her intercultural knowledge to mediate between Anglo and Indian worlds, even if she did not always feel fully accepted by either. Cultural disdain and discord were always present in Anglo-Iroquois relations, but there was an absence of racialized thinking in this early period. Given the high degree of interdependence between these groups, it made little sense to think in terms of fixed and insurmountable differences.[72]

The first century of relations with Europeans changed the lives of the Haudenosaunee forever, but it did not render them a broken or colonized people. The limited nature of the early English Empire granted the Iroquois important room to maneuver. Most important, they preserved a high degree of economic sovereignty. They literally maintained their ground by holding onto their homelands and hunting territories. Their access to valuable economic resources placed them in strong standing vis-à-vis the early English Empire.

The strength of their position secured them substantial political clout and ensured cultural self-determination. Despite experiencing much material change through extended contact with Europeans, Iroquois gender roles exhibited significant durability. In addition, they applied their kinship norms to their relations with English officials, traders, and settlers. Their stronghold in colonial New York also empowered them in their efforts promote an identity that championed their interests. Their importance as military and commercial allies encouraged the English to mentally integrate them into their conception of a broad Atlantic community. But the relative might of the Iroquois was ephemeral. As British commitment to an overseas empire magnified by the mid-eighteenth century, the Iroquois were exposed to increasingly injurious forces.

Chapter 2

The Ascension of Empire

American-born artist Benjamin West captured on canvas a famous moment in the 1755 Battle of Lake George when William Johnson intercedes to prevent a Mohawk warrior from scalping the captured French commanding officer (fig. 2). Recently appointed as supervisor of the Six Nations, Johnson embodies the civilizing force of Europeans in the New World. With one hand placed on the Mohawk, he gently but forcibly prevents the attack. With the other hand he points the Indian away, literally and symbolically relegating him to the sidelines of the imperial landscape now that a British victory has been assured and native martial power no longer required. The painting was a celebration of British imperial strength and virtue. Like many men of his generation, West was attracted to the events of the Seven Years' War, a momentous imperial conflict that marked the zenith of British imperial expansion in the eighteenth century. The Battle of Lake George, which occurred at the outset of the war, was of little military consequence, but coming in the aftermath of a dismal British defeat at the forks of the Ohio in western Pennsylvania, reports of colonial soldiers and Iroquois warriors valiantly repelling French forces were enough to solicit jubilation from victory-hungry Britons in the colonies and overseas. This battle caught the imagination of British audiences precisely because of the military involvement of around three hundred Mohawk warriors, including their famous headman Theyanoguin. Although the Iroquois were motivated by their own self-interests, West's image of the lone warrior reflects the way eighteenth-century Britons wished to think of them: as faithful and subordinate.

West's painting captures a moment of transition in the British-Iroquois alliance. The Battle of Lake George marked both an intensification in relations and a shift in power. The immediate result of the battle for Johnson was to catapult his rise in transatlantic fame, ensuring his receipt of money,

Figure 2. *General Johnson Saving a Wounded French Officer from the Tomahawk of a North American Indian,* by Benjamin West (ca. 1764–68). Oil on canvas. Derby Museum and Art Gallery, England.

title, and commission. The immediate result for the Mohawks was death and injury, the construction of forts on their hunting grounds, and the beginning of significant pressure to lend further military aid. The respective fates of Johnson and the Mohawks represent—albeit in exaggerated fashion—a much

broader trend. The Seven Years' War unleashed the disruptive forces of imperial expansion, which worked to augment British power in North America
at the expense of Iroquois autonomy. This war was distinct from previous
imperial conflicts fought in the colonies, marking as it did a change in the
way Britons conceptualized the meaning of an overseas empire and the way
in which they viewed the Haudenosaunee's relationship to that empire. Ultimately the war, beginning with the 1755 campaign, drew the Iroquois more
firmly than ever before into a widening imperial orbit by making increased
demands on their land and labor. In West's painting, the image of Johnson
motioning the warrior to step aside outside the frame of the picture is telling.
This mid-eighteenth-century conflict created a set of conditions by which the
Iroquois would be sidelined in the postwar era and their ability to influence
imperial forces undermined.

Well before the first muskets fired at the Battle of Lake George the respective
fates of William Johnson and the Mohawks had been moving along opposing but nevertheless interlinked trajectories. Johnson migrated to the Mohawk Valley from County Merth, Ireland, in 1738. His uncle, Peter Warren,
sponsored him to oversee his plantation on the south side of the Mohawk
River.[1] Attuned to the commercial opportunities flourishing in the transatlantic economy, Johnson soon carved out his own mercantile empire in the
New York hinterland. Foremost he prospered in the fur trade after establishing a trading post on the banks of the Mohawk River. He sent agents carrying
his goods to Iroquois villages and then gradually broke into the trade at Fort
Oswego, a British post on the southeast edge of Lake Ontario. Johnson was
equally committed to the accumulation and commercial use of land. Within
a year of his arrival he had purchased his own estate on the north bank of
the river where he settled tenant farmers, collecting their rent in grains. He
processed their crops in his own private mill before selling them to New York
merchants for foreign export. He built a large home, which came to be known
as Fort Johnson, on this site, where he lived with his German indentured wife
and three children. In 1751, he began to acquire his second estate, known
as Kingsborough, which lay twenty miles farther west. He would eventually
build an even grander abode on this land, dubbed Johnson Hall.[2]

By the time of Johnson's arrival in the valley, the Mohawks were no longer
the numerous and martial people they had once been. The construction of
Fort Oswego in 1727 had diverted trading activities west from Albany and
away from the Mohawks, undermining their importance as trading partners

and their former central role in diplomatic affairs. Furthermore, as the easternmost nation of the still-powerful Iroquois Confederacy, the Mohawks faced the greatest intrusion on their lands. Since the 1710s, a growing influx of settlers had moved into the valley, while other Albany residents wielded fraudulent deeds claiming ownership of Mohawk cornfields and hunting grounds. By the 1740s, the Fort Hunter and Canajoharie communities faced growing constraints to their power and prestige.

Johnson initially established relations with the neighboring Mohawks through his activities in the fur trade. His fair dealings with them and readiness to provide goods on credit engendered amicable feelings. Regular and close contact enabled him to become seasoned in their practices and beliefs. As he began to grow in wealth and political stature, the Mohawks looked to him as someone who could represent their grievances to the higher powers and who, through his public office and personal involvement in the fur trade, could provide them with access to the empire's wealth. Johnson further cemented ties by his common-law marriage to a Mohawk woman, Molly Brant, sometime after his wife died.[3]

For almost thirty years Johnson functioned as the principal conduit between the British Empire and the Iroquois nations, and his success in this role was due in large part to his adroit mediation of cultural differences. He was an extremely effective man-in-the-middle, borrowing and blending native and European forms. Johnson was both comfortable and highly capable of refashioning his cultural identity to fit situational needs. He strengthened and enlarged Indian ties through his willingness to act in accordance with their cultural norms. He appropriated Mohawk dress, customs, and values to appeal to their sensibilities, win their loyalty, and enhance his personal influence. He slept in their homes without complaint, graciously ate their cuisine, and fathered biracial children.[4] Johnson proved particularly proficient at mediating between Indian and British political cultures. The Iroquois always began meetings by symbolically erasing the grief of those who had recently lost loved ones. Notably the deaths of leaders were condoled and new ones selected to take their place. Understanding that the condolence ceremony was an "unavoidable" component of the diplomatic process, Johnson soon became expert at performing this rite. He made sure to incorporate the use of wampum belts in speeches and skillfully drew on their practice of employing metaphors and allegories to create a familiar rhetoric. Headmen thanked him "for speaking in Our own way, which is more Intelligible to us, because [it is] conformable to the Custom and manner of our forefathers." Johnson's

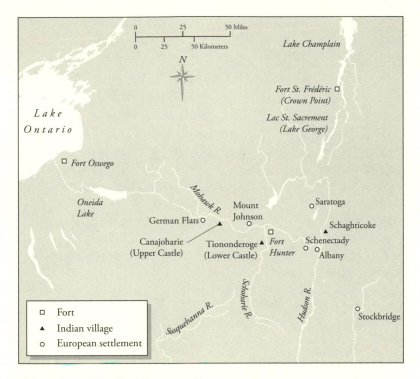

Map 2. The Mohawk Valley, ca. 1750s.

ease at enacting Indian forms won him the respect of many Iroquois. He was symbolically adopted by the Mohawks as a mark of friendship and given the name Warraghiyagey, "a man who undertakes great Things."[5]

Yet this description of Johnson as a benign and gifted broker reveals only a partial truth. Johnson was primarily an agent of empire who manipulated Iroquois practices and values to further imperial and private ends. He may have crossed cultural boundaries with great ease, but his political loyalties and cultural preferences remained firmly aligned with the empire. In his public office he was employed to fashion a British-Iroquois alliance that aided an imperial agenda: to promote a lucrative fur trade; to facilitate the colonial accumulation of Indian land; and to enlist Indian warriors against the French. In his private life as well, Johnson personified the accumulation ethos and cultural ideologies of the empire he served. He used his ties with his Indian relations to enhance his personal wealth and standing.

Throughout his career Johnson championed the view that the Six Na-

Figure 3. "Sir William Johnson, Major General of the English Forces in America," London engraving by T. Adams (1756). Library of Congress, Washington, D.C. This image was published to mark Johnson's new appointment during the war. Johnson's appearance, complete with fine wig and clothing, and the presence of a cannon signify his identity as a consequential-man-of-empire. But he stands against the backdrop of an American forest, indicating his connection to Native America.

tions' allegiance was essential to British fortunes in North America, even if he did not necessarily view them as his social equals. Through ties of commerce, religion, and intermarriage, Johnson held that it was possible to integrate the Iroquois into the empire. By highlighting their role as traders, consumers, land sellers, and soldiers, Johnson promoted the image of the Iroquois as valued fellow denizens of a British Atlantic community. Although Johnson did not subscribe to a racialized view of the Iroquois, he still understood his relations to them in terms of hierarchy. Johnson sought to establish patriarchal relations with his Mohawk neighbors. He readily viewed them as dependents, claiming to his uncle in 1749: "My Scituation among the Indians, and integrity to them, made those poor Savages Seek to me, so that I have a Superior Interest with them." Johnson wished to fashion an alliance in which the Mohawks assumed a subservient role as pliant and dependent clients. He often boasted of his power: "I have all my Counsellors the Mohawks and Canajoharees, with whose assistance I could bring them to do anything."[6]

He employed various measures to enhance Mohawk dependency and inflate his own patriarchal pretensions. To create a cohort of dutiful allies, he asserted his prerogative in appointing new leaders. On the death of a headman, the Iroquois conducted the condolence ritual and requickening ceremony in which a new chief was appointed to his place. Johnson began to enact this rite. In July 1753 he informed New York governor George Clinton, "It will be verry necessary to make Sachims now when I go up in Everry Nation (as there are severall dead) of those who are most hearty in our Interest. For which purpose I should want at least Eight, or ten Meddalls."[7] Asserting himself as male provider, Johnson sometimes requested warriors and chiefs to disrupt subsistence activities so that they could be available to him, reassuring them that he would supply their wants.[8] In fact, Johnson enhanced his role as patriarch through his ability to dispense goods. By lavishing gifts on key headmen, he expected loyalty and submission and was perturbed when it was not forthcoming. Johnson also asserted his manly dominance through physical and symbolic displays of virility, often donning the garb and song of a Mohawk warrior. At his first official appearance in Albany in 1746, a contemporary observed how he led the Mohawks to council "dressed and painted after the Manner of an Indian War-Captain." Johnson believed that a show of manly force and prestige was necessary to "Command" the respect and submission of the Mohawks. As he noted to his superior, although they were "somewhat warlike" they were "actuated by their fears at a small appear-

Figure 4. Portrait of Sir William Johnson, by John Wollaston (ca. 1750–52).
Oil on canvas. Gift of Laura Munsell Tremaine in memory of her father,
Joel Munsell. Albany Institute of History and Art. Eighteenth-century
portraiture was a popular way of indicating one's class. Positioned against
a dark background, which drew attention to the detail and finery of his
clothing, Johnson wore a rich scarlet suit, textured green waistcoat, and
cravat, hallmarks of his good taste, refinement, and social status.

ance of Power." Thus, when duty called, Johnson was certain to "talk very harsh" to Indian allies to get his way.[9]

If Johnson wished to treat Mohawk men as obliging patrons, he wished to remove native women from the political arena altogether. Embodying the patriarchal outlook of the British Empire, Johnson considered politics an exclusively masculine domain. Thus, he purposefully advised the New York governor not to invite native women to conferences, on the grounds that they had nothing meaningful to contribute. Yet, willing to acquiesce to Iroquois gender norms for the greater good of the empire, Johnson recanted on this position when circumstances necessitated. Learning of the powers and privileges of clan matrons, Johnson was obliged to endow them with gifts and flattery and to tolerate their participation in diplomatic exchanges. As long as it was politically expedient, he yielded to Indian practices. As one contemporary observed, Johnson "Knew that Women govern the Politics of Savages . . . and therefore always kept up a good understanding with the brown Ladies."[10]

While uncomfortable with the political role of native women, Johnson eagerly promoted their availability as sexual partners. Johnson relished the sexual opportunities available on the imperial frontier. He expressed his masculinized identity as a potent man of empire through his extravagant sexual relations with Indian women. By the mid-1750s, rumors circulated in London about the number of his Indian concubines while some reported that he had as many as seven hundred métis offspring. Johnson in fact fathered two documented illegitimate métis sons—Brant Kaghneghtago, also called Young Brant or Brant Johnson, and Tekawironte, also known as William of Canajoharie—with unknown women, before he took Molly Brant as his long-term consort, with whom he had a further eight children.[11] His frontier home became a place to facilitate sexual exchanges between Euro-American men and native women, whom he described as "a polite sett of ladies." Assisting sexual trysts, Johnson liaised between parties, such as when local militiaman Joseph Chew asked after "the young Ladys at the Castle," sending his compliments "to little Miss Michael at the Mohawks and madam curl'd locks at Canejesharry." Johnson also arranged meetings, informing one colleague that he intended to introduce him to "a Princess of the first Rank here, who has large possessions."[12]

In addition to constructing a gendered hierarchy with his Iroquois neighbors, Johnson also made sense of differences in terms of class. At generous moments he described Indians "as orderly a people as any of our Lower

A North View of Fort Johnson drawn on the spot by M.ʳ Guy Johnson Sir W.ᵐ Johnson's Son ?

Figure 5. "A North View of Fort Johnson drawn on the spot by Mr. Guy Johnson" (ca. 1759). Emmet Collection, Miriam and Ira D. Wallach Division of Art, Prints, and Photographs, New York Public Library, Astor, Lenox and Tilden Foundations. This engraving indicates the extent of William Johnson's wealth. Its inclusion in a London periodical reveals the growing interest Britons at home held for this frontier figure.

Class."[13] Their lack of private property, literacy, and Christianity led Johnson to conclude their social inferiority. Extremely status conscious, Johnson identified some Indians as more equal than others and sought out the friendship of the "better sort," namely chieftains, head warriors, and clan matrons who possessed status and influence. By courting these Indians, Johnson not only acknowledged their special social standing but enlarged it as well. His choice to form a long-term union with Molly Brant was well calculated. Brant was not just any Mohawk woman but the stepdaughter of Brant Canagaraduncka, a highly influential and wealthy Canajoharie headman.

Whatever social deficiencies the Iroquois possessed, Johnson held faith in their improvement. Through conversion to Christianity they could be Anglicized and absorbed into colonial society. Demonstrating little interest in protecting their cultural integrity, Johnson instead looked forward to their cultural assimilation. Throughout his career, he promoted the work of missionaries, believing that religious proselytizing laid the foundation for "civil" habits to develop. Indians would adopt European gender roles and economic practices through example. As Johnson observed, "when our increas'd Numbers place them more in our Neighbourhood . . . they [will] discover Superior Advantages in our Way of Living."[14] Johnson may have fathered biracial children, but he was determined to raise them as Anglicized citizens of the British Empire. His eldest son by Brant, Peter Johnson, was given his father's name and sent to Philadelphia at age thirteen to be apprenticed in the counting house of a wholesale business. William Johnson had no intention of allowing Peter to become a warrior-hunter, training him instead to become a New World merchant. To his other son, Brant Kaghneghtago, Johnson bequeathed land, a large sum of money, and livestock to enable him to become a farmer.[15]

Johnson intended to use his skills as a frontier diplomat to incorporate Six Nation allies into his vision of a commercially expansive, male-dominated, multiracial empire. He hoped also to enrich himself along the way. To achieve his aims, Johnson readily manipulated native beliefs and practices: adopting the language of kinship to cajole warriors into war, he constructed a network of personal alliances through lavish gift-giving and the appointment of chiefs. Although imaginative cultural borrowing flourished on Johnson's successive estates, it was not always symptomatic of mutually advantageous relations. Indeed, the ever-increasing size of Johnson's frontier homes symbolized his and indeed the empire's waxing strength. But Johnson's success depended on cultivating trust and friendship among the Six Nations. His role as super-

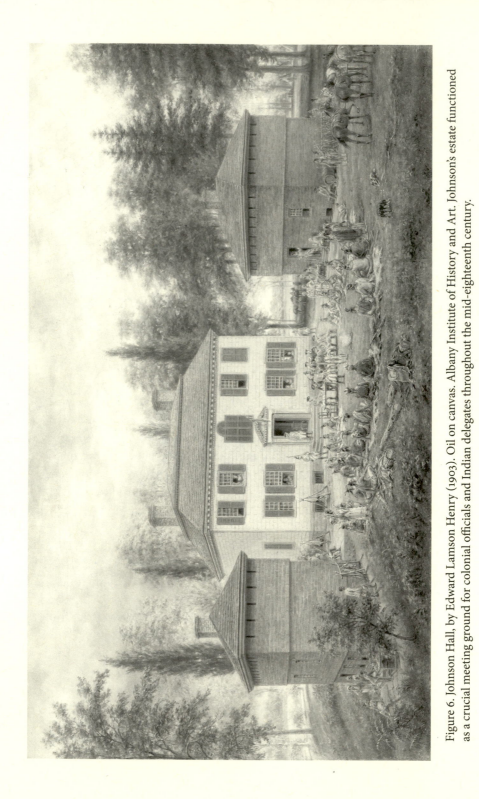

Figure 6. Johnson Hall, by Edward Lamson Henry (1903). Oil on canvas. Albany Institute of History and Art. Johnson's estate functioned as a crucial meeting ground for colonial officials and Indian delegates throughout the mid-eighteenth century.

intendent was meaningless unless he was willing and able to respect their etiquette, engage in their rituals, and respond to their grievances. Johnson was a forceful figure in Indian affairs, but his vision to remake the Iroquois as dutiful Anglicized subjects remained unrealized.

The Johnson-Iroquois alliance took form during King George's War (1744–48), an imperial conflict that reveals the limits of both Britain's ambition in North America and Crown control over native allies. When the French opened hostilities against an English settlement in Nova Scotia in May 1744, Governor George Clinton of New York hoped to enlist the Six Nations to defend the northern frontier. He found unwilling partners in the Albany commissioners, the men instructed the deal with Indian affairs. They preferred instead to promote Iroquois neutrality to ensure the continuation of the lucrative clandestine fur trade between Albany and Montreal. Dissatisfied with the commissioners' conduct, and on hearing of Johnson's close ties with the Mohawks, Clinton appointed him instead to manage Indian affairs. Johnson soon established his home as a base for recruiting, equipping, and sending out Mohawk scouting parties. But with an independent assembly refusing to back his agenda, Clinton lacked monies to finance Johnson's activities. He found little support from the home government. Fighting a costly war in Europe, the British Crown had little interest in diverting money to fund provincial soldiers and allied Indians in North America. Although Whitehall eventually commissioned a naval squadron to assist New England, she declined sending troops.[16]

The limits of imperial ambition were made abundantly clear in 1747 when Johnson received orders from Clinton to "prepare as many Indian Warriours as possible to assist our Forces in the Reduction of Crown Point." This was a French base, known by them as Fort St. Frédéric, on the northern tip of Lac St. Sacrement. Johnson shrewdly solicited Iroquois support without informing them of a proposed date. Already he had learned that promised British troops would not materialize. Now it looked increasingly unlikely that colonial soldiers would be ready to march anytime soon. Johnson was wary of incurring Iroquois censure should the invasion be aborted. Out of desperation Johnson organized his own independent campaign: "I am determined . . . to march against them with about 300 Indians, and as many Christians most of whom are volunteers." He was doubtful of much success but hoped to at least improve the reputation of the British. Johnson and his small army left Fort Johnson on August 28 and spent the next twelve days marching up to

Figure 7. William Johnson's coat of arms. William L. Clements Library, University of Michigan. The Johnson coat of arms reveals Johnson's familiarity with and exoticism of Native Americans.

Lac St. Sacrement and back down again. No attempt was made on the French fort. They saw little action and their efforts went largely unnoticed by the larger colonial and imperial world. By early next year, Britain made peace with France, returning the captured Louisbourg. Johnson soon after resigned from public office, irked by the assembly's refusal to reimburse him for costs incurred during the war. Ultimately King George's War, like previous colonial conflicts, demonstrated the Crown's reluctance to dedicate monies or troops to the colonies, to extend her territorial empire, or to oversee the management of Indian affairs.[17]

Despite Johnson's grandiose title during the war of "Colonel of the Forces to be raised out of the Six Nations," his influence was confined to the Mohawks and was limited even among this nation. The Mohawks were most responsive to Johnson's requests for martial aid because they were in the greatest need of a colonial ally. They saw the war as an opportunity to revive their flagging political stature in colonial affairs, to attain gifts and monetary rewards, and to impress powerful men like Johnson who would, in return, defend their grievances over land thefts. They understood the value of cultivating an alliance with Johnson, but they were unwilling to play the role of submissive dependents. Headmen showed contempt for the British who boasted of their intended grand invasion but did nothing while young Mohawk men died in frontier violence. Warriors angrily remonstrated when payments for their services were not forthcoming. Having whipped up their martial spirit, Johnson fretted that it might be redirected. "Should things miscarry, it will be the intire ruin of me," he warned Clinton, "for I can not pretend to live any where near them, as your Excellency may be sensible of they being a blood thirsty revengefull sett of people."[18]

Johnson met his match in Theyanoguin, generally known by the British as Hendrick Peters.[19] Theyanoguin was born in Westfield, Massachusetts, in 1692, the son of a Mohawk mother and Mahican father. According to the laws of matrilineal descent he was a member of the Mohawk Bear clan and spent his life living at Canajoharie. In adulthood he emerged as a skillful Indian diplomat. He represented a mirror image of Johnson: an individual who crossed cultural boundaries, adapting to the customs and practices of the other, to serve the interests of his own community. Most conspicuously, he became an outspoken critic of the land thefts that plagued the Mohawk frontier and regularly voiced objections at colonial councils.[20] As a shrewd diplomat of many "Political Talents," Theyanoguin used his ties with Johnson to enlarge his importance in Indian-colonial affairs, maintain a steady supply of imperial goods, and promote village interests. His active military involvement in King George's War secured him Johnson's respect and a disproportionate amount of gifts. Johnson gave him cash, clothing, and other prestige goods needed to sustain his social standing in Mohawk village politics. Through his skillful politicking, Theyanoguin kept goods flowing well after the war. He played on Johnson's fears of an Iroquois-French alliance to win advantages. In February 1750, he informed Johnson of French plans to attack the Iroquois because of the latter's refusal to abandon the British. By August, he accused the two empires of working in concert. By spreading such stories, Theyanoguin pressured Johnson to reconfirm British friendship through the symbolic act of gift-giving.[21]

Johnson expected something in return for his sponsorship of Theyanoguin. He utilized his friendship with the Mohawk headman to strengthen his own influence among the wider Iroquois community. He paid Theyanoguin to review his speeches and sought his political counsel. In his personal affairs, he relied on Theyanoguin to arrange a land sale.[22] But in his relations with Theyanoguin and the Mohawks, Johnson continued to insist on their political subordination. Toward the end of the war, when the Mohawks sought to negotiate directly with the French to secure the release of war captives, Johnson deterred them. Allowing them to deal separately with the French, he believed, would lead "to the great weakening of their dependence on this Province" and by extension their dependence on him. Consequently he was determined to use any means, "fair or foul," to render them politically impotent.[23]

Theyanoguin, however, resisted Johnson's efforts to subordinate him within a gendered alliance. He displayed his disdain toward Johnson, refusing to shake hands during one tense meeting and causing Johnson to complain of his "insolent" behavior. By attending intercolonial conferences in Albany and visiting officials in Boston and Philadelphia, he challenged Johnson's patriarchal dominance by seeking audiences, support, and gifts from other colonial sources of power. Demonstrating his instrumental attitude toward Johnson, he expressed indifference when the latter resigned from office. Upon learning that the Albany commissioners had been reinstated, he noted "that as there were now Several Commissioners, [he] hoped, their affaires would be better managed than by one Person."[24]

Not Johnson, the commissioners, or the governor could satisfy growing Mohawk discontent during the 1750s. Governor Clinton's failure to hold annual conferences and, in particular, to condole them for losses sustained during King George's War convinced many that he "had no love for them." Most significantly, the Mohawks were deeply embittered by the refusal of imperial authorities to address their mounting worries over fraudulent land claims. Matters finally reached a breaking point in 1753 when Theyanoguin symbolically broke the Covenant Chain while in conference with the governor. His actions sent a jolt to the London metropolis, where Whitehall officials promptly sent instructions for the colonies to organize an intercolonial conference to mend relations with the Six Nations. Despite their diminished status and size, Theyanoguin and the Mohawks were still significant enough to attract the attention of Crown officials.[25]

Theyanoguin had timed his actions well. By the mid-eighteenth century a discernible shift had occurred in Britain's stance toward her empire and Indian allies. Imperial policymakers had begun to invest their overseas territorial empire with greater significance, now more than ever associating mercantile interests with territorial acquisitions. This new understanding of empire was encouraged in part by the natural maturation of mercantile capitalism. Britain's strong agricultural base, growing laboring class, enterprising merchant community, and responsive financial institutions placed her at the forefront of European capitalist development. As Britain evolved into a leading mercantile manufacturing nation, her interest in a commercial and territorial empire heightened. Contemporaneously, her colonies underwent tremendous growth. A natural increase and significant immigration led to an almost fivefold rise in the colonial population in the first half of the century. A larger populace meant bigger markets for British merchandise and an enlarged colonial labor force to engage in production. Hence demographic growth was matched by an expansion of transatlantic commerce. Britain's trade with her West Indian and North American colonies grew by 225 percent between 1700 and 1750, demonstrating that the livelihoods of a widening number of men and women in Britain had become entangled in an expansive overseas empire.[26]

Britain's commitment to territorial empire was further prompted by the activities of the French, who in the 1740s began to claim possession of the Ohio country. As well as burying lead plates at strategic points that professed French ownership, the French also began erecting a line of forts in this region in 1753.[27] British colonial officials were disturbed by these activities, as the Ohio country had become an important source of economic interest. Pennsylvanian traders penetrated this region, carrying an array of goods to exchange for furs, and Virginian land speculators formed the Ohio Land Company in 1749 with the intention of expropriating the land from its native inhabitants to sell to would-be farmers for handsome profits. Recognizing the commercial value of this region, advocates of empire became increasingly territorial in their orientation. They believed that the growth and security of their colonies depended on continued access to markets and lands. But it now looked as though the French intended to confine English settlements to the eastern seaboard. Along with colonial officials, London merchants, who had organized into powerful lobbying groups, began petitioning Whitehall to take aggressive steps to defend their territorial and commercial interests against French encroachments.[28]

Receptive to the concerns raised by these interest groups, London officials began formulating a response to French activities. Coming to power in 1748, the new president of the Board of Trade, the Earl of Halifax, rejected old-style mercantile theory, which stipulated limited territorial expansion in order to consolidate existing trade networks. He instead promoted a new brand of territorial imperialism. The Duke of Newcastle, secretary of state, supported Halifax. Anxious in the face of growing French dominance in Europe, Newcastle viewed French activities in America as part of the same imperialist plan. Although the Ohio country marked the very outer limits of the British Empire, these men became convinced that British power and prosperity were intimately tied up with this region. Although London officials were reluctant to be drawn into a costly American war, French activities in the Ohio made Whitehall determined to take action.[29]

Within this new vision of empire, imperialists on both sides of the Atlantic attached greater importance to their Iroquois allies, whom they now deemed crucial to British interests. Through a series of earlier conquests the Iroquois alleged ownership of the Ohio lands. Their claim was insubstantial but nonetheless politically convenient. The geographic position of the Iroquois, situated between New France and the northern British colonies, and their reputation as martial warriors further underscored their importance. Imperialists produced pamphlets and memorials outlining Iroquois centrality to imperial concerns. In a 1751 pamphlet Archibald Kennedy, a member of the New York Council, advised that "the preservation of the whole continent depends upon a proper regulation of the Six Nations." Cadwallader Colden, another council member, agreed, observing that "the Indian affairs deserve the most serious attention as not only a very considerable branch of the British Commerce but likewise the Security of the Colonies in North America depends upon it."[30]

Britain's evolving attitude toward her North American empire and the new value she attached to her Iroquois allies manifested itself in the 1755 Crown Point expedition. The expedition began in late summer when Johnson and his provincial troops cut a road through the wilderness, marching from Albany to Lac St. Sacrement (map 3). At the lake, which Johnson dutifully renamed Lake George in honor of his king, they established camp and were soon joined by Mohawk allies headed by Theyanoguin. Johnson's army numbered 3,500. Warriors scouted the vicinity while Theyanoguin acted as translator and member of the war cabinet. On September 8, Johnson unwittingly sent about one thousand provincial soldiers and the majority of Mohawks straight into a French ambush. Fierce fighting ensued until Johnson and his men finally repelled the French, secured their camp, and captured the French general. The battle proved brutal, with over three hundred men dead on the British side. Theyanoguin was bayoneted to the ground and killed. Johnson was shot in his thigh, an injury that would plague him until his death.[31] The battle marked the beginning and the end of the Crown Point expedition as Johnson and his council of war decided that an attack of Fort St. Frédéric was unfeasible. Nonetheless, news of Johnson's "glorious victory" soon spread throughout the colonies and across the Atlantic. In New York City, the "Fort fired for joy." In South Carolina "all the Vessels in the Harbour immediately hoisted their Colours, and fired continued rounds of canon until night." London periodicals printed detailed reports of the battle praising Johnson and his Indian allies for their gallant deeds.[32]

The 1755 campaign marked an important moment of transition for the British Empire. In the space of eight years, Johnson had led two campaigns to Crown Point. Both involved a multiethnic force made up of Iroquois warriors and Euro-American colonists; both entailed Johnson assuming a primary role, using his home as a base to marshal Indian support and physically leading each campaign; and both shared in their failure of removing the French presence. Despite these similarities, far more significant are the differences that distinguished these two events. The 1755 campaign was part of a four-pronged assault planned for that year. Confronted by French advances in the Ohio country, the British Crown formulated a military response. By April 1755 they had sent over a commander in chief, Edward Braddock, with two Irish regiments to sack the French post, Fort Duquesne, in the Ohio Valley. Three other campaigns were planned for destroying Fort Niagara on the southwest shore of Lake Ontario, Fort Beauséjour in Nova Scotia, and Fort St. Frédéric at Crown Point.[33] Collectively, the summer campaigns achieved

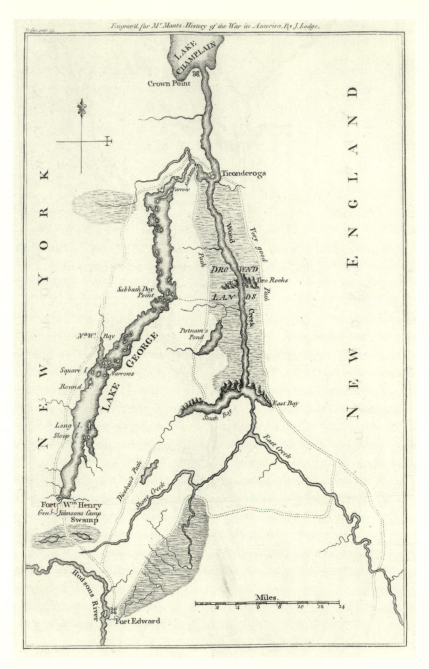

Engrav'd for M.ʳ Mants History of the War in America. By J. Lodge.

Map 3. The opposing forts of Lakes George and Champlain. Thomas
Mante, *The History of the Late War in North America* (London: printed
for W. Strahan; and T. Cadell in the Strand, 1772), opposite p. 33. John
Carter Brown Library, Brown University. Rather than removing the French
presence, the 1755 campaign resulted in the British and French constructing
additional forts in the vicinity of Lake George.

little military success, but Whitehall was now prepared to raise the stakes. Incrementally but decidedly, Britain deepened her commitment by sending more money and men overseas.[34] The Seven Years' War may have begun as a defensive war mounted to protect British colonies, but it quickly evolved into an offensive war fought to gain control of the land and resources of North America and epitomized Britain's new dedication to mercantile expansion, with dramatic consequences for its native inhabitants.

The 1755 Crown Point campaign serves as a useful device for illustrating and explicating a pattern of imperialization that occurred in British-Iroquois relations. This was an important campaign, not for what it achieved militarily (despite pronouncements to the contrary it was hardly a victory at all as the French remained firmly ensconced at Fort St. Frédéric and set about building a second fort) but because of what it signified in terms of imperial-Iroquois relations: the beginnings of a new centralized management of Indian affairs; a commitment to channel an extraordinary amount of funds for this endeavor; novel imperial pressure on Indians to serve as foot soldiers; a new inclination to build forts on Iroquois lands; and renewed efforts to incorporate the Iroquois in the cultural imagery of empire. The Battle of Lake George both symbolized and set in place a number of important themes for the rest of the war and beyond.

The Battle of Lake George solidified the home government's commitment to bringing Indian affairs under imperial control. In April 1755, after meeting with Edward Braddock in Alexandria, Virginia, Johnson received a royal commission granting him "sole Management and direction of the Affairs of the Six Nations of Indians and their Allies." The commission was intended to aid his efforts in leading a campaign against Crown Point.[35] Johnson promptly held a conference with just over one thousand Iroquois at his home in June to inform them of his new post. In a symbolic act of much significance he removed "the Embers which remained at Albany" and rekindled "the Fire of Council and Friendship" at Fort Johnson, thus marking a new era in British-Iroquois relations.[36] When some colonists questioned whether Braddock's death in July nullified Johnson's commission, the Crown responded by formally creating the office of British Superintendent of Indian Affairs in February 1756. Members of the colonial elite had been advocating the centralized management of Indian affairs for some years. Many pointed to the shortcomings of the Albany commissioners who, they claimed, put private interest before public concern.[37] Britain's new penchant for extending her dominion over North America, coupled with Theyanoguin's dramatic announcement in the fall of 1753, confirmed the necessity of Crown control of Indian affairs.[38]

The creation of the office of superintendent was a major development in Anglo-Iroquois relations. Administratively, Whitehall divided the colonies into northern and southern departments, appointing an officer to each. The superintendents were to report directly to the commander in chief and to receive from him an annual salary of £600 plus reimbursements for expenses. All other colonial authorities, including governors, had their right to deal independently with Indians rescinded. The superintendent was authorized to negotiate all treaties with Indians, regulate the fur trade, and supervise land sales and disputes. In the context of the war, as one official observed, the office assumed vital importance in its "great end . . . of fixing them [the Indians] steadily in our Interest, and engaging them in the service." For the first time in the colonies' history, control of Indian affairs was wrested from local control, organized into a unified set of policies, and centrally administered by a royally appointed officer.[39]

Johnson, whose "victory" at the Battle of Lake George ensured his selection for the northern office, quickly set about confirming the status of the Iroquois as useful and dependent subjects of an expansive British Empire.[40] He intensified Iroquois-imperial relations by encouraging their material dependence on the British by funneling large amounts of money and goods into their villages; entangling them in an endless succession of private meetings and public conferences; and pressing them to lend martial support and to permit the building of forts on their lands. To achieve his objectives, Johnson depended on a small army of local men—including Jellas Fonda, brothers Thomas and John Butler, Benjamin Stoddert, Arent Stevens, and Teady McGinn—who had been active in the Indian trade or provincial militia and were thereby experienced in Iroquois practices and language. They served as Indian officers and interpreters, spending the war years visiting Iroquois villages, assisting at conferences, and leading warriors to war.[41] Furthermore, Johnson depended on a sizable budget to carry out his work. Despite his efforts to remind the Iroquois of their duty to serve their king, they refused to act the part of devoted subjects. Ensuring their allegiance to the Crown necessitated ongoing imperial accommodation and considerable expense. Fortunately this time around, Johnson now enjoyed the financial backing of the Crown.

The large amount of monies the home government made available to Johnson during the Crown Point campaign was indicative of the new seriousness with which they now viewed Indian affairs. As part of the effort to bring Indian policy under Crown control, Parliament demonstrated a new readiness to allocate sizable funds to this branch of governance. At the June 1755 conference Johnson was authorized to brandish the wealth of the empire to impress potential Indian allies and secure their support. Throughout the proceedings, he provided generous feasts, distributed private presents to key chiefs, and made promises to equip warriors. As an indication of the type of compensation they could expect, Johnson doled out generous cash payments to some men employed during the preliminaries of the conference to scout the British-Canadian border. To make a lasting impression, Johnson marked the conference's end by a huge outlay of ruffled shirts, laced hats, silk stockings, knives, mirrors, razors, war paint, cloth, ribbon, threads, and buttons. This pattern of remuneration became typical throughout the war.[42]

Since the late seventeenth century, the Iroquois had periodically received goods from the English, but the Seven Years' War was distinct in terms of the sheer frequency and magnitude of goods dispensed. As part of the effort to construct a political and military alliance with the Six Nations, imperial officials acknowledged that substantial economic expenditures were inevitable. Not only were presents necessary as a mark of friendship, there were also practical reasons to dispense them: Indians had to be fed at conferences, warriors furnished for war, and villages provisioned in their absence. As superintendent, Johnson was responsible for facilitating the flow of three principal items from the empire to Iroquois villages: manufactured goods, food, and cash. Manufactured articles including clothing, jewelry, and an assortment of household wares constituted an important component of Indian gifts that were disbursed in bulk at the close of major conferences and more regularly in private councils. Johnson provisioned warriors for their military expeditions, prepared Indian war feasts, and fed his countless guests at Fort Johnson. Increasingly he provisioned villages with supplies of corn as war disrupted village economies. Finally, Johnson became the main distributor of cash to Indians during this period. He dispensed cash as a gift, as a means for Indians to purchase food on their way home from conferences, and increasingly in the form of payments for services rendered. His extravagant accounts illustrate how imperial directives formulated in London were revised on the edges of empire. Despite repeated instructions from superiors "to be as frugal as possible," constructing an alliance proved costly. As the war progressed, Johnson's expenses surged. From March 1755 to March 1757 he spent approximately £23,000. Between November 1758 and December 1759, he spent a further £17,000. Johnson justified his high costs on the grounds of necessity. A firm alliance with the Indians, he asserted, "cannot be obtained without a Continuation of Expences."[43]

But if Johnson was willing to run up significant costs in his effort to integrate the Iroquois into an alliance, he was unwilling to create an alliance of equals. Drawing on his experience with the Mohawks, he wished to subsume the rest of the Iroquois into a gendered hierarchy in which they would submissively defer to his—and by extension the Crown's—patriarchal rule. Although in speeches he referred respectfully to the king of England as their "Father," in practice he was more than comfortable to arrogate this role for himself. As patriarch supreme, Johnson adopted a two-sided persona. On the one hand, he assumed the posture of a stern and authoritarian father figure. He was exacting in his demands and domineering in his deliverance. He called for deference, ordering warriors to disobey their elders and chiding obstinate Iroquois for their "ungrateful" behavior. He used private councils not just to flatter and appease but also to bribe and browbeat defiant headmen. Instead of waiting for large congresses to consult the Iroquois in one body, he met with headmen beforehand to present proposed speeches for review and to solicit advice and support. If chiefs proved obstinate, Johnson bullied and pressured "to convince them of their Folly," sometimes causing them to protest his behavior. He also continued to create and install his own chiefs. In 1755, for example, without consulting the Mohawks, Johnson offered to make Peter, a former French-allied Iroquois, a chief if he promised to resettle in the valley and support the British cause.[44]

But when it suited him, Johnson also operated as a tender and generous father, acquiescing to Iroquois cultural practices and distributing gifts as a means to extend alliances. Notably he targeted head warriors, chiefs, and their female kin who through personal flattery, handsome presents, and private councils he entwined in an alliance. Johnson exercised his role as affectionate father through his control and distribution of goods. He was skilled in the ceremony of gift-giving. With a sound grasp of their cultural significance, Johnson understood that gifts could be used as a tool of entanglement: because the recipient was expected to reciprocate the kindness shown to them, gifts provided an essential means to forge ties of obligation. Through his lavish dispersal of gifts, Johnson breathed new life into the paternalistic power relations between the Iroquois and British.[45]

Assuming a fatherly posture, Johnson also kept an open house throughout the war, providing accommodation, medical care, and food. In 1757 he invited Aguiotta, an elderly Oneida headman, to live the remaining days of his life at Fort Johnson, where Johnson, as loving patriarch, promised "he should be well taken care of." As a dependent in Johnson's household, Aguiotta enjoyed comfort, sustenance, and physical safety in his old age. In return, however, Johnson expected Aguiotta to attend meetings and offer counsel. Furthermore, by taking Aguiotta into his household, Johnson assumed the right to exert influence over Aguiotta's family. He not only solicited the military support of his son and grandson, but when Aguiotta died in the summer of 1758 Johnson was involved in the selection of his replacement.[46]

Through his efforts as both a loving father and stern patriarch, Johnson crafted an extensive alliance system that moved beyond his immediate Mohawk circle. Headmen like Onondaga leader the Bunt, Ottrowana, a Cayuga headman and "an Indian who hath always distinguished himself in favour of the English," another pro-British Cayuga leader aptly called the Englishman, Canaghquiesa, Aguiotta, and Thomas King among the Oneidas, as well as three Seneca chiefs, the Belt, Seneca George, and Sayenqueraghta, provided Johnson with intelligence, protected Indian officers and traders living in their villages, gave military support or recruited warriors, and used their position to influence other Indians. Reflecting on past practices, Johnson noted in the late 1760s: "I have always made use of a few approved Chiefs of the several Nations, whose fidelity I have had the occasion to put to the test . . . and from whom I have obtained timely advices of almost everything of importance in agitation . . . I have made it their interest as much as I believe it is their inclination to be faithful."[47]

But Johnson grossly overstated his influence and the extent of Iroquois fidelity. With the exception of the Mohawks, delegates from all other nations continued to pay annual visits to the French governor. When chastised by Johnson they asserted their political sovereignty, reminding him that the French and British "talk together, and write letters without acquainting us of it."[48] The self-directed behavior of allies who refused to be subordinated is reflected in Johnson's relationship with the Bunt. Although Johnson may have considered him "a firm friend," this Onondaga headman spent much of the war seeking to constrain British power. At a meeting with the French governor in late 1756, he pledged neutrality and vowed to raze the fort built in his village by the British, a fort he had personally requested. In early 1757, he informed Johnson of an impending French assault of the German Flats. But the following year, unknown to Johnson, he gave the French two weeks' warning against a planned British assault against Fort Frontenac (now King-

ston, Ontario). Only once French defeat looked imminent did he fully side
with the British, joining them to witness the fall of Canada in 1760. By doing
so, he emerged from the war with his reputation intact as a dedicated and
trusted ally.[49]

The war did not permit Johnson to remold the Iroquois nations as dutiful and dependent subjects, but the creation of a centralized office did impose new constraints on them. No longer able to openly appeal to different
and competing colonial parties, the Iroquois lost important leverage. Theyanoguin's practice a decade earlier of securing goods and seeking redress by
petitioning officials from other colonies was no longer feasible with the creation of a single Indian officer. In the prelude to the Battle of Lake George,
the Mohawks had experienced the advantage of dissolved management when
William Shirley, governor of Massachusetts, undermined Johnson's authority
by soliciting Indian martial support independently of him. Two competing
army generals enabled the Indians to bargain for better rates of pay. But Johnson's strong insistence after 1756 that he was the sole agent for dealing with
Indians worked to close down alternative lines of appeal. Although he never
managed to exert unconditional authority in the management of Indian affairs, Johnson's forceful personality, his ability to dispense gifts, and Crown
support diminished negotiating opportunities for Iroquois headmen.[50]

In addition to ushering in a new era of centralized management of Indian
affairs, the 1755 Crown Point expedition was illustrative of new imperial demands made on Indian labor. From the outset of the campaign colonial officials envisioned employing a multiethnic army, hence their appointment of
Johnson as major general, a man of no military training but who was already
experienced in recruiting and leading Mohawk warriors. Governor Shirley
instructed Johnson to engage "every Warriour of the Six Nations that you
can by any means." Shirley planned for some of these warriors to assist in his
campaign against Niagara. Others were sent to accompany Braddock's forces
in the Ohio country. The ensuing rivalry that took place between Johnson
and Shirley for warriors demonstrates the high value that both men attached
to them. "Without Indians I think it will be madness to attempt Crown Point,"
Johnson remarked to a friend. To enlist their support, Johnson supplied warriors with guns and ammunition, provisioned their families, disbursed £1,370
worth of gifts to men in the aftermath of battle, and issued individual wages.
Theyanoguin received a special commission as an Indian captain and was
advanced "20 Dollars in part of his Pay." Thus Crown Point founded a lasting

pattern: for the rest of the war the Crown would make repeated calls to enlist native men for fighting and would be willing to expend significant monies for this purpose.[51]

Colonists had long considered Iroquois men to be adept in the art of warfare. Their major war exploits of the previous century had gained them a reputation as a ferocious and fearless people. Their knowledge of the terrain and experience in forest fighting caused many imperialists to agree with Johnson that they "might be made a verry usefull Body of men." Benjamin Franklin noted that "every *Indian* is a disciplin'd soldier. Soldiers of this kind are always wanted in the colonies in an *Indian* war; for the *European* military discipline is of little use in these woods." Other members of the colonial elite concurred, suggesting plans for Indians to scout the northern frontier and "to be kept there on constant pay, during the war." Shirley saw in the Iroquois a vast untapped and relatively inexpensive labor supply, commenting, "I should think if the Indians were kept in constant pay, they might be made as cheap soldiers." That the French continued to incorporate allied warriors into their war effort only encouraged the British to do so as well. Given their distinct modes of warfare, Indians were better suited to fight other Indians or, as crudely expressed by Johnson, "let dog eat dog and Indian fight with Indian. For the tame People of America, notwithstanding all their vaunts are not a Match, the French know it . . . they have turned the Indians upon Us."[52]

Appreciation of Indian martial skills meant that Englishmen had already established a tradition in the colonies of recruiting warriors in times of war. Such efforts had been largely informal, haphazard, and unassisted by the British Crown. For the most part, the Six Nations resented colonial attempts to embroil them in foreign conflicts and since 1701, with the exemption of the Mohawks, had pursued a strict policy of neutrality.[53] By 1754, as a new war with France looked imminent, colonial governors again attempted to enlist the services of their Indian inhabitants. To counteract French frontier assaults, the Massachusetts government recommended that the Stockbridge Indians be "received as soldiers in the province Service" and from late January to early July 1755 kept a company in pay and supplies. The New York governor was also anxious to organize ranger companies composed of "both whites and Indians," which he believed "would be of great Service," but was unable to secure funds from his assembly.[54]

Colonial initiatives to employ Indian warriors, however, were soon superseded by imperial measures. The Seven Years' War marked a major break with past practices as imperial policymakers made exceptional efforts to incorporate Indian warriors into the war. By establishing the centralized management of Indian affairs and allocating significant funds, the empire both endorsed and promoted the mass recruitment of Iroquois men. Repeatedly throughout the war, Johnson received orders from a succession of commanding officers to "use Your utmost endeavours, to procure as large a body as can be got." Indeed the vast bulk of his expenses were spent on outfitting, maintaining, and remunerating warriors. Even when campaigns were delayed or discarded, Johnson still needed to recompense enlisted men. He discussed with superiors the problem of incurring "a needless Expence" by holding Indians in readiness to march.[55] Johnson put into full effect his skill as cultural broker to recruit and integrate warriors into the British war effort. He drew on their cultural frame of reference, entreating them to go on the warpath for the specific purpose of obtaining captives and scalps to replace recently deceased kin. He appealed to their desire to live up to the warrior ethic, goading them to demonstrate their bravery and skill. By issuing cash wages and trade goods, he provided powerful economic incentives. Johnson also shored up military allies by co-opting the Six Nations' policy of adoption. To sustain tribal numbers, the Iroquois had long adopted Indian war captives and refugees into their lineages. Building on this custom, Johnson in 1756 encouraged the Mohawks to adopt a group of River Indians who had fled their home in Kingston, New York, after an English assault. By providing food and money, Johnson made this adoption possible. Not motivated solely by humanitarian concerns, Johnson believed that the "incorporation" of these natives would "strengthen our Indian Interest, and render a people before useless serviceable to the common Cause." He was involved in the resettlement of other remnants of New York and New England Indians and wasted little time arming and sending them out as scouting parties to fight in the war.[56]

Through inventive methods and sheer doggedness, Johnson succeeded in enlisting a considerable number of Indian men to the British cause. Undoubtedly the vast majority came from eastern villages. Encircled on all sides by colonial settlement and most dependent on Johnson for political patronage, these communities did not enjoy a strong bargaining position. However, warriors from all of the nations participated in the war, despite their official policy of neutrality. Warriors assisted in major campaigns, serving as auxiliaries for the British and provincial armies. In July 1758, almost four hundred warriors accompanied General James Abercromby as he led a disastrous expedition against Fort Ticonderoga. The next month, around forty warriors joined Colonel John Bradstreet in a far more successful assault of Fort Frontenac. Johnson enlisted just over nine hundred warriors to join General John Prideaux and his troops for the Niagara campaign in July 1759, although many refused to take part in the actual fighting. The following year, almost seven hundred warriors accompanied Johnson and General Jeffrey Amherst up the St. Lawrence River. Nearly two hundred traveled all the way to Montreal to witness the fall of Canada. Far more common, however, was Iroquois involvement in scouting expeditions: spying on French movements and obtaining captives for intelligence. They also served as messengers and transporters of supplies and cattle, and a number escorted Bradstreet's troops as they provisioned Fort Oswego in the spring of 1756.[57] By providing martial manpower, the Iroquois helped defend and enlarge resources essential to the British Empire.[58]

Martial entanglements proved costly, particularly for the Mohawks, who lost a substantial number of men. During the Battle of Lake George, twelve Mohawks were wounded and thirty-two died, including Theyanoguin. Increased contact with British and provincial troops also amplified the Mohawks' exposure to foreign disease. In early 1759 John Ogilvie, the Anglican minister at Fort Hunter, reported that in the Lower Mohawk Castle "Great Numbers . . . died of a malignant Fever that has raged amongst [them] for some Time." In 1760 Warren Johnson, William Johnson's brother, observed that an "Epidemical Distemper," most likely typhoid, had beset the Mohawks for the past two years, causing their numbers to be "prodigiously reduced." The Schoharie village also suffered demographic stress. When Johnson sought to replace the deceased chief, "old Seth," in 1757, he was informed by the community: "we look upon our Selves as a Poor reduced People not having one Man amongst us fit or worthy of that Post." Old Seth was not replaced until 1764.[59]

In addition to death, martial involvement exacerbated community tensions. By sponsoring Mohawk military cooperation, Johnson helped heighten intertribal disunity. Differences between the Mohawks and the other nations had already formed as a result of their participation in King George's War.[60] The Seven Years' War worked to widen this breach. The vast majority of the Iroquois resented the Mohawks' enthusiastic efforts to support the British. Following the Battle of Lake George, Indian agent Thomas Butler reported that the other nations sent a belt to the Mohawks, "signifying that they would not intermeddle, that the English & French had a design to kill them all. That the Mohawks might do as they pleased but if they join'd . . . [the British], they would kick them from them and have no more to say to them." They also sent a delegation to Canada to reaffirm their commitment to neutrality and

to disavow those "hot headed fellows who had lost all sense."[61] Political discord also occurred *within* nations, villages, and lineages. Silverheels, a Seneca Indian, earned considerable rewards for his martial services during the
war, but his willingness to labor for the empire aroused the contempt of his
countrymen, as he was soon "Looked upon as a Spy." Throughout Iroquoia,
families and friends became "much divided amongst themselves" as they disagreed over appropriate responses to the war.[62] Some communities dealt with
disharmony through their long-established practice of outward migration.
Pro-British Senecas resettled at Kanadesaga on the northern tip of Lake Seneca after the British constructed fortifications and a blockhouse at that site
in 1756. Staunch Anglophiles remained at Old Oneida, while other Oneidas
established a new settlement eight miles northwest of the old capital at a bend
in Oneida Creek. The village of Kanowarohare, also referred to as Oneida
Castle, eventually became home to about one-third of the Oneidas.[63]

The Crown Point expedition, intended to see the destruction of the French
post Fort St. Frédéric, resulted instead in the construction of two new British
military infrastructures, much to the Iroquois' displeasure. When the French
had first built their fort on the north side of Lac St. Sacrement, the Iroquois
had demurred, resenting a foreign intrusion in the heart of their northern
hunting grounds. According to Johnson, the Five Nations "were not only
ready to join but solicited the English to drive off the French from thence."
Many Iroquois hoped that the 1755 Crown Point expedition would achieve
what the 1747 campaign had failed to bring about. They were sorely wrong.
It was not long into the campaign that Johnson gave up plans to attack the
French at their base at Crown Point and instead concentrated his efforts on
building a counterfort at the opposite end of the lake. Johnson instructed
lands to be cleared while engineer Captain William Eyre began drafting plans
for what would be Fort William Henry. By the time it was completed in the
spring of 1756, this large earthen fort was big enough to garrison up to five
hundred men. To keep it supplied Johnson built the smaller Fort Edward sixteen miles south. Furthermore, a seventy-mile, thirty-foot wagon and cannon
trail had been cleared in the wilderness linking Albany, Fort Edward, and
Fort William Henry in an uninterrupted line.[64]

   The construction of Forts Edward and William Henry was indicative of
a major theme of the Seven Years' War: British military infiltration of Indian
hunting grounds. Previously officials had been content to simply acknowledge England's extensive landholdings without a need to militarily occupy

or settle them. Prior to 1755, the most ambitious imperial incursion in New York was the building of Fort Oswego, which had aroused Iroquois displeasure at the time. But this fort had been built primarily to protect access to trading routes and British control of the western fur trade, not to establish British settlements. It was also an isolated occurrence.[65] At midcentury, Britain's expanding mercantile capitalist economy with its drive to find new markets and resources, the French occupation of the Ohio country, and the political lobbying of interest groups encouraged Whitehall to review her relationship to overseas land. Lobbyists urged Whitehall to take a more aggressive stance in asserting Britain's ownership of western territories, advocating "we must *out-fort*, as well as *out-settle* them." Halifax acceded, arguing that Britain was entitled to "take care of our rights and possession in North America, by either building Forts on our boundaries to render theirs useless, or else by demolishing such as may have been clearly and notoriously built upon our ground." During the war, Britain firmly committed to the former option: erecting new forts. A defining trend set in place with the Battle of Lake George was the construction of a military infrastructure in the colonial hinterland. British soldiers captured a string of French forts and instead of destroying them rebuilt, strengthened, and garrisoned them, as well as building entirely new forts.[66]

The British justified fort building on Indian lands (in much the same way they justified their moral outrage at the French for doing the same) by highlighting their relationship with the Iroquois. By virtue of earlier conquests, the Iroquois claimed ownership of the upper Ohio Valley. Although these assertions were sketchy, Britain eagerly accepted them because they indirectly justified their own. Not only had the Iroquois placed part of their western hunting grounds under the protection of the king of England in 1701, the French had also acknowledged the Iroquois as British subjects in the 1713 Treaty of Utrecht. As subjects, both Iroquois people and their lands came under British jurisdiction. Johnson expressed a popular argument when he stated, "the Six Nations and their Country was allowed by Treaty to belong to Us." He furthermore concluded, "had the French been hindered" from infiltrating the Ohio country, "we could have treated with the Indians for those Lands."[67]

With economic motivation and political justification in place, Johnson played a key role in facilitating the militarization of the New York frontier. The war placed tremendous strategic importance on this region, as it comprised the borderland between New France and northern British colonies.

Even before the outbreak of hostilities, colonial officials promoted fort building and settlement in the area. Kennedy proposed that land north of Albany
and south of Lac St. Sacrement be settled: "I should advise the laying out of
those lands after the *New England* manner, in townships sufficient for sixty
families at least." He also encouraged "that a string of block-houses be erected"
and "a fort of some kind" be built among each Iroquois settlement. Looking
beyond the immediate concerns of defense, he noted that the Senecas inhabited "a fine country, where great encouragement ought to be given to settlers."
Johnson also viewed forts as essential to the security of the New York frontier
and a means to counteract the interfering presence of French priests and emissaries. He envisioned installing British traders, smiths, and missionaries at
these posts to enhance Iroquois allegiance.[68] Although neither Kennedy's nor
Johnson's more ambitious plans were achieved, a series of forts and block-
houses were nonetheless built throughout Iroquoia over the course of the war
and plans put into place to support postwar settlement. Johnson assisted in
this effort by advising on suitable locations and negotiating with the Iroquois
over their construction. His direct involvement in military campaigns meant
that he personally oversaw the building of new forts. After participating in a
major military campaign of 1759, Johnson began repairing fortifications at
Oswego without first waiting to receive royal approval. As he set about "felling, bringing in Loggs, and Levelling the Ground," he recommended to his
commanding officer "the necessity there will be for a good Respectable Work
here." He also strengthened the defenses of captured Fort Niagara, noting as
he did the need to maintain control of Lake Ontario, which would "secure to
us all the Conquests made [in] this campaign."[69]

Johnson faced the difficult task of convincing an increasingly skeptical
Iroquois of the virtue of supplanting French forts with British ones. He explained such measures in terms of paternalistic protection. "The great King
of England, your Father," he told them, desired "to protect your country, and
the lands which your forefathers have conquered." But the Iroquois remained
unconvinced. Suspicion over British intentions toward their lands was a primary reason why the vast majority pursued a formal policy of neutrality.
"Fully am [I] assured the Six Nations are sensible, that the deprivation of
what they deem their property, will be the consequence of either we or the
French prescribing Terms to each other, and hence the chief cause of their
indifference in our Quarrel," Johnson was forced to admit in private. "In regard to the settlements intended to be made at Ohio," Johnson noted, "they
don't like that either the French or English should establish themselves there,

it being their best hunting ground." The Iroquois grew more alarmed as the war progressed, aware that troops and forts would undercut their claims to sovereignty and hinder their economic subsistence. Forts encouraged settlers and livestock, which led to the loss of wooded land and wild game. A Canadian Iroquois echoed their fears when he asked in 1754, "Bretheren, Are you ignorant of the difference between our Father [the French] and the English? Go see the forts our Father has erected, and you will see that the land beneath his walls is still hunting ground . . . whilst the English, on the contrary, no sooner get possession of a country then the game is forced to leave it; the trees fall down before them, the earth becomes bare."[70]

Alongside material concerns of enlisting warriors and constructing forts, the Crown Point expedition also involved the cultural project of fitting indigenous people into the mental map of empire. The Battle of Lake George encouraged Britons at home and in the colonies to integrate the Iroquois into an imagined British Atlantic community. Johnson participated in this endeavor, keen to promote a discourse of Indian-English camaraderie. In his June 1755 speech to the Iroquois he constructed a sense of common heritage and shared identity between the Iroquois peoples and the British Empire that belied any notion of racial difference. "It is now almost 100 years since your Forefathers and ours became known to each other," he reminded them. "That upon our first acquaintance we shook hands and finding we should be useful to one another, entered into a covenant of Brotherly love and mutual friendship." Johnson described the Iroquois in the language of "brethren," "friends," and "allies," in contrast to the French, whom he vilified as "cruel Enemies" driven by their "Devilish and Blood thirsty Enmity." Although this was politically manipulative rhetoric, it nonetheless spoke to an actual history of Iroquois-English exchange that, while not devoid of conflict, had also been characterized by genuine cooperation and coexistence. Johnson both evoked and imagined this shared community, affirming to his Indian audience at Fort Johnson as well as his superiors in London that the Iroquois and the British had become "one body, one blood, and one people."[71]

Johnson was not alone in his efforts to emphasize themes of similitude and affiliation. Provincial troops "Saluted" Mohawk warriors "with a Round of guns" as the latter arrived at Lake George in the fall of 1755. Their contribution during battle aroused a sense of commonality and shared fate, especially when a number of leading warriors including Theyanoguin were killed. Contemporaries praised them for having "the *strength* and *courage* of a Lyon."

New England communities sent gifts of cattle to the lakeside camp to signify their gratitude, adding, "Hearty Respects to the young Moohawk prince the Surviving Son of Hendrick: and let Him and His people Share in our Small present." Another sent oxen "As A present to (the late famous) Handriks [and] his Indian Adherents." The presence of Mohawk warriors fighting and dying alongside colonial troops reinforced a sense of British-Indian unity and forestalled their racialization.[72]

These conciliatory sentiments expressed about Indian allies demonstrate that the business of empire building was partially ideological. Invariably, contact and exchange between Indians and Europeans throughout the colonial period involved the creative task of (re)defining collective identities. But the construction of difference, as embedded in cultural identity, took on a particular meaning in an imperial context. Whether the British wished to entangle Indians in military alliance and commercial partnership or, more basely, to remove them from their land, enslave them, or even kill them determined how they would construct discourses on Indianness. Material circumstance decided the content of British "knowledge" about the other. For much of the eighteenth century, Britain's economic, political, and military reliance on the Six Nations necessitated that they embrace an inclusive concept of empire, one that cast the Iroquois as trusted allies and integral members. As evidenced by the visit of the "four Indian kings" to London in 1710, Britons had shown a willingness to incorporate Indians into their ideological creation of empire. Although not everyone shared such a vision, Iroquois martial and political assistance during imperial wars prohibited racial precepts from dominating cultural discourses.[73]

The figure of Theyanoguin, in particular, aroused interest and appeal. Two portrait engravings circulated for sale in London, in the aftermath of the battle, reveal much about the divergent ways Britons constructed Indian identities at midcentury. At first glance, the 1755 engraving of Theyanoguin appears to depict him as a hybrid figure (fig. 8). He carries with him the accoutrements of native culture: in one hand, a tomahawk, identifying him as a warrior; in the other, a string of wampum, marking him as a man of diplomacy. The prominent facial tattoos also heighten his foreignness. But he is clad in European clothing—a long coat, hat, and ruffled shirt—thus suggesting his "Britishness." He is both exoticized and Anglicized. Theyanoguin's culturally mixed identity may explain his broad attraction, but with dress serving as a powerful marker of gender, class, and ethnicity, there are multiple ways of imagining how British audiences read this print. Another dominant

The brave old *Hendrick* the great *SACHEM* or Chief of the *Mohawk Indians*, one of the *Six Nations* now in *Alliance* with, & *Subject* to the *King* of *Great Britain*.

Sold by Eliz. Bakewell opposite Birchin Lane in Cornhill.

Figure 8. "The brave old Hendrick, the great sachem or Chief of the Mohawk Indians, one of the Six Nations now in Alliance with & Subject to the King of Great Britain." Anonymous engraving (1755). John Carter Brown Library, Brown University.

message embedded in this image is of Theyanoguin as a noble statesman. His fine suit of clothing reinforced his status as a man of power and importance. Visual icons are supported by the title of the engraving, which defined him as "the great Sachem or Chief of the Mohawk Indians." As they did with the 1710 visit of the four "kings," imperialists used Theyanoguin's status to legitimize their midcentury overseas ventures. In 1755, *Gentleman's Magazine* published his speech made at Albany the previous year in which he chastised the British for their slowness in meeting the French threat, thus identifying Theyanoguin as a participant in imperial discourse. Political interests were involved in the presentation of Theyanoguin as both a prestigious Indian chief and an advocate of empire.[74]

In addition to rank, Theyanoguin's dress also symbolized his Englishness. He is identified in the engraving as an acculturated Indian. European clothing undermined his Indianness and suggested his adoption of English values as well as material culture. Contemporaries frequently commented on Theyanoguin's dress because of its suggestive powers. When British officer William Hervey met him just prior to the Crown Point expedition, he noted that "he was drest after the English manner." He wore "a blue coat, a scarlet satin waistcoat laced with gold, leather breeches, blue woosted stockings and a gold laced hatt." Likewise, in his detailed description of the battle, Samuel Blodget found it necessary to mention that Theyanoguin rode to war "dressed after the English Manner." His clothing marked him as a political and cultural ally of the English. More than this, Theyanoguin's dress also denoted his subordinate status as royal subject. The English practice of distributing gifts of clothing to pro-British chiefs helped visually mark important headmen, enhance their status and power, and reward their loyalty. Regardless of how Indians interpreted these presents, for eighteenth-century Britons, by receiving and wearing a gift of English clothing, an Indian indicated his political faithfulness and submission to the Crown. A "great Sachem" he may have been, but as the title of the engraving also affirmed, Theyanoguin was a member of "one of the Six Nations now in Alliance with & Subject to the King of Great Britain."[75]

To fully appreciate the symbolic strength of clothing it is helpful to place this image alongside another print circulated in London the following year. In this engraving Theyanoguin is shown with minimal clothing (fig. 9). A blanket is draped across the shoulder of an otherwise naked body, a tomahawk in one hand. Why there are no facial tattoos in this image is unclear. It may have been a deliberate choice to make him appear less threatening. There is little to

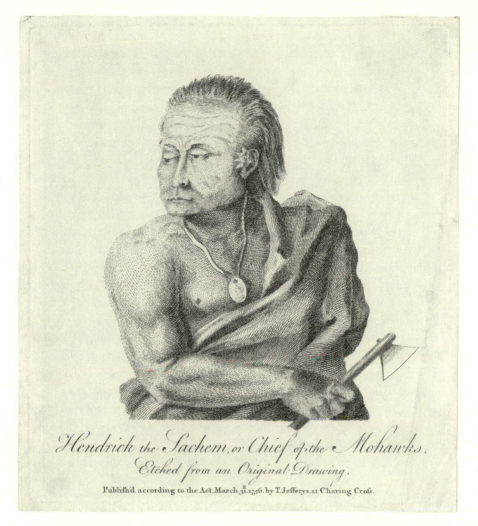

Figure 9. "Hendrick the Sachem, or Chief of the Mohawks." Etched from an
original drawing, published by Thomas Jefferys (1756). Negative no. 7722,
Collection of the New-York Historical Society, New York City.

indicate his status, and an unknowing viewer could easily mistake him for an
ordinary savage, rather than one of the noble kind. His Indian dress creates
a sense of the untutored and brutish. There is, however, one clue provided in
the engraving to suggest otherwise. Around his neck Theyanoguin wears a
medal bearing the image of the king. This article makes him reassuringly safe;

he is allied, subject, and subordinate. These multiple readings of Theyanoguin as noble Indian statesman, acculturated Indian, dutiful subject, and primitive but loyal savage demonstrate that British conceptions of Indianness were multiple and fluid. While there was a strong tendency to exoticize, there was still space enough in the ideological apparatus of empire to construct images and identities of Indians that pointed to alliance and commonality.[76]

As part of his unofficial duty as superintendent, Johnson was involved in promoting a perception of the Iroquois as imperial allies. Torn between political need and personal prejudice, he wavered between categories of similitude and difference. At a time when a racialized discourse directed at Native Americans was gaining a foothold in some parts of the colonies, Johnson eagerly upheld a view of the Iroquois as loyal subjects. His recognition of their commercial and martial value made him sensitive to endorsing such an image. He guarded against disparaging attitudes articulated by others, took great pains to humanize Indians by commenting on the personal attributes of individual men, and explained away repugnant Indian behavior on the grounds that "among them as amongst all other people there may be particular persons of bad Character."[77] Johnson's encompassing view of empire was captured in an engraving used on his Indian certificate, a pass issued to Indians during the war to allow freedom of movement (fig. 10). The image is marked by its symmetry. It depicts Johnson presenting a medal to an Indian under the tree of peace, hanging from which is the silver chain and heart of friendship. On either side, three colonists and three Indians sit in perfect balance, flawlessly mirroring each other in body pose and size. This pass, circulated among Indian allies and British officers, reinforced a sense of alliance and parity.

Political and martial allegiance, however, did not guarantee the Iroquois a permanent status as allies and respected members of the British Empire. As the war progressed and as British victory over New France looked imminent, the place of the Iroquois vis-à-vis the empire looked more uncertain. At the beginning of the conflict it had made sense to underline themes of kinship, affiliation, and common destinies that disproved any sense of racial difference. But as the British attained a new territorial empire in North America their relationship to Iroquois allies began to alter. The promise of military and political conquest offered new ways of envisioning Indian peoples—as peripheral, different, and even inferior.

Although only a minority of the Six Nations participated directly in the Battle of Lake George, this opening conflict of the Seven Years' War marked the

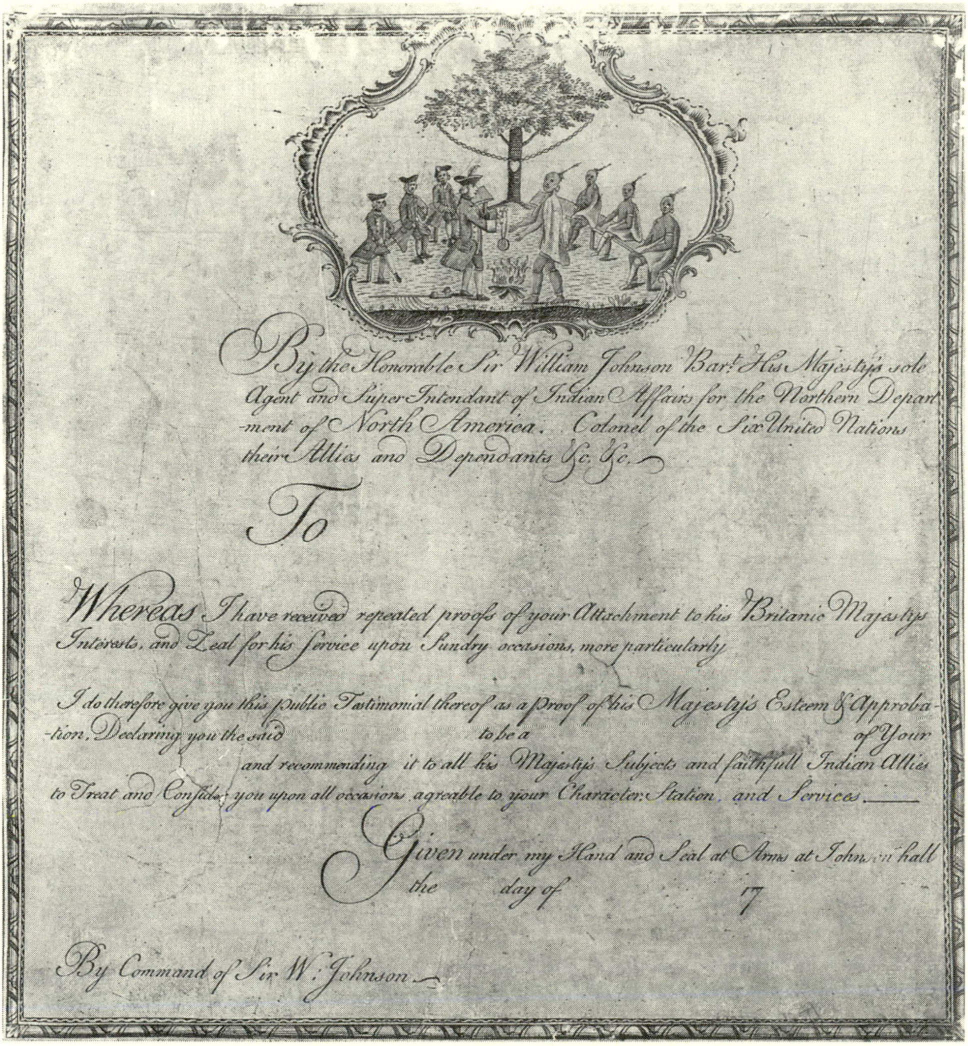

By the Honorable Sir William Johnson Bar.t His Majesty's sole
Agent and Super Intendant of Indian Affairs for the Northern Department of North America. Colonel of the Six United Nations
their Allies and Dependants &c. &c.

To

Whereas I have received repeated proofs of your Attachment to his Britanic Majesty's
Interests, and Zeal for his Service upon Sundry occasions, more particularly

I do therefore give you this public Testimonial thereof as a Proof of his Majesty's Esteem & Approbation, Declaring you the said   to be a   of Your
                         and recommending it to all his Majesty's Subjects and faithfull Indian Allies
to Treat and Consid.r you upon all occasions agreable to your Character, Station, and Services_____

Given under my Hand and Seal at Arms at John.n hall
the   day of   7

By Command of Sir W. Johnson

Figure 10. Indian testimonial given to New York State Indians by Sir William
Johnson in the eighteenth century. Engraved by Henry Dawkins. Negative
no. 2611d, Collection of the New-York Historical Society, New York City.

beginning of a new era for the entire Confederacy. The battle ignited the
forces of imperial expansion, which in turn would have major economic and
cultural repercussions for the Haudenosaunee. However, before the postwar
period of imperial entanglements is examined in greater detail, it is first nec-

essary to consider the extent to which the Iroquois mediated their changing world at midcentury. Throughout the 1740s and 1750s, the Iroquois mitigated the disruptive forces of imperial and colonial expansion. Notably, all the while Britain began plans to redraw the political map of the continent, the Iroquois were busily involved in navigating the economic landscape of the British colonies. As co-creators of new commercial forms flourishing on the frontier, the Iroquois experienced both novel opportunities and growing constraints on their economic autonomy.

Chapter 3

Trade, Land, and Labor

"An Indian makes 40£ & upwards yearly by hunting [furs] Winter, Spring & Fall," Warren Johnson observed during his tour of the Mohawk Valley at the close of the Seven Years' War. He detailed how hunters ventured to Canada, where furs were "plentier," to ensure a greater recompense. Native women also produced goods for the local cash economy. Warren noted their manufacture of shirts, which sold at 8 shillings apiece. Young men sold their labor to colonists. Warren remarked how some performed manual labor on his brother's estate. Many others exchanged soldiering skills for handsome "Rewards." Collectively, the Mohawks generated an additional livelihood as land sellers: "Of the whole country, which was formerly theirs they have now but a small Share." Land was a valuable commodity and one the Mohawks sought to benefit from. Warren presented them as gullible, describing how "they Sold their Land for Rum, & Trifles, like Sailors, who, when they have mony, are never Easy till they get rid of it." As well as selling natural resources, manufactured products, and physical toil, Indians were active consumers. Warren encountered Indians playing European fiddles and donning wigs. On one occasion, he witnessed a group of men patronize a local tavern, "soe they call every little house, which sells Rum," where they purchased a meal of bear and wild turkey "for which they at Once laid down ten Dollars, & paid for Rum besides, phaps twenty Dollars."[1]

By the mid-eighteenth century, as Warren Johnson's journal makes clear, the Iroquois were no strangers to a burgeoning commercial culture seeping into the Mohawk Valley. After one-and-a-half centuries of contact, the Iroquois were well practiced in the arts of price haggling, producing salable wares, and selling their goods and labor for cash.[2] The Iroquois still held onto older practices and values—including subsistence activities and an expectation for gift-giving—but in the complex economic landscape that evolved

in the New York hinterland, the Iroquois, much like their colonial counterparts, intermixed old and new economic tendencies.[3] As a consequence of
their widening array of commercial pursuits, the Iroquois experienced the
steady absorption of their land, labor, and resources into an emerging market
economy, but this was not an altogether negative trend. Even though Indians
behaved in increasingly commercial ways, they did not necessarily view this
to their detriment. Their ability to adapt to market pressures ensured their
survival in a rapidly changing world. Nonetheless, market-oriented behavior
did expose them to new dangers, as they became increasingly vulnerable to
the fickleness of the marketplace and the rising tide of colonial and imperial forces. The Seven Years' War, in particular, generated substantial difficulties as warfare disrupted village economies, increased Iroquois reliance on
commercial ventures, and allowed men like William Johnson to exact greater
demands. Yet, despite this trying period, the Iroquois still found ways to safeguard their interests. By playing off imperial rivalries, creatively adapting to
new commercial roles, and maintaining access to valuable resources, the Iroquois forestalled European economic domination.

At midcentury the economic frontier continued to function as a fluid arena
of interaction where neither Indian, colonist, nor imperial official could fully
dictate the nature of exchange. By this period, Fort Oswego had replaced Albany as the principal center of New York trade (fig. 11). Built in 1727 as a
counterbalance to the French trading post and garrison at Niagara, Oswego
had grown considerably by the 1740s. John Bartram, a Pennsylvanian bota-
nist who visited Oswego in 1743, described the fort as "a strong stone house,"
encircled by "a stone wall near 20 feet high and 120 paces round." Enclosed
within the walls was the trading town "where each *Indian* has his house to
lay his goods, and where any of the traders may traffick with him." During
trading season, Fort Oswego heaved with bodies and cargoes of goods, causing fort commanders to complain of having to work "under a Great Deall of
Noise of Druncken People and Indians." Oswego was not simply an imper-
sonal commercial zone but a co-created social space in which Indians and
Europeans fought, fraternized, and forged cross-cultural alliances, however
fragile at times.[4]

Conditions of frontier life encouraged expectations among both Indians
and Europeans that economic exchange be entangled—to some extent—in
personal relationships. Years of contact through trade facilitated legitimate
friendships. Many of the men involved in the trade at Oswego had long-estab-

Figure 11. "A South View of Oswego, on Lake Ontario, in North America." *London Magazine* 29 (May 1760): 232. William L. Clements Library, University of Michigan.

lished ties with the Iroquois. Captain Walter Butler had been commander at Fort Hunter since 1726, hence his two sons, John and Thomas, had grown up in the vicinity of local Indians. Probably Thomas's knowledge of Indian dialect and customs prompted William Johnson to commission him to lead warrior scouting parties during King George's War. Both Thomas and his brother were active in the trade. Other army officers including Benjamin Stoddert and Joseph Chew drew on friendships forged with Iroquois men during the war to carve out trading opportunities afterward. Arent Stevens (part Indian himself), Teady McGinn, and John Lindesay were local fur traders whom Johnson commissioned during the war to serve as Indian officers. Johnson recommended Lindesay to Clinton to serve as commander at Fort Oswego. Indians also traded with their German neighbors in the Mohawk Valley, demonstrating again that trade took place in the context of much wider social networks. Some traders carted their wares into Iroquois country, which provided opportunity and incentive to take Indian women as wives. Traders John Abeel and Edward Pollard both had Seneca consorts with whom they had children. Both foreign traders and the native kinship groups they married into hoped to embed exchange within familial social relationships.[5]

Yet despite the existence of trading networks based on kin and friendship ties, the ethos of the emerging free market increasingly conditioned the conduct of those involved in the trade. The Iroquois were far from naïve in their understanding of the capitalist economy. Decades of experience had taught them that the principle of supply and demand dictated the relative price of goods and not the personal feelings of traders. As early as 1715, one colonial governor informed a group of Iroquois, "the prices of Bever etc. does not all depend upon the pleasure of any man or number of men, but intirely upon the demands there happens to be for those commodities in the Europeans marketts. When the demand is great, that is when they are much wanted, the price raises; when it is not, that is when the marketts are glutted, the price falls." Some Iroquois shrewdly applied this principle to support their own interests. Onondaga headman Canassatego told the Pennsylvania governor in 1742, "Whenever any Particular sort of Indian Goods is scarce they constantly make Us pay the Dearer upon that Account. We must now Use the same Argument with them. Our Deer are kill'd in such Quantities, and our Hunting Countries grow less every Day by the Settlement of the white People, that Game is now difficult to find, and we must go a great Way in Quest of it; they therefore ought to give Us a better price for our Skins."[6]

The Iroquois were also familiar with a second main precept of the developing market economy that posited that the underlying objective of exchange was to secure a profit—that is, to accrue wealth in addition to the value of the good sold or exchanged. The profit motive generally entailed gaining a material advantage over the other person involved in the transaction. As one colonial official warned, "'tis the Method of all that follow it to buy as Cheap and sell as dear as they can, and every Man must make the best Bargain he can." The Iroquois experienced firsthand the relentless drive for profit that often encouraged Europeans to behave in underhanded ways. They also understood full well the enormous profits the British stood to gain. When the New York governor outlined to them the benefits Indians enjoyed at Oswego in 1740, one Iroquois wryly retorted, "we think brother, that your people who trade there have the most advantage by it, and that it is as good for them as a Silver mine."[7]

Like their colonial counterparts, the Iroquois were also keen to strike "the best bargain." Indians developed an understanding of themselves as free actors in an open marketplace and consequently shopped around, complaining when prices were not competitive enough. One French contemporary observed how Indians at Fort Niagara "compared and weighed" silver bracelets. Finding that those at Oswego were "of a purer silver and more elegant," as well as cheaper, they soon returned to Oswego to make their purchase. Clearly, concerns for price and not political or familial allegiance determined whom they traded with. As market-savvy actors the Iroquois played on imperial rivalries to create optimal market conditions. Headmen warned British officials that "the french Understand the Indian affairs Better then your People Does, they are more generous; and that Draws the Affections of the Indians (from you) to them." By outlining French generosity, the Iroquois pressured the British to offer better prices.[8]

Indeed, French economic overtures to the Iroquois were a constant source of irritation to the British. By 1749, a Jesuit priest had set up base at Fort Frontenac on the northeast side of Lake Ontario, opposite Oswego, where Indians were not only baptized but "Cloathed from Head to foot" and supplied with "powder and lead in plenty all for nothing." The Joncaire brothers, employed by the governor of New France to settle among the Senecas, became important gift-givers in their effort to cement an Iroquois-French alliance.[9] In the early 1750s the French governor, in a bid to steal Indian custom and, more important, political allegiance from the British, issued instructions for trade goods to be deliberately undersold at Fort Niagara. Economically, the plan made little sense—the king's treasury had to subsidize an estimated loss of

30,000 livres per year—but politically the French had much to gain. Thomas Butler soon complained of the "bad Markett" at Oswego as Indians bypassed this post on their way to Niagara.[10]

While the Iroquois readily showed themselves to be competent market actors, they did not shy away from older economic inclinations. Iroquois headmen, in particular, continued in their expectation for gift-giving. Exposure to market forces and colonial wars, which led to fluctuating prices and unmet needs, encouraged Iroquois headmen to pursue such strategies. In their dealing with the Haudenosaunee, British officials also came to rely on this form of exchange to strengthen political ties. The imperative to keep the Iroquois within the British camp meant that ritualized acts of gift-giving were commonplace at Oswego. The New York Assembly provided funds for an Indian commissary and interpreter to reside at the fort to engage in a general nursing of the British-Iroquois alliance. For this end they provided Indians with victuals, supplied goods for burial rituals, and distributed presents.[11]

An exchange between Onondaga headman the Bunt and the fort commissary John Lindesay in 1751 reveals the patchy development of market-oriented behavior, as both sides bypassed a commercial exchange in a place purposely built for that end. After reaffirming his ever-faithful allegiance to the British, the Bunt complained that "he was both hungry and poor" and urged the commissary to provide him and his warriors with victuals and clothes. He marked the end of his speech with a gift of three beaver skins. The use of such language was not necessarily literal but part of a diplomatic etiquette whereby guests were expected to exaggerate their hunger and poverty—almost to the point of begging—in order to enable the host to play the culturally valued role of provider without appearing to be proud. Such etiquette was particularly important in the context of unequal relations. Whether Lindesay understood this etiquette or not he played along. He noted in his journal that in response, "I gave him Provisions, and Cloathing etc. for his People, to the Value of Five Pounds above what he gave me, when he spoke, which was three Beavers." By prefacing his "gift" of three beaver skins with the rhetoric of political alliance and personal humility, the Bunt skillfully transformed what would otherwise have been a strictly commercial transaction into a culturally symbolic act of alliance and by so doing obtained goods over and above the market value of three beaver skins.[12]

In the minds of Iroquois headmen, profit making and gift-giving were not antithetical. On the contrary, they believed that British success at accruing wealth should make them more, not less, generous, and they were quick to chastise the British when this was not the case. Hence a group of head-men complained to interpreter Conrad Weiser "of the Covetousness of their Brethren of Albany," who "reaped a great profit of Thousands of pounds at the House of Oswego, but never would give them a meal of victuals." Despite their continual insistence for gifts, the Iroquois were not anti-capitalistic or "primitive." In the messy evolution of economic behavior, it was not unusual for the Iroquois to combine a belief in hospitality and gifting with a develop-ing commercial outlook.[13]

Market-attuned practices among the Iroquois underscored their adapt-ability to the changing world they lived in but equally exposed them to new dangers. By midcentury Iroquois livelihoods were fully bound up with com-mercial networks of trade, even if some headmen continued to refute their level of economic entanglement. In 1744, Canassatego chided colonists who, "by way of Reproach, be every now and then telling us that we should have perished if they had not come into the Country and furnished us with Strowds and Hatchets and Guns and other things necessary for the Support of Life." He denied their dependency, stating, "we lived before they came amongst us, and as well or better . . . tho' we had not Knives, Hatchets, or Guns, such as we have now, yet we had Knives of Stone and Hatchets of Stone, and Bows and Arrows and these Served Our Uses as well then as the English ones do now." But Canassatego grossly overstated the extent of their autonomy.[14]

Iroquois dependence on English goods left them in a vulnerable position. From the beginning of the fur trade, changing tastes in Europe, colonial wars, and the fluctuating rates of shipping insurance caused sharp increments and declines in the value of furs. Furthermore, decades of overhunting had ex-hausted local beaver supplies, and the growth of colonial settlements placed additional pressure on local game, forcing hunters to venture further afield or concentrate their efforts on hunting deer instead. What was more, as the eighteenth century progressed fur and skin exports became an ever-shrinking percentage of the New York economy. Superseded by the commercial produc-tion of grains and timber, fur dropped to less than 25 percent of total exports to London in the 1740s. By midcentury the center of the fur trade relocated west as the Ohio Valley assumed new prominence. Once central participants, by the 1750s the New York Iroquois found themselves considerably sidelined in the colonial economy.[15]

With the New York fur trade in decline, the Iroquois looked for alterna-tive means to access the trade economy. Some traded surplus supplies of corn at European forts; others produced a variety of Indian handicrafts, including baskets, moccasins, and leggings, to trade and sell in the local market.[16] In the early 1750s, most of the Six Nations joined in a booming ginseng trade. By collecting, trading, and selling this naturally grown root, Indians were not merely satisfying the demands of local exchange networks but participating in an international marketplace. Prized for its medicinal properties, ginseng was an extremely valuable export commodity, fetching high prices in China. Aware of the considerable financial gains to be made, Iroquois Indians, along with their colonial neighbors, devoted their physical labor and time to gathering this naturally grown root. "I cannot adequately describe what a furore there is around here over the famous root," a colonist noted in 1752. "Coll. Johnson has already bought over 1600 Bushells." Indeed, William Johnson was one of the main Mohawk Valley purchasers, employing entire Indian communities to harvest this wild crop and thereby promoting their involvement in an expanding market economy. "I have had most of all the five Nations for these 3 Months employed to gett me about four Hogsheads" of the root, he told a business associate in 1751. When Moravian minister John Martin Mack traveled through Iroquoia on his way to Onondaga in 1752, he noticed villages virtually abandoned as men, women, and children scoured the woods for the root. "The Indians sell them to the people hereabouts, or exchange them for goods with the traders," he reported. Missionary Gideon Hawley encountered a similar phenomenon when he visited the Mohawks that same year. Gathering the root throughout the summer, the Mohawks "got considerable by it, having collected it in great quantities."[17]

The timing of this activity is significant. Many communities were struggling in the aftermath of King George's War, which had impeded men's ability to hunt. At the close of the conflict the Onondaga speaker Ganughsadeagah complained to Johnson, "Wee think it very hard, being kept from Hunting now almost two years, (Except a trifle about Home)." The wartime shortage of goods had inflated trade prices, thereby diminishing Indian purchasing power. Ganughsadeagah exclaimed, "Goods are so dear . . . that we Can have nothing without paying three times as much as we used to do." Impoverishment forced some Indians to leave their children as pawns with traders until they could afford to settle debts. A postwar slump in the price of furs coupled with poor harvests prolonged Mohawk hardship. In the summer of 1752, Johnson reported that Mohawk families were forced "to leave their Castles and come among the Inhabitants there [in the Mohawk Valley] for relief." Others migrated to Canada. The ginseng trade provided economic relief during a period of strain. Missionary John Ogilvie noted that notwithstanding all of the Mohawks' difficulties, the "great Demand" for ginseng meant "they have had it in their power, to procure all the Necessarys of Life." He was less impressed by how they managed their earnings, as "most of them spent all the Profits arising from it, in strong Drink, and were Continually intoxicated, while they had a Penny left."[18]

In matters of land as well as trade, the Iroquois blended older customs with a developing familiarity with market forces. Although the Iroquois still enjoyed their territorial integrity in the early 1700s, they faced mounting pressure for their lands by an enlarging colonial populace. Consequently, the extent of their control over the process of land transfer steadily began to wane. The small trickle of Palatine Germans who arrived in the Schoharie Valley in the 1710s turned into a substantial stream during the 1720s. The construction of Fort Oswego on Iroquois soil in 1727 aroused consternation, prompting the Iroquois to complain to the British that they had "permitted them to come there only to trade" and not to build permanent sites. Demands were also made on lands beyond Iroquoia. Playing up to Six Nation claims of being overseers of a vast landed empire, the governments of Pennsylvania and Virginia lobbied Iroquois headmen to cede southern lands. The Iroquois confronted the issue of land cessions much like trade: as a means to construct alliances, to bolster their position vis-à-vis other Indian groups, and, increasingly, to extract gifts and money.[19]

The Iroquois Confederacy as a whole recognized that there were advantages to ceding land to Europeans. In a series of treaties with the Pennsylvania government during the first half of the eighteenth century, the Confederacy relinquished large areas in Pennsylvania that they claimed ownership of but which in fact Delaware and Shawnee Indians inhabited. Such cessions promoted a political agenda of strengthening their alliance with England, augmenting their status as "overlords" of smaller tribes, and generally reinforcing their centrality in Anglo-Indian affairs. Furthermore, these cessions generated significant economic gains. When the Confederacy released its claim to lands in Maryland and Virginia at the Lancaster Treaty of 1744, they received in return £220 worth of goods. Another land sale to Pennsylvania in 1749 earned the Six Nations £500. However, headmen did not always orchestrate these land sales from a position of strength but merely responded to situations not of their own making. In 1749, frustrated by the efforts of a determined band of invading colonists on the east side of the Susquehanna, Iroquois headmen found themselves "willing to give up the Land" for a monetary reward.

Unable to clear this land of unwanted intruders, the Iroquois hoped that the Pennsylvania governor would at least compensate them for their loss. Whatever short-term material and political gains they secured, Iroquois headmen like Canassatego understood that such exchanges were not equitable. As he told the Pennsylvanian governor in 1742, "We know our Lands are now become more Valuable; the white People think we don't know their Value, but we are sensible that the Land is Everlasting, and the few Goods we receive for it are soon Worn out and Gone."[20]

Giving away distant lands was one thing; confronting colonists within their own neighborhood was quite another. The presence of Fort Oswego was a constant reminder to the Six Nations that they no longer enjoyed uncontested control of their homelands. But turning a grievance into an advantage, most were content to enjoy the benefits of a place of commerce so close at hand. More troubling was the arrival of actual families wishing to fence and farm the New York hinterland. As the easternmost nations, the Mohawks and Oneidas faced the greatest threats to their territory as they confronted an ever-enlarging presence of German, Dutch, and English settlers in pursuit of freehold lands. Notably the number of German settlers swelled. From their base in the Schoharie Valley, German settlers pushed upriver, establishing new towns at Stone Arabia, Burnetsfield, and the German Flats, all lying west of Canajoharie and close to Oneida country.

Becoming increasingly sensitive to the commercial value colonists attached to land, the Mohawks and Oneidas gradually developed new methods for extracting revenues. Both communities assumed the role of landlords, requiring tenants to pay them for land use. One Oneida noted that although his village had made a gift of land to some Germans "in compassion to their poverty," they expected payment once "they could afford it." Renting tracts to German settlers also allowed the Mohawks to collect steady payments in cash and corn. William Johnson noted that local valley inhabitants "have for these Several years past, paid their Rent to the Indians."[21] In addition to renting, the Mohawks and Oneidas also sold land for money; for example, the Canajoharie community received "155 pieces of eight" for a plot of land sold to Jacob Glen in 1735. Colonists did not simply bully or trick Indians out of their territory; Indians did exercise free will. Headmen acknowledged their willingness to sell land just as long as they controlled how much and to whom. Land sales, like renting or loaning, were an important means of network building. By handpicking their neighbors, Mohawk leaders sought to safeguard their interests. It is not surprising that the Mohawks treated William Johnson as a preferred customer. Nevertheless, selling and renting was also an economic act. Money made from land sales and rent, much like the exchange of furs, ginseng, and handicrafts, permitted the Mohawks and Oneidas to access the local marketplace to procure other goods. The eastern Iroquois were not impoverished to the point that they had to sell land, but in the face of the declining value of furs or a bad harvest, lands sales provided an alternative means to supplement their livelihood.[22]

The growing number and sheer tenacity of settlers eager to secure their own homesteads undermined the ability of the eastern Iroquois to control the pattern and pace of land transfer on the New York frontier. Often Indians found themselves responding to circumstances beyond their control rather than acting out of free choice. Renting land was sometimes a means to make the best out of an unfavorable situation. Johnson noted that it was only after "the Indians finding that the Lands ... were settling fast" that "they applied to the Settlers for rent." Additionally, the Mohawks faced a series of fraudulent deeds and illegal occupations. The town of Albany laid claim to an area of rich meadow and forestlands called the Mohawk Flats near Fort Hunter. Although Governor Crosby had invalidated the deed in 1730, this claim soon resurfaced. One of the Dutch commissioners for Indian Affairs, Philip Livingston, was a principal claimant of a particularly iniquitous deed known as the Canajoharie Patent. Livingston and his partners claimed lands lying west of Fort Hunter and north of the Mohawk River, which encompassed the Canajoharie settlement and planting grounds. On hearing of the patent, the Canajoharie Indians exclaimed, "Livingston has murdered us asleep, for our Land is our Life." The equally nefarious Kayaderosseras Patent deeply troubled the Lower Mohawk Castle. This patent involved a group of colonists who claimed title to over four hundred thousand acres of prime Mohawk hunting grounds in Saratoga County, north of the Mohawk River and west of the Hudson.[23]

Added to these troubles, the Mohawks and Oneidas faced problems with their German neighbors, who by the 1750s had developed prosperous communities. Instead of honoring ties of friendship, this new generation acquired land through increasingly devious means: taking more land than the Iroquois had agreed to sell; claiming ownership of land that the Iroquois had only loaned; and squatting on new lands altogether. They complained of Conradt Gunterman, initially "a very poor man" whom they had sought to help. "We took [him] amongst us," they claimed, and "gave him a Tract of Land out of Charity." But forgetting their act of kindness, he now assumed additional lands, which they had "not given or sold him." Likewise, Captain Collins at

Canajoharie claimed woodlands when the Mohawks had only sold him low-lands. By contrast, they complained, they had "sold the Wood Land but not the Low Land" to Cornelius Cuylers, and so the list of disputes continued. The Mohawks were frustrated that German prosperity occurred at the expense of their own retreating land base. Gachadow, an Onondaga orator, commented on the reversal of fortunes by noting, "You know very well when the White People came first here they were poor; but now they have got our Lands and are by them become Rich, and we are Now poor."[24]

Mohawk frustrations over land thefts were publicly aired in a heated con-ference between Theyanoguin and Governor George Clinton in 1753. While Theyanoguin acknowledged the many legitimate land sales that had taken place, he condemned the practice of colonists taking up additional lands il-legally: "what we have sold we are well satisfied therewith and sensible, but it grieves us to have more taken up than we have agreed to sell." Ironically, the intercolonial conference that was held at Albany the following year, largely to resolve Mohawk land grievances, sowed seeds of a new land controversy. John Lydius, working on behalf of the Susquehannah Land Company of Con-necticut, plied a group of Mohawk Indians with alcohol and bribes to secure a deed for the Wyoming Valley on the northern branch of the Susquehanna River. This was an area comprising valuable hunting grounds. The Iroquois Confederacy was enraged when they learned of this insidious transaction. However, the outbreak of imperial warfare deterred colonists from settling in the Susquehanna Valley. For a while then, this growing sore point in the An-glo-Iroquois alliance was soothed, but war brought only temporary respite.[25]

Iroquois men and women formulated creative responses to meet the exigen-cies of a new economic order. The compelling desire to acquire foreign-made goods, the unpredictability of the fur market, the depletion of fur-bearing animals, and the growth of colonial settlement encouraged the Iroquois to develop novel ways to participate in a growing market economy. Notably the Iroquois began selling their physical labor for cash. Participation in new forms of paid employment was both casual and limited, but it was becoming more commonplace by midcentury. Serving as guides or interpreters, offer-ing safe passage across rivers and lakes, or supplying forts with food in ex-change for cash or trade goods provided a new way of securing a livelihood. Settlers, traders, and colonial officials commonly gave trade goods in lieu of services, but increasingly Indians expected and received cash. The exchange of labor for money marks a significant development in the economic and cultural behavior of Indians. By the mid-1700s, the Iroquois were moving away from an older understanding of the exchange of labor as part of a reciprocal arrangement to developing a nascent understanding of labor as a commodity, exchangeable for a specific monetary value.[26]

Indians living between river routes and near trading posts made a livelihood by transporting the canoes and packs of colonial traders and by supplying garrisons with food. Following the French construction of a fort at Niagara in the early 1700s, some Seneca Indians built homes nearby so that they could earn a living provisioning the French garrison. They also made sure to establish control of the Niagara River portage, by which they were able to "earn a good deal by transporting the Traders and Western Indians' goods." They received a variety of goods for their services including clothing and powder, but increasingly money became the dominant form of payment. Peter Kalm, who visited Niagara in 1749, observed large numbers of Senecas employed in carrying packs of deer and bear over the carrying place, remarking, "You would be surprised to see what abundance of such things are bro't every day over this place. An Indian gets twenty pence for every pack he carries over."[27]

On his way to Oswego from Onondaga in 1743, John Bartram encountered "a little town of about four or five cabins" near the Oswego Falls, where the Indian inhabitants "chiefly subsist by catching fish and assisting the *Albany* people to hawl their *Bateaus* and carry their goods round the falls." Similarly, Oneida Indians acquired cash as carriers at the Great Carrying Place. This was a valuable passageway between the Mohawk River and Wood Creek used by traders on their way to Oswego. As well as expecting a "gift" of rum or a blanket for the privilege of using the portage, the Oneidas charged a specific price for each cargo carried. When German settlers attempted to carve out their own niche in the carrying business in the 1730s by charging lower rates, the Oneidas aggressively sought to have them removed. In April 1739, the Oneida community collected as a body at the Carrying Place and tried to supplant the Germans by force. Tensions continued despite the moderating efforts of the Albany commissioners. In the 1750s, traders remonstrated against the intimidating behavior of the Indians, describing "the many hazards and difficulties" they confronted. "The Oneida Indians force our goods from us . . . and not content with making us pay a most exorbitant price, for each freight, but rob us of our Rum, stores and other goods." In addition, "they force away the High Germans . . . that we may be under a necessity of employing them, and paying whatsoever they please to demand." The Oneidas' actions were not part of an aggressive marketing campaign but an attempt to maintain control over a valuable form of employment. Their violent reaction when outsiders threatened to usurp their role signifies the importance of this commercial activity to their subsistence.[28]

The Mohawks, closest to European settlement, found numerous opportunities to engage in new forms of paid employment. In 1735, Peter and David were two Indians among a group of local men who received sixteen shillings for slaying twenty-four wolves threatening local livestock. Alternatively, the presence of Christian missionaries allowed Mohawk men to receive cash wages. The Society for the Propagation of the Gospel hired a handful of men to serve as catechists, readers, and schoolteachers. For men like Old Abraham, a noted elder and a man too old to hunt, laboring for the church was a viable way to earn an income.[29]

Warfare afforded Mohawk and Oneida men the principal means to sell their labor for cash. King George's War offered important opportunities for wage employment at a time when the pursuit of usual economic activities was rendered more difficult. Johnson employed some Indians "at an Extravagant price" to undertake the hazardous task of carrying supplies to the garrison at Fort Oswego. Most Mohawk warriors found employment through soldiering. In 1745, the New York Assembly issued bounties for enemy prisoners and scalps. Johnson was authorized to pay warriors ten pounds for an adult scalp and five for a child's, while an adult and child prisoner fetched twenty and ten pounds, respectively. Johnson approved of paying a set price for specific services as a cost-effective means to employ native martial power. As he explained to one colleague, a scalp bounty "is a verry good thing . . . if rightly applyed . . . Our government allowes a Sufficient Bounty for Such already and the Indians being therwith Content . . . Expect no More than what I paid them Last Fall."[30]

Warriors became vocal about how and what they wished to be paid. In March 1743, a delegation of Albany commissioners visited Mohawk warriors at their settlement "to persuade them to go up to Saratoga, and serve as outscouts, which their young men had refus'd to do chiefly on accott of their wages being too Small." Furthermore, these Indian employees were disgruntled because they "had been told by white People that the half of their wages was given by the Commissioners to their Sachems as Bribes to induce them to Send the young men out. This created a misunderstanding between the Sachems and warriors." Warriors demanded colonial authorities pay them directly and pay them well. When the New York Assembly proved slow to process funds, they grew agitated. Johnson complained to Governor Clinton of his situation: "I am quite pestered every day with partys returning with Prisonners and Scalps and not a penny allowed me to pay them, which is hard upon me and verry displeasing to them I assure you, for they Expect it, and demand it of me." The Mohawks not only pressured Johnson for the money he owed but specified how they wished to be paid. Johnson was obliged to inform Clinton that "The Indians would be pleased to receive their Money in Dollars." Perhaps their readiness to receive bounties was a consequence of their contact with the French-allied Kahnawake Mohawks, who had long experienced the commodification of captives.[31] In any case the Mohawks had good reason to be resolute in their demands for punctual pay. Having abandoned normal economic activities such as fishing and hunting, cash payments were essential to support themselves and their families. Yet despite the practice of selling martial services for cash, warriors resisted full entanglement in a strict system of commercial relations, as they continued to expect gifts of clothing and arms in addition to monetary rewards. They also required Johnson to maintain their families in their absence. British need for Indian martial assistance meant that Johnson made efforts to satisfy native expectations. But the experience of earning cash payments during King George's War set an important pattern for future imperial conflicts.

The Seven Years' War ushered in a period of tremendous economic strain for the Iroquois as warfare hampered farming, hunting, and trade. Acting as an agent for the empire, Johnson sought to turn economic difficulties into political advantage by promoting the commercialization of trade and making enlarged demands on Indian land and labor. Yet the Iroquois found ways to combat these constraints. This was not a period of imperial domination but of continued Anglo-Iroquois compromise. Many Indians found ways of overcoming hardships in trade and discovered a new penchant for wage labor that disturbed even Johnson.

Imperial conflict had a major impact on trade. The removal of additional places of commerce and sources of goods created new hardships for the Iroquois. For decades French Canada had provided the Iroquois with an alternative source of trade goods and diplomatic presents. At the beginning of the conflict the Iroquois sought to keep these economic channels open, pressing the French governor, at a conference in 1756, for a renewal of cheap trade at Fort Frontenac and control of the portage at Niagara. The governor also sent embassies among the western Seneca to dispense gifts. Economic ties with the French enhanced Iroquois influence in their dealings with Johnson. On more than one occasion they reminded him of their temptation to visit the French, who, they claimed, always "used us very kindly and supplyed all our wants."[32] Reeling under military defeat in the late 1750s, however, New France lost her capacity to serve as an economic alternative. Lack of control over the major water routes meant that the French could no longer channel adequate supplies to their forts. By April 1759, the Iroquois complained that the French had "greatly disgusted the Indians by not supplying goods at a reasonable price, or good in quality." Shrinking opportunities for trade diminished Iroquois bargaining power in their economic relations with the British. Despite British promises at the beginning of the war for subsidized trade, outlays of gifts, and the free provision of smiths, the declining power of the French lessened British need to continue the politically motivated distribution of goods and services to Indian allies.[33]

Added to Iroquois troubles, avenues for trade with the British also lessened as warfare destroyed important places of commerce. In August 1756, the French decimated fortifications at Oswego. While, for political reasons, some Iroquois welcomed the demolition, many lamented the loss of this vital center of commerce. Even the French were concerned that although the Iroquois appeared pleased by its destruction, "at the bottom of their hearts, they are not satisfied," as "it was a place where they found as much Rum as they pleased [and] goods much cheaper than with us."[34] To compound matters, the French subjected the German Flats to repeated assaults, causing Johnson to officially prohibit trade at this colonial settlement in 1757. Under the threat of frontier attacks, traders and smiths sent by Johnson to reside in Iroquois villages at the beginning of the war packed up their wares and headed back east to more hospitable climes in early 1757. The declining opportunities for trade caused strain. Throughout 1757 and 1758 Iroquois headmen regularly applied to Johnson to send traders back to their villages and to reestablish trade at the Flats.[35]

Warfare also hampered customary subsistence activities. Men's hunting was restricted as it became too dangerous to venture into usual hunting grounds. In addition to concerns over enemy gunfire, fear of getting "hurt or killed by the Ranging Companys who are constantly reconnoitring the Woods" also deterred the Mohawks from hunting north of Albany. The Tuscarora Indians, who had been living among the Iroquois since their adoption in the 1720s, complained to Johnson that their hunting was "entirely impeded" by the "quarrel" between Britain and France. Consequently, they added, "we have no way to supply our Families but by applying to you." Warfare also disrupted agriculture. The threat of French assaults left Indian women too "affraid to plant." Even the presence of garrisoned British troops proved to be to their detriment. Indians complained of the carelessness of soldiers who allowed army cattle to wander through fields destroying crops, and they accused soldiers of stealing their corn.[36]

Difficulties in farming and trade took their toll. In April 1757 Thomas Butler traveled through Iroquoia, noting widespread poverty: "I must acquaint you that Provisions among the Indians is very scarce and dear. . . . We have sent to the German Flatts several times for Provisions but whenever we eat of it was obliged to give the Indians [a] Share." The following month he wrote: "here is several of the Oneidas who say they have nothing to eat at home and are come here to beg Provisions . . . I am plagued with them." By 1760, most Iroquois communities relied heavily on food supplies from British posts. In March, Johnson warned the commander in chief, Jeffrey Amherst, of the "unavoidable expence of supplying great Numbers of Severall Nations" who were in "a famishing condition." He noted that Indians "from almost all parts" traveled to his home and neighboring forts for corn. While Johnson sent supplies of pork and corn upriver to the Senecas, the Mohawks and Oneidas secured aid from neighboring garrisoned posts. Johnson urgently requested more supplies as "Numbers of them, being comeing daily, and more expected."[37]

Economic stress caused by the war altered the nature of Anglo-Iroquois exchange. With the French no longer offering a viable source of trade goods and with their own subsistence activities hampered, Iroquois reliance on the British deepened. Imperial officials were pleased by this shifting balance of power and hoped that through economic relations they could subordinate Indian allies. Iroquois headmen unsettled by their impoverishment nonetheless expected Johnson to fulfill necessary familial obligations by providing for their needs. But Johnson increasingly moved away from Indian cultural etiquette. As British power grew, the inclination to satisfy Indian protocol lessened.[38] When in June 1757 the Onondagas, Senecas, and Cayugas formally reaffirmed their policy of neutrality, Johnson's immediate response was to tighten economic relations. He wrote to the Board of Trade: "I have told the Six Nations that I shall dispose of His Majesty's bounty and rewards only to such Indians as will actually go upon service. This I propose to make a fixt rule hereafter." This reflected a new pattern adopted by Johnson, who increasingly affixed the giving of gifts to identifiable services performed. The nameless Onondaga speaker requested that a trader be reestablished at the German Flats, reminding Johnson that "the ancient Covenant Chain was made for our mutual advantage, of which trade is a considerable part." But Johnson remained largely unsympathetic to Iroquois pleas, inferring that their neutrality was a chief reason why he could not reopen official trading: "Whilst our enemies are suffered to pass thro your country in order to come and destroy us, without their receiving any molestation from you, it will neither be safe or prudent for our traders to go that way." "Besides," he added, "as you have resolved to stay at home and smoak your pipes and leave us to fight the enemy, our people must be otherwise employed."[39]

In June 1758, when the Cayuga head warrior the Englishman turned up at Fort Johnson seeking provisions for the fifteen warriors who accompanied him, he found the superintendent unwilling to participate in the protocol of Indian hospitality. He reported that his warriors were "quite destitute of everything," particularly arms and ammunition, and entreated Johnson to supply their wants. "In return," he informed Johnson, "they have gathered among themselves some Skins which perhaps you may want for Shoes." The Englishman was not proposing a commercial deal. He hoped to situate the exchange of goods within the symbolic context of gift-giving. But Johnson refused to play along. Claiming that he had no goods of his own, he declined to provision the men. So as not to be indebted to them he returned their gift of skins, telling the Englishman, "I ought not to add to their Poverty by accepting it." Furthermore, Johnson used the occasion of their impoverishment to press them into military service. He claimed to be "much surprized" at their "great want and poverty." Given their neutrality for the last two years, he scoffed, surely "they had full Leisure for Hunting, by which means they might undoubtedly have supplied themselves." He claimed to be unable to help them since he had been instructed to give goods only "to such Indians as will go out with me to War" but concluded, "If your Warriors are willing to do this, they shall be fully supplied." If Johnson was not prepared to engage in the symbolic exchange of goods, the Englishman hoped that trade at the German Flats would at least be reinstated. As he reminded Johnson, "you well know Trade preserves our Common Welfare and in a Manner keeps up our mutual Friendship." Johnson, however, denied his request and instead stressed the Indians' status as free agents in a commercial marketplace. He told them, "Bever bears a high price at Albany and Schenectady and Goods are plenty. You are free and Welcome to go either place to buy and sell."[40]

Oneida headman Canaghquiesa experienced firsthand the commercialization of exchange. In December 1758 he visited Fort Johnson with a party of forty young men, women, and children. Early frosts had destroyed their crops, causing widespread impoverishment. On their way down to Fort Johnson they had stopped at Canajoharie in the hope that their Mohawk brethren would feed them. But Canajoharie crops had failed as well, which meant, according to Canaghquiesa, "they had not so much as a meal of Victuals to Give us on our way hither." Thus they arrived at Johnson's home on a cold winter's night "sick . . . fatigued and hungry." Johnson fed and quartered them, but such generosity was short-lived. The next day, Canaghquiesa evoked the language of humility, calling upon Johnson's "Assistance and Pity" in their "distressed Condition," telling him that "[we] beg you will appoint a place where we may get some Provisions." To ask to be pitied was to ask to be given goods without the expectation of having to reciprocate. Johnson refused to be obligated and instead placed the onus on them. He offered minimal assistance, informing Canaghquiesa that he would have been "much readier to relieve" them had their impoverishment "been occasioned by your Mens being employed in our Service." He noted the possibility of further aid but only "if you convince me of your deserving it." Johnson supplied gifts and goods from a position of dominance and as an opportunity to lobby for military aid.[41]

While he had Johnson's audience, Canaghquiesa also expressed concern over trade. That July, Amherst had ordered the construction of Fort Stanwix, a small garrison and trading post at the Great Carrying Place near Old Oneida. While the Oneidas harbored reservations about the presence of a new British post on their land, most welcomed the opportunity to trade. Contentment soon waned, however, when they found that goods were expensive. The costliness of waging war meant that the British could not afford to subsidize trade with Indians. Politically they had little reason to do so in any case. Canaghquiesa complained to Johnson about the high cost, reminding him of his promise "that the Goods should be sold us Cheap." He believed that because the Oneidas had demonstrated political allegiance, the British should reciprocate by rewarding them with inexpensive trade. Johnson retorted that his complaints were "ill grounded" and set about explaining to him the workings of the market economy: "You do not or at least are unwilling to consider that a Scarcity of any Commodity makes it dear. For Example your Bever and Skins are double the Value they have been when plenty." Furthermore, he added, "the War we are engaged in employs many of our Manufacturers and Artificers and of Course Goods cannot be altogether so Cheap as otherwise." The shifting balance of power permitted Johnson to abandon his usual rhetoric of reciprocity and replace it with instruction on the nature of commercial forces.[42]

But Johnson achieved only limited success wielding trade as a tool of coercion. The British remained dependent on the military support, or at least neutrality, of the Iroquois and therefore could not afford to alienate them. Despite his hard-line rhetoric Johnson was obliged to lend assistance. To ease their impoverishment he frequently supplied Indians with cash to purchase provisions. When Oneidas and Tuscaroras bemoaned their starving state in late 1758, Johnson "gave them some money to buy corn at Stoneraby, and other places about the River." Throughout his accounts he noted regular payments of cash given to Indians "to buy Provisions" or "to purchase Indian Corn" from colonists. Thomas Butler, stationed at Fort Stanwix, observed in early 1759 that Indians frequented the post to purchase dry goods and bread with money. Thus one major legacy of the war was to hasten the flow of cash into Iroquois village economies. By 1760, the Iroquois lived in an increasingly commercial world in which access to cash was fast becoming a necessity to maintain subsistence.[43]

The Iroquois also took matters in their own hands to compensate for difficulties in trade. By late 1758, French soldiers at Fort Niagara, finding themselves "in great Want," turned to the neighboring Senecas for provisions of corn, while others solicited Indians at Oneida Lake. With commerce restricted to the eastern towns of Schenectady and Albany, loss of competitive pricing ensued, causing some Iroquois hunters to venture south to Pennsylvania in the hopes of finding a better market for their pelts. To compensate for the deprivation of formal trading, some Oneidas became involved in an illicit trade flourishing between the German community at the Flats and the French Iroquois at Oswegatchy, just south of the St. Lawrence River. Acting as intermediaries, they carried German goods to the Oswegatchies in Canada. Others took advantage of the presence of troops in the valley, exchanging what furs they had for salt, meat, and rum and selling them fish.[44]

Alongside constraints in trade, the Iroquois faced continued pressures on their lands. As the French retreated, the British advanced, constructing a series of forts and roads in their imperialist march (map 4). To protect communication and supply lines and to secure native and colonial settlements, Johnson oversaw the militarization of the Mohawk Valley and beyond. The original Fort Hunter at Tiononderoge was strengthened and enlarged and Fort Hendrick was erected at the second, more westerly Mohawk village of Canajo-

harie. Fort Herkimer was constructed further upriver. By May 1756, forts
were also under construction at the Seneca, Onondaga, Oneida, Oquaga, and
Schoharie communities. Johnson was responsible for employing carpenters
and regulating their conduct with local Indians. In addition, the vital trading post at Oswego was fortified with the building of Fort Ontario in early
1755, and a road was cut out of the woods linking the fort to Schenectady.
Although fortifications at Oswego were destroyed in 1756, Johnson began
rebuilding work in 1759. Johnson also bargained with the Oneidas to permit
the building of Fort Williams and Fort Bull on the Oneida Great Carrying
Place. By securing this portage, supply lines could be maintained all the way
from Albany and Schenectady in the east to Oswego in the west.[45] Eventually,
the entire northern frontier was linked by a series of forts. Fort Edward and
Fort William Henry were constructed at Lake George, along with a new road
connecting Albany to the north. In central and western New York, British
troops built and seized additional posts, including Fort Stanwix, Brewerton,
Niagara, Erie, Presqu'île, and Le Boeuf. The British also established military
structures outside the immediate parameters of Iroquoia. Throughout the war,
after each successful campaign, British troops refortified and garrisoned captured French posts to assert territorial claims. To the south in Pennsylvania,
Fort Augusta was built at Shamokin and Fort Pitt on the ruins of the French
Fort Duquesne. Also within the Iroquois orbit of trade and travel, the British
eventually occupied the western posts at Detroit and Michilimackinac.

The Iroquois were exasperated by this method of conducting war. "When
we go to war our manner is to destroy a Nation and there's an end of it but the
English chiefly regard building Forts, which looks as if their only scheme was
to take possession of the Lands," they exclaimed. The Iroquois made sense
of the British military advance within their broader experience of colonial
land accumulation. The construction of forts and roads intensified Iroquois
concerns over their territory and heightened their distrust of the British. Although many Iroquois had solicited Johnson for forts to be built for their
protection, the issue still proved to be divisive. The Schoharie Indians, beset
with "jealousy and disagreement," split into two parties over the decision of
whether to allow the British to build a fort at their village. The fortification
of Oswego, in particular, aroused apprehension. As large numbers of soldiers
with their supplies traveled up the Mohawk River to this post, Johnson was
compelled to send two wampum belts among the Iroquois to soothe fears, but
many remained convinced that "the English have a mind to destroy them."
The presence of Fort Williams and Fort Bull greatly unsettled the Oneida

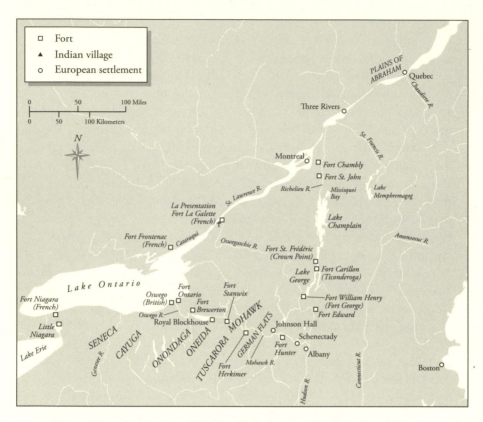

Map 4. The militarization of the New York frontier. The Seven Years' War brought significant military incursions into Iroquois homelands and western hunting grounds.

community despite Johnson's assurances that these posts were a temporary measure built in part for their defense. Captain William Williams, who oversaw construction of the fort named in his honor, complained of the tense atmosphere as "disaffected" Indians watched with hostility: "twas with Difficulty that I obtained Leave of them to clear and mend the Road . . . I lay Still in open camp [and] dare not cut a pickett, nor brake ground to intrench for fear of giving umbrage to my Jealous Neighbours." Resentment against these posts encouraged some Iroquois to participate in the French assault of Fort Bull in March 1756.[46]

Reassured by the presence of garrisoned posts, a small but steady stream of settlers continued to move into the Mohawk Valley. In 1758 Seth, a chief headman of Schoharie, complained to Johnson about "a number of Germans" who had illegally "settled on Lands belonging to the Indians of that Settlement." While Johnson appeared sympathetic to their plight, he was simultaneously involved in his own efforts to facilitate colonial accumulation of western lands. He worked strenuously to encourage settlers to remain on his frontier estate, boasting in 1761 that he had settled upward of fifty families. Men like Johnson looked to the war as a means to secure and enlarge a territorial empire. Lieutenant Governor James De Lancey issued a proclamation in 1759 promising free land grants to men who volunteered for military service, a strategy designed to bolster provincial forces and looked to the future prosperity and growth of the colony. The governor envisioned a newly extended colonial frontier made safe by a hardy stock of ex-soldiers inhabiting the region. To encourage settlement, De Lancey ordered that all "Wooden Hutts and Coverings" erected by troops be left in place for the use of settlers.[47] By 1761, British colonel Philip Skene had already purchased a tract of land on Crown Point near Lake Champlain, where he settled his regiment and their families. The advanced British military presence weakened Iroquois sovereignty and in the following decades would facilitate greater colonial incursions into Iroquoia once the French were defeated.[48]

As well as difficulties, the war years also offered new economic opportunities. A particularly striking feature of the war was the high number of Iroquois men who exchanged their labor for cash. In February 1757, two Seneca Indians named Silverheels and Johnny received "cash besides sundry goods" for intelligence gathering. On another occasion Silverheels, accompanied by Daniel, a Mohawk chief, piloted whaleboats from Irondequoit, on the south shore of Lake Ontario, for which they were paid six dollars each. Among the Oneidas, Gawèhe received a salaried commission as lieutenant of Indian warriors. David, a Schoharie headman, was outfitted and compensated with cash to lead "6 young Men to go to War" in the fall of 1756. The Oquaga head warrior, Thomas King, earned a wage for leading a party of Indians who assisted in the capture of Fort Duquesne in November 1758. Among the Mohawks, Daniel, Aaron, and Captain Dick found regular employment with the British army as Indian scouts.[49] These men engaged in dangerous and fatiguing work, but for their time and trouble they could expect generous pay. Their activities demonstrate how a major economic consequence of the war was the accelerated commodification of Indian labor. In larger numbers than ever before Indian men exchanged martial skills, physical labor, and mental toil for cash payments. The war created new opportunities for wage employment but also generated greater need for this activity, as warfare undermined usual economic pursuits. Indian men received cash payments for a variety of services: delivering messages, escorting interpreters, transporting goods, tracking down army deserters, and driving cattle to military posts. Most men earned cash by selling their martial skills. Obtaining prisoners, scalps, and intelligence were guaranteed ways of earning steady cash. In 1759, a party of warriors received £45 for securing three prisoners. Another group who returned from Canada with "a deal of Intelligence" pocketed £15 each. Indians who participated in major campaigns could also attain special commissions. Warriors at the Niagara campaign earned cash by destroying blockhouses surrounding the fort and escorting the captured French general to Fort Stanwix.[50]

To secure adequate wages for their work, Iroquois warriors first had to overcome a reluctant superintendent. Having experienced firsthand the problem of inadequate funds during King George's War and wary of incurring debt, Johnson was hesitant to rush headlong into a new policy of wage employment. Johnson's plans, however, were overturned by the activities of William Shirley and demands of Iroquois allies. In July 1755, Shirley and Johnson competed for military supplies as both prepared for their respective campaigns against Fort Niagara and Crown Point. Shirley sought to wrest Indian warriors from under Johnson's patronage by personally visiting the two Mohawk castles to promise generous wages if they joined his campaign. He also employed agents to scour the Mohawk Valley and entice Indians with handsome bribes. Carighwage, a Tuscarora headman, warned, "if these Methods of giving sumes of Money to the Indians were pursued . . . they would delude all the Indians." Mohawk headmen reported how "their Castles are tore to pieces with Discord Faction and riot" as conflict arose between those who remained loyal to Johnson and those who were swayed by the promise of monetary gain. These events incensed Johnson. He rebuked Shirley for not only undermining his authority with the Indians but creating market conditions wherein Indians could bargain for better wages between two competing employers. As one contemporary observed, "that Mr. Shirley in order to detach the Indians from Mr. Johnson has made them such large Offers, that Mr Johnson has been obliged to yield to very unreasonable Demands from them."[51]

The 1755 campaign set an important precedent by encouraging warriors to expect cash payments for their services for the remainder of the war.

In 1756, Canaghquiesa protested heartily to Johnson that economic necessity compelled his warriors to demand wages: "As we are now debarred from going to Canada where our wants used to be supplied and our hunting hindered by your dayly orders to hold ourselves in readiness to join the army we think it not unreasonable that those who go on such fatiguing and dangerous service should be well paid." He expressed annoyance at Johnson's attempt "to overset what has been so wisely thought necessary." He believed that if Johnson eradicated the wage system, warriors would "be very backward to move," and if he lowered their pay, warriors would "imagine that in a little time you will bring it to nothing." Therefore, he concluded, "we desire you may pay them as they have been paid by others." Canaghquiesa's insistence for cash may seem at odds with his later demands for subsidized trade and the continuation of gifts. He occupied what appeared to be a contradictory position, simultaneously embracing and rejecting aspects of commercial market relations. But this was not a flawed or inconsistent strategy; rather, it reflected an instrumental and pragmatic approach. He both resisted and pursued commercial behavior as and when it suited his needs. Canaghquiesa's advocacy of wage labor and noncommercial gifts illustrates the uneven and muddled process of economic change. Like so many Indians at the time, Canaghquiesa intermixed old and new economic behaviors and values.[52]

The Mohawks proved equally resolute to secure regular payments for their military services. In September 1756, Johnson was unable to deter a group of their men from drawing pay from a lieutenant of the rangers who, according to Johnson, "verry imprudently offered to engage some of the Mohawks and to give them 10 Dollars Bounty, with four Shillings p Day pay." The Mohawks refused to yield to Johnson's demand to give up wages. As he noted, "they told me they thought they deserved as much, if not more than the Rangers, as they were better acquainted with such service than any others." Johnson complained of the Mohawks' penchant for earning an income to the Board of Trade, remarking, "I have warmly remonstratted to the Indians upon the unreasonableness, and Novelty of this Custom of paying them by the Day, which they will not now give up." He chiefly blamed Shirley for the Mohawks' attachment to financial compensation, arguing that his "Lavish Bribery" raised "extravagant Expectations" among them. He also blamed it on their own natural inclination, "they being a verry mercenary people." The new wage system had simply "enflamed" their "natural avidity." Their desire for cash over other traditional gifts reflected their growing enmeshment in a commercial world. In the Mohawks' encounters with traders and colonial neighbors, cash was fast becoming a necessary commodity to obtain food, clothing, and powder. Hence, some head warriors even suggested the formation of a salaried Indian regiment. As Johnson wrote to his superior, Lord Loudoun, "they were of [the] opinion [that] forming them into companys with their own People Officers, would be the best Method we could follow to get a great Number."[53]

The persistent demands of the Iroquois for monetary remuneration eventually took effect on Johnson, as he soon came to view cash payments as a more efficient way of employing Indian labor. Given the staunch neutrality of many Iroquois, Johnson was disinclined to continue older practices. "I conceive giving presents in the old General way would be imprudent, and an ineffectual profusion," he told the Board of Trade in late 1756. Gift-giving was expensive and wasteful. As it had become "necessary to buy their assistance," given Iroquois insistence for cash payments, Johnson proposed to "make a sure bargain, and give to those Indians only, who will act with us, and for us." In his bid to cut costs and maximize Indian labor, Johnson took seriously Mohawk suggestions for a salaried regiment. Impressed by this scheme, he set about calculating the cost of a regiment of five hundred Indians and their officers. If Loudoun rejected this plan Johnson agreed to "follow the old Custom," but he believed that "Regimenting them . . . would be productive of good consequences" and less expense.[54]

Although plans for a salaried Mohawk regiment never materialized, cash payments for Indian labor became a widespread phenomenon for the remainder of the war. Johnson assumed the role as key paymaster, recruiting Indian labor, negotiating rates of pay, and disseminating funds. Serving as the official imperial employer, Johnson was responsible for supplying British officers with Indian laborers. He assigned some Mohawk warriors to Colonel James Mercer stationed at Fort Oswego, who paid them "twelve Dollars a piece" for their role as scouts and messengers. Colonel John Bradstreet, commissioned to supply Oswego, requested Johnson to send him some Mohawk scouts, noting, "I will with great pleasure pay them what ever you shall think proper a day or otherwise."[55]

This war differed from the previous imperial conflict because in addition to being paid scalp and captive bounties, Indians also received daily wages. In early 1756, warriors received a steady wage of four shillings a day for general scouting duties. In March 1758, Johnson's agents paid Indian scouts a daily wage of one dollar per day. Payments to Indians tended to be tiered, with head warriors, including the likes of Theyanoguin, Gawèhe, and Daniel, acting as salaried war captains, receiving a special commission in addition to wages. Rates of pay between Indians and colonists fared favorably well. Rank, not ethnicity, determined the level of remuneration. While Euro-American Indian officers received a higher daily wage, Iroquois warriors could expect to be paid the same amount as local Dutch and German men who joined them in multiethnic scouting parties. Thus in May 1760 Johnson paid two settlers and one Mohawk a dollar each per day for transporting horses to Niagara. Warriors enjoyed similar, if not higher, wages issued to provincial troops. In comparison to warriors who earned four shillings per day in 1756, privates in the New York provincial army received only one shilling and three pence in 1760. The considerable level of pay that warriors could demand was indicative of the high value the British attached to their martial skills.[56]

The experience of negotiating, receiving, and spending cash wages encouraged Iroquois men to develop an appreciation of the market value of their labor. They expected decent pay and "grumbled greatly" if was not forthcoming. When Johnson employed an Indian laborer in 1760 he was "obliged" to pay him one dollar per day, "which is the hire all People get here now from Suttlers [and] Traders." Indians knew the going rate and expected the British to pay accordingly. Demonstrating new market sophistication, the Iroquois refused to work if conditions of pay were unsatisfactory. Indian agent Thomas Butler reported of his strenuous efforts to enlist Indian warriors who were more concerned with obtaining sufficient pay than fulfilling reciprocal bonds: "when I talked or Mentioned to the Indians of Going a Scouting they asked for pay in C. [commission?] for the Same besides their dayley wages which I was obliged To do To some." He went on to complain, "there Seems no Such thing as Sattisfieing the Indians." Although the exchange of labor for cash never became a wholly commercial transaction—British need for Iroquois military support obliged Johnson to engage in a full range of Indian rituals to induce warriors to fight—participation in wage labor affected Iroquois economic morals. The war placed a commercial value on otherwise noncommercial and even sacred objects. In pre-contact Iroquois society, prisoners and scalps served important cultural and religious functions, but imperial war put tremendous market value onto these two articles that many Iroquois found difficult to ignore. Johnson paid twenty to two hundred dollars for a prisoner. Unsurprisingly, following the assault on Fort Niagara, warriors relinquished their claim to French prisoners and accepted cash payments instead.[57]

Johnson demonstrated an ambivalent attitude toward this new commercial spirit, actively encouraging it on the one hand and censoring it on the other. As he complained to the Board of Trade, the Mohawks gave military support "at a very expensive praemium," adding that "our present sittuation makes them very mercenary." He may have exaggerated their degree of market orientation, but clearly he was disturbed by new patterns of behavior. The presence of warriors throwing their weight around as independent actors in a commercial marketplace collided with his desire for hierarchical relations in which younger men dutifully deferred to his paternal authority. If headmen like Canaghquiesa oscillated between the ethics of moral and market economies, so too did Johnson. While he promoted the culturally uncomplicated transaction of labor for cash, he still urged the Iroquois to lend support on the basis of old-fashioned reciprocal bonds. As he reminded one group of men: "In former times when we went to war together . . . your ancestors never even thought of Pay."[58]

The degree of distress experienced by the Iroquois in the late 1750s proved impermanent. As the chaos of war subsided, communities made some form of recovery over the following decade. The war intensified trends the Iroquois had been experiencing for decades: the commercialization of forms of exchange; pressures to cede lands; and an increasing need to exchange labor for cash. In sum, the Iroquois experienced a growing absorption into a market economy. The Iroquois resourcefully confronted the forces of economic change by seeking to secure a foothold in both worlds: the monetized and nonmonetized. They continued to hunt and farm, even as they engaged in new forms of paid labor. While their adoption of commercial activities was a consequence of ongoing integration into a market economy, it was also a form of cultural adaptation: it was their attempt to maintain control over the process of economic change. As a consequence of material change, the cultural world of the Iroquois also began to alter.

Chapter 4

Gendered Encounters

In 1754, Theyanoguin employed a gendered slur to chastise the British for their tardiness in confronting the French threat. Deriding Britain's past military performance *"which was a shame and a scandal,"* he drew on sexualized imagery to criticize them further: "look at the French, they are Men, they are fortifying everywhere—but, we are ashamed to say it, you are all like women bare and open without any fortifications." Two years later William Johnson returned the insult when seeking to shame warriors out of neutrality and onto the battlefield; he accused them of behaving "more like fearfull and silly women than brave and honest men." Sharing a mutual appreciation of warfare as an inherently masculine pursuit, both sides resorted to gendered taunts to evaluate each other's manly performance, to justify their own position, or to coerce the behavior of the other. Iroquois clan matrons, however, had no intention of allowing Johnson to consider them "fearful" or "silly." As Canaghquiesa informed him, women were held in "Much Estimation Amongst Us" because "we proceed from them, and they provide our Warriors with Provisions when they go abroad." In public Johnson acknowledged women's political role, but privately he advised officials not to invite women to conferences as it "is only expensive, and troublesome and not the least Service [for] they have nothing to Say."[1]

As these varied exchanges reveal, the Iroquois and British, throughout the 1740s and 1750s, encountered one another upon a gendered terrain where ideas about gender roles and relations, sexuality, and kinship shaped the content and meaning of their interactions. Both sides carried with them partially overlapping but nonetheless distinct gendered attitudes and practices. Both sides drew on the language of gender to assign roles and responsibilities, as well as to impose or resist domination. At times their gender systems provided a meeting point where both sides could acknowledge their essential similitude. Yet more often than not, gender remained a contested arena in which competing ideas about the division of labor, allocation of power, and nature of hierarchy collided. During the Seven Years' War, protracted involvement with the British Empire imposed new strains on Iroquois gender roles, which, while not insurmountable, still proved onerous.

In a conference with the Six Nations, during King George's War, Governor George Clinton decried the "*unmanly* Murders" committed on New England frontiers by French soldiers and their Indian allies. He disapproved of the use of surprise raids, describing the "custom of murdering private People by Sculking Indians" as "inhumane." By adopting Indian modes of warfare the French had proved themselves to be cowardly. Rather than face the British army in open battle, "they dare not look them in the face in day light." Instead "like thieves" they "steal upon people who do not expect them in the night." He hoped that the French would end the war or at least continue it "in a *manly* manner and after the Manner of Christians." By contrast, he argued, the British had "acted like *Men of Courage*" because "they do not attack poor Farmers at their Labour but boldly attempted the Reduction of Louisbourg." Clinton ended his diatribe against the "unmanly" methods of Indian warfare by paradoxically appealing to the New York Iroquois to employ identical tactics against the French. Whatever reservations he had about Indian warrior masculinity, Clinton recognized its utility.[2]

The governor's exchange with the Iroquois is indicative of the general ambivalence Euro-Americans demonstrated toward Indian manhood. Imperialists and colonists alike acknowledged the martial character of Iroquois men. The brutal warfare waged by the Iroquois against western Indians and their French allies during the seventeenth century cemented such a reputation. They were, according to one colonist, "the most warlike people in North America." Given that European culture celebrated the virtues of brave and heroic soldiers, Iroquois warrior masculinity had the potential to elicit comparable commendation. Cadwallader Colden, in one of the first histories written on the Five Nations, praised the image of the virile warrior for having "manfully fought" in past conflicts.[3] But others were not so sure. Some denounced Iroquois methods of warfare that included ritualized torture, cannibalism, and scalping, forms of violence generally abhorred by Europeans. The Iroquois also relied on the guerrilla-style tactics of small-scale surprise assaults, which stood in stark contrast to European large-scale open battles and the use of heavy artillery.[4] Warfare was only manly, some held, if conducted in accordance with particular virtues. "It is *true Valour* we speak of; not a savage Ferocity, not a brutal Rage, not an insatiable Cruelty; but a manly Greatness, a sedate Firmness and Resolution in the Midst of Danger," the author of one 1758 pamphlet explained.[5] But it was not just the way Indian allies fought that provoked agitation. British need for Indian martial assistance raised questions about their own masculine identities: were they not man enough to fight their own battles? Imperialists and colonists embraced a dual impulse toward Indian allies, condemning them as cowardly at the same time they sought their assistance.

William Johnson, as linchpin between empire and Iroquois, was responsible for enlisting and integrating warriors into the British war effort during the mid-eighteenth century. This was a complex task that involved the careful mixing of Iroquois, colonial, and imperial gendered martial ideals. Johnson first gained experience during King George's War. Concentrating his efforts on the Mohawks, he stressed not only economic and political imperatives for their involvement but cultural ones as well by appealing to their warrior ethic. Johnson enthusiastically engaged in Iroquois war rituals to arouse their fervor for battle. In addition to providing food for large war feasts, he personally visited their villages where, as noted by one contemporary, "he dressed himself after the Indian Manner, made frequent Dances, according to their Custom when they excite to War, and used all the Means he could think of . . . in order to engage them heartily in the War against Canada." He adroitly played on the warriors' craving for personal status and distinction by bestowing handsome gifts of fine clothing.[6] When British soldiers failed to be sent over from Europe and as the provincial militia remained largely inactive, Mohawk disillusionment grew. Johnson led the campaign to Crown Point in August 1747, largely out of a desire to convince warriors of British military potency. He was skeptical of any success but noted, "it will nevertheless satisfye the Indians, being chiefly their desire" and thus give them "a better opinion of us." When the French murdered a group of warriors in 1746, the larger Mohawk community was incensed by the failure of provincial troops to assist them in tracking down the culprits. To exacerbate matters, the British made peace with the French without consulting the Iroquois and before the Iroquois had a chance to avenge the killings. Such conduct intrinsically violated the warrior ethic and greatly tarnished British manly credibility.[7]

At the outset of the Seven Years' War, Johnson faced an impressive undertaking of restoring Iroquois faith in British martial potency. At the summer conference of 1755, he reassured them, "It is not that the English are affraid

of the French or any of their Enemies, that I make you this offer." Instead
their involvement in war was presented as an opportunity for them to demonstrate their renowned martial spirit. Failure to assist would consequently
cause the English to suspect "that you [have] lost your ancient Bravery." By
contrast, Johnson emphasized the military vigor of the British. The king's
"Warriors," he informed them, "are now gathered together with their swords
in their hands, his great guns are loaded and all his warlike instruments are
sharpened and ready." Although "they are slow to spill blood, . . . when they
begin, they are like an angry Wolf." Thus he urged the Iroquois to "Be Men"
and state openly where their loyalties lay. By appealing to Iroquois desires to
exhibit the warrior ethic and at the same time making grand claims about
British military prowess, Johnson hoped to induce warriors to fight.[8]

He continued to employ gendered recruitment strategies for the remainder of the war, which saw the steady increase of Iroquois combatants. There
were important political and economic rationales guiding warrior behavior.
Some felt a genuine loyalty toward the British; many others were motivated
by a desire to rid the French from their territories. Assisting the British also
guaranteed money, clothing, and provisions. These factors aside, there remained strong cultural incentives to enlist. Engaging in battle—albeit the
battle of others—provided Iroquois men with the opportunity to perform a
much cherished gender role and thereby achieve social status within their
communities. Warriors at the Battle of Lake George had little reason to be
disappointed. One contemporary noted how victorious warriors "passed
thro' *Albany* with many scores of *scalps*, mostly *French*, fastened on poles,
and carried along in solemn triumph. They seemed highly pleased also with
the *laced hats* and *clothes*, the *guns*, the *watches*, the *pocket-money*, and *other
plunder*, our people were willing to let them have for their encouragement."
Johnson skillfully played on their cultural proclivities. In large conferences
with the Six Nations, he incited their martial spirit. Appealing to their collective pride, he urged them to "retrieve" their "pristine fame" so that "the
very name of the six nations . . . will be a terror to their enemies!" When they
refused, he questioned their manhood.[9]

The ability to recruit warriors depended on an appreciation of their gendered cultural practices. Reflecting their culture as a whole, which placed a
premium on personal autonomy, Iroquois war parties were generally egalitarian in nature. Although some warriors enjoyed greater respect and leadership than others due to previous war exploits, no warrior held authority over
another. Village chiefs were also unable to exert coercive powers. It was up

to individual warriors to decide whether or not to engage in military ventures. This was in stark contrast to the British army, which was immensely hierarchical. As part of their manly conduct, regular soldiers were expected to be deferential and subordinate. The Iroquois' lack of hierarchy perplexed Johnson, who viewed their beliefs about freedom and independence as "extravigant," claiming that "they are a people under little, or no subordination." He recognized the difficulty of imposing a tiered structure on warriors. As he explained to Governor William Shirley at the outset of the conflict, "To establish the Indians into Companys of 100 Men each with Captains, Lieutenants and Ensigns, is impossible that sort of regularity cannot be obtained amongst those People."[10] Yet Johnson deftly took advantage of their cultural traits. The lack of rigid hierarchy enabled him to procure warriors regardless of the sentiments of the larger community. Despite the Six Nations' determination to remain neutral during the war, Johnson still sent his deputies into Iroquoia to appeal directly to warriors, usually head warriors who enjoyed a large following. These deputies were instructed to use promises of military glory and material rewards to "spirit up the Indians" and "prepare the Warriors' minds for War." Johnson also continued his practice of appealing to warriors' desire for status by giving them elaborate clothing, war medals, and other articles of distinction. Rather than attempt to integrate warriors into the army, he encouraged their role as independent scouts.[11]

A high degree of cultural negotiation took place between Johnson and warriors. For much of the war he had to acquiesce to their gendered practices of warfare. Warriors continued to perform valued war rituals such as the war dance, an important custom designed to arouse martial fervor. Impressed by this ceremony, Colden described how each warrior "sings the great Acts he has himself performed, and the Deeds of his Ancestors; and this is always accompanied with a Kind of a Dance, or rather Action, representing the Manner in which they were performed." Through this ceremony of male bravado, "they work up their Spirits to a high Degree of warlike Enthusiasm." Warriors also insisted on taking captives and scalps, important trophies of war through which they acquired status. Johnson in fact took advantage of this practice. To persuade warriors to go on the warpath he frequently requested them to engage in battle for the specific purpose of obtaining scalps or captives to replace recently deceased friends and kin. Thus, in June 1757, Johnson gave two war belts to Peter, a head warrior, "to bring him a Prisoner in the room of Captain Teddy McGin deceased, agreable to the Indian Custom."[12]

All the while Johnson extolled and encouraged warrior masculinity he also sought to control and contain it. As patriarch supreme, Johnson ultimately desired warriors to defer to his manly command. Although he promoted their aggressive masculinity, he still attempted to subordinate them within a hierarchical alliance. Johnson's self-assigned role as "head warrior" received imperial sanction when he was appointed major general of several campaigns. Most famously he led the joint provincial and Indian force against Fort St. Frédéric in 1755. Demanding subordination among his multiethnic army, he told enlisted warriors that "they are not to go a Scalping as in the late War, only to March with me where ever I go." Away from the battlefield, Johnson asserted his patriarchal rule by chastising those who refused to adequately defer. When a group of Onondaga warriors chose to follow the advice of their headmen and remain neutral instead of taking up Johnson's call for arms, Johnson chided them for their defiance. "I . . . never expected you could be prevailed on to drop the Design [of war] at the request of the Sachems," he told them. Refuting the long-held authority of chiefs, he added, "it was very wrong of them to act in that manner." Although warriors continued to behave in accordance with individual and familial interests, they found it necessary to enact public shows of deference in their dealings with Johnson.[13]

In contrast to the previous conflict, the Seven Years' War brought a much larger number of Iroquois men into contact with provincial and British troops. Once on the battlefield soldiers assessed the manly virtues of their Indian allies. When they first encountered Iroquois warriors they were struck by their physical appearance. The lack of clothing, colorful body paintings, and absence of facial hair challenged their perceptions of what they considered a manly demeanor. To some observers the warriors' appearance signified their savageness. Others were more impressed by what seemed to be a rather majestic semblance. A young soldier, James Gilbert, felt unable "to Describe The oddness of Their Dress," which included "Jewels in Their noses [and] Their faces painted with all Colors." Yet, he observed, when the Mohawks engaged in their virile war dance at the encampment at Lake George, "They had the eyes of many To view There with Great Admiration." Charles Lee, a young commanding officer, noted their refined nature when he wrote, "they acquire something of an ease and gracefulness in their walk and air which is not to be met with elsewhere." Thus he jested in a letter to his sister: "I assure you that if you were to see the young Warriors dress'd out and arm'd you would never allow that there was such a thing as gentillity amongst our finest gentlemen at St. James!"[14]

The notable lack of hair on the Iroquois generated debate. In eighteenth-century Europe, facial hair was an emblem of masculinity. Guy Johnson, Indian agent and son-in-law of William Johnson, claimed that their lack of hair was "owing to themselves, and not the Effect of Nature." He went on to explain, "it is a general Custom with them, on its first Appearance to pluck it out with a twisted Brass Wire, and afterwards to apply Ointments to the Parts which at length overcome the Hair."[15] However, to less knowledgeable Europeans a lack of facial hair could be interpreted as a sign of immaturity or effeminacy.

Europeans were also intrigued by Iroquois sexual behavior. The presence of European women at eighteenth-century military camps was commonplace. Wives of soldiers, washerwomen, prostitutes, and female cooks frequently followed the army from one engagement to the next, which meant there was much opportunity for sexual exchange to occur.[16] In actual warfare European soldiers raped female prisoners. By contrast, warriors avoided contact with women and there are no records of Iroquois men ever sexually assaulting female captives. This was due in large part to their beliefs concerning the contamination of male and female energy. It was also a result of their practice of adoption. The rape of a potential sister or cousin touched on the taboo of incest. The warriors' lack of sexual interest became in itself a source of interest. When researching his famous *History of America* (1777), the historian William Robertson found it necessary to inquire into the sexual behavior of Indian men. He asked, "are the Indians defective in the Animal Passions for their females, and are they inferior to the People of the Ancient Continent both in desire and ability?" In response Indian agent George Croghan assured him that "the Indians are No way Deffective in the Animal Passions" but "have as Great Desires and abilitys I belive as any Nations can have." Guy Johnson agreed. He explained that warriors refrained from sex because they believed "it debilitated them, and drew their Attention from the Pursuit of Glory and Military Atchievements."[17]

The actual conduct of warriors during the war aroused mixed views. At one end of the spectrum the Iroquois were highly valued. Many colonial officials believed that the presence or absence of Indian warriors would make a crucial difference to the outcome of a battle. Officials also reluctantly acknowledged that Indian military tactics were better suited to the North American terrain. This lesson was learned early. In the aftermath of Braddock's defeat in the Ohio Valley, New York lieutenant governor James De Lancey concluded, "the Success of the French was entirely owing to the European Troops being unaccustomed to and unacquainted with Wood Fighting." Warren Johnson noted that most officers "reckon 300 Indians . . . [were] a Match for 1000 Regulars, in the Woods, [as] they are very great Walkers, bear Fatigue, and [are] quick sighted." Consequently, William Johnson encouraged the adoption of Indian military tactics by colonial men. In the hundreds of scouting parties he sent out, he employed local men to fight alongside warriors so that skills and methods could be easily transferred. On a more formal level, the commander in chief authorized the formation of ranger companies, which modeled themselves on Indian-style warfare. Throughout the war, Anglo-American men adopted the modes and manners of Indian warriors. Warren Johnson observed how "some white People" copied Indian dress, physically marking their bodies through the process of tattooing, "which is done by pricking the Skin with Pins, till the Blood comes, and then applying Gunpowder to it; which will remain for ever." Although "'tis a great Torture," soldiers engaged in this practice along with Indians because "it makes them look desperate, and besides is A Considerable Addition to their Fury."[18] Guy Johnson also noted how "White Men employed in the Indian service . . . followed the same Method [as Indian men] and got rid of their Beards." Certain forms of Indian violence also crossed cultural boundaries; some soldiers took up scalping. By appropriating the physical appearance and military techniques of their Indian allies, soldiers assumed facets of Iroquois warrior masculinity. But this was not always a case of innocuous cultural borrowing. British and colonial men adopted and ultimately turned Indian modes of warfare, such as guerrilla-style tactics, against the original practitioners.[19]

An undercurrent of disquietude underscored and sometimes undermined efforts to commend the manly virtues of Iroquois men. By praising, copying, and relying upon Iroquois warrior masculinity, British subjects and officials cast doubt over their own masculinity. At midcentury, the British were especially sensitive to accusations of weakness and degeneracy. Imperial rivalry coupled with strong anti-French and anti-aristocratic sentiment underlay a growing sense of national malaise and fueled a public preoccupation with "effeminacy," which according to contemporary dictionaries meant the "admission of the qualities of a woman, softness, [and] unmanly delicacy." Social commentators warned that immoderate luxury and aristocratic overassociation with the French had corrupted the manners and morals of men and emasculated the body politic. Englishmen had "impaired their vigour by Excess" and had "made themselves soft with all Manner of Delicacy." Britain's poor performance in the initial campaigns of the Seven Years' War seemed to confirm that Englishmen had indeed lost their manly virtues and had "sunk in Effeminacy."[20]

Given this broader cultural context, Britain's reliance on the martial skills of an indigenous people whom they considered less than equal left imperialists feeling awkward. The image of the virile Iroquois warrior, whose aggressive masculinity reminded the British of their own military weakness, aroused both admiration and contempt. Officials found themselves in the contradictory position of simultaneously promoting Iroquois masculinity at the same time that they belittled it. Johnson's own discomfort at advocating the manhood of men he wished to subsume as his dependents led him to disparage their manly virtue when he claimed that "British soldiers have infinitely more bravery than any Indians." Similarly, as commander in chief Lord Loudoun issued funds to enlist warriors, he also insisted that colonial rangers were "much stronger and hardier fellows than the Indians," who, despite being tall, "are a *loose-made indolent* sett of People" and doubted "a good deal of their *Courage*." Army officers claimed Indian allies to be "Trifles and of little Use" while they requested more warriors to scout for them, and whenever warriors refused to scout they confirmed English perceptions that "they seem fearful." Some officers felt that the martial spirit of the Iroquois was less a sign of their manliness than of their depravity. Reporting on the Indian involvement in the British assault of Fort Frontenac, an anonymous observer derisively noted that the majority of the Indians "kept at a mile's distance during the attack"; after the French surrendered, they "came running from the woods, where they had been conceal'd; like ravenous beasts, full of the expectations, of satiating their blood-thirsty fury on the captives." The use of animal imagery in discussions about Indian masculinity was common throughout the colonial era and reveals in this instance the compulsion of Englishmen to deny the humanity, let alone manliness, of men they fought alongside.[21]

Ideas about gender similarly shaped the attitudes and behaviors of Iroquois men. Warriors embraced their own set of gender norms, which guided their conduct and affected how they viewed the behavior of others. For the Iroquois, warfare was the epitome of manhood and they took great pride in their fame as a warlike people. They used their martial spirit as criteria for assessing the masculinity of others at the same time that they remained sensitive about their own reputation. Thus, to counteract accusations that they had "fled like Cowards," Mohawk men felt obliged to reassure Johnson in September 1755 that their prompt retreat from battle "was not from Fear or treachery, but in compliance with their constant Custom" to mourn for their dead. Both collectively and individually Iroquois men resisted the efforts of Johnson and others to impose denigrating gendered identities upon them. When the French governor taunted an Iroquois delegation for their subordinate status vis-à-vis Johnson, suggesting that Johnson made them "tremble" in their villages, the Iroquois refused to be emasculated, retorting, "We, the Five Nations, fear no man on the face of the earth." Extended contact with Europeans, however, exposed the Iroquois to new ways of thinking about gender roles and relations. They were intrigued, bemused, and occasionally troubled by British gender practices: the harsh discipline commanding officers exercised over soldiers contradicted their understanding of warrior status and autonomy, while the dismissive attitude British men held toward women's political prerogatives caused Iroquois headmen to regularly remind Johnson of the special status the Iroquois accorded women.[22]

But Iroquois men also found British gender constructs to be useful. For example, on one occasion an Onondaga headman sought to deflect Johnson's censure for failing to respond to a message by blaming Johnson's use of "foolish people and women" as messengers. Such people "either don't remember or designedly alter your meaning," he told Johnson.[23] This headman reaffirmed Johnson's belief in the unsuitability of women in diplomacy, not necessarily because he believed it but because it suited his particular interests at that time. The Iroquois never simply and unthinkingly adopted English gender norms, nor did they stubbornly cling to their own. Instead they selectively and no less creatively co-opted and combined both. In the diplomatic and martial exchanges with others they modified and applied gender discourses in very deliberate ways. In the long run, however, the process of cultural adaptation and synthesis was not always under their control or in their best interest.

The reconstitution of gendered meanings was most visible in the realm of diplomacy where the Iroquois utilized European notions of gender hierarchy to reenvision their relationship with other native groups. In the early 1700s, Iroquois relations with the Delawares altered significantly as the former assumed a position of dominance by assisting colonial authorities to dispossess the Delawares. Iroquois headmen manipulated gender metaphors to suit the realities of this new relationship and to justify their actions. Whereas a century before the Delawares became "women" and the Iroquois "men" to suggest a reciprocal political agreement, by the 1740s the meaning had shifted. Drawing on a European definition, Iroquois headmen called the Delawares "women" to place them in an inferior status, to suggest the limits of their power, and to naturalize a new relationship of domination. Hence in 1742, Canassatego refuted Delaware land claims by asserting, "We conquer'd You, we made Women of you, you know you are Women, and can no more sell Land than Women." Attending clan matrons would have been perturbed by Canassatego's illegitimate claim that men, not women, controlled the land. Throughout the Seven Years' War, the Iroquois continued to employ the metaphor of "women" to remind the defiant Delawares of their subservient status. In 1756 a Mohawk chief avowed, "We, the Mohocks, are Men; we are made so from above, but the Delawares are Women and under our Protection, and of too low a kind to be Men." Implicit in this statement, with its reference to various positions of "above," "under," and "low," was a hierarchical understanding of gender relations.[24]

The Iroquois also borrowed from Europeans discourses on women's sexuality when they employed the metaphor of the lascivious madam to denigrate others. In contrast to Iroquois culture, which held lenient attitudes toward female sexuality, English and colonial society throughout the seventeenth and eighteenth centuries demonstrated a proclivity to prescribe, police, and punish women's sexual behavior. The adulterous wife and lusty bawd were common metaphors used to imply social disorder and to evoke the image of the emasculated male. By the 1740s, this sexual discourse had begun to enter Iroquois political language. In 1742, Canassatego censored the Delawares for their readiness to entertain a low opinion of the English, telling them in council: "Your Ears are ever Open to slanderous Reports about our Brethren. You receive them with as much greediness as Lewd Women receive the Embraces of Bad Men." To convey a sense of outrage and betrayal when the Delawares sided with the French during the Seven Years' War, an Oneida headman likened them to adulterous women: "we charged you to be true to us, and lie with no other Man; but of late you have suffered the String that tied your Petticoat to be cut loose by the French, and you lay with them, and so became a common Bawd." Reflecting the consequences of extended contact with the English, some Iroquois speakers resorted to new metaphors of women—divorced from the land, a lower kind, and sexually promiscuous—to put down political opponents.[25]

In the context of warfare, the Iroquois continued to reinforce and redefine the meaning of gender. Warfare was an inherently gendered activity that made it difficult to disentangle from a discourse on masculinity. Gender metaphors were a regular feature of rebukes between Iroquois warriors and Indian foes. Explaining to the British in 1744 why they were unable to make peace with the Catawbas, Onondaga headman Gachadow noted that the former had "sent us word that we were but Women; that they were men and double men for they had two P—s; that they could make Women of Us, and would be always at War with us." Similarly, Delaware enemies demonstrated aggressive defiance to the Iroquois during the Seven Years' War when they threatened to "cut off" their "private parts." These references to "women" and "men," which were grounded in sexual bodily differences, did not necessarily infer gender hierarchy. The nature of men as warriors was derived from their physicality. To lack a penis suggested that they were not warriors and therefore not properly men. However, as in the diplomatic sphere, the woman metaphor was increasingly used in warfare as an insult to suggest weakness and fear. Hence Iroquois warriors declared that "it was not looked upon as a warlike Action" to obtain a Cherokee scalp, because their Cherokee enemies were considered to be but mere "old Women."[26]

In a like manner the Iroquois cast an equally critical eye over the manly performance of European men. In the early 1750s, Johnson was hard-pressed to secure the friendship of a pro-French Cayuga head warrior. "The reason he gave me," Johnson explained, "was, that the French he thought were a more warlike people then we, and being the Head Warriour of the five Nations himself, Said he had a veneration for all those of his own disposition." During the middle decades of the eighteenth century, the Iroquois regularly expressed doubts about British manliness. Britain's performance during King George's War provoked derision. Peter Wraxall, secretary of Indian Affairs, noted that the war campaigns "tho' introduced with formidable appearances and swelling boasts made us lose all credit for Military Virtue among the Indians." He concluded, "when the warlike Genius and disposition of the Indians are considered this source of the Declension of our Interest and influence among them will appear to have weight."[27]

The Seven Years' War generated similar denigration from the Iroquois. British methods of warfare seemed at odds with Indian notions of masculinity. The drawn-out campaigns that involved extended periods of inactivity, the practices of fort building and prisoner exchange, and the rigid hierarchical structure of the army aroused scorn. Furthermore, Iroquois fears about Britain's motives for waging war colored their perception of British men as dishonest and unmanly. Johnson explained to his superiors that a British show of fortitude would win Iroquois respect, whereas the appearance of weakness would lose them to the French: "Certain I am that if the Indians should find We Bully, and threaten without Executing our Just Vengeance upon the French, and make good that Superiority we Boast. . . . We shall not have an Indian upon the Continent left in our Interest." Braddock's military debacle posed problems for Johnson, requiring him to take "much care" when informing Indian allies of events. Further defeats continued to dismay Iroquois allies.[28]

However, the Iroquois were very instrumental in their accusations of "unmanly" behavior. While some Anglophile Iroquois were genuinely disappointed by the apparent weakness of the British forces, others used gendered taunts to serve a political agenda. By accusing the British of lacking manly vigor, Iroquois men provided themselves with a ready excuse for not fighting in a war for which politically they had little desire. Most Iroquois communities pursued a firm policy of neutrality during King George's War. They could repel British pressure to provide support by pointing to English inactivity. In 1748, the Cayugas claimed to be appalled by the colonists' poor war effort. After chastising them for having "sat still and . . . [done] nothing," they refused to lend assistance until "you fight yourselves like men." For many Iroquois who had no intention of joining the Seven Years' War, British slowness to battle and initial defeats afforded them a convenient pretext not to participate. Those providing the harshest criticism of the British war effort were often those with the least interest in alliance. In April 1756, Seneca warriors made only a tacit commitment to join Johnson at Oswego "to go out fighting with him," adding, "they hoped he would not do as was done there last year, sit still, eat, drink and make excuses." "The English begin but do not go through with any thing," they complained, concluding that "such like things . . . do not become a Warrior." Following the loss of Fort Oswego in 1756, Iroquois headmen visited Johnson to provide a lengthy critique on the British "want of vigour, and good management" in military affairs. Johnson took their charge quite seriously, concluding after the meeting, "Could we but give such a convinceing proof of our Prowess" it would "turn them with such destructive Rage upon the French." But it was possible that such a rebuke was used by the Iroquois to absolve them of their failure to rush to the defense of Oswego.[29]

The Iroquois also creatively employed gendered arguments to influence other aspects of the war. Following the French assault of Fort Bull at the Oneida Carrying Place in March 1756, the Iroquois reproached the French governor for his chosen method of warfare. "It was not manly but deceitful," they complained, conducted "in a base and cowardly manner." They urged the governor to assemble his troops at Oswego or Lake George and confront British forces in open battle and "in a man like way." This gendered description of warfare, which is almost identical to the one Governor Clinton used in

1746, is illustrative of Indian manipulation of a European gender discourse. The attack of Fort Bull was conducted in typical Indian fashion: it was a small-scale surprise raid on a frontier post in which a significant number of French Indians participated. The decision to describe an Indian-style attack as un-manly was deliberate. It seems that they were less upset by *how* this attack was carried out than by *where* it was carried out. Fort Bull was in the heart of Iroquois country, an area that the Iroquois wished to keep clear of military conflicts. A European-style battle fought at Oswego or Lake George was not necessarily more "manly," but it was preferable because it directed conflict away from Iroquois settlements. The Iroquois played on what they under-stood to be European notions of unmanly and manly warfare to serve their own ends. Alternatively, it is possible that this exchange between an Iroquois headman and the French governor never actually took place. The conversa-tion was reported to Johnson and may consequently embody a different set of political objectives. By employing this gendered description of warfare, the Iroquois speaker crafted a familiar and appealing discourse for Johnson, one that emphasized the common manliness of Iroquois and Englishmen who preferred to engage in open and manly battle at the same time that he emas-culated the French and their Indian allies as cowardly. This Iroquois speaker may have adopted English gender norms to score some political points with the British superintendent.[30]

Entanglement with the British Empire placed new pressure on Iroquois war-rior masculinity. As Johnson maximized the role of the Indian warrior to serve the needs of empire, facets of this cultural construct became unhinged. Fighting alongside British and provincial troops at times undermined the ability of Indian warriors to wage war according to their own cultural dic-tates. Not only were methods of warfare modified but their behavior as men in the arena of warfare was as well. Iroquois men largely resisted external pres-sures that circumscribed their warrior masculinity, but they were not entirely successful. Furthermore, as Johnson augmented his leadership role among warriors by sponsoring their activities and dispensing goods and wealth, he aggravated tensions between Iroquois men.

The role of the Indian warrior was traditionally grounded in a complex nexus of social and religious meaning and ritual. Extensive engagement in imperial warfare eroded these cultural moorings. Before embarking on a military expedition, warriors typically performed a series of rituals includ-ing war feasts, dances, songs, and the ceremonial sacrifice of dogs. Once they joined the British war effort, however, warriors found it more difficult to control their own military and cultural agendas. Having to be ready to march when instructed by Euro-American commanding officers meant that there was very often a lack of time and opportunity to perform religious rites. In 1758, the Mohawks complained to Johnson of his impatience to march, noting, "it was very contrary to our established Custom and manners to be as it were thus drove out to War." Johnson also exerted pressure on warriors not to leave immediately after battle, despite their practice of mourning.[31]

Purification rites, once central to pre-contact warrior culture, soon lost sway. Historically, warriors ingested purgatives to cleanse their bodies before battle, but during the 1750s they increasingly engaged in practices that were at odds with notions of purity. Alcohol use was common among warriors and its impact debilitating. Officers and Indian agents reported that warriors were "of little service" because of drunkenness. An army officer with a party of Mohawk men sent on a scouting expedition in March 1756 returned prematurely: "The Party he had with him got drunk at Lake George, and disagreed which intirely disconcerted their Scheme." Excessive drinking triggered violence. In May 1756, a group of Mohawk warriors had to disband from their martial activities "oweing to their haveing too much Drink which Ocationed ill blood between them as they often quarreled in their cups."[32] Intoxicated warriors less able to perform threatened the manly prestige once attached to the role of the stoic warrior.

Formerly, concerns over purification had also applied to sexual abstinence. Perhaps through the influence of alcohol or through extended contact with British and provincial soldiers, the sexual mores of some warriors loosened. Guy Johnson recalled how in the early 1760s, Iroquois leaders complained to Johnson about "the Degeneracy of their Warriors, who then pursued [sexual] Intrigues." A French officer also noted this change in behavior among the Iroquois. While he observed that there were many men who, "wishing to be warriors," refrained "from sexual activity or indulg[ed] in it only in moderation," he added, "Not all the young men think thus." He noted the existence of "libertines unconcerned by military glory who, through their dissolute behavior, seem to constitute a class apart." Similarly, Warren Johnson implied a change in warriors' sexual mores when he observed in 1761 that "Indians *formerly* did not Sport or marry untill 30 years of Age, for they imagined it infeebled them."[33]

The desire to conduct war according to their own preferences led some warriors to ignore Johnson's call for arms. Teyohaqueande, an Onondaga warrior, concentrated his energies during the Seven Years' War on fighting an age-long battle against the southern Catawbas. This conflict, which dated back to at least the seventeenth century, was part of the mourning-war complex whereby captives were sought for adoption or torture in order to assuage the grief of the recently bereaved. Just as important, war against the Catawbas provided a vital means for men to demonstrate martial prowess. Missionary Henry Barclay noted of the Iroquois, "their only inducement to war is glory, and [they] esteem it the greatest honor the farther distant they seek an enemy from their own country." For Johnson, anxious to recruit warriors for his own war, the Catawba conflict was a waste of martial manpower. He issued cash bribes to deter warriors from heading south. But this conflict was culturally satisfying for warriors like Teyohaqueande because it allowed them to enact a masculinized identity in ways similar to previous generations. Consequently, warriors who turned up at Fort Cumberland in Maryland in September 1757 did so not to aid the British but because they had heard that there were Catawbas in the vicinity. As Johnson attacked Fort Niagara with the assistance of large numbers of Iroquois warriors in the summer of 1759, Teyohaqueande led his own assault against Catawba foes. He was among a group of Onondagas who passed through Pittsburgh with five captives. Yet, Teyohaqueande finally bent to imperial pressure and redirected martial skills toward the British war effort, even though such involvement required cultural compromise. The desire for material rewards or perhaps the longing to secure Johnson's political backing caused Teyohaqueande to cut short the appropriate time to mourn the loss of his recently deceased child to join imperial forces at Oswego in September 1759.[34]

Warriors found that they were often prohibited from performing older customs of captive taking and scalping, activities that gained them military glory. Commanding officers generally sought to curtail this aspect of the warrior ethic. In the aftermath of the Battle of Lake George, Johnson managed "with great Difficulty" to prevent the Indians from scalping and killing the captured French general. After the seizure of Fort Levis in 1759, General Jeffrey Amherst, in a bid to protect prisoners, forbid warriors from entering the garrison. Enraged by Amherst's actions, many warriors left in disgust. Ironically, they were later censured for having "basely" and "shamefully" abandoned him. Their actions, however, were motivated by a resentment of having been denied the right "to prosecute the war agreeable to their own custom." They had wanted "to take full revenge of the French, for the former insults their Ancestors had received." Furthermore, the acquisition of captives and scalps would have demonstrated their bravery and martial virtue to their families back home. Officers attempted to satisfy the Indian desire for captives, blood, and scalps by offering them material rewards instead. During the assault on Fort Frontenac, Colonel John Bradstreet prevented his Indian allies from molesting prisoners by turning their attention to plunder: "The search for valuable goods, became then their entire pursuit." Similarly, Johnson was only able to redeem French officers captured by the Iroquois at Fort Niagara in 1759 by offering "ransom" and "good words" instead.[35]

The shift from captives to material plunder is significant because it reveals how economic concerns came to overshadow once dominant cultural and religious motives for warfare. This was part of a seventeenth-century trend whereby the Iroquois had waged war against their Indian neighbors to rob them of peltries and to secure access to hunting grounds. Engagement in imperial wars during the mid-eighteenth century took this economic concern to a new level. During the Seven Years' War, the payment of wages and commissions to Indians became widespread, causing the cultural criteria for measuring manly credentials to alter. Personal prestige was gained not just by the number of captives and scalps brought home but also by the size of financial earnings. In this respect, Iroquois men took on certain facets of European definitions of manhood insomuch as their performance as men was increasingly evaluated on the basis of economic success.[36]

The new tensions Iroquois men confronted when fashioning a masculine identity on an imperial frontier are evident in the experiences of Sahonwagy, a Fort Hunter Mohawk and son of Theyanoguin. At midcentury Sahonwagy enacted a masculine identity that set him apart from an earlier generation. While his forefathers had performed their manhood strictly in the realms of warfare, hunting, and diplomacy, Sahonwagy's masculinity was shaped in part by his extensive contact with Europeans. In July 1753, the Society for the Propagation of the Gospel in Foreign Parts (SPG) hired Sahonwagy, known by the British as Paulus Peters, at an annual salary of £7 and 10 shillings to serve as a schoolteacher. Missionary John Ogilvie hoped that Sahonwagy might also "officiate as Clerk, and read Prayers to the Indians in . . . [my] Absence." Up to forty children attended his schoolroom by June 1755. Sahonwagy had perhaps been encouraged to take up this line of work by his uncle Old Abraham, a noted headman and Indian missionary whom Europeans praised for his pious and sober nature.

The outbreak of the Seven Years' War generated new opportunities to both redefine and reinforce masculine gender roles. Attracted by the promise of higher wages and by the desire to pursue more customary modes of masculinity, Sahonwagy gave military support to the British. Following "several Complaints that he was so taken up with War-parties, that he had greatly neglected the Instruction of the Children," the SPG suspended his salary in February 1759. For the rest of the war, Sahonwagy was a committed warrior. Yet, abandoning the schoolroom for the warpath did not represent a clear-cut choice between new and old. Fighting with the British involved cultural change: the need to be on call to march undermined Sahonwagy's warrior autonomy; serving as part of a multiethnic scouting party meant that it was not always possible to perform in typically Indian ways; and the all-too-easy flow of alcohol held the potential for warriors to abandon the stoicism and honor long associated with their role. Furthermore, the usual channels for acquiring status, through captive taking and scalping, were not always feasible, as Johnson insisted that prisoners be delivered up. Instead new ways of attaining merit were pursued. In the summer of 1756, Sahonwagy received his first set of wages as an Indian war captain. In 1758, he earned the healthy sum of a dollar a day, plus the promise of a fifty-dollar reward for obtaining a prisoner. His wages provided him with not only a livelihood but an important means to acquire prestige.[37]

Increased integration with the British Empire reinvigorated the role of the Indian warrior. Courted and patronized by Johnson to engage in military campaigns for which they were handsomely rewarded, young Iroquois men experienced an elevation of their gender role in the mid-eighteenth century. However, this was an adulterated process as both incentives for engaging in warfare and the methods of doing so altered.

Furthermore, Iroquois involvement in the Seven Years' War had a detrimental impact on gendered relations between men. By soliciting the support of warriors and encouraging them to behave in ways that were not necessarily sustained by the larger community, Johnson disrupted the delicate balance of power between elder headmen and young warriors. Although warriors had always been free to act independently, the social prestige and authority enjoyed by hereditary chiefs meant that their wishes were usually considered, if not obeyed. While the social status of hereditary chiefs may have already been declining by the early eighteenth century, they still exerted influence over warriors. When the Mohawks were called to war in 1745, for example, "the younger Indians offer'd to dance the Warr Dance imediately and receive the Hatchet and make use of it, but the older restrain'd them and obliged them to hold their Peace." Ongoing British interference encouraged a steady shift in power relations between elder headmen and younger warriors. Following the Battle of Lake George, Ogilvie observed that "the Sachems positively refused" to lend further support. British officials, however, continued to apply pressure, appealing "in private Conversation with the Fighters." Ogilvie noted, "We encouraged them all we could, and I make no Doubt but twenty or thirty principal Warriours will go out." Tensions increased as warriors acted against the wishes of village elders. An Onondaga Indian reported that "the Young Men of his Nation blame the Sachems for their backwardness and say it was their faults that Sir William was now angry with them." The warriors claimed to be "ashamed" of their chiefs, "adding that had the Sachems left it to them or even desired them to exert themselves, they would have done it long ago, and let them smoak their Pipes." Blaming elder headmen for their own "backwardness" was of course a convenient way for warriors to deflect Johnson's annoyance with them for failing to fight. Even so, Johnson's insistent pressure and handsome bribes to persuade men to war created a climate for tensions to arise between elder men who relied on social deference and moral suasion to keep their younger male relations in line and these heady warriors in search of personal status, wealth, and autonomy. By enacting their gender identity as "men of war" in imperial conflicts, men exposed themselves to the corrosive forces of cultural dislocation, generating not just political tensions within communities but generational and gendered tensions as well.[38]

In the early 1750s, an article appeared in a New York publication titled "A Letter from Yariza, an Indian Maid of the Royal Line of the Mohawks, to the Principal Ladies of New York." After praising the general state of peace between her people and the English, Yariza made a special plea to her English female counterparts. In a style of meek deference, she proclaimed the desire of Iroquois women to serve the ladies of New York, noting, "How gladly, O lovely Sisters! would the Indian Maids attend on you in your high wigwams, to learn something of your gracefulness and Goodness." Yet, Yariza concluded they were "not worthy, till better fashioned." Consequently she urged that some "skilful Females" be sent to teach them English so that "wherein you utter your commands and meanings . . . we may perfectly understand, and be the more fit to attend to them."[39] This letter, supposedly translated by a "plain countryman" of New York, is less useful as an insight into the values and aspirations of Iroquois women on the eve of the Seven Years' War than as a record of (male) European attitudes toward gender and ethnicity. In an emerging racial and gendered pecking order, colonists deemed it appropriate

Figure 12. "Guerrier Iroquois." Hand-colored etching by J. Laroque, from Jacques Grasset de Saint-Sauver, *Encyclopedie des voyages . . .* , vol. 2, Amerique (Paris, 1796). Library and Archives Canada/C-003163. This image depicts the quintessential Iroquois warrior, although his iron weaponry, bayonet, and indeed much of his attire are a consequence of colonization.

for Iroquois women to be subservient not only to men (Indian and colonial) but to Anglo-European women as well.

The image of deferential Iroquois women wishing to serve as handmaid-ens would have appealed to English colonists who were otherwise troubled by the reality of native female gender roles. The central part Iroquois women played in the Iroquois economy was perplexing for European men. The inde-pendent female farmer was a cultural anomaly in a British-colonial culture in which men farmed and women *assisted* under male supervision. The Iroquois division of labor struck colonists as perverse and was construed as evidence of male idleness and female exploitation. Colden noted that Iroquois women "perform all the Drudgery" while "the Men disdain all Kind of Labour." John Bartram made a similar comment when he described Iroquois men as "lazy and indolent at home" and "the women continual slaves."[40] In the political realm as well, colonial men, wedded to the belief that war and politics were the sole provinces of men, were astonished and no less discomforted by the power of clan matrons. Warren Johnson noted with keen interest in his jour-nal that not only do "Indian Women assist at Councils" but that they also exercised "great Influence" over warriors. William Johnson's associate Golds-brow Banyar was baffled to learn that "it is a Custom for the old Women even to preside" in village councils. Many officials simply remained ignorant of women's political status.[41]

Yet whatever their objections to the role and status of Iroquois women, European traders, settlers, soldiers, and diplomats often found themselves dependent on their services and skills. As women traded at forts and set-tlements, produced desired commodities, requested the hired labor of set-tlers to assist with farming, attended political conferences, and acted as hosts and consorts, they played a central role in generating and mediating cross-cultural exchanges. The benefits colonial men derived from women's eco-nomic and political contributions prompted their reconciliation to Iroquois gender norms.

Women had a visible and vibrant presence on the imperial frontier partly through their market-oriented activities. Trading in furs and liquor, produc-ing shirts, wampum, and moccasins for sale, and selling surplus supplies of corn and other wild produce, women found ways to access a market economy. By midcentury Iroquois women were particularly noticeable in the liquor trade. The Indian demand for alcohol enabled women to carve out a profit-able niche for themselves by facilitating the flow of alcohol from its colonial importers to its Indian consumers. Moravian missionaries traveling through

Sauvagesse Iroquoise

Figure 13. "Sauvagesse Iroquoise." Hand-colored etching by J. Laroque, from Jacques Grasset de Saint-Sauver *Encyclopedie des voyages* . . . , vol. 2, Amerique (Paris, 1796). Library and Archives Canada/Acc. No. R9266-3501. This is one of the few images European men made of Iroquois women, despite the latter's vital and visible presence on the imperial frontier.

Iroquoia in the 1750s noted the arrival of Indian women from British trading posts with kegs of rum to sell. The rum trade offered women economic advantages but also generated a host of social ills including domestic violence. Although the matrilineal nature of Iroquois society offered women various forms of protection and support, it was relatively powerless to shield them from the drunken violence of men. Ogilvie noted that inebriated male kin threatened the safety of women. He recorded how one "worthy woman, the wife of a Sachem," was "barbarously murdered" by a drunken male. Another European commentator noted that women were "generally well treated by their Husbands when Sober."[42]

During periods of hardship women's propensity to enter a market economy waxed. This was particularly true of the Seven Years' War, which proved immensely disruptive to Iroquois economies. Eastern Iroquois women struggled in their long-esteemed role as farmers as the threat and reality of frontier assaults disturbed the normal farming cycle. Women neglected cornfields when they found they had "to hold themselves in readiness . . . to fly to the Woods in case they hear of the Enemy's approach." The troublesome presence of neighboring British troops inhibited the ability of Canajoharie women to farm. They complained in 1757 of "Soldiers Stealing our Corn" and of the damage caused by their cattle "always Running and Pasturing in our Corn fields." Closer contact with Europeans facilitated the spread of disease among the eastern Iroquois, thereby weakening the female workforce. Women could also no longer rely on male relations to assist them as they usually did during the arduous periods of the farming cycle, as war made substantial demands on men's time and labor away from villages. Difficulties in agriculture were not confined to the Mohawks, as other communities found themselves struggling.[43]

In the regular and extended absence of male kin during the Seven Years' War, women relied instead on the assistance of colonial settlers. In March 1756, Onondaga women assigned a male speaker to ask Johnson to "order some people to come up and plow our Corn Lands which are grown so stiff that our Women can scarce enter them with their Hoes." Johnson promised to send up some German settlers. The Cayugas made similar requests. Mohawk women went even further by appealing for the assistance of colonial men to fence, protect, and even farm their cornfields. In February 1756, the Canajoharies of the Upper Mohawk Castle complained to Johnson about the commander of the garrison stationed at their village, Hendrick Fry Jr. Although they had initially approved of him, they now desired his removal.

Warriors admitted to Johnson, "we were mistaken in our choice; for alto' he made us the fairest promises, that he would, during our absence, take care of our lands and the crops then in the field, he was altogether deficient in the performance, by which neglect, we entirely lost our crops!" In return for their readiness to join military expeditions, the Lower Mohawk Castle requested help with farming a few months later. They claimed "that as now the planting time is coming on whereon our sustenance throughout the year depends that you would be pleased to see our Corn Land secured. We should be glad that you would appoint somebody that understands our Language to take care as well of our Castle as our planting Ground." In response, Johnson sent local settlers to fence their cornfields and help plant. Assisting women in agriculture provided Anglo-American men with a useful source of income during the war years.[44]

Continued difficulties in farming encouraged women to pursue alternative strategies to secure a livelihood. They compensated for their poor performance in agriculture by increasing their participation in a commercial trading economy. Women had long been active in the Indian trade, but their involvement intensified during the war as men's productive labor was redirected toward warfare. Consequently, when an Onondaga Indian named Red Head came to trade at the German Flats in November 1756, he was outnumbered by the ten women in his party. The following year when Johnson prohibited official trading in the valley, the Cayuga community was first informed of the ban "by a Squa" who had been trading at the Flats. In response to Johnson's prohibition the Onondagas noted, "our women who chiefly carry on that article will be disappointed."[45] Women also remained highly active in the liquor trade. Keen to enlist the service of sober warriors and chiefs during the war, Johnson grew frustrated by women's efforts to supply rum. In 1758 he wrote, "The Indians in general are so devoted to and so Debauched by Rum, that all business with them is thrown into Confusion by it and my transactions with them unspeakably impeded." Despite imperial efforts to ban its sale, female traders continued to traffic alcohol. "Notwithstanding all the Care [that] has been taken to prevent the Selling [of] Rum to Indians," Johnson complained to his superior, "here [it] is as great plenty as ever. I am told it was brought from Albany by the Squaws." Johnson was particularly rankled by the fact that it was native women who defied his wishes. When Indians at his home became intoxicated, Johnson once again complained of the defiant behavior of female traders, "for liquor was as plenty among them as Ditch Water, being brought up from Schenectady by their, and other Squaws."[46]

Women also responded to new economic opportunities created by the war, such as the high demand for Indian moccasins and snowshoes needed by scouting parties. Johnson, in particular, paid local women to produce these goods. In February 1759, he paid a Cayuga woman twelve shillings for three pairs of Indian shoes. In March, he purchased a further eight pairs from two Onondaga women. Johnson made frequent purchases of moccasins, such as the 208 pairs bought for £41 in April, but he did not always list the manufacturer. If Indian women were the prime producers of Indian shoes, then this was a lucrative business for them during the war. In addition, local native women also sold Johnson prepared animal skins and wampum belts, the latter being essential for the numerous Indian conferences he held. Western Iroquois women also found opportunities to earn cash. When French soldiers at Fort Niagara experienced a shortage of provisions, "Indian Squas" from the neighboring Seneca town brought them supplies of Indian Corn, "which they sold at a great Price."[47]

Despite new commercial opportunities, heightened economic hardship during the war meant that women had to request aid directly from Johnson. When the Canajoharies found themselves in a "melancholy situation" after Hendrick Fry Jr. left them bereft of corn, Johnson came to their aid. Taking over the usual role of women, he promised to furnish the community with "three hundred skipples of corn" and assured them, "you shall have a further supply, until you are able to raise your own grain." Native women and Johnson attached different meanings to his role as provider. Through their male speaker, women often employed a deferential rhetoric of neediness to ensure that goods were forthcoming. Their language was symbolic, not literal. Hence, when a Cayuga speaker requested that Johnson provide women of his village with "Petticoats to cover their Nakedness," he did not mean that they were actually naked but that they lacked sufficient clothing. When they "*pleaded* a scarcity of Corn etc. and *begged*" for rum, they exaggerated their impoverished state to obtain gifts in a socially sanctioned way. Beleaguered women did not consider themselves to be in a position of dependency. They understood their request for clothing and food in the context of reciprocal relations. In exchange for their personal or familial support of the war, they expected Johnson to fulfill his obligation to supply their material wants. For Johnson, although the presence of "begging" women was an economic burden, in cultural terms they made sense, reinforcing his patriarchal self-image as provider and his belief that women were naturally dependent.[48]

Women's inability to produce adequate crops during the war years did not undermine their power relations with their male kin. While they may have struggled with farming, women successfully found other ways to contribute to the family and village economy through their involvement in trade and petty commodity manufacture. All across Iroquoia, men and women continued to swap and share resources. When impoverished Cayuga women appealed to Johnson for aid they marked the end of their speech with a gift of animal skins, an article obtained from warriors. When Iroquois men visited Fort Johnson, they brought moccasins and shirts to sell, goods manufactured by female kin. Despite disruptions to agriculture, a communal pooling of resources persisted throughout the war.[49]

In addition to their economic activities as traders and producers of goods, women provided other vital services for colonial men in the context of war. By serving as messengers and suppliers of intelligence, by encouraging male kin to lend martial support, and by offering food, shelter, and safety to Euro-Americans, Iroquois women reaffirmed their importance in Anglo-Iroquois relations. Women traveled from their villages to British forts bearing important news. In April 1759, Thomas Butler, stationed at Fort Stanwix, reported how "a squa from Oneida, told me she was come from the Castle all the men being drunk or not at home, to let us know, that a french army was at the oswego falls on their way to Attack this place." In March 1757, "Several Onondagas, Tuscaroras and Oneidas" who were "mostly Women" arrived at Fort Johnson to report of French movements. Another Indian woman provided detailed information on the French assault of Fort Oswego. Johnson sometimes turned to elder women to broker disputes with head chiefs and on at least one occasion employed an Indian woman to serve as an interpreter.[50] British and colonial men who ventured into Indian settlements sometimes depended on native women for their sustenance and even survival. In 1754, two Moravian missionaries residing among the Onondagas spent an evening without food because "the woman of the house was not at home, and the son was not empowered to deal out provisions." Men's lives sometimes depended on female protection. Women offered shelter and forms of escape from drunken violence and politically motivated intrigues. When two French-allied Senecas set out to murder the Dutch trader John Abeel in 1756, an Indian woman saved his life by warning him of the danger and aiding his escape. Army deserters could secure their place in Indian villages through intermarriage.[51]

Women also made their presence known in the Anglo-Iroquois alliance through their political deliberations in large conferences, informal meetings, and village councils. Aware of European gender norms, head women made sure, usually through their male speakers, to remind Johnson of their influence. In 1755, the Mohawks informed Johnson that upon learning about his intended visit to New York, "both Men and Women" had "met together in Council" and decided to use the opportunity to send a message with him to the governor. On another occasion he was told directly by a headman that "it is no new thing to take women into our councils particularly amongst the Senecas." Johnson was made equally aware that the political views of women were highly respected. One Mohawk informed him, "Brother our women are very dear to us and their request and opinions are always regarded by us in an especial manner." When Johnson inquired among some Mohawks as to the best way to retrieve British prisoners held by the Six Nations, they advised him to consult with "their Sachems, Chief Warriors, and leading Women." In 1758, Mohawk clan matrons advised Johnson not to attend the Onondaga conference as they feared for his safety. If he had any doubt as to the gravity of their words, they cautioned him, "We flatter ourselves you will look upon this our speech, and take the same notice of it as all our men do, who, when they are addressed by the women, and desired to desist from any rash enterprise, they immediately give way."[52]

A key political power Iroquois matrons held was their influence over male warriors. With the outbreak of the Seven Years' War, Governor William Shirley urged Johnson to engage as many warriors as possible by appealing "to each Man, or to any or all of their Chiefs," thus ignoring the influential role of clan matrons. Possessing a keener understanding of Indian diplomacy, Johnson opened the June 1755 conference by announcing that as he was to make an important speech the following day, "I desire that none will absent themselves either Men, *Women* or Children." Women attended this speech and asserted their authority throughout the conference. John Lydius, who was there on behalf of Shirley to enlist men for the Niagara campaign, experienced firsthand female political privileges. Lydius attempted to recruit Nicholas, a chief of the Canajoharie and husband to Sarah, a member of the Iroquois nobility. When he asked Nicholas to go with him to Niagara instead of Crown Point, Nicholas "replied, pointed to her, there is my wife . . . ask her Consent." For the rest of the war Johnson was reminded of women's special relations with warriors. At a 1756 meeting attended by four Iroquois chiefs and two Seneca women, the speaker informed Johnson, "As women have a great influence on our young Warriors, I must desire that the women now present in particular may be acquainted with what news you may have and with all public affairs relating to the five Nations, for their Influence is a matter of no small consequence with our Fighters." In 1758, Johnson sent Zachurias, a Mohawk Indian, to recruit warriors among the Senecas. At their village, "a large number of Men and Women" assembled to hear his message and delivered a joint response.[53]

Women became involved in the matters of war and politics because their personal and familial interests were at stake. In the extended absence of warriors, concerns over their physical safety were paramount. Women utilized their ties with Johnson to safeguard security needs. In the fall of 1755, a group of Mohawk women encamped at a little creek below Johnson's home. In 1756, they petitioned Johnson for forts and militiamen. A Mohawk speaker informed him, "Our Women of the two Mohawk Castles have given it as a solemn charge to us that we should use our utmost Interest that a strong guard be left to defend them in our absence." Some sought lodgings and medical assistance from Johnson when ill. Women also maintained an active interest in the war because of the opportunities it offered, including the acquisition of spiritually valued scalps and captives. With men frequently away, women continued to play a central role in the selection, adoption, and assimilation of English captives, such as the two Seneca sisters who traveled independently to Fort Pitt on the Ohio to obtain Mary Jemison, an eight-year-old captive of the Shawnees. They adopted the Pennsylvanian girl to replace their deceased brother. Women equally prized scalps. Following the Battle of Lake George, Myndert Wempel, a blacksmith stationed at the Senecas, reported to Johnson that "the Women rejoices verry much of the News, we received 6 Scalps here they thank'd the General for doing so."[54] By aligning themselves with Johnson, women also found a way to access the wealth of the empire. Careful to secure the favor and support of politically consequential women, Johnson engaged in a liberal distribution of gifts throughout the war. Just prior to the Battle of Lake George he issued "Some Hints for a Commanding Officer," which included, "when you make presents to the Indians let them be such as will be most acceptable to their Wives and Mistresses." Johnson took special care in supplying appropriate gifts for women. Of particular value to them were functional items such as working implements, copper kettles, strouds, and stockings. Yet they also enjoyed more decorative articles such as jewelry, ribbon, threads, and buttons. Johnson's account books reveal that he also made frequent cash gifts. In distributing these articles he targeted the female relations of high-ranking chiefs and head warriors.[55]

One native woman who benefited enormously from her relationship with Johnson was Molly Brant, Johnson's common-law wife. Molly was born in relative poverty and obscurity to Christian parents in Canajoharie in the mid-1730s.[56] She spent some of her childhood in the Ohio country but returned to Canajoharie at a young age where she was exposed to English influences. The presence of a nearby Anglican missionary at Fort Hunter provided her with access to Christian teachings and literacy skills. Her mother, Margaret, after being twice widowed, married Brant Canagaraduncka in September 1753 when Molly was about seventeen years old. This marriage marked the beginning of Brant's upward social climb. Her stepfather was a prominent and elderly headman of the powerful Turtle clan of the Lower Mohawk Castle and a man of considerable wealth. Brant and her younger brother Joseph now moved into the higher stratum of Mohawk society. After the marriage, the family settled at Canajoharie, where her father built one of the largest homes in the village. He also owned horses and cattle. As one of the headmen it was only fitting that Brant Canagaraduncka host important visitors. Whenever Johnson ventured into Canajoharie, he stayed at the Brant household. Through this means Molly met her future husband.[57]

Brant had much to gain from her union with Johnson. It enhanced her social status and provided her with considerable wealth and security. During the war years, when many of her community suffered impoverishment, she experienced relative comfort at Fort Johnson. Her husband's heavy workload permitted Brant considerable autonomy in the management of household affairs. Akin to native women generally, Brant played an important role as hostess and housekeeper. During the numerous visits made by Indians she was responsible for ensuring that they were fed, housed, and entertained. Consequently she was given her own accounts to manage with local traders. But if marriage to Johnson brought certain advantages, it also required compromise. Removed from the matrilineal order of Iroquois culture, Brant spent her married life as a member of a patriarchal household where the presence of indentured servants, black slaves, and Euro-American stepchildren made for complex lines of hierarchy that she needed to negotiate carefully. Whatever freedoms she enjoyed as housekeeper, she remained economically reliant on her husband, having no independent means of generating a livelihood. Unlike Iroquois culture where children were raised by mothers, it is questionable how much input Brant had over her children's upbringing. According to English custom, her children were given their father's name and were sent away to learn Anglo gender-appropriate skills and trades. Marriage to Johnson entailed that she modify gender practices. Despite a significant degree of acculturation, Brant never forsook her Indian heritage, managing to merge aspects from both cultures. Hence contemporaries noted how she "dressed after the Indian Manner, but her linen and other Cloathes [were] the finest of their kind." Both in her material reality and cultural outlook, Brant kept her feet firmly planted in Anglo-American and Indian societies and by doing so maintained a level of influence among the Mohawks.[58]

Johnson too sought to make this union serve his own political agenda. Although seemingly a love marriage, Johnson understood that his choice to take an Indian woman as his common-law wife enhanced his reputation among the Indian community. His marriage gained him admission to Mohawk kinship networks, through which he forged important alliances. Johnson used his status as a member of an extended Indian family to exert influence. Furthermore, Brant's significant relations made her an asset. In addition to her stepfather, her stepbrother Nickus Brant was a noted headman. Johnson courted his favor by bestowing him with gifts. Her brother, Joseph Brant, would also emerge as a distinguished Indian leader. Johnson was quick to recognize his potential power, commenting that he would become useful because of his "connection and residence." As one contemporary observed, Molly Brant's kin made her "of great use to Sir William in his Treaties with these people." The social standing and authority Iroquois culture assigned to women rendered Brant a useful partner, regardless of her family ties. To utilize her power and position, Johnson was obliged to make cultural adjustments, tolerating, if not encouraging, her political involvement. Contemporaries noted that throughout their marriage, Brant assisted Johnson in his diplomatic dealings with Indians, using whatever influence she had. As one remarked, "she has always been a faithful and useful friend in Indian affairs. . . . When treaties or purchases were about to be made . . . she has often persuaded the obstinate chiefs into a compliance with the proposals for peace, or sale of lands."[59]

More generally Johnson understood the gains to be had through an alliance with Iroquois women, but he was not always willing to cultivate this resource. Recognizing the political clout of clan matrons and the wives of head warriors, Johnson made occasional efforts to court their support. He respectfully listened to their speeches, thanked them for their advice, and outwardly demonstrated a willingness to accept their political prerogatives. Expressing an understanding of the communal nature of Iroquois politics, which included a consideration of women's views, Johnson ended a speech to the Six Nations by stating, "Let all your youngest people hear what I have to say, and your men *and women* seriously consider it." But in addition to these conciliatory and inclusive strategies, Johnson also sought to create an alliance of men by divorcing women from the political process and by undermining their involvement in decisions about war.[60]

Partially through the actions of Johnson, clan matrons experienced an erosion of their influence over warriors. During the numerous military campaigns, Johnson appealed directly to the warriors without first securing the support of clan matrons. He sent Indian officers to personally petition warriors, advising them that "the best way to engage Indians, is to Secure in your Interest the head Warriours who can bring their party along with them." Armed with money, gifts, and wampum belts, these officers traveled throughout Indian country soliciting the military support of individual men. Following the Battle of Lake George, Mohawk matrons rallied against warriors lending further support, "saying their Loss is already heavy, and that perhaps they would have no body left to take Care of [them]." Johnson and his agents, however, continued to apply pressure, and warriors continued to enlist despite the wishes of their aunts and mothers. This pattern persisted throughout the war. Economic dislocation in Iroquois villages had already disrupted relations between women and warriors. Women exercised influence over warriors partially through their production and control of crops. By withholding these supplies, they could deter warriors from engaging in military ventures. But their ability to produce and thus deny foodstuffs lessened as war progressed. When Cherokee women in a special peace message in 1758 urged the women of the Six Nations to live up to their role "to furnish the Warriors with Provisions whenever they go upon any Exploit," Iroquois women assented. However, their role as sustainers was fast becoming more ritual than material. Johnson, in fact, took over this function. Throughout the Seven Years' War, he provided hundreds of warriors with arms, clothing, and, most significantly, food.[61]

Johnson also sought to physically exclude women from male spaces. In August 1759, he sent a letter to Molly instructing her not to meet him at the army camp at Oswego. Heavily pregnant with their first child, she had planned to join Johnson in the aftermath of his successful campaign at Niagara. Along with soldiers and warriors, a large number of native women and children also encamped at Oswego. The presence of women at military camps was quite customary in Iroquois culture, for they collected firewood, prepared meals, and provided a source of companionship. With a scarcity of food in their villages during the Seven Years' War, it made sense for women and their children to join their male kin. Yet for Johnson, their presence violated gender ideals. Women represented an invasive and disruptive presence in what he deemed to be a wholly masculine terrain.[62] When Mohawk women arrived with warriors just prior to the Battle of Lake George, Johnson sent them back to Schenectady on wagons, though some women managed to remain. When the battle broke out, an observer reported how a group of warriors retreated to their camp "to take Care of the Squaws and Children they had brought with them."[63] In the midst of a recruitment campaign in 1758 Johnson ordered his Indian officers to obtain as many men as possible and at the same time "prevent Women and children from coming with them." When women began to arrive, Johnson instructed his Indian officers to "give the Women Provisions to carry them home." Women were a costly and unwanted intrusion. Thus when he urged the Six Nations to leave their women behind, he reminded them, "we must think of nothing but War." Despite Johnson's wishes, Indian women continued to be present at military encampments, forcing Johnson to turn this to his advantage by employing their services as messengers and scouts.[64]

Uncomfortable with the political involvement of women, Johnson sought to restrict their presence at conferences as well. Guided by his patriarchal belief that women had nothing worthy to contribute to political matters, he viewed their presence as a pointless expense. The necessities of war had on occasion prompted Johnson to address and include women in diplomatic meetings, but he avoided doing so whenever possible. By the close of the war he went even further by publicly disputing the political value of clan matrons. At a conference held with the Six Nations in 1762, Johnson specifically demanded that Iroquois women not attend. The women complied but sent a message via an Oneida speaker of their disappointment at being excluded. Johnson, in response, explained, "I really could not Discover any Necessity there was for the presence of Women and Children, and therefore I Called none but those who were Qualified for, and Authorized to proceed on business." Only six years earlier, however, during the height of the war he had gracefully acknowledged the political importance of matrons when he told some Senecas: "I am sensible your Women are of no small consequence in relation to public affairs and I shall be always disposed to consult and inform them of our public Business."[65] In the new political climate of British victory over the French, Johnson was better able to set the terms of intercultural diplomacy.

Throughout the 1740s and 1750s, gendered relations between the Iroquois and British were marked by a high degree of mutual accommodation and cultural synthesis. To secure the friendship of the Six Nations, Johnson and others were obliged to tolerate and adopt their gendered practices and values. But Johnson was also involved in efforts to manipulate Iroquois gender norms and he achieved some success. Neither men nor women experienced a radical makeover, but entanglement within a British imperial orbit generated new pressures and constraints on their gendered way of being. It was not just gender identities that were being challenged at midcentury. While Iroquois men and women mediated gendered encounters with a patriarchal British Empire, they also confronted new ethnic and nascent racialized ways of understanding human difference.

Chapter 5

Indian and Other

At the height of the Seven Years' War, William Johnson complained to his superior of "the intemperate, and imprudent sallies of prejudice and resentment which escape from many of our European Bretheren," aimed toward Iroquois allies. He warned that "if not curbed," such malicious expressions would "weaken the little Indian Interest we have left." Indeed, throughout the war, incidences of discord and violence erupted along the New York frontier as soldiers, settlers, and Indians clashed. Tensions soared when each side resorted to killing the other. In July 1757, Johnson reported "the most difficult Jobb" he had attempting to quell Iroquois fury following the murder of two Oneida men by an English trader, Thomas Smith, who had "knocked their brains out" with a pole. The larger Indian community was "so enraged," Johnson reported, "saying these made five now murdered by Us within a Year." The following year the Iroquois were put on the defensive when a Cayuga warrior, Tanighwanega, killed and scalped John McMickel, another English trader. Johnson rebuked the Cayugas for this most "black affair," observing that during the war, "some of every one of the Six Nations, except the Mohawks have privately spilt our Blood."[1]

At first glance these incidences of cross-cultural murder appear to confirm an image of the frontier as a rigid racial dividing line characterized by mutual hostility and disdain. On closer inspection, however, a more nuanced picture emerges. Far more common than acts of violence were patterns of intercultural exchange and cooperation. The two men murdered by Smith were on their way to scout the Canadian border; like hundreds of other Iroquois warriors during the war they fought alongside the British against the French. Furthermore, to appease the bereaved community, Johnson could rely on his close friend and political ally, Seneca chief the Belt, to present his speeches. Undermining their sense of Englishmen as a collective other, Johnson persuaded them "not [to] judge of all your Bretheren by the Behaviour of One worthless Fellow."[2] While Tanighwanega saw fit to murder McMickel, other Indians forged genuine friendships with European traders. During the mid-century, Iroquois men and women welcomed traders into their villages, protected them against the French, provided them with intelligence, food, and shelter, and entangled them in webs of kinship. Without idealizing or romanticizing this early phase of colonial encounters, it is important to recognize that relations could be based as much on codependency and collaboration as on conflict and violence. On the New York frontier, cultural misunderstanding, self-interest, or a simple lack of consideration created tensions and distrust between natives and newcomers, which sometimes culminated in bloodshed. But acknowledging these less savory aspects of Indian-European interactions does not disprove the idea of the frontier as a porous zone of cultural interaction. Cultural prejudice and ethnocentrism there may have been, but full-fledged racism did not yet exist. If violence and discord occurred it did so alongside prevalent themes of comradeship. The Seven Years' War worked to supercharge the dual discourse of difference and similarity by creating new sources of division, as well as an equally great imperative for alliance. While there was real conflict, there was also a pervasive theme of friendship and mutual assistance. Throughout this period race did not yet provide the dominant prism through which either side constructed group identity, even though by the close of the war attitudes had begun to harden.[3]

Powerful ties of commerce, war, religion, and family bound Indians and colonists together in webs of interdependency along the Mohawk Valley. This was an ethnically diverse region comprising Dutch, Palatine German, Scotch-Irish, and English immigrants, African slaves and freemen, and Iroquoian and some Algonquian Indians. Ethnic diversity made for a melody of "mingled languages." One visitor to the region noted how "it is common to hear High and low Dutch, Irish Mohawk, Oneida and English spoken amongst the settlers." But the coming together of diverse peoples also made for discord. Nonetheless, although Anglo-Indian relations occasionally soured, for much of the first half of the eighteenth century cross-cultural encounters were based more on convergence than divergence. For Indians and settlers living in close proximity and reliant on one another for goods and services, alliance—however tenuous at times—rather than hostility better served their mutual needs.[4]

The economic exchange of manufactured goods and natural resources facilitated a multiethnic partnership. Although incidences of deceitful trading practices and land thefts engendered ill feeling, the exchange of goods was more successful at bringing groups together than at keeping them apart in this early period. Impoverished German settlers, who found the Mohawks and Oneidas willing to loan or rent them land, had good reason to develop amiable feelings. In turn, Indians looked to settlers to satisfy their own material wants. Men like George Weaver at the German Flats and Lodowick Crane at Canajoharie opened up their homes to the Indians as trading posts, resting places, and taverns. Reflecting on the value of local Germans, the Oneida sachem Canaghquiesa noted, "we get a great deal of Provisions . . . and reap many Advantages from our Neighbourhood with the Settlers there—besides when the 5 Nations come our way and are hungry it is from the German Flatts they are fed." Regular and personal contact between the eastern Iroquois and their German and Dutch neighbors permitted a variety of social ties to develop. Indians frequented the home of local settlers to socialize and drink. A popular stomping ground was the home of George Kast, "the last plantation inhabited by white people" before Oneida country. One contemporary noted how "the Indians visited him quite often and never departed empty-handed." Although overfamiliarity could also breed contempt as drunken revelry led to scuffles, all in all, daily and intimate contact between these groups undermined a sense of impermeable difference.[5]

The ever-present military threat of New France and her Indian allies also fostered comradeship along the Mohawk Valley. Although not all Iroquois opposed the French, for those who did, their opposition provided a source of commonality with the English and Dutch. Colonists and Indians were deterred from developing racialized attitudes toward one another by the existence of a cultural other against which they could unite, or at least appear to unite. This sense of coalition was reinforced when Indians and British colonists fought alongside one another. During the planned invasion of Canada in 1709, over four hundred Mohawk, Oneida, Onondaga, and Cayuga warriors volunteered their military support. During King George's War, large numbers of multiethnic scouting parties composed of "Christians and Indians" killed and scalped together. The experience of battle bolstered a feeling of mutuality and shared experience. A local German settler, recounting his memory of the late war to Conrad Weiser in 1751, invoked this common heritage: "Over the evening meal he told us about the cruelties that during the last war were committed against the *Christians and Indians* in this region" by the French. When New England missionaries made overtures to the eastern Iroquois in the late

1740s to move to their colony for religious instruction, New York colonists opposed. John Ogilvie, missionary to the Mohawks, observed, "Our province in general dislike the Indians Removal as it would lead to divert the trade from us and leave our frontiers naked and defenceless."[6] Clearly, colonial reasons for desiring Indian neighbors could be self-serving, but while military and economic needs persisted, the construction of new racial identities was stalled.

Religious worship was another arena in which Indians and colonists found a common ground. In the early eighteenth century a series of Protestant ministers proselytized among the Mohawk nation. In addition to the chapel built especially for their use at Fort Hunter, the Mohawks attended services at Albany, Schoharie, Schenectady, Canajoharie, and the German Flats. The Mohawks resisted complete conversion, selectively adopting aspects of Christianity that made sense to them, but even so this form of Anglicization undermined their otherness. Colonists were impressed by the Indians' readiness to participate in Christian baptisms and weddings. Ogilvie recorded how he baptized some Oneida women "in the presence of a numerous Crowd of spectators, who all seemed pleased with the attention and serious behaviour of the Indians upon that solemn occasion." Colonists also participated in these ceremonies by serving as sponsors and witnesses. Some became actively involved in efforts to instruct Indians. John Jacob Oel, a Palatine immigrant living near Fort Hunter, served as Ogilvie's assistant during the 1750s. Anne Grant, who spent her childhood in Albany, recalled how Dutch women sought to "diffuse" Christian doctrines "among the elderly and well-intentioned Indian women." Frontier Christianity provided a common language and set of practices that allowed Indians and colonists to come together.[7]

The creation of real and fictive familial ties also bridged the cultural divide between Indians and Euro-Americans and worked to prohibit racial consciousness. Cross-cultural sex was a common feature of frontier life. Loneliness, attraction, and political and economic motivation encouraged European men and Indian women to join in sexual partnerships. Anglo-Indian unions gave rise to a new generation of métis individuals, who in turn provided a permanent link between communities. Warren Johnson, during his visit to the Mohawk Valley in 1761, observed Indian-European intermixture when he took stock of variations in physical appearance: "if a [Indian] Child is got by a white person its Hair is never black but brownish." Missionary Jeremy Belknap hinted at the degree of miscegenation that occurred in the seventeenth and eighteenth centuries when he noted in 1796 that "among the Oneidas there is scarcely an individual who is not descended on one side from Indians of other nations, or from English, Scots, Irish, French, German, Dutch and some few, from Africans." Because of their cross-cultural skills, métis individuals often assumed the role of cultural broker, further facilitating exchange and communication across the frontier. Arent Stevens, who became a provincial interpreter in 1747 and a trusted aide to Johnson, was the son of an English colonist and a woman of mixed Indian-European descent.[8] The Mohawk Valley was not neatly divided into "Indian" and "European" worlds but comprised a more culturally ambiguous human landscape.

William Johnson's own family exemplifies this pattern of ethnic fusion. In June 1742, Johnson's son Brant was baptized at the Fort Hunter chapel. This was not the first time a Johnson progeny had received this ceremonial rite at the Anglican Church. In 1740, Johnson's first child, Ann, had been baptized there, the following year John, and three years later Mary. But these were children born of Johnson's German wife. Young Brant, or Brant Kaghneghtago as he came to be called, was part of Johnson's Indian family. Johnson probably did not attend the baptism, but he did arrange for his close friend (and eventual father-in-law) to act as a surrogate father. Church documents record Brant Kaghneghtago as the son of Brant Canagaraduncka and his second wife, Christina. It is very probable that Christina was not only Kaghneghtago's adoptive mother but his biological maternal great-aunt as well. Sources indicate, though do not conclusively prove, that her niece Elizabeth was Kaghneghtago's mother and Johnson's Indian consort. Brant Kaghneghtago, like many métis individuals, spent most of his life inhabiting a cultural borderland positioned between Mohawk and colonial worlds. He most likely spent his childhood living with his mother or surrogate parents. When his adoptive father went to Philadelphia in 1755, Kaghneghtago was among the party. But he also remained close to his birth father, accompanying him on his travels, and was generously provided for in Johnson's will. Kaghneghtago felt the pull of both his Indian and European roots.[9]

Perhaps his hybrid identity encouraged him to marry a woman with a similarly mixed cultural background. Margaret Campbell, the daughter of a Virginian settler, was a former Indian captive. Abducted at a young age, she had lived long enough among the Indians to learn several languages. Western Indians had eventually delivered her up to the Indian superintendent, and it was during her time in the valley that she met Brant Kaghneghtago. Their wedding day was a truly family occasion, for in addition to marrying Brant

and Margaret, the minister Reverend Theophilus Chamberlain also performed a Christian marriage ceremony for Joseph Brant and Peggy. Joseph
was Kaghneghtago's step-uncle and William Johnson's brother-in-law, that is,
the brother of Johnson's Mohawk wife, Molly. Brant Kaghneghtago and his
new bride set up home in the valley, where Brant rejected the hunt to take up
husbandry. Part Indian and part European, Brant Kaghneghtago, his Indian
captive wife, and their four daughters carved out hybrid identities for themselves in the Mohawk Valley. The multiethnic households of William Johnson
and Brant Kaghneghtago may not have been the norm, but they were not
significant aberrations either. The material necessities of life meant that many
early North American frontiers allowed for a high degree of cultural interaction and synthesis.[10]

Fictive familial ties also crisscrossed the frontier. Mutual need for one
another encouraged both sides to impose or accept pretended familial identities. The practice of symbolic adoption was native in origin but welcomed by
Europeans who understood the advantages it conferred. In the early 1710s,
Conrad Weiser, a German immigrant, was sent by his father to live among
the Mohawks for the winter. During this time he was adopted into one of
their lineages. Understanding the importance of the Mohawks as allies and
the need for effective communication, Weiser's father desired his son to become conversant in their language and customs. Weiser did indeed become
an official colonial interpreter. Through adoption, the Iroquois believed they
had "divided him into two equal Parts." He would repeat tradition later in
life by sending his own son to live among the Mohawks. John Lydius, whose
Dutch father had served as an Indian missionary at Albany, was adopted into
the Turtle clan. Lydius Jr. used his Indian familial ties to obtain land deeds
from the Mohawks and to encourage his Turtle clan brothers to fight alongside General William Shirley's forces during the Seven Years' War.[11] Although
Indians and Europeans may have attached different meanings to these kin
identities, the creation of familial ties—even fictitious ones—undermined
a sense of permanent otherness. Rather than comprising culturally distinct
communities, the Mohawk frontier was characterized by multiple and shifting ethnic identities and allegiances.

The material conditions of the New York frontier deterred colonists from
constructing racial identities for their Iroquois neighbors, but it did not prevent all traces of cultural disdain. Some colonists, who perceived little value
in cultivating relations with Indians, chose instead to articulate arguments

of Indian savagery. According to Ogilvie, their conduct toward the Iroquois "give the most convincing proof that they regard them only as meer *Machines* to promote their secular interest; and not as their fellow creatures, rational and immortal agents, equally dear to the Father of spirits, capable of the same Improv'ments in Virtue, and the purchase of the same precious Blood."[12] Yet such attitudes did not yet dominate. In the early 1700s, British colonists failed to ascribe to a fully worked-out racialized conception of Indians. Instead they drew on religion and class to make sense of human differences. Whether out of genuine feelings of amity or calculated self-interest, colonists projected an identity among Iroquois as valued—albeit culturally different—allies.

The numerous positive assessments colonists and imperial officials offered of Iroquois culture indicate that they did not view them as wholly alien and inherently inferior. Notably, to create a sense of shared community and common interests, colonists often focused on points of similarity when discussing Iroquois cultural practices. While benign comments existed alongside more derogatory sentiment, they nonetheless reveal the absence of a rigid and universal racial ideology. Attitudes toward the Iroquois spanned an entire spectrum that encompassed both derision and respect.

Iroquois martial skills were one aspect of their culture that solicited praise. Cadwallader Colden, when describing their "noble Virtues," likened them to another ancient civilization: "The Five Nations . . . in their Bravery in Battle, and their Constancy in enduring Torments, equal the Fortitude of the most renowned Romans." Almost paraphrasing Colden, another commentator, William Smith, praised them for their gallantry and commitment to liberty, noting, "herein, perhaps, they may be thought worthy [of] the Imitation of politer Nations."[13] Iroquois political culture seemed to entertain a level of sophistication that invited approbation and again provided a point of comparison. Euro-Americans were impressed by the existence of a political confederacy with Onondaga operating as a capital. Philadelphia printer Benjamin Franklin commended the Iroquois' ability to achieve this degree of organization by reflecting on the colonies' own failure to fashion an alliance during the Albany Conference of 1754. He lamented, "it would be a very strange Thing, if *Six Nations* of ignorant Savages should be capable of forming a Scheme for such an Union" when the British colonies were not. The oratorical skills of the Iroquois also drew acclaim. According to Smith, their fluency with words and graceful articulation offered "Proofs of the Indian Genius, Sprightliness of Imagination, and many other Shining Qualities." The manner in which they presented themselves in council was also admired. John Bartram, who visited Onondaga in 1743, described them as "a subtile, prudent, and judicious people in their councils." Warren Johnson described a Mohawk council as a "Solemn and decent" event and likened it to the Houses of Lords and Commons.[14]

The Iroquois were also complimented for their cordial and courteous manners. Reverend Henry Barclay, who served as an Indian missionary, found the Iroquois to be "good natur'd and Hospitable." Charles Lee, an English commanding officer who spent time among the Mohawks, asserted, "I can assure you that they are a much better sort of people than commonly represented; They are hospitable, friendly, and civil to an immense degree." Moravian missionaries who traveled through Iroquoia in the 1740s and 1750s noted the kindness they met with. Despite being strangers, they were offered food, protection, and shelter by Iroquois villagers. Missionary John Christopher Frederick Cammerhoff described his Cayuga hosts as "kindly disposed" and "pleasant and polite," and claimed to be "very much edified by their behaviour." Cammerhoff was also one of a number who lauded the Iroquois' physical appearance, asserting they were a "fine looking people, who made an agreeable impression." Lee was equally impressed by their countenance and physique, noting "in their persons they are generally tall, slender, and delicate shapes . . . their Complexion is deep olive, their eyes and teeth very fine, but their skins are most inexpressibly soft and silky. Their men are in general handsomer than their women, but I have seen some of them very pretty."[15]

In the absence of rigid racial categories, notions of class and social rank influenced European perceptions of Indians. Signs of status and hierarchy among the Iroquois generated a sense of commonality and encouraged colonists to distinguish between the ordinary rank and file and the nobility. William Johnson consciously sought the friendship of members of the Mohawk elite, as exemplified by his marriage to Molly Brant. Other class-conscious colonial men also chose to intermarry with leading families. John Lydius married the niece of the famed Madame Montour, a powerful cultural broker who lived on the Pennsylvania and New York frontier. A German immigrant named Peter Spelman married the daughter of the Shawnee leader Parinosa. Charles Lee married a Seneca who was not only a "very great beauty" but the daughter of an important Seneca chief, "the famous White Thunder who is Belt of Wampum to the Senekas which is in fact their Lord Treasurer." Boasting of his wife's high status, he told his sister, "I shall say nothing of her accomplishments for you must be certain that a Woman of her fashion cannot be without many." Irish Indian interpreter George Croghan married the daughter of Nicholas, a leading sachem of Canajoharie, and Sarah, a member of the nobility. Their daughter, Catherine, would eventually become the second wife of noted Mohawk leader and British ally Joseph Brant.[16]

While Euro-American men often times pursued marriage or sexual unions with Indian women for self-serving reasons, this practice nonetheless reveals the limits of racial consciousness. Lax attitudes toward intermarriage reached the highest levels of imperial policy. In 1709, the Board of Trade, writing in favor of Palatine emigration to New York, proposed that these immigrants would "in [the] process of time by intermarrying with the neighbouring Indians (as the French do) . . . be Capable of rendring [a] very great Service to Her Majesty's Subjects." In a similar fashion, although writing almost fifty years later, Peter Wraxall, secretary of Indian Affairs, recommended in his memorial to the board that soldiers be encouraged "by some gratuitys and advantages" to marry Indian women as an effective means to promote cross-cultural ties. He did not consider—as many would a century later— that mixed marriages would lead to moral degeneracy. His only stipulation was that Indian wives be baptized in the Christian faith. Nor did Bartram consider it a "horrid crime" for Englishmen to take Indian women as wives. If they dressed and cleaned themselves as English women he believed they "would make as handsom, dutifully industrious, loveing and faithfull wives." However, he also noted it would be preferable if the English "could whiten their Scin A little and perswade or compell them not to use strong drink." While this last comment reveals a disdain for Indian complexion, it also demonstrates his belief in the impermanency of skin color.[17]

The terminology employed by British subjects to refer to the Iroquois also indicates a lack of racialized thinking. The Iroquois were most commonly referred to as "Indians" or more specifically by the name of their nation. Although they were also called "savages," this term did not originally carry with it racial connotations denoting a fixed inferior state. Rather, "savage" was applied to groups who lacked Christianity and therefore "civility." In much the same way, the term "squaw" was used primarily as a marker of gender distinction. There is little to suggest that its eighteenth-century usage contained a derogative racialized meaning. Most telling of all was the absence of an established color category to describe the Iroquois. This physical marker of difference did not yet obsess early eighteenth-century colonists. Although they were aware of their differing skin complexion, they rarely employed color terminology when referring to the Iroquois. When and if color categories were employed they varied considerably. On the odd occasion the Iroquois were referred to as a "Copper Colour" or "the Tawny People," but they were not associated with one specific color. Johnson once described an Iroquois named Hans Croyn as "a whiteish Indian." His Indian officer, John Butler, in attempting to differentiate between two men informed Johnson that, "the blackest of these two Indians is the one I recommended to you."[18]

Colonists were not averse to the idea that Indians and Europeans were derived from common origins. The popular belief of the times held that Indians constituted the lost tribe of the Israelites. According to this theory of monogenesis, Indians were the descendents of Shem and thus part of the same biblical family as Europeans. During his travels through Iroquoia, Bartram felt little need to debate whether or not the Iroquois had been created by the same god but instead on how they came to be in America. Although he found it "reasonable to suppose the almighty power provided for the peopling of this, as well as of the other side of the globe, by a suitable stock of the human species," he was more convinced by the theory that they had originated elsewhere, such as north Europe or Egypt, and ended up on the American continent through misnavigation of the seas.[19]

Despite colonists' positive appraisals of Iroquois culture, their relaxed attitudes toward miscegenation, their failure to employ a fixed color category to describe natives, and their belief in common origins, they rarely regarded the Iroquois as their social equals. Even settlers who enjoyed close and daily contact with the Iroquois readily found fault with their manner of living. Moravian missionary David Zeisberger and his companion met with a critical reaction when they informed Kast of their plan to live among the Onondagas. Zeisberger recorded in his journal that Kast exclaimed, "Why did we wander around in the woods, and not live like other Christians? For we would derive no benefit, but be obliged to live like cattle among the Indians, and spend a miserable life."[20] All aspects of Iroquois culture, from eating habits to gender roles, from religious beliefs to child-rearing practices, were condemned as culturally inferior. The point is, however, that whatever shortcomings colonists accused the Iroquois of possessing, they did not consider them to be permanent. The dominant consensus in the 1740s held that the sources of Iroquois character deficiency were external and therefore alterable.

Among the causes given for Iroquois savagery, the machinations of the French featured high. Many colonial officials described the Iroquois as naïve, gullible, and thus susceptible to manipulation by others. Imperialists believed that the French took advantage of this situation to disseminate trade, gifts, and religion among the Iroquois in an effort to "Spirite them up against" the British. William Johnson argued that the "Naturall disposition" of the Iroquois "would lead them to rejoice at our prosperity," but contact with the French "corrupted and poisoned" their minds.[21] Colonists also blamed alcohol abuse for the degeneration of Iroquois character. Both Barclay and Ogilvie complained about excessive use of liquor among the Mohawks, which led to violent and debased behavior. Johnson, too, readily blamed intoxication for Iroquois misconduct, explaining, "though sober they are a manageable people, they are perfect Brutes when drunk."[22]

Colonial commentators highlighted "the ill examples of Christian professors" as another corrupting influence. In reference to the Mohawks, Bartram remarked, "I am sorry to say their morals are little if at all mended by their frequent intercourse with us Christians." Archibald Kennedy, in his pamphlet outlining the need to cultivate a union with the Six Nations, agreed that their poor character was a result of having "been debauched by the Christians." Traders in particular were blamed for setting a poor example. Imperial officials accused them of teaching the Iroquois a host of bad habits including a taste for liquor. As Ogilvie summed up, "The disolute lives of the greatest part of those, who converse with them upon account of trade, seem to have a very ill-effect upon their Minds."[23]

Colonists held that the absence of Christian Protestant religion constituted the main cause of Iroquois savagery. Though some Indians had shown a willingness to convert, their numbers seemed small and their commitment was evidently lacking. Euro-Americans disregarded Iroquois religious beliefs as "very confused and much mixed with superstition." Conrad Weiser, despite spending his youth among the Mohawks and holding sympathetic attitudes toward them, still urged the necessity for "true conversion." By indoctrinating the Iroquois with Christian principles, colonists hoped that improvement of moral habits would follow. The Society for the Propagation of the Gospel in Foreign Parts supported the efforts of a number of Anglican missionaries. Barclay, who served from 1738 to 1746, initially found the Indians to be "Tractable" and believed that "were proper methods taken they might easily be civilized" as their "Natural Capacities are very Good." Ogilvie, who succeeded him, maintained that through educating Iroquois children it was possible to "change their whole Habit of thinking and acting and tend to form them into the condition of a Civil Industrious people."[24]

Men other than missionaries also believed in the possibility of morally improving the Iroquois. Colden stated that the Iroquois had been "bred under the darkest Ignorance," which caused their savage state, but added, "It is wonderful, how Custom and Education are able to soften the most horrid Actions." Lee defended the character of the Mohawks. While he acknowledged their tendency for violence, he argued, "the Indians may indeed be excus'd more than the French, for they are bred up in these bloody notions." All that was needed to improve their character was "good breeding," by which they could even "infinitely surpass the French." Smith, who referred to the Iroquois as a "valuable Part of our Species," compiled a collection of articles designed to promote a positive image of Native Americans. In his introduction he wrote that it was a "very great Mistake to think those People . . . are barbarians." He blamed a lack of religion and abuse of alcohol for their failings and urged that by teaching them Christianity and useful arts it was possible to "cultivate their fine natural parts."

William Johnson, too, was a staunch supporter of proselytizing among the Iroquois and throughout his career solicited the Board of Trade for funds to support the work of missionaries. He believed that not only was it possible to improve their moral and religious character but also that through religious and cultural conversion the British could secure their political allegiance away from the Catholic French.[25]

In their discussions of the Iroquois, British colonists and officials assigned to them a homogenous identity that was more a cultural fiction than material fact. As the tumultuous events of the seventeenth century had demonstrated, Iroquois identity was far from cohesive or static. A demographically changing tribal population meant that the Iroquois were constantly redrawing ethnic boundaries. Cultural and political fracturing led to outward migration from Iroquoia. From the 1720s onward, many Senecas, disturbed by the expansive presence of the French and British on their lands, relocated to the upper Ohio Valley. Decades of separation from the Iroquois proper and ongoing cultural integration with Delaware and Shawnee inhabitants of this region encouraged these Senecas to develop a new, distinct ethnic identity as Mingos.[26] In New York, the Iroquois continued to incorporate outsiders, most famously adopting the southern Tuscaroras as the sixth nation in 1722. Additionally, new multiethnic communities sprang up in lower-central New York. By 1713, the mixed town of Oquaga had been established on the banks of the upper Susquehanna. Composed predominantly of Oneidas but also Nanticokes, Mahicans, Shawnees, Cayugas, Tuscaroras, and Mohawks, Oquaga villagers set about inventing new traditions and common practices to bind them together. An assortment of Iroquois and non-Iroquois Indians also founded Otsiningo in the Chenango River Valley (present-day Broome County) around 1723 and Unadilla, also in the upper Susquehanna Valley, in 1753.[27] The profusion and convergence of these different ethnicities reshaped the contours of Iroquois identity.

Yet despite their diverse ethnic blend and protracted history of inward and outward migration, members of the Iroquois Confederacy by midcentury had begun to construct a new holistic definition of group identity. Premised on a doctrine of separate origins from Europeans, some Iroquois orators went as far as to state that the Great Spirit had spiritually ordained such differences. Undeniably, the nature of Iroquois interactions with Europeans over the course of a century and a half had steadily engendered a growing sense of difference.[28] Notably, challenges to their territorial integrity caused some Iroquois to revise notions of selfhood by emphasizing a link between origins and land. New renditions of their origins story stressed this connection. In the Iroquois origins myth Sky Woman's daughter gave birth to twin sons. The elder son, called Sky-Grasper, went on to transform Iroquoia by calling on the spiritual energy of the material and celestial worlds to create plant life, rivers, animals, and human beings. There are countless variations to this myth. In one popular version the turtle is acknowledged as the supernatural force that impregnated Beloved Daughter. The turtle represents the land as he provides the foundation of North America. He is also the father of Sky-Grasper and assists him in the process of human creation. Thus a subtle but significant link was made between the land (the turtle) and Iroquois identity.[29]

Iroquois headmen and speakers articulated a more explicit connection between land, origin, and identity in their political oratory with the British. The first recorded account of this discourse occurred in Pennsylvania in 1744 during the Lancaster Treaty conference. When the Maryland government asserted its right to a tract of land on the basis of lengthy possession of it, the Onondaga headman Canassatego responded: "what is one hundred years in comparison to the length of Time since our Claim began?—Since we came out of this Ground? For we must tell you that long before One hundred years Our ancestors came out of this very Ground, and their Children have remained here ever since." By contrast, Canassatego emphasized the colonists' separate origin and lack of right to the land: "You came out of the Ground in a Country that lyes beyond Seas." Gachadow, an Iroquois speaker, went even further when he contended that the Great Spirit created Indians and Europeans in distinct locations and with alternative destinies in mind: "The World at the first was made on the other side of the Great water different from what it is on this side, as may be known from the different Colour of Our Skin and of Our Flesh." Clearly the Great Spirit intended for them to live apart. Although the king of England may have sent the English over "to Conquer the Indians," Gachadow contended, "it looks to us that God did not approve of it, if he had, he would not have Placed the Sea where it is, as the Limits between us and you." The Lancaster council minutes reveal a new definition of Iroquois group identity based on a doctrine of distinct genesis.[30]

Separate origins and habitations made for dissimilar modes of living. Headmen like Canassatego proudly asserted "our different Way of living from the White People." Gachadow noted differences in laws: "that which you call Justice may not be so amongst us. You have your Laws and Customs and so have we." Political processes also varied. An Iroquois chief named Scagwar-easarah explained that the Iroquois had a particular way of holding councils that involved a great deal of deliberation, "for . . . they are not like the white people to detirmine Emeadiatly." Some Indians noted the incompatibility of modes of warfare. An Onondaga headman refused to lend military support during King George's War on the basis of cultural differences: "If you who are of one color think proper to fight, it is well, we do not incline to concern ourselves with it, because when we once engage in a war, we can't easily make it up, our blood growing too Hott, but you white people easily make up matters, and sometimes in a year or two are at peace again."[31]

The doctrine of separate origins represented a novel racialized way of understanding group identity, but in the 1740s, such a discourse remained confined to the diplomatic sphere, articulated by Iroquois speakers during conferences with the British. In their actual on-the-ground relations with colonists, the Iroquois continued to support a more fluid concept of otherness. Rather than embrace a worldview that comprised fixed categories of "them" and "us," the Iroquois entertained a view of outsiders as potential kinsmen. Such a view could be motivated by political self-interest or legitimate cordial feeling, but either way it demonstrates that the notion of separate origins remained more political rhetoric than an actual lived reality. To counteract colonial threats, Iroquois speakers emphasized a discourse of difference, but the necessities of frontier life encouraged ordinary Iroquois men and women to seek out or even manufacture points of commonality.

The Iroquois possessed a set of tools and practices to potentially dissolve barriers of difference. Their long-established application of kinship terms, such as "brethren," still functioned in the eighteenth century to foster a sense of intimacy and obligation in their relations with Europeans. Their custom of renaming, likewise, could work to undermine a sense of otherness. Issuing a European with an Indian name was a highly personal act designed to make foreigners feel welcome but also to make them appear less foreign. Sometimes renaming occurred for practical purposes. The Moravian missionaries August Gottlieb Spangenberg and Zeisberger noted how their Indian guides "saw fit" to give them Mohawk names "as they said ours were too difficult for them to pronounce." In this instance renaming was a means of making strangers seem less strange. Renaming was also politically motivated. Continuing a seventeenth-century tradition, the Iroquois granted New York governors with the generic title of "Corlaer," named after the esteemed Dutch leader Arent Van Curler. By assuming this designation the governor was expected to perform a particular role: to host the Iroquois at regular diplomatic councils, adopt Indian protocol, condole deaths, distribute gifts, and address their grievances. Renaming may have engendered familiarity, but headmen used it primarily as a means to influence the behavior of others.[32]

The Iroquois practice of adoption precluded a fixed sense of difference and extended ties of kinship to Europeans. Through symbolic adoption the Iroquois indicated their high regard for an individual and established certain expectations for his or her behavior without necessitating that the person actually live with them and become an Indian. For example, Colden, a permanent resident of Albany, nonetheless enjoyed his status as an adopted member of the Mohawk Bear clan. One particular aspect of symbolic adoption was the granting of symbolic sachemships, an honor saved for European men of standing. Receiving a sachemship was the greatest mark of esteem, as these European men were permitted to sit in councils. But it also allowed the Iroquois to forge alliances with powerful individuals who could bring political benefits to their communities. In 1746, at a meeting with the Mohawks, Johnson "had the Honour of a Sachem conferred on him." Recognizing his growing economic and political stature in the valley, the Mohawks were keen to claim partial ownership of him. "That the one half of Coll. Johnson belonged to his Excellency, and the other to them," the Mohawks told the New York Council in 1751. The Mohawks also granted a sachemship to his brother, Warren Johnson. "I had this Day the honor, at Fort Johnson, to be made a chief Sachem, or Prince, in a grand Council of the Six Indian Nations, being the first white Man ever admitted to that Rank (my brother Excepted) amongst them," Warren proudly noted. While he was confident of their "good Opinion" of him, he also quietly acknowledged that his political title was largely due to his famous brother: "They look upon me, as their great Mate, being Brother to Sir William." Charles Lee described to his sister how he had "the honour to be adopted by the Mohocks into the Tribe of the bear under the name of Ounewaterike." He was under no illusions as to why he had been selected: "I do not flatter myself that I am so much indebted to my own merit for these dignities as to my alliance with one of the most illustrious families of the Six Nations." It was less his English connections than his Indian ones that rendered him so attractive, as he had already married into a noble Seneca family. His adoption "entitled" him "to a Seat and the privilege of Smoking a pipe in their Councils."[33]

The most radical methods used by the Iroquois to transform outsiders into kin were literal adoption and marriage. The Iroquois transferred their pre-contact policy of adoption to Europeans. Through a series of rituals—running the gauntlet, symbolical washing, and redressing in Indian attire—European captives were stripped of their former identity and adopted into Indian households to replace deceased family members. Following King George's War, William Johnson experienced much difficulty removing adopted French war captives from Iroquois villages. Indians believed that by inducting Europeans in native ways of living they could be Indianized. In reality, it was generally women and children who proved to be more susceptible to acculturation.[34] Although prior to the Seven Years' War British captive taking was minimal, the Iroquois nonetheless had a cultural mechanism in place for transforming colonists into Indians. Marriage as well enabled the Iroquois to turn Europeans into kin. Like their colonial counterparts, Iroquois women and their families could be just as instrumental when selecting potential partners. They valued cross-cultural unions as a means to foster alliances with a foreign but useful people. Forging relations with Anglo-American men secured them gifts, assistance with farming, and religious instruction. By becoming wives and consorts to traders, women sought to embed economic exchange within familial networks.

The use of kinship terms, renaming, literal and symbolic adoption, and intermarriage highlight the limits of racialized thinking among the Iroquois. Despite the emergence of a separatist political doctrine, in their day-to-day encounters with colonists the Iroquois demonstrated that they did not believe group differences to be rigid and absolute. Evidently the Iroquois were becoming increasingly sensitive to cultural distinctions between themselves and Europeans, but they had not yet abandoned the belief that people's values and behavior could be altered. On the contrary, decades of missionary endeavors made them painfully aware of the possibility of cultural transformation.

Christianized Indians not only prayed differently but behaved and thought differently as well, causing social fissures. The Iroquois emphasized their cultural distinctiveness partly as a response to external pressure to become more like Europeans. Hence, when Shickellamy, an Oneida Indian, confronted the enthusiastic efforts of missionary David Brainerd in the 1740s, he responded, "We are Indians, and don't wish to be transformed into white men."[35]

The Iroquois belief that Indians could be "*transformed* into white men" made them particularly wary of allowing their children to be taught by Christians. Ogilvie noted the opposition of Mohawk parents to having their son educated by a missionary, as they feared "he would learn to despise his own nation." At the Lancaster Treaty, commissioners from Virginia presented a plan to the Iroquois for removing some of their children to a school where they would be "instructed in all the Learning of the White People." In response, the Iroquois reminded the commissioners, "you, who are wise, must know that different Nations have different Conceptions of things." Several of their sons had already been educated by colonists, "but, when they came back to us, they were bad Runners, ignorant of every means of living in the Woods, unable to bear either Cold or Hunger, knew neither how to build a Cabin, take a Deer, or kill an Enemy, spoke our Language imperfectly, [and] were therefore neither fit for Hunters, Warriors, nor Counsellors." They declined the Virginians' offer and instead made the counteroffer to educate their sons, noting, "we will take great Care of their Education, instruct them in all we know, and make *Men* of them." By men, they meant *Indian* men.[36]

Perhaps reflecting a growing practice among Englishmen who referred to themselves as "white" in relation to others, the Iroquois too made greater linguistic use of this term by midcentury. However, the ethnic diversity of colonial New York, not to mention distinctions between colonies, deterred the Iroquois from fully conceptualizing non-Indians as a collective other. Despite the popular use of the term, the Iroquois continued to identify discrete groups among the colonists. English, French, Dutch, and Germans were distinguished by a number of visible ethnic markers including language, religion, and foodways. Ethnic and colonial rivalry also discouraged the Iroquois from perceiving Euro-Americans as a monolithic entity. Thus when a group of Virginians murdered some Iroquois warriors in 1744, the Onondaga war chief Jonnhaty urged his men not to seek revenge on the grounds that "there were different Sorts of white People." Similarly, even as the Mohawk community in the winter of 1745 was panic-stricken as rumors spread of an impending British attack, they resisted viewing all colonists as a unified enemy. The Mohawks distinguished between those situated in the east, the "Albany people," who "have cheated us our Lands," and local settlers, "our Bretheren the English," who "always were kind to us." They believed that "the Albany people" had "agreed to kill us, or drive us away from Our Lands, which they covet," and claimed they had been informed of this plot by "our friends among the white people." The use of color categories did not yet indicate the development of racial consciousness.[37]

The presence of African Americans in the Mohawk Valley further complicated the development of racial thinking among Indians. The Iroquois encountered this group in a variety of contexts: as slaves of local settlers, runaway fugitives, church attendees, and assistants to traders, as well as the "many free Negroes" in the valley "who have good Estates."[38] The Iroquois were aware of the derogative status many colonists assigned to their slaves. Indeed the French used this to their political advantage. In 1748, Johnson reported that the French told the Six Nations "that we looked upon them as our Slaves or Negroes, which affair gave me a great deal of trouble at that time to reconcile." Some Iroquois adopted English racialized attitudes. Anne Grant claimed the Iroquois treated African American slaves "with contempt and dislike." In May 1754, an Onondaga Indian and his wife brought the Albany commissioners an English prisoner redeemed from the French and "demanded a negro man in Exchange." Perhaps they desired this "negro" for a slave. But the Iroquois were just as likely, if not more so, to forms ties of alliance with African Americans, as the assimilation of runaway slaves in their villages suggests.[39] Iroquois attitudes toward African American slaves, like their attitude toward British colonists, were malleable and shifting and characterized by a lack of racial rigidity.

Although the Iroquois acknowledged sources of difference in their relations with colonists by midcentury, they continued to utilize a language of both distinction and similarity. The Iroquois discourse on separate origins served an instrumental use. By emphasizing their distinct origins and way of life, the Iroquois hoped to fend off colonial pressures on their lands and maintain cultural autonomy. Although this separatist doctrine originated prior to the 1750s it remained confined to political discourse and did not yet influence daily interactions with colonists in any meaningful way. Furthermore, throughout the 1740s, the Iroquois were equally inclined to articulate an alternative discourse of brotherhood. The desire for British military protection, trade goods, and gifts prompted the Iroquois to remind the British of their historical alliance and to emphasize bonds of commonality. Overlooking cultural dissimilarities, they instead reaffirmed the Covenant Chain of Friendship that intimately intertwined Indians and Englishmen in an economic and political union. As they told Johnson, "Our firm Resolution is to stand by you as Brothers."[40]

The Seven Years' War aggravated preexisting sources of cultural friction at the same time that it created new opportunities for cross-cultural cooperation. Incidences of discord and violence between Indians, soldiers, and settlers abounded as the war caused attitudes on both sides of the frontier to harden. The bloodshed caused by Indian war parties incited ferocious anti-Indian sentiment throughout the colonies. In New England, where Indians were denounced as "miscreants" and worse, missionary Eleazar Wheelock found it next to impossible to raise funds among wealthy colonists for his Indian school. As he explained to Johnson, "the Ravages made and cruelties Used by the Natives on our Frontiers . . . has raised a Temper [among] many very contrary to Charity." Indians and colonists from Pennsylvania and the Ohio country, through word and deed, also demonstrated a growing contempt for one another.[41] But the situation in New York differed. If the war heightened mutual disdain, it also amplified the need for cross-cultural alliance. In fact the Seven Years' War supercharged a dual discourse of amity and hatred, pushing people further apart at the same time that it encouraged Indian-colonial unity. In colonial New York, the imperial frontier persisted as a fluid zone of interaction rather than a strict racial dividing line. Colonists and soldiers continued to differentiate between allied and enemy Indians, condemning the latter and exonerating the former. The Iroquois also made distinctions between various European ethnic groups. Their growing distrust of British troops promoted their ties with local settlers. Furthermore, a significant amount of crossing occurred along the frontier. Warriors enlisted to support British and provincial armies, while traders, smiths, war captives, and army deserters spent time among the Iroquois. Although there were real points of contention and distrust, there remained powerful incentives for coexistence.[42]

Relations between Iroquois Indians and British and provincial troops were especially prone to conflict. Adam, an Iroquois Indian from Oquaga, reported how his people "had been ill used by some Soldiers between Albany and Schenectady who took from them a Cag of Rum and a Blanket." This was just one of a number of reports of soldiers stealing money and goods from Indians.[43] The British regular army garrisoned next to the Mohawk villages at Fort Hunter and Fort Hendrick was a source of vexation. Throughout 1756–58, the Mohawks regularly complained of abusive conduct, noting that these men "do not behave like Brothers to us." Soldiers physically assaulted Indians, sexually harassed women, stole corn, damaged crops, and confiscated rum. On one occasion, soldiers at Fort Hunter taunted Canajoharie Indians that they would not be permitted entry if the French attacked. On another occasion soldiers pushed one unfortunate Indian to the ground with the butt of a rifle when he attempted to enter the fort and proceeded to pour the contents of a chamber pot over his head.[44] Commanding officers also behaved offensively. Captain William Williams, fort commander at the Great Carrying Place at Wood Creek, soon made himself "a very disagreeable person" to the local Iroquois. He disregarded their military intelligence, accused them of being spies, removed their guns, and threatened to have them imprisoned. As Johnson noted, "I am affraid he is not disposed to, or not skilled in that kind of Behaviour which is necessary to gain the Confidence and good will of the Indians."[45] Complaints were also leveled at the provincial commander John Winslow and his officers at Lake George. Winslow rebuffed a group of warriors returning from a successful scalping expedition. To add injury to insult, his military officers "turned them out" of the camp "like Dogs."[46]

Cultural prejudice and misunderstanding rather than ingrained racism shaped colonial and British behavior toward their Indian allies. A lack of familiarity with the Iroquois provided fertile ground for pejorative attitudes to flourish. The war marked a tremendous influx of provincial and British troops into the region, most of whom had never encountered the Iroquois and were unversed in their customs and language. Many New England soldiers came from towns in which local Indians were remnant groups living on the fringes of society. Consequently New Englanders associated them with a marginal impoverished status, and it was this knowledge they brought with them in their dealings with the Iroquois. Newly arrived British troops and officers were completely unskilled in Indian relations. Many who had fought in the Jacobite Rising a decade earlier may have viewed Indians in a similar fashion as they did Highland Scots: as a savage, rebellious, and dangerous people living on the fringes of empire and in need of the civilizing force of the army.[47] Deficient cultural understanding caused breakdowns in the military alliance. William Johnson often cautioned that the soldiers' lack of knowledge in Iroquois language and custom would cause "Differences and misunderstandings" to arise. Lack of familiarity sometimes proved deadly when soldiers literally mistook allied Indians for the enemy. In April 1757, a soldier from the Royal Americans misguidedly shot a friendly unarmed Mahican Indian traveling to Albany, which "occasioned no small Uneasiness" among the larger Indian community.[48]

Overfamiliarity also bred discontent. Alcohol was a major cause of friction between soldiers and allied Indians. The availability and widespread use of rum meant that casual fraternizing between men could end in confrontation. Commander in chief James Abercromby encountered disharmony among Iroquois warriors and army rangers collaborating on a scouting venture. "Having Drunk together," he complained in April 1758, they soon "fell to Handy-cuffs." To maintain harmonious relations Johnson pursued a policy of separation and sobriety. He issued orders to commanding officers to ensure that "none of the Soldiers do molest, Insult or drink with any of the Indians who may fall in their way." He also sent instructions to fort commanders to "keep your Party Sober, and in good order and prevent their haveing any unnecessary Intercourse with the Indians, least any difference might arise between them from too much familiarity." Indian warriors were kept as detached auxiliaries to minimize contact with soldiers. To ensure that soldiers would recognize Iroquois allies, Johnson had them wear red headbands and mutter the secret password, Warraghiyagey, Johnson's Indian name.[49] Despite such measures, violence still occurred, sometimes quite deliberately. In June 1756, British soldiers from the 44th Regiment killed and mutilated a Tuscarora warrior named Jerry. Yet even this brutal act of violence was not a consequence of clear-cut racial hatred. It soon emerged that the previous year Jerry had enlisted as a scout on Edward Braddock's ill-fated campaign. As British defeat in this battle looked imminent, Jerry switched sides and proceeded to scalp and kill former allies. British soldiers killed Jerry to avenge an act of treason.[50]

The war also aggravated tensions between the Iroquois and neighboring colonists. Again, the misuse of alcohol rather than deep-seated racial hostility underlay discord. In the early eighteenth century, Indian alcohol consumption was largely confined to the western post of Oswego or within the confines of Iroquois villages. During the war a greater number of Indians visited the German Flats, Schenectady, and Albany. One observer noted how local inhabitants took advantage of this situation by "perpetually making the Indians drunk with Rum, which they sell in most unreasonable quantities." Johnson also remarked on the pernicious practice of Albany "Townpeople" who exchanged rum for Indians' clothing and arms. The local rum trade engendered bad feeling on all sides. Indians who awoke from a drunken stupor to find themselves naked and unarmed or bereft of furs and corn became angry. Headmen alarmed by the harmful effects of alcohol use in their communities resented the enthusiastic efforts of colonists to keep their Indians well plied. For local inhabitants not involved in the rum trade, intoxicated Indians in their settlements were a source of annoyance. Drunken behavior caused disturbance and violence and sometimes led to the destruction of property. In November 1758, "several Irregularities and violences" were committed by Oneida warriors "on the Property and Persons" of local settlers. Tensions were fraught and Johnson warned of "fatal Consequences" if this behavior continued. The Oneida headman Nickus, quite powerless to regulate his young men, blamed their ill conduct on the "Flood of Rum in the Country."[51]

The killing of livestock by Indians also antagonized relations. Whether this action was motivated out of hunger or through drunkenness made little difference to Dutch and German settlers, who resented this impolite conduct. In 1758, the small Oneida community residing at Schoharie "were in a starving Condition owing" not just to the "the scarcity of Game" but also to "the Sullenness and ill temper of the Inhabitants of that Settlement on Account of some Pigs etc. which were killed by some Indians lately." Colonists usually assisted Indian neighbors in times of need, but the rude behavior of warriors during the difficult time of war caused good feelings to dissipate. Johnson, however, through skillful mediation resolved the conflict.[52]

Animosity between Indians and colonists occasionally climaxed in murder. The killing of two Oneida warriors by English trader Thomas Smith in 1757 and the scalping and slaying of English trader John McMickel by a Cayuga Indian named Tanighwanega in 1758 engendered contempt and distrust on all sides. Yet such acts of Indian-colonial hostility were small in number and largely devoid of racial overtones.[53] The reasons for Smith's actions remain unknown, but Johnson suggested that the Oneidas were to blame through drunken misconduct. As he noted to their family, "your People are often over bearing in their Cups and not to be bore with." While such a claim may have been self-serving, it may also have been truthful. Whatever the cause behind the violence, Johnson made a formal apology to the Six Nations through an enactment of appropriate protocol: he condoled the deaths, metaphorically removed the British hatchet out of their heads, and distributed handsome gifts. By such measures he "made them easy" and held the

Anglo-Iroquois alliance, however fragile, in place.[54] The apparent motiveless murder of McMickel caused Johnson to consider it an affair of "extraordinary villainy." However, the Cayuga Nation, which offered full apology for Tanighwanega's act, provided a political reason for the killing by insisting that he was working in concert with the French. The fact that Tanighwanega stole McMickel's watch and money but not a letter containing army intelligence suggests an alternative economic incentive.[55]

Although bloodletting and murder took place on the New York frontier, more common were mutually beneficial relations. In the late 1750s, Indians, Europeans, and Euro-Americans crossed the frontier in acts of friendship and codependency. Allied warriors who gave military assistance during the war cultivated good feeling. The Battle of Lake George, in particular, promoted a sense of Anglo-Indian unity, reinforcing the status of the Iroquois as valued members of the British Empire. Throughout the war news of Iroquois warriors on their way to join British forces "gave great joy to all the Troops." A substantial number of Iroquois warriors joined local militiamen in scouting parties, temporarily putting aside cultural differences as they borrowed and enacted each other's martial rituals.[56]

In the reverse direction, Europeans and Anglo-Americans also crossed over into Indian country for an array of reasons. Despite the murderous affairs involving Smith and Tanighwanega, genuine friendships also existed between traders and Indians. English traders traveled and resided among the Iroquois in the early years of the war, and when conditions grew more dangerous British-allied Indians offered them protection, shelter, and forms of escape. After being helped to safety from the murderous intent of two Seneca Indians, trader John Abeel found refuge among the Onondagas. Similarly, Albert Ryckman spent the winter of 1757 on a hunting expedition with the Onondagas in order to avoid the French. Blacksmiths as well as traders also formed friendships. Barent Wempel "was well acquainted with the Sinakass and cou'd Speak thire language." His father, Myndert, had served as a blacksmith to the Senecas during the 1740s. It is very probable that his son lived with him, learning the language and trade. When war broke out, the Senecas "desired that some of Myndert Wemp[el]'s sons . . . might reside" with them as they "understood their language, [and] were known to them." By 1757, Barent was serving as blacksmith and interpreter at Kanadesaga, a new Seneca village on the northern tip of Lake Seneca, but when his safety could no longer be guaranteed, Indian friends cautioned him to leave. The English interpreter and blacksmith William Printup lived near the Lower Mohawk

Castle but during the war served as a smith for the Onondagas, who gave him the Indian name Sagudderiaghta. His son, by an Iroquois woman, participated in scouting expeditions. Johnson noted that "he is verry much looked upon" by the Onondagas "on Acctt of his Father haveing lived among them Severall Years in the Country's Service. He also talks the Indian language best of any in the Province."[57]

Also evident of this fluid frontier was the phenomenon of war captives among the Iroquois. Resolute in their belief that it was possible to assimilate foreigners into their communities, the Iroquois continued their policy of adoption. In early 1757, a group of Onondaga Indians turned up at Johnson's home with "an English Drummer who was taken Prisoner at Oswego last spring and given to them by the French Indians in the room of an Onondaga who died." During the same year reports surfaced of a young German girl taken at the German Flats by enemy Indians but who had ended up among the Iroquois. In April 1759, the Cayugas under great pressure from Johnson delivered up a group of captives consisting of James Perry, a thirty-year-old Welsh man, Robert Wilson, a thirty-five-year-old London-born man, a young girl named Elizabeth Armstrong, a German woman named Catherine Hilz, and a Highland soldier. These are just a few of the numerous captives who lived among the Iroquois during the war. The Iroquois claimed that Ohio and French Indians supplied them with war captives to replace their deceased. Johnson, however, warned them of the impropriety of holding British subjects, noting, "keeping our Flesh and Blood as Prisoners will look very ill and not like Brothers." He employed a variety of measures to secure their redemption, but the immense difficulty he faced reveals the intensity of ties formed by the Iroquois to their newly adopted kin.[58]

Whether captives felt the same attachments to their captors is another matter. Most were held against their will. Nonetheless, women and children taken captive were far more likely to assimilate. The most famous case of this phenomenon was Mary Jemison. In 1758, Shawnee Indians captured Jemison in Pennsylvania when she was eight and passed her on to the Senecas residing on the Genesee River, where she spent the remainder of her life. She married twice, had eight children, and expressed a high degree of contentment with her life. While her experience was by no means typical, it was not unheard of either. A number of captives chose to remain among their captors even when offered the chance of freedom.[59]

Army deserters also traversed cultural boundaries. The strict discipline, scanty provisions, and harsh conditions of army life caused a significant number of soldiers to abandon their posts throughout the war. In early 1756, provincial troops from Pennsylvania and Maryland sheltered with the Six Nations after absconding from Oswego. Their decision was based on pragmatism rather than cultural preference. Deserters took refuge among the Iroquois usually as a temporary measure until it was safe to return home. Unsure as to whether such men could be trusted, Indians were not always hospitable hosts. Soldier James Clark deserted from the Carrying Place at Wood Creek in 1756 and made his way south to Oquaga where he resided with at least one other soldier and a number of war captives. Some of these outsiders intermarried and found safety, but others were not so lucky. Clark witnessed "many barbaritys Commited" on the prisoners including one "poor German Girl" who "lost her life." Clark finally managed to escape, but instead of returning to colonial society he found refuge at Onondaga in the home of the Bunt, where he was protected. While some Iroquois undeniably demonstrated hostility toward agents of the British army, many welcomed deserters into their communities, if for no other reason than because these men provided additional strength in numbers. Captain William Williams understood all too well the advantages the Iroquois stood to gain from accommodating ex-soldiers, grumbling how "one of these Divilish Deserters" forged an order enabling Indians to obtain liquor from a nearby fort. He also blamed army absconders for encouraging their Iroquois hosts to kill cattle and steal from carpenters passing on their way to Oswego. The Iroquois did not require much encouragement to engage in such exploits, but they no doubt benefited from the soldiers' literacy and knowledge of personnel. Because each side could offer the other real benefits, genuine friendships formed. Some deserters were adopted into the tribe, and a few chose to remain after the war, such as "Jemmy Campbell an Irish lad" from Oswego, who married "an Oneida Squaw" and resided with her family.[60]

For the most part, contact with deserters inhibited Indians from developing racial categories. Army deserters often expressed hostile attitudes toward the British. Because of their negative experience in the army, their need to justify their desertion, and their desire to win native approval many spoke harshly about the cruel and oppressive nature of the British, even making up stories about Britain's imperialistic designs to destroy the Iroquois. In May 1756, Johnson noted "uneasinesses and jealousies" of the Six Nations. The Oneidas and Tuscaroras reported that "Several Soldiers from Oswego and the Carrying Place have come amongst us" with a report that the British army was collecting at Boston in preparation for an assault of Iroquoia. Surrounded on all sides by a growing military presence, many Iroquois were prone to believe such reports. While the propagandist activities of deserters aroused Iroquois suspicion against the British, it discouraged them from perceiving all Europeans and Euro-Americans as a collective racial other.[61]

The Iroquois were further deterred from collectivizing non-Indians into a single conceptual category by their diverse interactions with a motley crew of neighbors. Indeed, the complex relations that existed between various ethnic groups residing in the Mohawk Valley belied the concept of a racial frontier. Throughout the war, the Iroquois continued to distinguish between different ethnic bands. While Mohawk Indians denounced the behavior of British soldiers stationed at Fort Hunter and Fort Hendrick, whom they generically labeled "Red Coats" on account of their brightly colored uniforms, they favored local Dutch militiamen. Experience had taught them that the latter group was far more sympathetic in their attitudes and conduct. In their complaints to Johnson, the Mohawks urged that local men replace the Red Coats "as they are People we are acquainted with and can agree better together." Over years of contact many Iroquois had formed friendships with local militiamen, adopting members and giving them Indian names. Hence, when the Onondaga nation desired a fort to be built for their protection they requested "our brother Otawandanawa (Lieut Mills) as officer there."[62]

While relations with "Red Coats" remained strained, friendly alliances persisted between the Iroquois and their German and Dutch neighbors. The Dutch community of Schenectady offered a valuable center for trade, and men of Dutch descent were employed by Johnson to work as traders and smiths in Iroquoia. The Iroquois had also forged important social and economic ties with the German communities of the German Flats. In addition to providing trade goods, settlers provisioned the Iroquois in times of need and even assisted Iroquois women with their plowing. Furthermore, throughout the war, both German and Dutch men fought alongside the Iroquois in scouting parties.[63] In November 1757, following months of rumors of an impending large-scale assault, a body of French soldiers and their allied Indians devastated the region. According to one report, as many as forty farmhouses, barns, and outhouses were destroyed and innumerable livestock killed. Only eight bodies were found, leaving over one hundred inhabitants unaccounted for. Flames had consumed some, but most had been taken into captivity. Rather than fueling anti-Indian hatred, German-Iroquois relations persisted. In the two weeks preceding the assault, the Oneidas had given three warnings of a possible attack. In the aftermath of the attack they visited the Flats to condole their German friends on their losses. Such gestures helped deflect anger and hostility away from the Iroquois community.[64]

Johnson and his superiors worried about the potential dangers inherent in these multiethnic relations. During the war, the British colonial elite often reflected on the fidelity of German and Dutch settlers within New York. It was not long into the conflict, however, that rumors stirred of disloyalty. In June 1757, Lord Loudoun instructed Johnson to "keep a watchful eye on the Germans and Dutch" suspected of "carrying on a treasonable correspondence with the Enemy." Loudoun and others feared that these groups would use their influence to turn the Iroquois against the British. Indian agent Thomas Butler was certain that "bad ignorant people of a difrant Extraction from the Engilish" sought to cause "Troubles" between the British and the Iroquois by "telling idle Stories."[65]

The war fueled tensions between German colonists and the British Empire. Like the Iroquois, many Germans resented British troops in the Mohawk Valley. British garrisons failed to provide much in the way of defense because of their small number and refusal to scout the area. Yet local inhabitants were still expected to maintain them, which they considered an imposition. With their own reasons for opposing the presence of military personnel, many Iroquois sympathized with German complaints. This shared grievance formed an important source of commonality that worried Johnson. Reports soon surfaced of Germans corresponding with the French via Iroquois messengers. Oneida Indian Gawèhe was suspected of carrying letters from German inhabitants to the French in which they described their difficult existence, poor treatment by English troops, and desire for French protection. Others employed Oneida middlemen to carry on an illegal trade with the French Iroquois. Johnson also learned of the activities of one prominent German family, which was "taking all opportunities to create an animosity between the Officers, Soldiers and the Indians." Johnson felt compelled to keep John Butler stationed at the German Flats "to prevent any Misunderstanding from arising between the Troops posted there and the Indians."[66]

Since the English conquest of New Amsterdam in 1664, tensions had dominated Anglo-Dutch relations. The Seven Years' War added fuel to the fire. British soldiers, administrators, and traders overran Dutch enclaves such as Schenectady and Albany. This caused much resentment, especially when attempts were made to quarter troops in Dutch homes. The Dutch vented their frustrations to the Iroquois. In April 1757, Johnson reported to the commander in chief that "the Indians are taught to make a Distinction between the English and Dutch, and are told that the former oppress, and endeavour to root the latter out of the Country." He concluded, "Those things have a bad Tendency." One group of Dutch men informed the Iroquois that "the Engilish are very Severe on the people at albany taking from them what they pleas breaking open their doors when they will." These Dutch settlers also recounted a quarrel that broke out between themselves and English soldiers, explaining, "The quarrell was because they wou'd not allow the Engilish To be Masters and take from them all they had," adding, "the English wanted to drive them about like dogs." This story enhanced Iroquois anxieties over the security of their own land. The large number of British troops stationed in the valley and the construction of forts and blockhouses had already generated significant alarm among them. In December 1758, Canajoharie Indians protested to Lieutenant Archibald McAulay at Fort Hendrick when local timber was cut down for the garrison. Skeptical that the Canajoharie had legitimate grievances, McAulay instead blamed the origin of their complaints on "ill advised Malicious Dutch, who enternally studies to make variance between His Majesty's Garrison and the Indians." The Dutch struck a chord with the Iroquois by suggesting that they shared a similar plight: British threats to their property. Some Iroquois even considered aligning themselves with the Dutch against the English. Thomas Butler reported to Johnson on the events of a hunting trip taken by Lieutenant Peter Schuyler, a Dutch militia officer, and a young Onondaga Indian: "The Indian knowing him to be of Dutch Extrackt began to Speak words reflecting on the Engilish and told Schuyler it woud be Good that the Albany people or Dutch with the Indjans Shoud joyn and drive the Engilish out the Country."[67]

The harsh reports leveled against the British by army deserters and German and Dutch settlers provoked Iroquois concerns over their land and sovereignty. Many viewed the British and French with equal distrust. A group of Iroquois headmen protested to the French governor in 1757: "The English your Brothers and you are the common Disturbers of this Country I say you white People together . . . You both want to put us Indians a quarreling but we the Six Nations know better, if we begin, we see nothing but an entire ruin of us." Other Indian groups promoted this emergent racialized way of thinking. Stories circulated that the French and British actually worked in concert with the intention of embroiling the Iroquois in their war in order to destroy them. Groote Junge, a pro-French Seneca, reported that "the present War between the English and French was but a pretended one and that by and by they would make Peace and unite to destroy the Six Nations." When the

Delaware and Shawnee Indians of the Ohio country attempted to persuade the Six Nations to join their campaign during the war, they drew on their developing sense of racial identity. They told the Iroquois that "it was best not to War one with another, but to take up the Hatchet against the White People, without distinction, for all their Skin was of one Colour and the Indians of a Nother, and if the Six Nations wou'd strike the French, they wou'd strike the English."[68] With the exception of the western Senecas, who were more sympathetic to racialized appeals, most Iroquois did not yet embrace such a pronounced pan-Indian identity and instead continued to make distinctions among Europeans. Decades of contact with both empires had informed them of significant religious and political differences between the two. As long as the war permitted, the Iroquois chose to play off French and British rivalries for their own gain.

The complex array of exchanges that took place between the Iroquois, Dutch, German, British, and French demonstrates the high degree of cultural fluidity that existed in the mid-eighteenth century. Although the Seven Years' War hardened attitudes on both sides of the Anglo-American frontier, it did not cause this frontier to solidify into an impermeable racial divide. Mutual need and dependency encouraged boundary crossing and collaboration. As long as these forms of interaction dominated, racialized identities remained in nascent form. But change was coming. By the very act of assisting the British to victory, the Iroquois helped shift the balance of power in North America. Reliance on Indians as martial, economic, and political allies had held in check the formation of racist sentiment, but as British victory seemed imminent, some Anglo-Americans began to question the value of Iroquois allies. Johnson recalled how, during the 1760 campaign, "a gentleman imprudently Cursed an Indian who was passing by his Tent, saying that on our return from Canada we should soon extirpate all of their colour."[69] The shifting socioeconomic conditions of the 1760s would cause such sentiments to gain ground.

Chapter 6

Economic Adversity and Adjustment

The close of the Seven Years' War may very well have brought peace to the New York frontier, but it did not bring peace of mind to Oneida headman Canaghquiesa. "We have for sometime past heard that our Brethren the English were wanting to get more Lands from us," he sighed in council with Johnson in 1762. The war was not yet officially over, but already settlers were petitioning for new lands and encroaching onto Iroquois hunting grounds. Speaking on behalf of the Six Nations, he pressed Johnson to "prevent your People from Coming amongst us . . . as we begin already to be greatly Confined, not having sufficient left us for our hunting." To the east, Canaghquiesa watched with alarm as his Mohawk neighbors faced three fraudulent deeds that threatened ownership of their cornfields, villages, and hunting grounds. To the south, he witnessed diminishing hunting opportunities as colonists streamed into the upper Susquehanna Valley. Closer to home, he confronted new settlements around Fort Stanwix. "We have had our Lands from the beginning of the World, and we love them as we do our lives," he reminded Johnson. Land guaranteed economic autonomy, community survival, and some degree of political parity with colonial and imperial powers. But pressures to cede land continued. In 1766, his community relinquished two large tracts to New York governor Henry Moore. Two years later, Johnson coaxed and coerced the Oneidas to yield additional lands at the Treaty of Fort Stanwix (map 5). Once encompassing millions of acres, the Oneida land base had shrunk substantially by the late colonial period. Reflecting on the changing physical landscape, Canaghquiesa remarked, "when our Young men wanted to go a hunting the Wild Beasts in our Country they found it covered with fences, so that they were weary crossing them, neither can they get Venison to Eat, or Bark to make huts, for the Beasts are run away and the Trees cut down."[1]

Despite emerging from the Seven Years' War as allies of the victorious

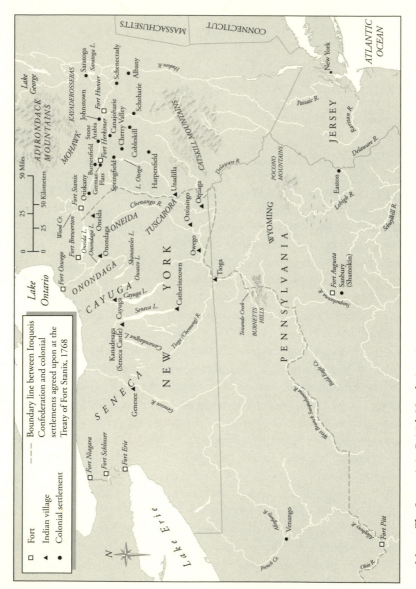

Map 5. The Iroquois in British North America, ca. 1770.

British Empire, the Six Nations soon discovered that there were few "spoils of war" to enjoy. As the experience of Canaghquiesa and the Oneidas demonstrates, the postwar period brought with it renewed economic constraints. The 1763 Peace of Paris marked the pinnacle of British power in North America. Military victory led to massive territorial gains, including French Canada, Spanish Florida, and additional West Indian islands. New lands encouraged greater settlement, commercial trade, and the commodification of natural resources. Although British power remained fragile throughout this period, as colonists, natives and officials battled over what form their new empire should take, the gathering pace of imperial and colonial forces had a tangible impact on the Haudenosaunee.[2] Military and colonial incursions onto their lands, the further erosion of the New York fur trade, the loss of the French as an alternative trading partner, and the strengthening pulse of commercial forces presented the Iroquois with substantial challenges. As ever the Iroquois displayed tremendous tenacity in the creative ways they dealt with economic adversity. While they could not avoid the widening grip of a burgeoning capitalist system, they still had some choice as to how to engage with it on a daily basis. But a shrinking land base and increased reliance on external markets marked an erosion of their economic and political sovereignty. As subjects of a new British North American empire, the Haudenosaunee carefully negotiated the forces of economic dislocation, but now more than ever their economic well-being was enmeshed within the larger world in which they lived.

Following the fall of Canada, the most immediate and visible threat to Iroquois lands came in the form of military occupation. Despite wartime promises that European forts would be destroyed once the conflict was over, General Jeffrey Amherst secured recently acquired territories by refortifying abandoned French posts and constructing new military installments. The Iroquois were chagrined. The Onondaga speaker Teyawarunte in a speech to Amherst remarked, "instead of Restoring to us our Lands, we see you in Possession of them, and building more Forts in many Parts of our Country." All along Iroquoia, the British ensconced their military presence. On the east side of Lake Oneida stood Fort Schuyler, the Royal Blockhouse, and Fort Stanwix. On the west side of the lake and in Onondaga country were Fort Brewerton and a post at Oswego Falls. Despite the French destruction of Fort Oswego a new post had been built in 1759 and the French post at Niagara refortified. On their southern border in Pennsylvania new forts were raised. One Indian speaker, a Cayuga chief, complained to Governor James Hamilton that the Six Nations and their tributaries were "penned up like Hoggs. There are Forts all around us, and therefore we are apprehensive that Death is coming upon us." Garrisoned posts reinforced long-held Iroquois fears of British intentions to conquer and expel them.[3]

Amherst's policy of encouraging settlement around New York posts undermined Iroquois subsistence activities, further exacerbating tensions. Amherst hoped that residents would help with transportation and grow foodstuffs for soldiers. The Senecas were disgusted to learn that he had authorized a settlement by Captain Walter Rutherford and others at the Niagara Carrying Place. These men disrupted Seneca livelihoods when they assumed control of the portage from which the Senecas had for decades extracted revenue by charging travelers a toll for its use and by carrying the goods of traders. Seneca cries that "the General is giving away their Country to be Settled" soon circulated throughout Indian country.[4] The Oneidas and Onondagas grew troubled as carpenters erected outhouses and lodgings in their vicinity and as soldiers cleared land for cattle and vegetable plots. "At Fort Brewerton, we daily see your People clearing large Fields of our Land—the Same at Oswego Falls," they remonstrated in May 1763. Officers stationed at either end of Lake Oneida prohibited Indians from fishing and hunting in the area and oftentimes confiscated any victuals they obtained.[5]

Indians feared that the mere presence of posts would encourage further settlement, a concern that was not unfounded. Paralleling the military infiltration of western lands was the incursion of a new body of colonial settlers. Peace restored to the frontier gave way to a burst of western settlement. By 1761, New York authorities began processing new petitions for land patents, while claims that had lain dormant during the war years were vigorously pursued. Notably, colonists attempted to acquire territory bordering the Canadian frontier, lands previous deemed too dangerous to settle. Little Abraham, a chief of the Lower Mohawk Castle, was distressed to learn that the partners of the Kayaderosseras Patent were intent on pursuing their claim. Adamant that the original deed had been forged, he informed Johnson of their determination not to part with essential hunting grounds. But by August 1763, Mohawk warriors had discovered "that a Number of People were Settled and still Settling on Lands" around Saratoga and "cutting Saw Logs."[6] The controversial Canajoharie Patent was also rekindled. Although most men involved in the patent including Philip Livingston had relinquished their claim by 1760, one German immigrant and longtime resident of the Mohawk Valley,

George Klock, held steadfast in his right to Indian lands at Canajoharie. He alleged ownership of their village, cornfields, and rented lands—in the words of one Indian, "the very Lands on which they live, and out of which they get their maintenance." The Canajoharies were panic-stricken. Johnson informed Cadwallader Colden, the surveyor general, "in all my life I never saw People so enraged as they were at it . . . [they] concluded it was better for them all to dye at once, than to live in misery, and at last starve, which they foresaw was to be their fate." Klock's activities hindered the ability of the Canajoharie to maintain their role as landlords as he set about evicting their tenants and forbidding them from paying rent to the Indians.[7]

Collectively, the Iroquois Confederacy faced threats to their southern hunting grounds in the Susquehanna Valley. These lands fell into a region that was part of a border dispute between the colonies of Pennsylvania and Connecticut. The Susquehannah Land Company of Connecticut was determined that this land be settled by New Englanders, even though they did not enjoy their government's backing. Undeterred and acting on the pretense of a deed illegally obtained from the Iroquois during the 1754 Albany Conference, the company began supervising the migration of New Englanders to Wyoming in the upper Susquehanna Valley in 1761. Despite sending a strongly worded warning to clear off their land, the Iroquois found that more settlers arrived. This caused major consternation among the nations, who claimed that "they must be Ruined, it being their best Land as well as their Chief Hunting Country." The Six Nations rallied Johnson and sent a delegation to meet the Connecticut governor in May 1763 but to little avail.[8]

Steadily the Iroquois employed intimidation and force to defend their territory. In the summer of 1762, Thomas Baugh complained of the aggressive behavior of the Oneidas at Fort Schuyler when "a large number . . . Insulted the Soldiers" and then "Endeavoured to gett over the Stockades, threatening to kill," and plundered the home of a settler. A month later, Lt. Hugh Wallace, stationed at Fort Brewerton, reported that neighboring Indians had broken into the garden opposite the fort and "carryed away every kind of Roots." Motivated by their strong aversion to posts in their country and feeling defiant, they informed Wallace "that they would take every thing that was planted or would be planted there, until they were paid for the ground." The issue of garrisoned posts pushed some Iroquois to take increasingly violent measures.[9]

It is within this context of British occupation of Indian lands that Seneca participation in the Anglo-Indian War is best understood. In the summer and fall of 1763 a variety of western Indian groups engaged in a series of separate though overlapping military strikes against the British. They destroyed all western forts with the exception of Niagara, attacked illegal colonial settlements including Wyoming, and pushed back the line of settlement. Among these warring tribes, the westernmost community of Senecas located at Chenussio along the Genesee Valley played a prominent role. In June, a party of Chenussio warriors approached Fort Venango, in Franklin, Pennsylvania, pretending to be allies. As soon as they gained entrance, they unleashed a violent assault, killing the entire garrison except a few men who were taken prisoner, only to be killed later at an Indian town. The following month, they carried out similar attacks on Fort Le Boeuf and Fort Presqu'île in northwestern Pennsylvania. Then in September, three to five hundred warriors, chiefly from the Chenussio settlement, ambushed a convoy of British soldiers as they transported goods along the Niagara Carrying Place.[10]

Economic concerns and grievances fueled Seneca actions.[11] Their attack of British forts demonstrated a desire to rid the British from their western hunting grounds and to forestall what they perceived to be a British design to dispossess and conquer them. As they told one commanding officer just before they executed him, the maintenance of British forts "gave them Reason to think that they [the British] were determined to possess [their country] . . . for which they would destroy them." The Niagara Carrying Place became a particular focus of their hostilities because of the economic benefits they had once derived from this spot. The French at Niagara had generously bestowed gifts, periodically subsidized trade, and permitted Seneca revenue-gathering practices at the Carrying Place. Johnson argued that the principal cause of Seneca aggression was "the difference they found between the present and former possessors of Niagara." Indeed it was only shortly after Rutherford had been granted control of the portage that the Senecas began circulating war belts among the western Indians inviting them to war, spreading the word that "The English treat us with much disrespect, and we have the greatest reason to believe by their behavior they intend to cut us off entirely; they have possessed themselves of our Country . . . there is no time to be lost; let us Strike imediately."[12]

The Anglo-Indian War failed to achieve any long-term benefits for the Senecas or the Six Nations as a whole. The Senecas ceased hostilities by the winter of 1763, and in the peace they negotiated the following spring they surrendered the tract of land along the Niagara Carrying Place, a further blow to their already hampered economic position. The war temporarily halted migration and prompted the Crown to issue the 1763 Proclamation that restricted settlement east of the Appalachian Mountains. But Crown efforts proved futile. Once warfare ended, migration resumed.[13] For settlers interested in New York lands, the Anglo-Indian War was something of a distant sideshow that did little to impede their plans. New York's fertile soil and pleasant climate attracted a steady stream of colonists. Touring the valley in 1764, one European visitor noted, "All the land on the Mohawk is counted good, and Sells very high, it wants nothing but Industry, and Inhabitants to make it a rich, pleasant and Independent Country." Colonial settlements, like Cherry Valley, bloomed in south-central New York during the 1760s.[14]

Migrating colonists altered the landscape, disturbing wild game and the migratory movement of fish and wildfowl, causing Indians to protest, "We know not where to go for subsistence tomorrow . . . good hunting is no more known amongst us, since the encroachments of the white people." Settlers brought with them new types of vermin that destroyed crops. Indians also complained of "the White People's Cattle" trampling their cornfields.[15] The influx of settlers with their livestock and pests vitiated the efforts of Iroquois farmers and hunters and promoted cycles of impoverishment throughout the postwar period. In 1765, hundreds of hungry Indians descended on the home of William Johnson. "There was no preventing their coming so numerous," he complained, "owing to their great scarcity at Home, for many of them come on no other Acctt. but to get provisions." In 1767, missionary Samuel Kirkland, residing at the Oneida town of Kanowarohare, reported on their "extreme Poverty." Vermin had destroyed the previous year's harvest, while "Worms threaten the Destruction of one half of the present Crop." A poor harvest in 1769 again left many communities in "Distress for the want of Corn."[16]

Closest to European settlement, the Mohawk and Oneida communities at Schoharie, Tiononderoge, Canajoharie, Old Oneida, Kanowarohare, and Oriska experienced significant threats to their territorial integrity and consequently the greatest disruption to subsistence activities, thus hastening their movement toward market-orientated behavior. The Schoharies wrangled with local settlers over land rights in a dispute that was not settled until 1772. The Tiononderoge Mohawks were caught up in a protracted struggle with the town of Albany over ownership of the Mohawk Flats and faced unrelenting incursions onto their northern hunting grounds. The Canajoharies faced numerous challenges to their land by the double-dealings of a handful of unprincipled neighbors, while the Oneidas contended with mounting pressures to cede land around Fort Stanwix. Pursuing drawn-out litigation battles, soliciting the help of powerful men, and occasionally relying on brute force, the eastern Iroquois demonstrated that they were not to be simply turned out of their homes.[17]

The Canajoharies appealed to Johnson in their ongoing battle with George Klock. Johnson offered support because of his close familial ties to the Canajoharies—his in-laws were key residents—but also because he understood that these lands were crucial to their subsistence. Johnson was also abhorred by Klock's illegal behavior, not to mention his refusal to defer to imperial authority. But Klock's determined and surreptitious dealings proved too slippery even for Johnson to curtail. Klock remained resolute in his demands, insisting that the Canajoharies "had no Right to a foot of land whereon they lived," and continued to interfere with their tenants. Most of the Canajoharies' meetings with Johnson were taken up by their remonstrations against "that old Rogue, the Old Disturber of our Village." Some became so distressed living under his threat that they migrated to Canada. Klock pressed his claim right up until the Revolutionary War, and through his perseverance he eventually secured land in the 1790s.[18]

The Fort Hunter Mohawks, by contrast, found Johnson to be far more lukewarm in opposing the Kayaderosseras Patent. The discovery of "a great number of new Settlements" on their hunting grounds around Fort Edward, Saratoga, and Lake George horrified them. In January 1765, Little Abraham notified Johnson that hunters had encountered "a considerable number of men from different parts, cutting down, and Carrying away Saw loggs, and the best of Timber from off their land." The following month, they sent a delegation to warn off these unwanted intruders. They also made a formal complaint to the rest of the Confederacy in a bid to prompt Johnson to take up their cause. Johnson expressed some concern for their loss, but he recognized the tremendous value of these lands and, accordingly, in a mood of fait accompli, encouraged a compromise. They resisted. Abraham had been one of the many Mohawks who had accompanied Johnson and Amherst to Montreal, but he now felt a sense of betrayal as he realized that assisting the British to victory had opened up the northern frontier to settlement. As he told Johnson, "it is only since you have got the better of the French that you have made Settlements thereon, imagining as we suppose that you think you could now do as you please." Although they refused to be "bullied" out of their land, under pressure from Johnson to sell and already hindered in their hunting as settlement and logging dispersed wild game, the Mohawks finally agreed to relinquish a section of the Kayaderosseras Patent in exchange for five thousand dollars in 1768.[19]

Realizing their relatively powerless position to stem the tide of settlers, the eastern Iroquois pursued other strategies to safeguard their interests. All the while they protested against illegal deeds and settlements, they continued to sell and rent small parcels of land. Years of exposure to advancing market forces had encouraged them to develop a new understanding of land as a commodity that could be bought, sold, and rented. They engaged in land sales, haggling over prices to gain an advantageous deal. In September 1766, the two Mohawk villages "dispose[d] of sundry tracts to Schohare people and others." The following year, Thomas King at Oquaga negotiated a land sale with a group of speculators from Cherry Valley. Alongside land sales, the Iroquois continued to earn money as landlords, renting lands around Fort Hunter "to different People every Year."[20]

Johnson condemned their developing market sophistication, noting, "The Indians in General certainly give us great trouble about Lands as they are become better acquainted with their Value." He complained of the Mohawks who demanded what he considered the exorbitant price of £50 per acre for a parcel of "poor Stoney Land" near Schoharie, observing, "The Indians are grown so cunning, and tenacious of their property, that in short it is verry difficult to get Land from them without paying too much for it." But Johnson exaggerated their commercial proclivity. The Mohawks were not budding entrepreneurs but a people with ebbing economic options who attempted to secure additional revenue as hunting lands diminished. They also continued to be selective regarding whom they sold and rented to, causing Johnson to comment, "they certainly can give preference to whom they like." However, because potential buyers first needed to acquire a license from colonial authorities before they could obtain an Indian deed, Mohawk ability to choose their own neighbors was undermined. They deplored their situation, complaining that authorities issued licenses to people they were unacquainted with.[21]

Farther west, the Oneidas faced fresh land threats. By this period the Oneidas were settled at three communities in the vicinity. Located near Oneida Lake was the oldest village of Old Oneida, home to Canaghquiesa. Eight miles away was the largest settlement, Kanowarohare, and a little further east at Oriskany Creek was Oriska, home to around ninety Indians. The combined total of all three villages was roughly 480.[22] In May 1766, Thomas Gage, the new commander in chief, ordered all forts along the Mohawk Valley to be abandoned but left a single officer in place at Fort Stanwix (present-day Rome) to maintain the buildings and forward supplies over the Carrying

Place. The abandoned fort and blockhouse soon attracted settlers. Tensions fomented between squatters and local Indians, and Johnson feared violence. The Oneidas "are sorry to find that the Soldiers have been Succeeded by Settlers," Johnson informed Gage in June 1766. They viewed settlers as more threatening than a garrison because unlike the latter, the former "encreases and overspreads the Country." The Oneidas pursued a campaign of intimidation, systematically razing all other abandoned forts and threatening to "turn Everybody away from" Fort Stanwix.[23]

Johnson was aware that lands around Fort Stanwix had been patented "many Years ago" and therefore viewed eventual colonial occupation as inevitable.[24] To hasten this process he encouraged the Oneidas to sell two large tracts in the fall of 1766. Over eighty Oneidas collected at his home to negotiate a major land sale that ultimately bolstered the economic interests of members of the colonial elite. In attendance was Governor Moore, who, having applied to the privy council in London for a direct land grant for his children, depended on Johnson to secure him a sizable plot. Gage had also instructed Johnson to obtain him land. Johnson shrewdly employed his skill and influence to secure two large tracts, one on the south side of the Mohawk River, the other on the north side above the German Flats. This "verry valuable and extensive Tract" contained two hundred thousand acres. Johnson commended himself that "with regard to Soil and Scituation" it was "the verry best" and reserved a fifth part for himself. Canaghquiesa and his community hoped that they too had gained something from this sale. With settlers already illegally squatting on these lands, the Oneidas were determined to be at least compensated for their loss. By selling land to powerful men like Johnson and Moore, they also intended to secure influential allies who could help them in future land threats. Finally, by ceding this extensive tract and requesting "that they might not be applied to for any more to the Westward," they hoped to have established a firm boundary between their country and colonial settlement.[25]

But Oneida efforts were short-lived when in 1768 Johnson orchestrated one of the largest colonial acquisitions of Indian land with the Fort Stanwix Treaty. Since the 1763 Proclamation had failed to arrest migration, talks had been under way to establish a new line. By 1765, the Iroquois Confederacy had agreed in principle to a fixed boundary, enshrined in treaty, as a feasible solution to the unmanageable level of land theft and violence that plagued the frontier. They were not, however, prepared to permit the top section of this line to extend into the heart of their country. Even the Board of Trade

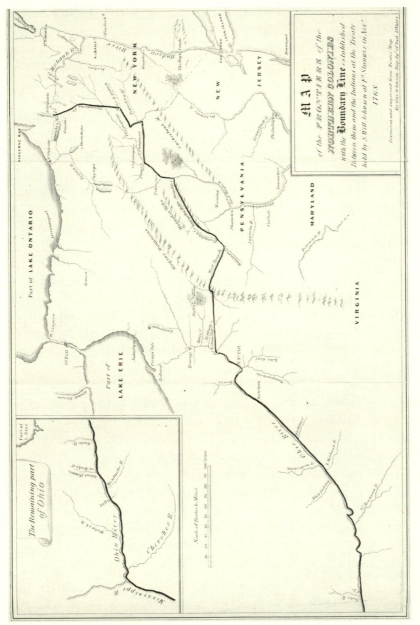

Map 6. Portion of Guy Johnson's map of 1768. William L. Clements Library, University of Michigan. As the map illustrates, the top end of the line was brought all the way up to the Oneida Carrying Place. The Mohawk communities fell east of the line.

instructed Johnson to avoid negotiations involving western New York, cautioning him to end the northern tip of the line at Owegy, just north of the New York–Pennsylvania frontier at the confluence of the Susquehanna river and Owegy creek. At the Fort Stanwix treaty conference in September 1768, attended by over three thousand Indians and numerous colonial officials, Johnson went much further than either the Iroquois or Board of Trade desired. Through Johnson's intense pressure, sharp reprimands, and handsome bribes, the Oneidas eventually agreed to yield to his demand that the northern tip be brought right up to their territory at Wood Creek, thus permitting lands around the Carrying Place to fall east of the boundary (map 6). In exchange the eastern Iroquois were guaranteed access rights to hunting grounds, carrying places, river ways, and roads lying east of the line, and the Mohawks, residing on the colonists' side of the boundary, were to have their villages legally secured to them by deed.[26]

The Fort Stanwix Treaty was a tremendous blow to the economic sovereignty of the eastern Iroquois. The treaty formally opened up lands in central and south-central New York for colonial accumulation. Between 1769 and 1771 speculators raced to survey and patent lands around Fort Stanwix in north-central New York and along the Delaware, Susquehanna, and Unadilla valleys to the south.[27] While much of the land in central New York by the eve of the American Revolution may still have been physically unoccupied, it was nonetheless patented and owned by colonial Americans (map 7). Indian agent George Croghan managed to obtain over 250,000 acres of land, almost all of Otsego County in central New York. Colonists had already patented hundreds of acres of land in central New York prior to 1768, but the treaty worked to encourage the physical development of these lands. Hundreds of settlers poured into the upper Susquehanna Valley, bringing livestock, damning rivers, felling trees, and slowly changing the forested landscape into agrarian homesteads.[28] William Johnson was one of the biggest beneficiaries of the treaty, securing an additional 100,000 acres of land in the upper Susquehanna Valley. He quickly set about clearing lands, settling families, building mills, and creating transport links to connect his new settlements to Schoharie and the east.[29]

Rather than soothe Iroquois concerns, the Fort Stanwix Treaty seemed to confirm their worst fears. Unhappy by the terms of the treaty, some Mohawks left their villages to resettle west of the line at Oquaga. But even those at Oquaga were disturbed to learn that the boundary line came up much closer to their settlement than expected, forcing Guy Johnson to admit that an inac-

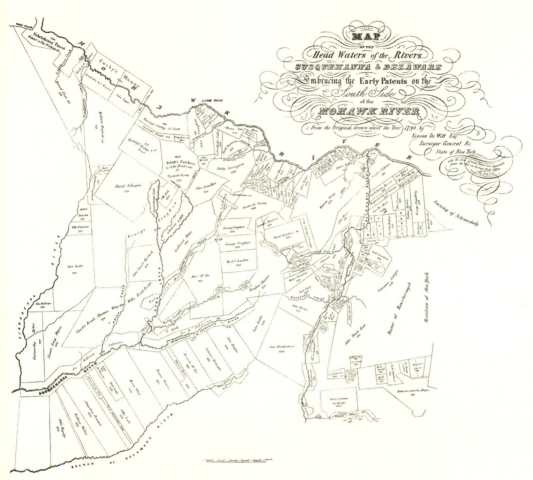

Map 7. Land patenting in New York. From the original drawn ca. 1790 by
Simeon Dewitt Esq., surveyor general. Reproduced from Francis Whiting Halsey, *The Old New York Frontier: Its Wars with Indians and Tories, Its
Missionary Schools, Pioneers and Land Titles, 1614–1800* (New York: Charles
Scribner's Sons, 1901). By the late colonial period the New York hinterland
looked like a patchwork of legally bound tracts of land. This map reveals the
extent of colonial landownership on the south side of the Mohawk River.

curate map had been used during the treaty conference. Indian hopes that the
treaty would help hold back the tide of would-be settlers were soon dashed.
By 1771, Gage reported, "I am told it is a fact that people have already passed
the boundary settled in 1768 and are building in the Indian country over

the rivers Susquehanna and Ohio." By the mid-1770s, the mixed-Iroquois
towns along the Susquehanna Valley encountered trespassers who, as Adam
of Oquaga complained, "made encroachments upon our lands, by surveying
our hunting-grounds close up to our habitations."[30]

The Fort Stanwix Treaty not only failed to prevent further colonial incursions onto Indian lands, it also diminished Iroquois political potency. For
political convenience Johnson relied solely on the Six Nations to negotiate the
treaty, thereby reinforcing their status as spokesmen and overlords of lesser
tribes. But their centrality in Indian-colonial affairs was only temporarily
heightened. By ceding thousands of acres of land, Six Nation headmen gave
away a critical resource that buttressed their power. In one stroke they alien-
ated thousands of Native Americans who now viewed them as little more
than "slaves of the white people." By giving the British what they wanted, the
Iroquois undermined their own importance in Anglo-Indian politics. Ever
since the close of the Seven Years' War colonial officials had begun to doubt
the power and consequence of the Six Nations. In 1765, the New York governor noted, "I have often thought that the Six Nations assumed too much
to themselves in directing affairs with all the other Nations" and hoped that
"some method . . . be taken to check their ambition." Following the Fort Stanwix Treaty, particularly as western Indians began to organize a powerful pan-
Indian alliance, this view of a politically irrelevant Confederacy seemed to be
confirmed.[31]

In the immediate postwar environment, the reinvigorated drive of commercial forces combined with new restrictive imperial directives to further sever
trade from rituals of alliance and diplomacy. The reduction of New France
opened the way for British traders to infiltrate and monopolize the Great
Lakes fur trade, causing opportunities for profit to swell. William Johnson,
caught between his own entrepreneurial disposition on the one hand and his
need to serve his imperial master on the other, advocated a fur trade based
on the principles of a market economy but tempered by system of regulation. He advised that traders be licensed, that trade be confined to a limited
number of posts where it could be supervised by specially appointed officers,
and that prices be fixed and standardized. Johnson wished to maximize the
role of Indians as productive hunters and consumers of a multiracial, newly
enlarged British Empire.

     Johnson's superior, Jeffrey Amherst, in fact went much further than
Johnson advised. Aware that Indians could no longer turn to an alternative

European trading partner and keen to curtail costs to the Crown, Amherst advocated a policy of strict frugality. He authorized Johnson's plan to confine commerce to posts, affix prices, and appoint commissaries. To encourage productive behavior he also banned the alcohol trade and, generally distrustful of natives, limited sales of ammunition. Johnson was concerned by some of these measures. As Indian subsistence depended on access to powder, "they must suffer greatly if they can't have some from You," he warned Amherst. In addition to new prohibitions in trade, Amherst instructed the abolition of gift-giving. Motivated largely out of a desire to protect his own military budget, Amherst also justified this policy on the grounds that gifts cultivated values antithetical to the ethos of a market economy. Dependency on presents, he remarked, "can only Serve to render the Indians Slothfull and Indolent," whereas the obliteration of this expensive practice "will oblige them to Supply themselves by barter." In principle Johnson supported the eradication of gifting. During the Seven Years' War he had already begun transforming gifts into a form of payment for specific services. But Johnson was wary of the dangers of an abrupt change in policy, cautioning that Indians "must be gradually weaned from" gifts.[32]

Iroquois livelihoods suffered as a consequence of this new stringent trading environment. Price-fixing and confining trade to a small number of forts undermined their bargaining power. Limiting supplies of ammunition hindered their ability to hunt and thus to procure wild game for consumption and commerce. When Johnson suggested to Amherst in the winter of 1761 to set prices at Oswego to ensure a 50 percent profit margin, he demonstrated that financial gain and not alliance was the principal goal of trade. Indeed, at each of the western posts the price of goods rose. In March 1761, Anaroongo, an Onondaga speaker, protested, "we are now (by the dearness of goods sold to us in our Country, and at the different posts), obliged to pay such exorbitant prices, that our hunting is not sufficient to purchase us as much cloathing as is necessary to cover us, and our families." Complaints continued in the ensuing years.[33]

Compounding Iroquois hardship was Amherst's policy of eradicating gifts. Despite years of exposure to a commercial marketplace, Iroquois headmen still desired and expected European officials to indulge them in the etiquette of gift-giving. As well as symbolizing friendship, gifts provided an important means of obtaining much-needed goods in times of hardship. But headmen quickly discovered that presents were no longer forthcoming. When Seneca chief and British wartime ally the Belt visited Fort Niagara with a large group of Indians in the winter of 1761, he presented the commanding officer, Major William Walters, with "three Belts of Wampum" and "a few skins" to verify his words of "Brotherly friendship." However, when he asked Walter to reciprocate by a gift of clothing to the women of his party, the commanding officer insisted that the Belt take back his furs and "purchase a Blanket or two from the Traders." Walter also attempted to return the wampum, "teling them it had cost them money." Unlike the Bunt's interaction with Colonel John Lindesay a generation before, the Belt's effort to keep trade bound up with diplomacy failed. The refusal of fort officers to provide gifts of food, powder, and clothing elicited censure from all six nations, who complained of their unbrotherly behavior. Denying gifts not only affronted Iroquois sensibilities but, more important, exacerbated economic difficulties. "If we were Starving with Hunger (which is often Our Case)," Canaghquiesa remonstrated in 1762, "they will not give Us a Morsel of Any thing."[34]

Expensive trade, the lack of gifts, and a scarcity of ammunition rendered the early 1760s a precarious time. Not yet recovered from the upheavals of war, many communities were poverty-stricken. In December 1761, Johnson noted the "misery of several Indian familys, occasioned by sickness, and a failure of their Crop of Indian Corn," adding, "many of them must inevitably perish without assistance." The following summer, the Oneidas claimed to be "very poor." "Destitute of almost all kinds of Provisions," they were "obliged to catch what few Fish they could, in the River and Creeks." In the fall of that year the Onondagas were reportedly "almost starved having nothing to live upon but what they get by Hunting." By 1763, the Onondaga community living at Otsiningo bemoaned that they were in a "deplorable Situation, having no Ammunition wherewith to Hunt for the Support of themselves, and their Old People." The Iroquois employed a variety of strategies to ameliorate hardships, including appealing to Johnson for aid, resorting to bows and arrows, and continuing their wartime practice of killing livestock from neighboring colonial settlements and forts.[35]

Distressed by this new economic order, the Iroquois sought to reinstate a play-off system that would garner them some leverage. If the British no longer had to compete against the French, the Iroquois hoped to at least encourage economic rivalry between colonies. In August 1761, they appealed to Pennsylvanian authorities against Johnson. As Tokahaio told Governor Hamilton, "We are very poorly off, as we have no Trade stirring among us . . . the things we buy from General Johnson are very dear." He urged Hamilton to set up a series of trading posts in Pennsylvania, explaining, "if your Goods are sold reasonable, we suppose that General Johnson will also sell his goods cheaper than he now does." His proposal was backed by Onondaga headman Ashenoch: "Our Brother General Johnson, and those who live near him, sell their Goods very dear, and give us nothing for our Skins; but as I have heard our Brother of this Province gave better prices for our Skins, I have brought them here, and hope my Brother will see Justice done me in the Sale of them."[36]

At a Pennsylvania conference the following year, they continued in their efforts to influence trade relations. They suggested not only locations for new trading houses but also which "honest Men" should operate them. Still holding out for ideals of kinship and reciprocity to govern intercultural exchange, they recommended men like John Harris, who was "very well known" to them "as his Father was before him." To encourage economic competition, and thus Iroquois bargaining power, they suggested alternative places of commerce. They hoped that one store of goods would be kept at Shamokin and another with Harris so that "they will sell at different prices." The Iroquois, however, were fighting a losing battle. Concerns over profitability, not cultural accommodation, guided the behavior of colonial officials. Hamilton informed Iroquois headmen, "it is not in my power to fix any certain price upon our Goods." Explaining to them that the value of goods could only be determined by whether "the risque and demand for them is greater or less," he emphasized the forces of the market economy over interests in alliance.[37]

Iroquois dissatisfaction with the new trading structure intensified and found its most violent expression with the martial exploits of the Chenussio Senecas in the summer of 1763. Along with the issue of western posts, grievances against the new trading policies galvanized the western Senecas to war. Before killing the commanding officer at Fort Venango they ordered him to write down a list of their protests. Foremost they remonstrated against "the Scarcity and Dearness of Powder," which had hindered their ability to subsist over the previous two years. They were incensed at having to pay "two Deer Skins for a Gill" of powder. This inflated price was "in Proportion" to the high price of most other trade goods and "when they Complained of the Dearness, and Scarcity of everything, they were ill treated" and told to go elsewhere. But if economic pressures incited the Senecas to war, they also caused them to sue for peace. By late 1763, the Senecas were in need of British provisions and ammunition, items they no longer had access to. When three Chenussio Indians arrived at the German Flats in November "to purchase Powder and other things," Johnson promptly instructed that they be escorted by guard to Albany. All across the western backcountry, Indian groups ceased hostilities as supplies of powder and food ebbed. Colonial officials noted triumphantly that the Indians "begin to feel that they cannot subsist without us." By December the Senecas had capitulated. During the peace negotiations that followed, Johnson made a point to remind them of their declining economic autonomy by chiding them, "You are not ignorant that we can reduce you to Beggary without fighting, by only Debarring you of Trade."[38]

The Anglo-Indian War did little to improve trading conditions for the Iroquois. By 1764, partly out of a desire to assuage native grievances and based largely on Johnson's recommendations, the Board of Trade had drawn up a comprehensive plan for trade regulations. But the Plan of 1764 failed to receive royal backing, and by 1768 it was officially rescinded as imperialists redirected funds eastward to deal with rebellious colonists.[39] The consequent removal of Indian commissaries from key posts had a notable impact on the Iroquois, further eradicating the practice of gifting. Already a much watered-down version of its previous form, gift-giving virtually disappeared at western posts by the late 1760s. When Johnson toured western Iroquoia in July 1769 he met with Seneca and Cayuga Indians disenchanted by the "reduction of favors." When they complained "that they were refused a Morsel of [pro]visions at Fort Pitt," military officials dismissed their grievances as "trifling." Complaints against the commanding officer at Fort Niagara, John Brown, also fell upon deaf ears. Indians censured him for his parsimonious nature and reluctance to adhere to Indian protocol. He was "Verry Indifferent" to the Senecas during one council, two traders observed. He not only interrupted their speech but gave them "very little" provisions for their journey home. The lack of gifts signified to the Iroquois shifting relations. No longer could they compel the British to acquiesce to their customs; instead they were obliged to play by the rules of the empire.[40]

Encouraged by the Proclamation of 1763, which declared the Indian trade to be "free and open to all our subjects whatever," a new breed of trader had saturated the Indian trade following the Seven Years' War. With little experience of intercultural exchange and unversed in Indian protocol and language, many relied heavily on the rum bottle to facilitate the traffic in furs.[41] The departure of fort commissaries in 1768 provided further scope for traders to engage in unethical practices. "One of the principle Complaints of the Northern Indians for some time past," Johnson informed his superior in 1773, "is the Irregular method of carrying on the Indian Trade, and the neglect of some of the Colonies . . . to make proper regulations for its better government."[42] During this late period the roguish behavior of colonial trad-

ers elicited universal censure from imperial officials. Johnson cursed them as
"a Sett of verry worthless fellows." Officer James Stevenson stationed at Fort
Niagara and then Detroit described them as "a sad set for they would cut
each others throats for a Racoon's Skin." He noted their lack of intercultural
skills and worried that colonial officials obtained their knowledge of Indian
customs from men "who's Ideas do not extend beyond the Circumference of
a Beaver Skin."[43]

If officials were unable to curtail the underhanded schemes of traders, Indians had even less luck. They remonstrated against an array of baneful practices that collectively pointed to the refusal of traders to act in accordance
with kinship principles. "Ill natured" traders cheated them out of their furs,
overcharged them for goods, and sold them fake silver and watered-down
rum. In 1774, the Seneca chief Serihowane charged that the absence of regulation had thrown the Indian trade "into utter confusion." Traders, "being left
to their own will" and driven by an unrelenting "pursuit of gain," followed
them into their hunting grounds, plying them with liquor and imposing on
them "at pleasure." Similarly, a Cayuga war chief noted "how disagreeable it
was to their nation to have Traders continually among them who sell rum, and
thereby occasion much mischief, and trouble." The trafficking of alcohol became a particularly abhorrent aspect of the trade and one that village headmen
lobbied against. Colonial traders pushed alcohol sales with increased vigor as a
means to wed native peoples to the marketplace. Even Johnson was disturbed
to find that traders "carry little or nothing else because their profits upon it are
so considerable." This increased reliance on alcohol did not go unobserved by
village elders. Headmen from Oquaga in 1770 noted their dismay when traders arrived at their villages in canoes loaded with "nothing but a heap of Caggs
and Barrels filled with Rhum, which at once made us tremble."[44]

The traffic in rum generated a host of ills. Johnson's longtime ally Red
Head died in 1764 "by excessive drinking" while trading at Fort Ontario.
Similarly, Gawèhe succumbed to "hard drinking" at Fort Stanwix. Drunkenness also resulted in violence. At Fort Niagara in 1767, a drunken brawl between Garugahigoagh and another Indian resulted in Garugahigoagh's death
after having received "Blows about his Breast." Fort commanders were at a
loss as they witnessed scenes of drunken revelry. Allan Grant, commissary
at Fort Ontario, grew apprehensive in 1769 as intoxicated Indians arrived.
"Such Drunkenness I never saw the like [of in] all my life," he reported. Alcohol abuse also led to impoverishment in some cases as both men and women
neglected subsistence activities.[45]

The rum trade did not create new cycles of debt and dependency among the Iroquois, but it was one of a number of articles that consigned them to the market economy.[46] By the late colonial period, Iroquois material culture had dramatically transformed. Cups and saucers, candlesticks, ruffled shirts, and wooden furniture were commonplace in Oneida and Mohawk homes. If women regularly made shoes for sale in the 1750s, then they commonly purchased them during the 1760s. In 1768, missionary Eleazar Wheelock was hard-pressed to acquire Iroquois artifacts "without the least Mixture of foreign Merchandize." The Iroquois were reminded of their dependence upon the transatlantic economy when the colonial boycott of British goods in 1770 left them "scarce without provisions." However dissatisfied they were with the state of the fur trade, they remained reliant upon it.[47]

Although dependent on foreign trade, the Iroquois were not prepared to become mere victims of its abusive practices. As Indians failed to receive redress in the fur trade they increasingly took measures into their own hands. In demonstration of their displeasure that forms of exchange were moving further away from Indian ideals, the Iroquois engaged in numerous acts of protest and resistance. From vandalism and theft to violence and murder, Iroquois warriors expressed their anger and frustration against the new order. Theft at forts, in particular, became a persistent problem. Indian Commissary Normand MacLeod, stationed at Niagara, was obliged to seek Johnson's advice on the matter: "I wish I knew what ought to be done with any Indian or Squa who is guilty of theft, they have stole lately here a Feusil, a watch and a pair of shoes." Seneca warriors regularly engaged in horse theft around the fort and the Carrying Place, causing MacLeod to hold a special congress with them on the matter in August 1767. The fort's interpreter, Jean Baptest De Couagne, was sent into Seneca country to collect the stolen property, but within weeks the Senecas succeeded in stealing additional horses and pigs. They caused further uproar when Seneca chief Castesh killed a bullock. Although the rest of his community claimed to be ashamed of him, looting and vandalism endured. In 1770, a group of drunken Seneca warriors dug up the picket fence surrounding the fort's burial ground to make a fire. A few days later, two Indians ran off with one of the fort commander's cows. In April 1772, Johnson was still requesting Seneca and Cayuga warriors to return stolen horses and rifles.[48]

In addition to targeting forts, Iroquois warriors directed hostilities specifically at traders. In September 1767, commissary Michael Byrne was obliged to "fence up" two "Breaches" between some traders and Onondaga men after the latter had "forced Some Keggs of rum at the falls." In 1770, a party of five Senecas plundered a group of traders near Fort Erie.[49] Then in 1772, two Seneca warriors killed four French traders as they traveled in a birch canoe on their way back from Fort Niagara. According to one account, "the Indians robbed the Canoe of Thirty Packs, which they buried and afterwards returned to their Village." The outcome of this event stands in contrast to the murder of a trader committed by two Senecas in 1762, wherein the culprits evaded punishment. A decade later, the British allowed no latitude. They placed enormous pressure on the entire Confederacy until they handed over the warriors to be jailed and compensated the family of the deceased through the repayment of furs. The success of the British in forcing the Confederacy to comply with their procedures is indicative of the weakened status of the Iroquois. Their loss of economic autonomy manifested itself in their diminishing political might.[50]

As trade moved away from Indian protocol, it also gravitated away from New York, further undermining Iroquois bargaining power. Already in decline in the 1740s, the New York fur trade continued to shrink following the Seven Years' War. As the Canadian fur trade opened up to the British, New York merchants and traders increasingly bypassed Fort Ontario and Niagara in their effort to secure a foothold in the Great Lakes region. Although the trade in furs remained an important part of the Iroquois village economy, it had become sidelined in the colony of New York, wherein the value of furs steadily declined. Fur exports had originally amounted to more than 25 percent of the total value of New York's exports to England in the first half of the century, but by 1750 this figure had dropped to 16 percent and then had further declined to a little over 2 percent by 1775. Pressure mounted on the Iroquois to diversify economic interests.[51]

The account book kept by an unidentified Mohawk Valley trader in the early 1770s reveals much about the altered economic existence of the Iroquois in this late period. The trader kept accounts for over eighty Iroquois customers—predominantly Mohawks and Oneidas but including those from all six nations—who frequented his store. Like a generation before, his Indian clients exchanged beaver pelts and other skins for an array of European wares, but his book documents notable differences in both the content and nature of exchanges that took place. Indeed, trade frequently took place in the absence of animal skins altogether. In February 1774, two Mohawk men named Thomas and Seth brought peas and corn to the trader's store. The following month Seth brought an additional "three scipples" of peas and "two scipples" of wheat. Thomas and Seth were not unique. Throughout the late 1760s and early 1770s, Mohawk men regularly brought peas, corn, and wheat to sell or exchange for goods. These men had not swapped their role as hunter for farmer—as Iroquois women continued to dominate agriculture—but their reliance on food staples as trade goods indicates the reorientation of family economies. Employing European farming tools and techniques, the eastern Iroquois had both intensified and diversified crop cultivation. Like their colonial neighbors, the Mohawks no longer farmed purely for home consumption; they also had an eye on the local marketplace.[52]

In addition to food staples, the Iroquois also sold their labor to the Mohawk Valley trader in exchange for cash or goods. In the fall of 1773, Seth received payment for going four days in search of the trader's "Negro," while two Indians named Peter and Laurence on separate occasions received goods "by riding 8 Loads of wood." The trader recompensed other men like Decanhachquasa, an Onondaga, and Captain Gorus, a Cayuga, for supplying him with fresh venison. The trader paid another Indian known as the Wise Cayuga for assisting his two agents in selling merchandise in Cayuga country. Fifty-six days' worth of pay was deducted, however, because the Wise Cayuga failed to "attend" to his duties. No longer solely dependent on hunting, men exchanged their physical toil for goods and cash.[53]

Perhaps an even more significant marker of change was the extent to which money circulated as a medium of exchange between the trader and his Indian clientele. In the 1770s, Indians regularly used cash to procure goods; in May 1774, for example, Hanse Crine settled his account by paying the trader "19 dollars." Cash moved in both directions. The trader often issued payments to Indians for their furs and crops. In 1773, for his "share in beaver" an Indian named John was paid "cash in full." When the trader sold a wampum belt pawned by a Seneca Indian named Sawetowa for a greater sum than Sawetowa actually owed, the trader was obliged to make up the difference in money. "I have paid him 1 Dollar and all is settled," he recorded in his book. Similarly, when Thomas brought goods to close his account in May 1775, the outstanding balance was in his favor, prompting the trader to pay him "cash in full." Thomas was also one of many Indians who went to the trader to borrow money. In June 1773, the trader noted under Thomas's account "cash lent to buy tobacco."[54]

The production of salable crops, the tendency to sell one's labor, and the predominance of cash circulating demonstrate that Iroquois material circumstances had transformed significantly by the late eighteenth century. Entanglement in the widening grip of a transatlantic mercantile economy resulted in the diversification of Iroquois village economies, wherein the Iroquois balanced subsistence modes of production with an increasing commercial need to sell goods and labor in a local marketplace. Decades of economic pressures meant that by the 1770s, the Iroquois had come to inhabit a transitional order; a frontier exchange economy based on barter and reciprocity persisted in the New York hinterland, but it did so alongside an emerging cash economy. The Iroquois still heavily engaged in subsistence activities—fishing, hunting, and farming—but they also depended on market-oriented pursuits. Furthermore, these pressures dislodged, although did not fully eradicate, age-old values of hospitality and reciprocity among some Iroquois.

The Canajoharies, Johnson observed to a colleague in 1769, "are already sensible that their Children must from being surrounded on all Sides have recourse to Farming of some sort." Indeed, as hunting opportunities diminished and colonial settlements increased, the eastern Iroquois modified agricultural practices to improve their subsistence. "The Mohawks have lately followed Husbandry more than formerly," Joseph Brant informed a visitor to the region in the late 1760s. Other colonial observers noted new practices, referring to the Fort Hunter Mohawks as a people "who subsist by Agriculture." The Mohawk and Oneida communities had long adopted European iron farming tools to increase crop production. They also diversified produce, cultivating a range of crops that included peas, wheat, and corn. During his visit to Oquaga, ex–army officer Richard Smith took stock of the degree of agricultural innovation. In addition to Indian corn, villagers harvested "Beans, Water Melons, Potatoes, Cucumbers, Muskmelons, Cabbage, French Turneps, some Apple Trees, Sallad, Parsnips, and other Plants." He further observed that the town had "Two Plows." Other communities, including the Onondagas and Tuscaroras, hired local Germans to plow their lands. Intensified agricultural production served the needs of home consumption, but it also provided a supplementary means to tap into the local marketplace. Increasingly, the Iroquois exchanged harvested yields for trade goods and cash. Their ownership of wooden barrels for storage and sleds and wagons for transportation indicates their practice of producing surplus for the purpose of trade.[55]

Another novel aspect of this modified agricultural economy was the pursuit of animal husbandry. While at Oquaga, Smith observed "Horses, Cows, Hogs, and Poultry." Both the Mohawks and Oneidas owned a substantial number of domestic animals by the mid-1770s. Nor was the adoption of livestock peculiar to the eastern Iroquois. The Senecas too raised chickens, hogs, horses, and cattle, although in lesser numbers. The Iroquois strategically adopted animal husbandry as a means to enhance their subsistence; it provided them with new forms of meat to consume and another means to acquire foreign goods. Indians hired out horses and sold livestock and poultry to traders and local colonists. The adoption of livestock did not signify unqualified acculturation. Poultry and pigs were generally allowed to move and mix promiscuously and treated as another form of wild meat, while efforts to fence cattle and harvest hay were oftentimes lacking.[56]

The need to enter the marketplace to obtain foreign wares encouraged the Iroquois to produce other salable goods. Throughout the 1760s and 1770s, the Iroquois engaged in petty-commodity production. Smith noted the production of moccasins and garments embroidered with wampum for sale and observed that Indians demanded "high Prices for their Labor." Similarly, Patrick M'Robert on his travels through New York in 1775 encountered the "Indian manufacture" of "belts, sashes, baskets, magazines, [and] band boxes." He remarked, "this trade was formerly very advantageous" to colonists, "but the Indians of late are much wiser, and not so easily hoodwinked as formerly."[57] Indians also found a livelihood by turning natural resources into commodities. Indians at Oquaga sold maple sugar to passing colonists. The Mohawks collected wood ashes, an impure form of potassium carbonate used in the manufacture of potash. Wild roots including ginseng and ginger were locally traded. In the mid-1760s, the Onondagas collected and sold roots to a local widow, while in the early 1770s, valley merchant Jellas Fonda sent agents into Onondaga and Cayuga country to "Buy Jinsang" from the Indians.[58]

Indicative of the changing economic landscape was the increased commodification of Indian labor, particularly among the eastern villages. Few Indians became wholly dependent on wage labor in this period. But if Indian employment had been limited and sporadic in the early 1700s, it had become far more quotidian by the 1770s. Iroquois men received payment for transporting traders and their goods over rivers and portages. In 1762, at least twelve Mohawks found employment in the bateaux service. They earned four pounds a trip carrying goods and people from Schenectady to Fort Stanwix, and two pounds hauling cargo around the Little Falls at Oswego. The Oneidas, having secured their access to the Oneida Carrying Place during the Fort Stanwix Treaty, earned a living transporting the packs of traders. Seneca men also found work as bateaux men. While most received cash wages, some accepted goods for their services.[59] Local settlers also made use of Indian labor. One resident of the German Flats paid an Oneida to steer his sheep "in the woods." Another, in the summer of 1766, paid an unnamed Indian four dollars for driving cattle from the Royal Blockhouse to his farm at Burnetsfield. George Croghan hired local Indians at half a dollar a day to perform various tasks on his new estate near Otsego, previously prime hunting grounds. Indians also supplied traders with fish and venison, transported loads of firewood, tracked down runaway slaves, and carried goods to forts in exchange for cash rewards. Knowledge of the land meant some men sold their services as guides.[60] The series of missionaries who settled among the Oneidas and Mohawks in the 1760s encouraged paid work. A handful of Oneida men earned a livelihood through their services to the church as catechists, schoolteachers, and missionaries. Deacon Thomas, an Oneida, earned £20 a year for his work as a catechist and schoolmaster from the New England Company for the Propagation of the Gospel. Kirkland paid "50 shillings to his brother (*Quedel*); fifty to *Wirom*; and five pounds to the Tuscarora Catechist" and "promised some small consideration" to Doniat and Thahnehtoria, two Oneidas, for "singing of Psalms every other night in the week."[61]

The expanding presence of the British Empire aided the commodification of Indian labor. To carry out warfare, conduct diplomacy, and maintain forts the British required the hired help of Indians. During 1761–62, a few Mohawk warriors accompanied Captain Quinton Kennedy's ranger company to fight in the West Indies. Others found employment hunting down British army deserters.[62] The outbreak of the Anglo-Indian War again offered the opportunity to exchange martial skills for cash, although on a much smaller scale than it had during the Seven Years' War. Still, Daniel received £62 for 155 days of military service.[63] Following the end of hostilities, British forts operated as sites of Indian employment. Native men sold their services as guides, interpreters, messengers, and manual laborers. Seneca warriors were "well paid" for supplying the garrisons at Fort Niagara and Fort Erie with venison and turkey.[64] William Johnson continued to function as a principal employer on the New York frontier. In his official capacity as superintendent he paid Indians for delivering correspondence to western posts, providing intelligence, and escorting army officers and supplies. "Bradley an Indian" received $6 per diem in 1765 for carrying dispatches to Niagara, Fort Stanwix, and Fort Ontario. Some forms of Indian employment remain unspecified, such as the "3½ Dollars" paid to Thomas of Canajoharie "for Services."[65] Johnson also hired Indian labor in a private capacity, employing Indians to work on his estate. "Job the Indian and his son" received £7 for performing manual labor at Johnson Hall in the summer of 1770. He paid other Indians to assist surveyors and to fetch goods from neighboring stores.[66]

By the late colonial period, Indians had developed a heightened awareness of the commercial value of their physical toil. They had come to expect to be paid for their labor and voiced complaint when it was not forthcoming. Indian expertise in intelligence gathering and traversing vast distances granted them leverage. Payments had to be negotiated. When Johnson hired Indians to carry correspondence to Niagara in the winter of 1771, he was "obliged to advance them something more than" formerly agreed "in Consideration of the Extraordinary difficulties they met with during the late general Snow Storm, when they were obliged to hire others to accompany them on Snow Shoes." Indians complained if they felt they were unfairly paid. Peter, a Mohawk who had "quitted his Wages and place" of work with a Frenchman to engage in "public Service" for the British, protested when he was paid less than his partner. In addition to a blanket, stockings, and shirt he received for carrying valuable intelligence he also expected to be paid $60 from an army officer and another $40 from some merchants. Years of providing services meant that Indians had established practices for price setting. Smith, after paying his Indian guide "James the Mohawk" half a dollar per day in 1769, noted, "The Indian Custom, probably derived from the Dutch, is to be paid for the time of returning as well as going." He further observed, "The Oneidas and most other Indians are said to be extortionate and very apt to ask high Prices especially when they perceive a Necessity for their Assistance."[67]

Although the Mohawks were the most accustomed to paid forms of work, the Senecas also combined their insistence on noncommercial forms of exchange with a growing appreciation of cash-for-labor exchanges. In the winter of 1764, Seneca chief Karandowana and two others accompanied Allan Grant from Niagara to Johnson Hall. This was no simple demonstration of friendship but a chargeable service. Needless to say they "were greatly Surprized at his going away without . . . paying them." Also troubling Karandawana was the conduct of commander John Brown at Niagara, who refused to treat his men as free actors in a commercial marketplace. The Senecas were involved in a profitable enterprise of selling fresh meat to the garrison. But Brown undermined their commercial endeavors when he instructed soldiers to confiscate their goods at the fort entrance and pay them only in bread and a small sum of money. The Senecas were appalled at being prevented from negotiating prices and selecting customers. "We are a free People, and acustomed to Sell whatever we have to whom, and where we liked best," Karandowana retorted. Never simply unwitting participants, Seneca men embraced the ethos of the market economy to promote their interests.[68]

The commercial sale of their labor was just one of a number of activities that increased Iroquois exposure to cash. In the late colonial period, money frequently circulated as a form of exchange, indicating the extent to which the Iroquois had become entangled in a market economy. Imperial expansion promoted an infusion of cash into Iroquois hands with Johnson serving as key paymaster. In addition to paid employment, Johnson promoted the transmission of cash through the numerous land sales he mediated. At the conclusion of the Fort Stanwix Treaty he distributed over £10,000 to the Six Nations. Indians also regularly received cash for selling manufactured goods. As the Iroquois engaged in a greater number of activities that resulted in the exchange of money, they were drawn more tightly into a market economy. The need to obtain money to acquire desired goods strengthened their commitment to market-oriented activities.[69]

Indians had long used their own multipurpose forms of currency, such as furs, corn, and wampum, and resisted European coins as the sole monetary system. In the seventeenth century, it was just as common for Indians to wear coins as decoration as it was to use them as payment. Even as late as the 1740s, some Iroquois demonstrated that they valued the *gift* of money as much as the article itself. At a conference with the Iroquois in 1744, Witham Marshe noted how his companion "flung a handful of English half-pennies" among a group of native children, which "pleased the elder sort very much" for "they esteem it a great mark of friendship, if the white people make presents to their children."[70]

However, by the 1770s, foreign money had become indispensable when dealing with colonists. Access to pounds and dollars was fast becoming a necessity if Indians wished to purchase the goods they had long become dependent upon. When Indian guests visited his home on the frontier, Johnson was obliged to provide them with money to purchase food on their journey home. When crops failed in 1769, many Indians "lived thro the Winter and Spring on the Money received at the Treaty of Fort Stanwix," Smith observed. "They were continually passing up to the Settlements to buy Provisions and sometimes shewed us money in their Bosoms." Similarly, Allan Grant, at Fort Ontario in August 1769, observed that "Dollars are here now as plenty as dirt." Trader account books reveal the frequency of cash payments in ordinary times as well. Much like local Euro-American settlers, Indians relied on a mixture of cash and crops to acquire trade goods.[71]

The Iroquois sought to limit their reliance on cash by using coins in tandem with alternative and preferred forms of currency. During his travels, Smith encountered a group of Oneida women who wore "Silver Broaches each of which passes for a Shilling and are as current among the Indians as Money." Throughout Iroquoia, native women wore broaches, which served a dual function as both a monetary unit and decorative article (fig. 14). Alternatively, army officer Joseph Bloomfield noted that wampum was "the current money" among the Iroquois. "As the Indians live far from the Sea," he observed, "our people make and sell the Purple [wampum]" from marine shells and enjoy "a handsome living by that Trade." Because both broaches and wampum were articles of European manufacture, the Iroquois still needed to first enter the market to sell goods or labor in order to trade in the currency of their preference. The Iroquois experienced only partial integration into a cash economy, but it still marked a chipping away of their economic autonomy.[72]

In a story related to an English captive during the height of the Seven Years' War, a Seneca headman warned how avarice and self-interest had once almost destroyed the Iroquois. At the beginning, the Great Spirit endowed each of the nations with a particular natural produce. The Mohawks received corn, the Oneidas, nuts and fruits, the Onondagas, squash, grapes, and tobacco, the Cayugas, nuts and roots, and the Senecas, beans. While the Great Spirit desired them to enjoy their special bounty, he also expected them to "love and take care of one another" by sharing their reserves. For a long while the Five Nations peacefully followed these rules, but soon after being counseled by an evil spirit they adopted a new mode of conduct. Beginning this trend, the Mohawks declared, "We abound in corn which our brothers have not; let us oblige them to give us a *great deal* of fruits, beans, roots, squashes, and tobacco, for a *very little corn*; so shall we live in idleness and plenty, while they labour and live hardy." The four remaining nations soon followed suit, each seeking to gain an advantage over the other. A period of strife ensued. Incensed by their misconduct, the Great Spirit punished them by darkening the skies, emptying the rivers, and removing all forms of animal life and vegetation. Nine summers of distress finally brought the Iroquois to their senses and they repented for their misdeeds. Recognizing their change of heart, the Great Spirit restored order to the earth and "from that time down to the present day," the Seneca headman concluded, "it has been an inviolable

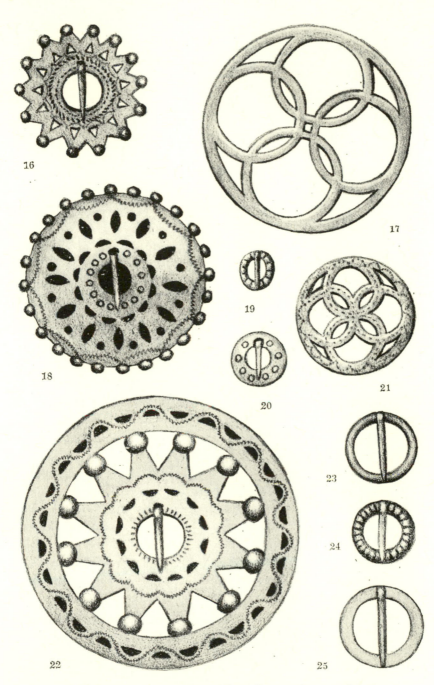

Figure 14. Eighteenth-century Mohawk broaches. From *New York State Museum Bulletin* 73: 101, plate 3. Courtesy of the New York State Library. Broaches like these were immensely popular in the late colonial period, used as both a decorative article and a form of currency.

rule and custom among the nations, that every Brother is welcome to what a Brother can spare."[73]

The Seneca's story functioned as a cautionary tale to his audience of male warriors, containing as it did implicit instruction on how men should engage in socioeconomic relations with one another. The Seneca headman went on to contrast Iroquois behavior with that of Europeans. Reflecting on current conditions in North America, the headman claimed, "the English and French, though they called the Indians brothers, had long practiced the same wickedness towards them, making everything dear that they exchanged with them." Not only this, the French and British treated each other in a similar manner. Referring to the duties placed on trade, the Seneca observed how "Corlaer," the governor of New York, made "Onontio," the governor of New France, "pay dearer for strouds and blankets; then Onontio makes Corlaer pay as much dearer for beaver; what at best, can either of them get by this, but his own inconvenience and the other's ill-will?" the headman asked. He believed that the Seven Years' War was a direct consequence of these baneful economic practices. "The Great Spirit of the white people is now angry with them," he warned, "and has left them to lift the hatchet, brother against brother, to destroy their own habitation, and bring misery on both their countries."[74] The headman's story was a forceful warning against the dangers of allowing economic exchange to take place outside the realm of kinship. Lack of brotherly regard between Europeans had led to bloodshed.

This didactic narrative was premised on an idealized account of the original state of Iroquois society devoid of inequality and greed. The Seneca headman was not alone in employing such a device. Throughout the eighteenth century, Iroquois headmen trumped up the egalitarian nature of Indian society as a means to contrast themselves with the "grasping" and "competitive" spirit of Europeans. Such sharply drawn distinctions were part fabrication. Pre-contact Iroquoia was a ranked society. Differences in wealth paralleled social demarcations, as hereditary chiefs and their families generally occupied the largest longhouses and enjoyed the greatest access to prestige goods. Yet, even if pre-contact society was ranked, social practices centered on gift-giving and communal ownership prevented extremes of wealth from developing. Clan affiliation also served as an important device to ensure that all individuals, through a pattern of reciprocal obligations, enjoyed access to assistance and goods. While eighteenth-century headmen may have idealized their society, they were not wholly inaccurate when outlining themes of sharing, mutuality, and brotherly regard that structured socioeconomic relations.

The practices and values attendant to a mercantile capitalism alarmed some members of the Iroquois Confederacy, who warned younger members against such conduct. Yet, decades of entanglement with a burgeoning market economy left an indelible mark on cultural norms and reshaped the way some Indians interacted with each other. The Seneca chief may have told this story precisely because he was worried about the changing economic morals of his fellow villagers. Involvement in market-oriented practices eroded older values of reciprocity, generating new commercially tinged attitudes. The shift in values and conduct was neither universal nor absolute, but it was real.

In 1770, chiefs from Oquaga voiced an unusual complaint when they highlighted the rude conduct of Native American traders. "One thing . . . we very much dislike," the headmen announced, was "Indians coming and trading among us." This new class of trader behaved ruthlessly: "Indians devour us, they extort from us every thing we get with great pain and Labour in the Woods, for little or nothing . . . if we desire them to be reasonable in their demand, it has no impression upon them." Similarly, in 1774, a Cayuga war chief expressed his desire "that neither the White People, or *Indians* be allowed to come to Cayuga to trade" because of their pernicious traffic in rum. Native women traders were notorious for their sharp dealings. Missionary David Zeisberger noted how they sold rum "at a considerable profit to the Indians, often taking from the latter everything they have, sometimes even their rifles on which they depend for subsistence." The Indians described here may not be typical, but they suggest a change in economic behavior at least among some sectors of Indian society.[75]

Iroquois concerns for self-gain eroded older communal practices of sharing and redistribution. In December 1768, a deputation of Oneida Indians from Kanowarohare came to Johnson "to accquaint him with the hard treatment their Village (in particular) had met with" because the Confederacy had failed to fairly distribute monies received from the Fort Stanwix Treaty. The Iroquois custom of hospitality was reportedly in decline. Indian agent George Croghan claimed that whereas in earlier times the hospitality ethic meant "the Community Can Never Suffer for Want," this practice had waned "since they become more acquainted with Europeans." If the Iroquois had ever once given freely to each other, they no longer always did so by midcentury. When crop failure hit the Iroquois in the 1760s, impoverished families were obliged to buy corn from each other. Kirkland noted how a poor harvest among the

Senecas in 1765 left "some families entirely destitute." A number "have been to Cayogon [Cayuga] to purchase corn and could get but a little by giving an enormous price." Two years later, Kirkland observed that impecunious Oneidas procured corn from the Tuscaroras: "They carry each a new stroud Blanket worth twenty Shillings, and tell me they expect to get no more than a Skipple of Corn a piece." By the 1770s there was an impoverished class among the Mohawks who relied on the British Crown for their support. Johnson buried a number of these indigent Indians, "destitute of friends." He provided aid to "a sick Mohawk unable for these 2 Years past to help himself" and supported "the Oldest Sachem of the Mohawks" and his family, they "being very Poor." That Johnson assumed responsibility for what would have once been a communal obligation to look after one's own reveals something about changing preoccupations of the Mohawks on the eve of the Revolution.[76]

A new penchant for accumulating personal property further points to the erosion of communal values. Indian agents familiar with the Iroquois observed how individual families had began to accrue private wealth. Guy Johnson remarked, "they have no Property in Common, the Product of the Labour and Hunting of each Individual, being at his own Disposal." Croghan agreed, noting that "Every family have thire Distinct property." The new value attached to personal wealth encouraged some Indians to no longer bury belongings with the dead.[77] Decades of contact with European practices and goods played a major role in altering attitudes. The introduction of horses and livestock had encouraged the Iroquois to revise their understanding of private property. In December 1764, Johnson berated the Oneida community after an Indian named Nickus killed some sheep belonging to a settler. Refuting the Indians' well-versed argument that wandering livestock were communal, Johnson noted how "that very Rascal Nickus" had made claims to his own private property only a few months before. Nickus had "made a great deal of noise," Johnson reminded them, when a cattle driver appropriated his horse and "would not rest until he got Lieutenant Colonel Campbell to pay him £16—for the horse." Thus, Johnson concluded, "if your People are so tenacious of their Property, why should not ours, who have a better notion of it, than you." However, Indians were clearly developing "a better notion of it" as they regarded both livestock and horses as personal assets by the 1770s.[78]

Along with domestic animals, the Mohawks also came to privately own land. Although the Mohawks still held the majority of land in common, by at least 1777 some individual Canajoharies had begun to procure allotments. The primary documents are frustratingly quiet as to how and why this pattern of land ownership occurred. Historian David Guldenzopf suggests that they had "begun to purchase lots from the clans." Some Indians also bought land from colonists, and on at least one occasion Johnson deeded land to an Indian. In many respects, individual landholdings were a logical outcome of adopting European legal definitions of private property. Private family plots marked a major break in tradition with the Canajoharies' not so distant past.[79]

Perhaps even more startling than new patterns of private resources was the degree to which property ownership was unequal. As a consequence of growing entanglement in a nascent capitalist system, the eastern Iroquois experienced economic stratification by the late colonial period. The war loss claims filed by the Mohawks following the Revolutionary War provide an invaluable insight into their material world on the eve of this conflict, demonstrating the existence of an economic elite. In terms of total wealth, encompassing land, standing property (houses and barns), farming implements, and livestock, the smallest claim made was for £25 and the largest was over £1,200, pointing to a sharp division between the haves and have-nots. The value of standing property ranged from £15 to £250, with 60 percent owning standing property worth £50 or less. Archaeological evidence further supports the existence of an elite pattern of residential houses. Excavations of the Brant family home in Canajoharie and the Enders House site at the Lower Mohawk Castle, both dating to the 1760s, indicate that some Indians lived in larger homes built of stone. Ownership of land, like everything else, was unequal. Approximately 80 percent of the Mohawks who filed claims owned just 36 percent of all private lands. The smallest individual landholdings began at three acres and climbed upward to almost 600 acres.[80]

Similar discrepancies of wealth are also evident among the Oneidas. In 1794, U.S. government agent Timothy Pickering carried out a detailed report of the losses sustained by the Oneidas and Tuscaroras during the Revolution. Unlike the Mohawks, they possessed less property, they did not privately own land, and they experienced less extremes of wealth. Nonetheless, like the Mohawks, private property was widespread and generally unequal. In terms of total wealth, Oneida claims ranged from £1 to £287. Nearly all claims were for £65 or less, with the exception of a small elite of seven family heads who claimed over £65. Especially evident in Pickering's report were differences in housing structures. At the lowest end of the scale and in the largest quantity were simple "Indian" or "bark" houses. Totaling forty-four, they were valued at £2 to £8. In the middle range, there were seven homes built with hewed logs, a housing structure more highly valued. The third and most expensive group comprised framed houses, totaling twenty-two. Even these varied in size and value. The home of Indian chief Skenendo was worth £44. The most expensive house, valued at £48, was a "large well finished house and store, cellar walled with stone."[81]

To some extent Johnson promoted this pattern of economic inequality. Throughout his career, he engaged in the unequal distribution of gifts to Indians who demonstrated loyalty. For example, in September 1770, he dispersed $280 in private cash presents to key headmen. Through this practice he facilitated the creation of an economic elite composed of pro-British families.[82] But Iroquois economic stratification also resulted from the nature of the new economic order. Involvement in a market economy provided opportunities to acquire wealth, and some individuals and families were more successful than others in this endeavor. The Mohawks and Oneidas who claimed the greatest wealth were head warriors and their female relations.[83] Warriors enjoyed ample access to the market economy throughout the 1740s–70s by exchanging their martial skills for monetary rewards. This wealthy elite owned a disproportionate amount of barns, plows, hoes, and livestock. Such fixtures of Euro-American agriculture were not purely an indication of wealth but also a *source* of wealth, as the production of crops and pursuit of animal husbandry enabled them to procure foreign goods.

Although pre-contact Iroquois society had contained a socioeconomic elite, Iroquois enmeshment within a market economy transformed the nature of this hierarchy. By the 1770s, the older ranked society, made up of elite families, had given way to a new type of stratified society. In some respects this new society was more egalitarian in that a greater portion of the population had access to "prestige goods" through their involvement in a market economy and trade with Europeans. Wealth and status were no longer confined to a finite number of elite lineages. But in other respects, this newer society was just as restrictive, if not more so. As older practices of sharing resources and redistributing wealth waned and as men and women demonstrated a growing attachment to accumulating private property, positions of relative wealth and poverty became more fixed and extreme.

Discrepancies in wealth encouraged the development of quasi-class identities. Mohawk men and women demonstrated their high social standing through their visual displays of wealth. By adorning their clothes with silver broaches, purchasing horses and cattle, or choosing to drink tea out of porcelain teacups, this Mohawk elite cultivated a new cultural identity for themselves that set them apart from less wealthy Indians. Clothing and personal adornments, in particular, were an important means for establishing status. During his travels through eastern Iroquoia, Smith observed variations in dress between "the common sort," which included "a Shirt or shift with a Blanket or Coat, a Half-Gown and Petticoat," and leading headmen and their families who wore more expensive fabrics in imitation of the English manner. Bloomfield was struck by the very visible distinction between "the almost naked Savages" who attended a conference, "the Men haveing a Clout only round them and the Women a skirt and Blanket," and "the Heads and Chiefs and their squaas who were elegantly dressed with mockinsens, Leggings etc." Moravian missionary John Heckewelder noted how "the wealthy adorn themselves besides with ribands and gartering of various colors, beads and silver broaches." Women of these families "line their petticoat and blue or scarlet cloth blanket or covering with choice ribands of various colors, on which they fix a number of silver broaches, or small round buckles." If silver broaches and buckles denoted a specific monetary value, then the desire to put them on physical display can be construed as status-seeking behavior.[84]

Clearly, important themes of continuity coexisted alongside profound cultural change. Developing market-oriented pursuits while holding onto subsistence agriculture and hunting, Iroquois economic culture was in a state of flux. Although a desire for profit gained the upper hand among some Indians, notions of kinship also continued to shape the way the Iroquois structured socioeconomic relations with one another. Indians exhibited new commercial values at the same time that they clung onto distinctly noncommercial practices. At the mixed town of Oquaga, Smith visited a shad fishery where "all persons present including strangers, such is their laudable Hospitality have an equal Division of fish." He further noted how "Debts and Theft seem to be almost unknown among them, Property being in some Degree common to all."[85] While values attendant to an emergent market capitalist order had made inroads into Iroquoia, they had not yet thoroughly dislodged older concerns of fulfilling familial obligations.

In the late colonial period, Iroquois Indians continued to live outside a market economy but not beyond its reach. The Iroquois creatively responded to encroaching commercial forces in ways that lessened their disruptive impact. Change was immense but not entirely detrimental. By continuing to hunt and farm throughout the eighteenth century, by Indianizing European goods, and by using native forms of currency alongside European coins, the Iroquois mediated structural changes through their own cultural practices. Resisting total dispossession and impoverishment, they found a viable way to live in this new transitional order. But as they became increasingly reliant on foreign markets, goods, and currencies at the same time that colonists and imperialists became less dependent on them for their furs, land, and martial labor, Iroquois political status receded. The shifting socioeconomic realities of their situation had a significant impact on their cultural realm of experience. In the process of becoming entangled in this imperial commercial world, the Iroquois continued to modify gendered practices and ethnic identities.

Chapter 7

The Iroquois in British North America

In the 1770s, Iroquois "brethren" from neighboring settlements chastised the Kanowarohare Oneidas for failing to "live like true Indians." Ever since the arrival of missionary Samuel Kirkland to their village in 1767, Kanowarohare Oneidas had undergone rapid baptism and religious conversion, causing others to urge them to "revive . . . old customs." More was at stake than mere spiritual conviction. Under the stewardship of Kirkland some men began to take a more active part in farming and animal husbandry. Others became schoolteachers or Christian ministers. By appearing to relinquish the tomahawk for the plow, pen, and bible, Kanowarohare men threatened the basic fabric of Iroquois ethnic and gendered identity. "You . . . are now going to become praying people, like those in the East," Indian critics warned. "By this you will lose your warrior spirit and become like silly women and children." While the Kanowarohare Oneidas began to identify more with the practices and values of the English, other Iroquois were deepening their commitment to a racialized *Indian* identity that emphasized their distinctiveness from *whites*. They lamented the existence of Indians who "have always been fond of *White people* and their manners and appear to love them more than they love Indians."[1]

In the late colonial period, the Haudenosaunee people embodied diverse ways of being Iroquois. The pressures of colonization led Iroquois men and women to develop multiple, oftentimes conflicting, ways of enacting gender roles and ethnic identities. Despite retaining unifying aspects of a deeply embedded Iroquoian culture—including a rich spiritual heritage, clan affiliation, and an emphasis on the matrilineal—significant cultural differences between and within the five nations emerged. The formulation of new cultural identities was a product of both coercion and agency. Indians made choices, but the larger imperial-colonial world determined what options were available.

Growing dependence on a market economy, land loss, the influence of missionaries, the growth of colonial settlements, and the emergence of novel
forms of inequality all had an unavoidable affect on the Iroquois cultural
realm of existence. As residents of a new British North America, they demonstrated remarkable resilience, holding onto cultural forms even as they
reshaped them in the process. Men and women recrafted gendered, ethnic,
and racial identities that spoke to the demands of their changing world but
still remained anchored within their own cultural frame of reference. But the
Iroquois were becoming increasingly inconsequential in a colonial landscape
in which Euro-Americans were gaining control over lands and resources.
While the Six Nations avoided total subjugation, Anglo-American pressures
on them constrained their postwar efforts to define their cultural worlds.

The compulsion to perform their long-cherished warrior ethic remained
strong among the Iroquois throughout the postwar period. Following the
Seven Years' War, warriors from all six nations resumed their longstanding
conflict with the Cherokees, which was motivated by a desire to secure captives, scalps, and, most important, manly prestige. Johnson was acutely aware
of the cultural benefits young men derived from southern raids. "To keep
up a Spirit of War amongst their People is a Maxim of Politicks which they
never Forget," Johnson informed Gage. Because of the "nature of their Warfare" and owing to "the length of their Journeys and the Difficulties they have
to Surmount," Iroquois warriors believed "they atchieve more reputation in
Quarrels amongst themselves."[2] Throughout the decade and beyond, warriors
also enacted their manhood by mounting southern raids against the Catawbas and Choctaws, often against the wishes of village elders and clan mothers. Directing their martial skills against Euro-Americans provided warriors
with a further opportunity to celebrate their manliness and to acquire social status. After murdering trader John Newirk and his servant in 1762, two
Seneca warriors toured triumphantly through western villages, "boasting of
their Manhood." A decade later, news of the Seneca murder of French traders
on Lake Ontario aroused admiration. Samuel Kirkland reported that when
"the scalp or death shout" was carried into Kanowarohare by some western
Indians, "the martial spirit of the young warriors soon waked up from its
long slumber and they shouted and halloo'd till their spirits were raised to a
prodigious pitch."[3]

However, economic and political realities of the postwar period obstructed
men's attempts to achieve a martial masculinity. Imperial interference served

as one impediment. Once recognized by the British as an important resource to be cultivated and harnessed for their own ends, the warrior spirit was now considered a liability. In the 1760s, Johnson was concerned with suppressing the activities of warriors for a variety of political reasons. British imperialists felt that Iroquois-Cherokee hostilities created too much havoc among the latter, which in turn disrupted the precious balance of power in the South between the Cherokees and martial Catawbas. A more pressing problem concerned the resentment of Virginian settlers. Violence frequently erupted when Iroquois war parties passed by their settlements on their way to Cherokee country. Consequently, Johnson placed significant pressure on the Iroquois to abandon this war. A peace was eventually brokered between the two groups at Johnson Hall in 1768.[4] In 1770, Johnson again intervened when the Cherokees sought a military alliance with the Iroquois against western Indians living along the Wabash River. The potential of a military union between two powerful nations aroused consternation among imperial officials, who feared that such a union could be used against the British. A large conference was held at the German Flats in the summer of 1770 at which Johnson successfully compelled warriors to desist involvement.[5]

It was not simply the meddling efforts of Johnson but more specifically the warriors' own reduced situation in relation to colonial society and the British Empire that made their pursuit of ancient battles more problematic. When warriors formally agreed not to enter into a military alliance with the Cherokees in 1770, they did so in part because they recognized the danger of engaging in a military venture without imperial sanction. For practical reasons they required Johnson to provide them with passes so that they could travel unimpeded through colonial settlements to the Wabash River. Warriors also needed to be provisioned. Although they claimed this was their right, "as they had formerly assisted the English," it was also a matter of necessity given the failure of crops the previous year and "the distress they were in for clothing, etc.," owing to the colonial boycott of British goods. Furthermore, warfare against southern tribes was made more dangerous by the hostile Virginians they had to pass and became simply less feasible as the Catawba population diminished.[6]

Subsiding opportunities to wage war generated cultural anxiety. When in 1765 Captain Onoingwadekha, a Seneca head warrior, appealed to the young men of his village to go on the warpath against the Cherokees "as a testimony of their military valour," he encountered resistance. Discounting the usual propensity to seek the manly glory of warfare, they confessed "they had doubts in their minds, both as to the expediency and justice of the measure." Annoyed, Captain Onoingwadekha warned them that "they would soon lose all their martial spirit" if they failed to uphold customary gendered pursuits. On another occasion he lamented the loss of martial opportunities and its dismal impact on New England Indians: "How many remnants of tribes to the *East* are so reduced, that they *pound* sticks to make brooms, to buy a loaf of Bread or it be a shirt. The warriors, which they boasted of, before these foreigners, the white people crossed the great Lake, where are they now? why their grandsons are become *mere women!*"[7] Mary Jemison, the adopted Seneca captive, recalled the long peace of "twelve or fifteen years [when] the use of the implements of war was not known, nor the war-whoop heard, save on days of festivity." In the absence of real warfare, the ritualized celebration of the warrior ethic became an important social event. As Jemison remembered, "the achievements of former times were commemorated in a kind of mimic of warfare, in which the chiefs and warriors displayed their prowess, and illustrated their former adroitness . . . thereby preserving and handing to their children, the theory of Indian warfare." But for some, merely ritualized enactments of warfare were not enough. On the eve of the American Revolution, the commander at Fort Niagara noted the concerns of some Seneca men: "The old ones . . . when in their cups [i.e., drunk] and off their guard can not help saying that this long peace will be the ruin of their nation, that their warriors are loosing their manhood and that their youth must become women, having no opportunities of exercising themselves in war."[8]

In addition to diminishing opportunities for warfare, the eastern Iroquois faced the added pressure of missionary influence on their gender norms. Protestant missionaries who sojourned in their villages in the 1760s and 1770s brought with them definite ideas about appropriate gender roles and a clear agenda for transforming "lazy" Indian men into pious, industrious farmers. In 1765, David Fowler, a young Montauk settled at Kanowarohare to teach the English language and instruct men in farming and animal husbandry, wrote to his sponsor, Eleazar Wheelock, "I beleive I shall perswade the Men in this Castle at least the most of them to labour next Year: They begin to see now that they would live better if they cultivate their Lands than they do now by Hunting and fishing." Yet, two years later he was still struggling to commit men to agriculture and soon after left complaining that "these Indians dont labour" but instead are "continually going from Place to Place."[9] Kirkland faced similar difficulties when he moved to Kanowarohare. He also encouraged Indian men to imitate an Anglo-Christian model of manhood by becoming godly husbandmen. He purchased European farming utensils for the Oneidas' use, hired a local man to "assist them in plowing," and personally joined them in "their fields, to instruct them in their husbandry." Despite his efforts, age-old patterns of female agriculture and male hunting persisted.[10]

Despite resisting missionary efforts to remake them in accordance with Euro-American gendered ideals, eastern Iroquois men found that difficulties in hunting and an abiding involvement in the market economy necessitated their recourse to new patterns of masculine behavior. Alongside paid forms of labor, they also took up other novel pursuits in husbandry, carpentry, and Christian ministering—activities long associated with European modes of masculinity. The Mohawks and Oneidas did not experience all-out cultural transformation but careful negotiation and piecemeal transition. If and when they took up new "manly" trades they did so in a casual and temporary fashion, with an eye to secure whatever advantage they could and a determination to abandon the practice when and if it no longer suited their interests. Involvement in new manly pursuits offered men important benefits, and through the selective and partial adoption of such practices they could minimize, but not elude, disruptions to longstanding gender norms.[11]

By the late colonial period, wage labor had become a wholly masculinized activity, performed solely by Iroquois men. Because these men oftentimes worked alongside male colonists, the impression that the exchange of physical toil for cash was a distinctly masculine enterprise was reinforced. Male wage labor did not mark a radical departure in Iroquois gender norms. By engaging in physically demanding work that relied on their knowledge of the land, personal agility, strength, stamina, and even martial skills, men performed what they already culturally deemed to be "men's" work. But wage labor also led men to enact a new kind of manhood because of the rewards attached to this activity. As opportunities for warfare diminished and paid labor increased, the means for assessing a manly performance altered. Increasingly, men's status as men was no longer derived purely from their skill as warriors, hunters, or orators but more so by their ability to acquire cash and material wealth. Paid labor did not redefine the meaning of Mohawk manhood, but it did add another dimension to this gender construct.[12]

Men learned new skills and trades to compensate for their shortcomings in hunting. Some took a more active part in agriculture as suggested by their purchase and ownership of farming tools. Men also owned livestock, indicating their increased involvement in animal husbandry. William Johnson encouraged the masculinization of this activity by targeting men for gifts of cows, poultry, and pigs as well as purchasing these articles from them. Because livestock was generally allowed to roam free and treated more or less as another form of wild meat, men's partaking in animal husbandry served as a natural extension of their role as hunters.[13] Partly as a means to lessen their dependence on colonists, the Mohawks and Oneidas developed other European vocations. Kirkland commented on the "proficiency" of Oneida men in carpentry: "with a little assistance they are able to finish a house." They also applied to the New York governor for a smith to be sent to their village so that "some of [our] young men might acquire a small degree of skill in the trade." Remarking on the degree of Mohawk acculturation, missionary Charles Inglis noted in 1771 that they "are in some measure Civilised. They cultivate lands; several of them have learned trades; all have fixed habitations; they have also cattle of various kinds, many of the conveniences of polished life."[14]

Cultural involvement in Christianity also offered new ways for constructing masculine identities. A number of Mohawk and Oneida men abandoned usual masculine pursuits to become catechists, schoolteachers, and missionaries. Church-oriented men embodied a novel model of masculinity grounded in Christian ideals of piety, sobriety, and submissiveness, which stood in stark contrast to the bellicose warrior-hunter. Yet, most men defied a complete absorption of Christian gendered norms. The Iroquois engaged in a discerning appropriation of Christianity. In addition to whatever satisfaction they derived from its theological tenets, joining the church could enhance one's personal authority within the community, provide a source of welfare or employment, and enable the Iroquois to acquire literacy—an empowering skill to possess in the Atlantic imperial world.[15]

Indians borrowed and learned from missionaries only as long as it served their interests. William Johnson's own métis son, Tekawiroñte, repelled efforts to refine his gendered behavior at Wheelock's school. His teacher noted that although he seemed "capable of making a very likely man . . . his Pride and the Violence of his Temper . . . rendered him troublesome." He soon quit the school. John Davies, a young Mohawk, did not allow his education at Wheelock's academy to stand in the way of his pursuing culturally preferred activities. In May 1769, he left his paid employment as a guide to Richard Smith "to march against the Catawbas in company with a few of his Countrymen who take this long Tour merely to gratify revenge or Satiate Pride."[16] Mohawk and Oneida men switched between gendered modes of conduct as situational needs dictated. Whatever encouragement Kirkland made to turn warriors into pious and productive Christians, he was well aware that their primary concern remained with matters of war and the hunt. In 1771, he fretted that one of his schools would have to be closed down because the Indian schoolteacher was about to leave for the spring hunt. In 1772, he observed how "reports of an Indian war very much soured the minds of the Young Warriors, that they gave very little heed to the things of religion." The nameless young man hired by missionary John Stuart to serve as his private tutor and public interpreter at Fort Hunter demonstrated that he could be just as selective when choosing his employment. Stuart depended on his assistance for Sunday services but worried about how long he would be able to retain him, "as I cannot afford him a sufficient maintenance to induce him to neglect Hunting and reside Constantly here." When the young interpreter eventually quit, Stuart suspected it was because he had grown "weary of confinement, and [the] regular manner of living."[17]

As Iroquois men adapted to the pressures and opportunities of residing in British North America, they devised novel ways of enacting masculine identities. Joseph Brant, the younger brother of Molly, embodied this hybrid gendered identity that melded old with new. In his youth, Joseph pursued a well-trodden path appropriate to his station and sex. He was raised to embrace the warrior ethic and at age fifteen took part in his first martial exploit at Lake Champlain during the Seven Years' War. As he came from "a Family of Distinction," Brant was selected by Johnson to attend Wheelock's school in the summer of 1761. When he first arrived he "was considerably cloathed, *Indian*-fashion, and could speak a few words of *English*." Over the next two years, however, Brant was made over as he was schooled in the dialect, dress, and decorum of an English gentleman. He made substantial headway learning the English language and became well versed in the Bible. Impressed by Brant's progress, Wheelock described him as a possessing "a manly and genteel Deportment." Plans were afoot for Brant to assist in a new missionary school in Canajoharie where it was hoped he would instruct other young men to learn European gender norms. Yet Brant resisted total acculturation. In 1763, concerned with "gaining the Displeasure of his Friends," who resented his remaining so long at Wheelock's school, he returned to his home in Canajoharie where he resided until the outbreak of the American Revolution.[18]

Despite his desire to live as a Mohawk man, Brant in fact constructed an alternative model of masculinity. Not wholly dependent on the hunt, he earned his livelihood by engaging in a range of commercial pursuits. He worked as an interpreter for the British at Fort Ontario and sold his services as a guide to colonial visitors. He also farmed, owning land, livestock, and cattle. His large purchases of goods, particularly wampum and paint, suggest that he may have acted in the capacity of an Indian trader as well. Through involvement in wage employment, agriculture, and possibly trade, Brant acquired considerable wealth. His economic pursuits illustrate that enmeshment within a commercial Atlantic system presented Iroquois men with new ways of constructing masculine identities at the same time that it posed obstacles to performing traditional "manly" roles. Yet Brant did not fully abandon older notions of Iroquois masculinity either. He was an able warrior, as demonstrated by his aggressive stance toward antagonistic settlers and by his legendary martial role during the American Revolution. Furthermore, despite his new wealth, Brant's rise in political power was still rooted in "kin-based traditions of leadership" and his ability to control "external relationships that delivered material goods." Thus Brant embodied a gender identity that combined new practices with older forms.[19]

Women also experienced increased pressure on their cultural patterns of behavior at the same time that they retained core aspects of their gender identity. The most visible sign of cultural continuity in their lives was their ongoing dominance in husbandry. Agriculture remained central to the Iroquois economy. Diversifying crops and producing for local markets and home consumption intensified women's farming activities. Jemison among the Senecas provides the only firsthand account available on the working life of female agriculturalists in this period. Initially living in the Ohio region, she noted how "we had no ploughs . . . but performed the whole process of planting and hoeing with a small tool that resembled, in some respects, a hoe with a very short handle." She compared their labor favorably to that of women of European descent, recalling how, "in the summer season, we planted, tended, and harvested our corn, and generally had all our children with us; but had no master to oversee or drive us, so that we could work as leisurely as we pleased."[20]

Women oftentimes used their ties to the colonial world to enhance their position as farmers. In the early 1760s, the two daughters of Cayuga headman Tokahaio asked the Pennsylvania governor for a horse. In possession of "two plantations, at which they plant Corn," they desired a means to transport crops. As they had done during the Seven Years' War, women continued to ask colonial men to plow their cornfields. Through an appointed male speaker, Onondaga women in 1767 complained to Johnson of being "in a Starving

Condition" and requested "that two good men might be sent with Horses, and Ploughs to their Country to plow their lands." They were prepared to pay these men "but hoped it might be at a moderate price." Rather than view male farm laborers as an infringement on their sphere of influence, women more likely considered outside help a successful strategy to improve their productivity. Despite their rhetoric of impoverishment, the fact that these women had money to pay for such services suggests that they enjoyed a basic level of subsistence. These were not desperate and needy women but calculating economic actors who saw an opportunity to improve their situation.[21]

Imperial and colonial expansion did not nullify women's position as farmers, but it did alter this role. Among the Mohawks, women's relationship to the land shifted. Although women were declared to be its "properest Owners," the breakdown of communally held lands into smaller privately owned plots in Canajoharie negated their power to make decisions about how lands should be distributed and used. It also meant that women did not always labor in large female-related work gangs. The activities of drunken and deviant Indians who signed away allotments without first securing permission and the unscrupulous conduct of colonial squatters further abraded women's jurisdiction over their soil. The most significant way women's role as farmers changed had to do with the degree to which farming had taken on new commercial concerns. Mohawk women increasingly produced crops for an external marketplace in addition to domestic use. In January 1775, an Iroquois woman named Catherine purchased three ells of ribbon, two pairs of shoes, and black stroud from a local trader with a payment of "4 scipples" of maize and some cash. This was not the first time she had used corn and cash to procure trade goods. Catherine may have obtained cash from her husband's involvement in wage labor, but it is also apparent that like other Indians she sometimes used supplies of corn as currency.[22]

Although women were determined not to be "reduced to make Brooms," their dependence on foreign markets and goods cemented their commitment to commercial enterprises. In addition to selling crops, eastern Iroquois women also supplemented farming with petty-commodity production. The increased rarity and thus exoticism of Indian handicrafts enhanced their market value. Furthermore, difficulties in agriculture in the postwar period encouraged women to remain active in other economic activities. European visitors were keen to acquire Indian "curiosities" as they traveled through Indian country and paid handsomely for such goods. Smith purchased "a few curiosities of Indian Manufacture" while visiting Oquaga, "among which

[was] a Pair of embroidered Moccisons" costing him ten shillings. In 1776 Joseph Bloomfield noted the presence of "Squaas" at his military encampment in the Mohawk Valley. He observed that "they are here almost as much at home," producing "Mockinsons and "other Things" to sell to soldiers. For the most part, the production of salable goods remained a casual activity and secondary to women's role as farmers. Mohawk and Oneida women confined manufacturing to the quiet months between harvesting and planting new crops. Hence, when missionary David Fowler went in search of some Indian handicrafts among the Oneidas in late 1766, he had trouble locating any. "These Women dont make such till winter then they have wherewithal to make them. I shall get them very easy in the Spring," he observed. Mohawk and Oneida women, still in occupation of their cornfields, engaged in petty-commodity production as a complementary activity to fit around husbandry.[23]

A few native women abandoned farming altogether, seeking an alternative livelihood via commercial trade. Sally Ainse, a woman of Oneida descent, emerged as a principal trader on the New York frontier by the 1760s.[24] She held accounts with several Dutch merchants from whom she purchased large quantities of food and alcohol. Transporting her merchandise westward, she sold these goods to her Indian and colonial customers at her trading base at Fort Stanwix. Operating as a middleman in the profitable ginseng trade, she purchased this naturally grown root from locals and then sold it in bulk to eastern merchants. Ainse was also an important supplier of alcohol in the region.[25] Through her business enterprise she secured a substantial subsistence, which held her in good stead when her marriage to colonial interpreter Andrew Montour dissolved. In 1762, she acquired a parcel of land for her son from the neighboring Oneidas. As they recalled, "She was desirous [the land] should be near the old Oneida Castle as thereby the English would be prevented from taking it." Like the other Iroquois, she was weary of colonial encroachment on Indian lands. Her connections to the Oneidas worked in her favor. Her request being granted, she "Treated" the headmen "with Wine." As the fur trade moved west, so too did Ainse. She relocated to Fort Michilimackinac and then Detroit in the late 1760s and early 1770s, taking English trader William Maxwell as her common-law husband. Although this union also expired, wealth generated through trade enabled her to purchase her own western homestead in 1780.[26]

Because women continued to find ways to participate in a commercial marketplace, they sustained socioeconomic parity with men. While paid labor was becoming distinctly masculinized, women found an alternative means to access a cash economy by producing Indian handicrafts, trafficking rum, and selling surplus crops. Women's ability to participate in cash-generating activities helped avert a new system of gender subordination.[27] Women's production of salable produce enabled them to acquire goods they desired from Euro-American traders without having to rely on male kin. The account book of a Mohawk Valley trader reveals that a number of women—including "Yellow Belly's Wife," "Madelen," "Lydia," and "Christine," also known as "Drunken Marie's daughter"—held their own private accounts. Women turned up at forts, settlements, and trading stores with cash, harvested crops, and wild fruit to procure foreign-made wares and services, such as "Cattreen the squa," who purchased "one gallon of Rum and a Cagg" from valley trader John Butler, and "Peggy the Squa," who paid a local shoemaker for his services.[28] Women's involvement in commercial trade networks may point to the growing dependence of Indians on foreign markets, but equally it highlights women's ongoing interdependence with male relations.

Despite their active participation in commercial activities women did not generally act as independent economic actors but rather as contributors to an increasingly conspicuous nuclear family economy. A significant cultural development in Iroquois society by the late colonial period was the partial reordering of household relations. The basic unit in Iroquois society had always been the "fireside" or nuclear family, but the movement to smaller dwelling places gave greater physical visibility and social prominence to this kinship unit and in particular the spousal bond.

Throughout the eighteenth century, under the impact of demographic strain, political dissension, colonial influence, and in the absence of military threat, Iroquois homes and households decreased in size. This trend, already in place by the 1740s, accelerated following the Seven Years' War and was most evident among the eastern nations.[29] At Oquaga, housing structures changed significantly. Multiple-family dwelling places were still present in the 1760s, as Smith recorded during his 1769 visit "that 6 or more families sometimes reside together." But in the years that followed, the community was busily involved in the construction of smaller single-family homes. By 1776, a colonist remarked that the village contained about fifty houses "some built after the ancient Indian manner, and the rest of good hew'd logs properly dove-tailed at each end," a distinctly European style of architecture. An American soldier during the Revolutionary War described their homes as "good log houses

with Stone Chimneys and glass windows."[30] Similarly the Oneida community
at Kanowarohare was diligently engaged in building single household dwelling structures in the 1770s, encouraged in part by Kirkland who provided
carpentry tools. One headman lived not in the traditional longhouse but in
one of the twenty-two framed houses built in that village that had two chimneys and windows, described by one contemporary as "a good house built in
the Dutch fashion."[31]

Framed houses for nuclear dwelling places were most common among
the Mohawks. In 1750, Conrad Weiser stayed in the home of Brant Canagaraduncka at Fort Hunter, one of the first framed houses among the Mohawks.
He described the home as "a well built, 2 story house, provided with furniture
like that of a middle-class family." Following the Seven Years' War, influenced
by the presence of colonial settlers and missionaries, the Mohawks built more
of this style. Johnson noted the presence of "good framed houses belonging to the Indians" at Fort Hunter and frequently provided boards for their
construction. Bloomfield, visiting the Mohawks in 1776, noted that "their
habitations are Very small, consisting only of a little cottage, in the middle
of which is their fire-place: here both they and the Animals they breed, live
promiscuously." Another observer in the 1780s also detected European influence when he described the homes of two Mohawk chiefs as "framed" and
each with "a good barn."[32] Among the western nations as well, smaller houses
became more commonplace, while older longhouses were used primarily for
public meetings. Archaeological evidence reveals that by the 1770s, many
Senecas lived in small log cabins complete with leaded glass windows and
metal-hinged doors.[33]

The spatial rearrangement of kinship groups encouraged a new focus in
the economic life of the Iroquois, particularly the eastern nations, for whom
evidence is the strongest. Labor and resources became concentrated within
a smaller nuclear unit, thereby displacing a village or clan economy. In the
early seventeenth century, the Iroquois had fished in large communal groups
on clan-owned fishing grounds. By the mid-eighteenth century, it was more
common for them to fish in small groups or individually.[34] Patterns of trade
further reveal the prominence of the nuclear household economy. According
to the accounts kept by one Mohawk Valley trader, members of a "fireside"
family exchanged and consumed goods in ways that demonstrated their close
economic ties to one another. Individuals often purchased goods for other
members of their immediate family. It is unclear whether the wife and daughter of an Indian named Hendrick ever patronized this trader's store in person,

but Hendrick often purchased goods for them on their behalf. Another Mohawk Indian named Canategarie along with his three sons frequently bought
articles for one another, and for a while Canategarie shared the same account
with one of his sons. To pay for goods Indians regularly drew on the funds
and resources of other family members. When Lydia purchased a variety of
wares in the winter of 1773, she charged the cost to her son's account. More
often, Indians acquired goods by paying with the crops grown by their wives
and daughters or with beaver skins hunted by their husbands or sons. Parents
sometimes objected to the costs incurred by their children. Adam, after his
son Jacob failed to pay for his goods bought under his account, requested the
trader remove Jacob's outstanding debt and list it separately. Wives sometimes disapproved of purchases made by their husbands; the trader was
obliged to pay back some cash to Hendrick "which his wife would not allow
at settling."[35]

These various transactions reveal the extent to which the economic lives
of members of a nuclear household intertwined. Although the Iroquois continued to attach cultural importance to the relationship between uncles and
nephews, and between mothers and daughters, ties between fathers and
sons, and husbands and wives had become more pronounced. The number
of fathers and sons who bought and sold goods together or for one another
overshadowed entries for uncles and nephews. Village and clan membership
remained paramount throughout this period, but in regards to economic activities at least, the primary source of identification lay with one's most immediate family members.

The move to smaller households was accompanied by other cultural
shifts, including certain types of descent being structured within the father's
side of the family. English surnames, which had become commonplace by
midcentury, were transmitted through paternal lines. Individuals took either
their father's Indian name or, more commonly, his Christian name. The son of
Hendrick Peters (a.k.a. Theyanoguin) was Paulus Peters (a.k.a. Sahonwagy).
Molly and Joseph Brant used their stepfather's first name for their surname.
Children of Dutch and English fathers often received their father's first and
last names.[36] Property, in addition to names, could also follow patterns of
paternal descent. When the Oneidas reported material losses sustained during the Revolutionary War, they did not define any of their property as clan
owned. Instead it was listed as privately and predominantly male owned. Furthermore, these documents reveal that it passed through the paternal line as
often as it did through the maternal line.[37] A patrilineal emphasis was also ev-

ident in residency patterns, as wives began living with their husband's family after marriage. When Joseph Brant and his wife, Peggy, visited her relations in Oquaga they "did not lodge with her Father . . . but with her Sisters," indicating the continuance of matrilocal patterns. However, their permanent place of residency was not with her family. Brant and Peggy lived in the home of his former stepfather and mother in Canajoharie. Similarly, while at Oquaga Smith observed a "handsome Bride" and her "young Mohawk" husband "on a visit to *her* Relations," indicating again her actual place of residency with her husband's family.[38]

The Iroquois had never been strictly matrilineal. In pre-contact society, the nuclear fireside family "in essence was bilateral and provided the individual with two lines of appeal, first to the mother's line, and second to his father's." While surnames and wealth may have come to pass through the male line, clan affiliation and hereditary titles continued to pass through the female line. Instead of a clear shift away from the matrilineal toward the patrilineal, late eighteenth-century cultural patterns reveal a new emphasis on a system of bilateral or double descent.[39] Furthermore, the movement toward smaller households did not mark the demise of the matrilineal lineage. Even as families began residing in smaller groups, these kinship units continued to live collectively in the same settlement so that members of an extended lineage were in proximity. Along with the persistence of the female-headed extended family was the continued importance of the Iroquois clan structure. Well into the nineteenth century and beyond, clans continued to perform reciprocal duties within the community and serve as an important form of identification.[40]

While the matrilineal bend of Iroquois culture remained pervasive, on a more immediate level of the day-to-day other forces worked to enlarge or at least alter men's roles within the household. Physical separation from the extended lineage and the patriarchal bias of influential Europeans persuaded some Mohawk and Oneida men to take on new responsibilities in the instruction of their children. For Johnson, men were the undisputed lords of the household. Thus, when required to select boys for Wheelock's missionary school in Connecticut in the early 1760s, Johnson deemed it appropriate to consult only with grandfathers and fathers. Throughout the mid- to late eighteenth century, missionaries exclusively chose young men to train as ministers and teachers of children, again encroaching on women's roles as mothers. After decades of contact with European customs, some women came to expect their husbands to assume a more dominant role in supervising household members. Among the Oneidas, Kirkland reported how a recently remarried widow with a dozen children "came to me with a heavy complaint, that her husband would not assist her in the government and instruction of her Children, that the burden all lay upon her, that she alone was obliged to correct [them]." Some women found the decline of the extended female-headed household to their detriment. In 1766 Johnson sent Margaret, "the Wife of *Daniel* a Mohock," to seek refuge at Wheelock's school. Having been mistreated by her husband, she was in need of "retiring from his Resentment for a time." One can only suspect that new residential patterns necessitated her removal. Had she been living, as many Mohawks were, in a nuclear family unit, then she would have been under the immediate wrath of her husband. Spatial separation from female kin could result in a loss of physical protection.[41]

But the situation of Margaret was extreme and, according to the documents, uncommon. It also stands in contrast to the experience of another Mohawk woman named Margaret, the mother of Joseph and Molly Brant. By the late 1760s, Margaret's household was a small one. Her husband, Brant Canagaraduncka, had passed away and Molly now resided at Johnson Hall. But living with Margaret, son Joseph, daughter-in-law Peggy, and grandchildren may have been others, including Canagaraduncka's godson, Brant Kaghneghtago. By Iroquois practice, Margaret was still the head of the household, although male colonists begged to differ. In the mid-1760s, missionary Theophilus Chamberlain lodged at the Brant home, but, perturbed by the unfriendly reception of "the old woman," as he referred to Margaret, he left. He noted her displeasure. She "took me by the Throat and bid me come home," Chamberlain recorded. "She did this in a manner so faint that I easily read from it the meaning of her heart. She very well knows that Joseph will never be pleased at my living out of his house, unless I had one of my own; and his return is shortly expected." Chamberlain assumed that Margaret was concerned by her son's reaction to his moving out. But it is just as likely that Margaret enjoined Chamberlain to return because she was keen to maintain her community-sanctioned role as gracious hostess, or she may have been angered that he had insulted her hospitality. That a native woman could cause a European man to pack his bags and leave further points to her domestic power. If Margaret retained authority over the household, her female line retained ownership of the actual house. Following her death, her daughter Molly inherited the home, thus demonstrating the persistence of matrilineal descent.[42] External pressures may have altered the form of matrilineal structures, but they did not destroy this core aspect of Iroquois culture. The sustained power of the matrilineal lineage—even if it was now separated among smaller households—and women's ongoing economic centrality provided important bulwarks against patriarchal forces.

Another indication of the continued status enjoyed by women in Iroquois society was the high regard assigned to clan matrons. During the Anglo-Indian War, Thomas King from Oquaga reassured Johnson that head women would "use their Endeavours . . . [to] keep their Sons, and Husbands at home." Women's words, King promised, would "be of some Service" to Johnson "as they have a great deal to say in our Nation." Women from other communities used their influence to encourage male relatives to act "the manly part" and join British forces.[43] Clan matrons asserted themselves in diplomatic affairs especially when issues of land were involved. At a meeting with Johnson in 1761 to discuss the activities of George Klock, Canajoharie headmen attended with "the first Woman of the Wolf Tribe, named Esther." At a later meeting in 1763, "33 of the principal Women of Conajoharee" were present.[44] The high status attached to women, particularly female heads of clans, was notably evident among the Senecas. At the outbreak of the Anglo-Indian War, "the Women of the Seneca" appealed "to the Women of other Nations" to persuade their men to take up arms against the British. Similarly, when the Senecas sued for peace, "a great number of women" accompanied the delegation to Fort Johnson to negotiate the terms of surrender. Seneca women continued to express their views on matters of war. In 1767, "the old women of the Sinecas" warned "their Young Men from going to War" against southern Indians. Fort commanders and commissaries paid special attention to native women of influence. In 1771 John Brown at Niagara reported to Johnson of having met a Seneca woman "*of great Consequence*" who lived in the Ohio Valley. "I am informd that the Woman has very great influence over three Villages," he noted. Queen Catherine, otherwise known as Catherine Montour, was a Seneca woman of particular renown. Her village at the head of Seneca Lake was generally referred to as French Catherine's Town.[45]

Yet, despite outward signs of cultural continuity, the situation of clan matrons had altered over the course of the eighteenth century as they found that social prestige did not always translate into actual tangible power. Part of the challenge they faced came in the form of patriarchs like Johnson, who continued his two-pronged approach of courting and curtailing women's political prerogatives. He praised women for "their Sagacity and cordial Esteem" and made it his job to identify and reward head women.[46] But he also actively discouraged their involvement in political affairs. In 1768, he sent headmen word not to bring women to attend the Fort Stanwix Treaty "as business is best carried on when none but fit men go about it." He also sought to interfere in the selection of hereditary chiefs by insisting that such men be brought before him. Guy Johnson noted in the 1770s that men who were in line to assume hereditary titles were "generally brought to the Superintendant, to be approved of, and receive his Medal." On at least one occasion Johnson sought social sanction for this role when he "marched on at the Head of the Sachems singing the condoling song which contains the names, laws, and Customs of their renowned ancestors."[47]

For the most part Iroquois communities continued to reject Johnson's attempts to divorce women from the political process. But entanglement in an imperial system meant that it was not always possible or advisable to allow indigenous gender practices to shape diplomatic exchanges. In order to protect their own interests, chiefs and clan matrons found that it was sometimes necessary to bow to patriarchal practices. When the Canajoharies desired an accurate account of their landholdings in 1760, they requested their land be surveyed "in the presence of our Young Men and Boys in order to prevent contention and Debate for the future."[48] That "men and boys" took charge in what had always been a female sphere of influence demonstrates the Canajoharies' understanding of British gender norms.

A deeper threat to the authority of clan matrons arose as a consequence of the transforming nature of village politics. Ever since contact with Europeans began in the seventeenth century, the rules for obtaining power and leadership among the Iroquois had been shifting. In pre-contact society, the nobility had occupied political offices and carried much influence over village affairs. The rise of the Iroquois Confederacy encouraged men other than those in line for hereditary offices to attain positions of power. By demonstrations of their oratory skills, shrewd diplomacy, or martial valor, these Pine Tree Chiefs won local support and achieved dominance in village politics. Growing entanglement with the British Empire intensified this internal political transformation by providing men with additional means for acquiring wealth, status, and power. Patronage by British officials and participation in imperial wars and a market economy gave rise to a new generation of independently wealthy warriors and chiefs. Johnson deliberately sponsored merit chiefs throughout his career. Through the distribution of money, medals, and clothing, he provided head warriors with the material backing needed to obtain political influence. Because those who acquired new wealth were not necessarily those who already enjoyed a prominent social position, established sources of authority were challenged. In the late eighteenth century, it was wealthy warriors and their families, not necessarily clan matrons and hereditary chiefs, who determined the course of village politics.[49]

The emergence of a warrior elite whose martial exploits and personal wealth translated into political potency contested the influence of female clan heads. Enjoying a new source of power and prestige, and perhaps feeling less duty-bound to their maternal aunts as a consequence of no longer living in extended households, warriors were less concerned about having their actions endorsed. Despite their repeated calls on warriors to "lay down their Arms," clan matrons found it "extremely hard to prevail on the generality of the Warriors" to heed their words. By the 1770s, clan matrons' authority over warriors had in many instances become more ceremonial than substantial. In council after council, spokesmen assured Johnson that head women "who have much influence" over "young men" recommended them to pursue peace while younger male relations continued to engage in frontier violence. The rhetoric of women's restraining power can be partly explained as a political device designed to placate Johnson. It also reveals that regardless of their actual power to affect political change, clan matrons continued to hold a highly esteemed and ritually vibrant role within their communities.[50]

As warriors conducted themselves as an autonomous force in their own right they also challenged long-held kinship patterns between men. Warriors had customarily referred to their male elders as uncles, thus acknowledging social deference. Yet warriors increasingly behaved in nondeferential ways. Asserting warrior autonomy and power, Thomas King informed the Pennsylvania governor in 1762 that "Counsellors can do nothing unless the Warriors should give their Consent to it." Seneca warriors displayed similar disregard for their male elders. They claimed that warriors were "the People of Consequence for Managing Affairs," not their chiefs, who were "a parcell of Old People who say Much, but who Mean or Act very little." Among the Oneidas, Kirkland observed that "the Warriours for the most part are uncontrouled by the *Sachems* or Lords." Oneida headmen agreed, noting, "we are poor Creatures [and] have no strength and authority. If we say that which is good and right so far as we know, we are not regarded."[51]

Although there may have been a tradition in Iroquois political discourse to emphasize the respective rise and decline of warrior-chief status, the frequency and quality of this claim waxed over the course of the eighteenth century. To be sure, invoking self-impotence could serve a political convenience. By professing a debilitated status, headmen shrugged off responsibility for the aggressive behavior of young men from their villages. But equally chiefs had good reason to believe that their ability to control younger men had weakened. The Seven Years' War after all encouraged new ways for warriors to obtain wealth and prestige, which undermined the importance of deference and hereditary status that had once played a far greater role in ordering relations between men. In addition to lamenting their loss of power, civil headmen began searching for new ways to regain their sanctioning powers over warriors, some by appealing to Johnson. In 1764 Oneida headmen from Oquaga asked the superintendent to provide them with paper passports so that they could control the movements of younger men. By assuming the right to dispense passes they could compel warriors to obtain "the Consent of their Councellors" before they left their village. Headmen called on Johnson in 1770 to deter warriors from going to war with the Cherokees, causing warriors to be "not well pleased." Older men were also drawn to Christianity as a means to augment their authority over unruly warriors, particularly with its message of temperance, submission, and restraint. Through preaching and practicing the gospel, they hoped to regain the respect of warriors, thus bringing them back into their fold. In a noted act of deference, Oquaga warriors in 1764 told their headmen, "Your Example of Piety has entirely, reclaimed us, insomuch, that we are to assure you we shall quit the immoderate use of Liquor, and other Vices, and be entirely directed by your Councils."[52] Yet such statements often lacked substance as warriors continued to resist constraints. This generational conflict between warriors and chiefs was not simply about the right of younger men to wage war when they wanted but pointed to much larger issues about how power was to be attained, distributed, and exercised along gendered lines in Iroquois society.

As Iroquois men and women—to varying degrees—renegotiated gendered roles and relations, they were also involved in the no less complex task of reconceptualizing their ethnic identity and relations with non-Iroquoians. The Iroquois had long applied kinship terms to describe their connection with European settlers. Through fictive and actual adoption they incorporated outsiders into their lineages. Dependent on Iroquois neighbors as economic partners and martial allies, frontier settlers had responded in kind. Consequently, for decades the imperial frontier was characterized by a high degree of cultural fluidity. A striking feature of the post–Seven Years' War period was the degree to which cultural fluidity gave way to a more rigid racial divide. Hostility and confrontation came to mark relations between the Iroquois and colonial settlers as both sides began to refashion group identities.

In the 1760s, a virulent form of Indian-hating gripped the colonial populace living on the fringes of empire as they engaged in acts of violence against native peoples. The rise in Indian-hating was particularly acute in the colonies of Pennsylvania, Maryland, and Virginia, where the murder of Indians became all too common.[53] Johnson, troubled by the state of affairs, noted that colonists treated "Indians with contempt, much greater than they had ever before experienced." He observed that older forms of cultural accommodation with natives were now impossible given "the utter aversion our people have for them in general, and . . . the imprudence with which they constantly express it." Colonial Indian-hating found its most frightening expression when a group of frontier inhabitants, dubbed the Paxton Boys, callously murdered twenty friendly Christian Indians in Conestoga and Lancaster, Pennsylvania, in 1763 and then attempted to kill a further 140 Moravian Indians seeking refuge in Philadelphia. The event was rendered more troubling by the response of local inhabitants who applauded the Paxton Boys' efforts and shielded them from the authorities.[54]

Implicit in this Indian-hating was the genesis of a racial doctrine. By the 1760s, a new ideology focusing on internal physiological factors overshadowed an older belief that environmental conditions such as religion and climate were the primary source of human difference. Increasingly native peoples were dehumanized and denounced as savages who were naturally and thus permanently inferior. Frontier warfare played a part in racializing Anglo-American attitudes toward Indians. Indian raids, scalping, and captive taking during the Seven Years' War and Anglo-Indian War fueled racial hatred and ignited a desire for revenge. Yet previous episodes of Anglo-Indian warfare in the seventeenth century had also ignited virulent denunciations of "Indian savagery" but did not give rise to a fully developed and widely embraced racial doctrine. Former outbreaks of hostility proved to be ephemeral and sporadic. The 1760s stands apart from earlier periods precisely because pejorative attitudes began to mature into a racist discourse. This discourse did not abate but gained coherence and universal appeal over the following decades. By the early nineteenth century, racial thought was fused with pseudo-scientific theory.[55]

A particular set of socioeconomic conditions developed in the second half of the eighteenth century that made it possible, and indeed preferable, to cultivate and sustain a racial ideology. The growth in racism coincided with unprecedented and for the most part illegal efforts to settle the west. The defeat of New France provided British colonists with a novel opportunity to stake claims to western lands. Although Indians still inhabited this region, colonists made confident by their swelling numbers ventured west with boundless determination. The frontier inhabitants who attacked Indians and who "openly avow, that they will never find a Man guilty of Murther for killing an Indian" were the same individuals who built homes and communities on Indian lands. These two acts of racializing Indians and expropriating their resources went hand in hand. Johnson frequently cursed frontier settlers because they "not only perpetrate Murders whenever opportunity offers, but think themselves at liberty to make settlements where they please." The rise in racial hostility cannot be disentangled from this economic phenomenon. Constructing racial models to dehumanize Indians provided a means of absolving acts of dispossession.[56]

An emergent racial model that posited that Indians were naturally inferior and treacherous provided a framework for colonists to view all Indians including the Iroquois. In the 1760s, Iroquois Indians who ventured onto southern frontiers frequently became victims of indiscriminate violence. An Iroquois chief was murdered in 1765 as he traveled between Fort Cumberland and Fort Bedford in Pennsylvania. A year later a Mohawk was killed and scalped by Samuel Jacobs near Fort Cumberland as he returned home from Cherokee country. Jacobs fled to the backcountry of Virginia where he found protection among settlers.[57] In April 1766, Robert Seymour murdered an Oneida Indian trading in New Jersey. Adam, the Oneida chief at Oquaga, noted that the deceased "had always been a firm friend to the English, accompanying their Armies every Campaign," and concluded that Seymour had murdered "without any Cause, but from mere dislike to Indians." Johnson agreed, informing Gage that the murder resulted from "the ill timed resentment of the Country People, who think they do good Service when they Knock an Indian in the Head." He further added, "I am well informed they intend to do so with all they meet in small partys."[58] The Fort Stanwix Treaty did little to stem the tide of violence. In July 1769, German settler Peter Reed reportedly murdered the son of Johnson's longtime ally Seneca George near the Susquehanna River. In 1770, Johnson paid a large gift to an Oneida family after colonists murdered the father and his two sons. Mathew Haley murdered two Senecas near Fort Pitt in 1771, and two years later a mini-war broke out between Ohio Indians and Virginians after Michael Cresap and others murdered over thirty Shawnee and Seneca Indians near the forks of the Ohio River.[59]

Although the southern frontiers provide the most extreme cases of rampant Indian-hating, racial disdain also became more pronounced in postwar New York.[60] Along the Mohawk Valley, relations between the eastern Iroquois and their colonial neighbors soured as the latter group, secure in their numbers and desirous of procuring greater resources, continued to dissolve ties of reciprocity. While some genuine friendships persisted, a growing number of settlers viewed Indians at best with indifference, at worst with hostility. Their increasingly hostile behavior caused the eastern Iroquois to reassess the usefulness of kinship metaphors to define relations. As headmen noted, those who threatened to dispossess them were "those whom we always considered as our Children." Such settlers had "formerly regarded us whilst we were men, and they then were children," observed another, but "now they are by our means, by Land [and] trade etc. become rich, and powerful, and are now endeavoring to deprive us of what little Land we have Left."[61]

Racial discord was apparent soon after hostilities ceased between the British and French. Despite their "good behaviour" during the war, Mohawk warriors complained how they were "met with a bad return" from their neighbors. George Klock, the German settler involved in illegal land claims, deliberately spread inflammatory propaganda in which he accused the Mohawks of "Scalping and other depredations" in order to arouse anti-Indian feeling. In early 1763, two local men, Richard Allen and Mr. McKnight, used the butt end of a whip and a stick to beat an Indian passing their wagon "in a most unmerciful manner." There was no apparent motive for the attack according to a Dutch eyewitness who claimed that had he not intervened, "they would have beat the Indian to Death." Despite having recently fought together against the French, a growing strain of racial contempt marred the outlook and behavior of some frontier settlers. The Anglo-Indian War breathed new life into racial animosity as colonists proved receptive to reports of Indian treachery. New York newspapers printed stories that Mohawk warriors had participated in frontier violence in Pennsylvania. The distinct caps they wore supposedly verified their identity. Johnson, outraged by these false reports, fumed that the Mohawk did not even wear head caps. In 1764, the Mohawks complained of the violence perpetrated by several neighbors who "use them vastly Ill, by turning their Cattle into the Indians' Corn fields, and beat their Women and Children when Driveing them out." Johnson noted to his colleague that "this has been often done, but more so of late in the absence of their Young Men." Such violence drove a wedge between communities.[62]

Even after the passions of war abated, tensions in the Mohawk Valley continued. Klock with an array of accomplices and on two separate occasions inveigled a number of drunken Indians to accompany him to England. Keen to exploit their perceived exoticism by London audiences, he literally put them on show to make money. The wider Mohawk community was incensed by Klock's exploitative enterprise and vowed revenge. Another neighbor, Cobus Maybe, incited animosity. When Theyanoguin's widow refused to lend Maybe a sled he let forth a torrent of verbal abuse, threatening the entire community "that they would soon be sent a packing from thence by the Governor as having no right to the lands." Men like Klock, Maybe, and others involved in illegal land claims continued to spread malicious reports designed to arouse anti-Indian feeling. In June 1767, the Mohawks learned that complaints against them "of a very serious nature" had been sent to the governor. Creating an atmosphere in which Indians were regarded as untrustworthy, naturally violent, and less than human made it easier to dispossess them of their property. By the early 1770s, the Mohawks could no longer depend on the once-taken-for-granted hospitality of German neighbors. After meetings at Johnson Hall, the superintendent was obliged to provision the Mohawks for their journey home. As he noted in his journal, "the Inhabitants wou'd not give them a Morsel since the War." This aggrieved the Mohawks, who had been promised by "them formerly (when they sold and gave them lands) that they shou'd always be welcome to their Houses." Hostility sometimes manifested into violence. In 1773, Johnson paid for the burial of a Mohawk chief who was "supposed to [have been] drowned by the White People, and which caused much uneasiness." The ill manners of valley inhabitants convinced many Mohawk that "some evil designs" had been formulated against them. Concerned about their physical safety, they appealed to Johnson to interpose to prevent their being "murdered treacherously and basely" just as the Conestago Indians had been in 1764, for "they imagined [that] was what their neighbours intended" for them.[63]

Charles Inglis noted the swelling tide of racism in his memorial to the Board of Trade in 1771. Wishing to secure funds for a missionary program, Inglis first needed to make a strong counterargument against the charge that the Iroquois were racially inferior. Inglis was worried by the prevalent belief among colonists that the Iroquois were "incapable of being civilised or brought over to Christianity." He refuted this sentiment: "I grant the Iroquois are ignorant, when compared with civilised Nations; but certainly we should distinguish between Ignorance and Dulness—between the Want of Knowledge and the Want of Capacity to receive it." The Iroquois were capable of change, he affirmed, as "Whoever has any Acquaintance" with them "must know they are not deficient in Point of Understanding." Human differences were not rooted in the body, rather "Culture, with other external Circumstances, constitute the principle Difference between the various Parts of Mankind."[64] The opinion of Inglis, however, was losing appeal. Colonists had little interest in promoting the Christian conversion of Indians. Instead, emphasizing points of difference was a necessary first step in the process of racializing and abusing onetime allies.

Despite the refusal of a growing number of colonists to live up to kinship ideals, many eastern Iroquois resisted the temptation of viewing them through the lens of race. Ever since a chapel and fort had been built among the Tiononderoge community and four "kings" had visited Queen Anne in 1711, the Mohawks had been acquiring an identity that was increasingly "British" and "imperial." They expressed their identification with Britons in new patterns of housing, dress, and gendered familial arrangements. Christian conversion among the Oneidas also inhibited racialized ways of constructing group identity. At the ethnically mixed settlement of Oquaga, Christianity served as a powerful component in newly emerging ethnic identities. The presence of a Christian mission on the site since 1748 had made tremendous inroads in articulations of group identity. So considerable was the effect of Christianity that by the 1770s the principal source of tension in the community was not between pagans and converts but between Anglicans and New Lights adherents.[65] Although critical of the behavior of colonists, many eastern Iroquois continued to stress their common humanity and shared history. They recounted the wars in which they had fought alongside one another, pointed to economic ties of trade and land that bound them together, and most of all they upheld their Christianity as evidence of their cultural similarity. This effort to highlight their sameness was not a mark of weakness or sign of subservience but a means to shame and chastise the "unbrotherlike" conduct of colonial neighbors.[66]

By contrast, however, a far greater number of Iroquois residing in central and western New York readily abandoned a familial language to define intercultural relations. Troubled by the aggressively expansive presence of the British and generally being "in a Very discontented state on account of all the late ill Conduct of the Frontier Inhabitants," many Senecas, Cayugas, and

Onondagas tried and tested new racial models of understanding. Violence and theft committed by traders, settlers, and soldiers confirmed to them the futility of kinship terms and encouraged them to instead embrace a racialized language of difference. Rather than identify with Euro-Americans and their culture, the western Iroquois increasingly advocated a doctrine of racial separatism.[67]

The move toward separatism, however, was a drawn-out and untidy affair. In particular, the presence of English captives, deserters, and children of mixed racial descent living among them complicated the process of (re)defining group identity. English captives became a mounting source of friction within Indian communities as residents began to reassess whether kinship or race was more significant in determining Iroquois membership. The wars of the mid-eighteenth century had created ample opportunity to secure captives for adoption at the same time that it rendered this practice more troublesome, heightening tensions with the British but also between Indians. By the 1760s, the Senecas had become far more cautious when adopting Europeans, recognizing the limits to successful integration. Total assimilation required captives to adopt not only Indian language, dress, gender roles, and lifestyle but Indian identity as well, and even this might not guarantee full acceptance by the rest of the village. Although she spent the vast majority of her life as a Seneca woman, Jemison was suspected "for a long time" of being a witch by the wider community.[68] Fighting alongside warriors against the British provided one way to establish one's Indian credentials, but it did not ensure permanent Indian residency. In 1764, during the Anglo-Indian War, Johnson learned of "a White Man" residing among the Senecas for several years who had committed "Treachery" against the British at the Niagara Carrying Place. Despite his staunch pro-Indian sentiment, this acculturated captive could not prevent villagers from delivering him up to the British. Even after he escaped and fled back to the Senecas, he was again returned. While the British exerted immense pressure on the Senecas to relinquish captives, some Iroquois equally felt that non-Indians no longer belonged.[69]

The Senecas exhibited an increasingly instrumental attitude toward Euro-American captives. Instead of transforming captives into kin and adopting them into Indian lineages, the Senecas found nonfamilial uses for them. The Chenussio Senecas held onto captives following the Anglo-Indian War in the hopes that British troops were less likely to attack their villages if they contained English women and children. Captives also possessed important skills that enhanced their value, such as blacksmithing. Instead of being adopted into households, captives could be kept in a form of servitude. Following the Anglo-Indian War, one Seneca village returned most of the captives taken during that conflict except "two Young Girls whom they want for Work."[70]

Despite a shared hostility toward the British army, the Senecas did not automatically welcome or trust the presence of deserters in their villages either. Experience had taught them that soldiers often desired to live among them out of self-interest instead of a real sense of kinship and common identity. Christopher Strobel fled to the Senecas after deserting from Oswego in 1756, but once the Seven Years' War ended he left their community to settle along the Mohawk River. His voluntary removal from the Indians earned him significant grace from Johnson, who urged Gage not to punish him for desertion, at the same time that it reaffirmed to the Senecas the impermanency of kinship ties forged during the exigencies of war.[71] The ability of deserters to ingratiate themselves among the western Iroquois depended on how "Indian" they behaved. Lewis Andrews, who by 1774 had "lived many years" among the Iroquois after deserting from the 46th Regiment, managed to affix himself to their community by having "married one of their Women," with whom he had "several Children." However, his Indian family recognized that he continued to hold strong ties to the British and went on his behalf to appeal to Johnson that his crime of desertion be annulled.[72] A notorious deserter named Sherlock reportedly went about painted as an Indian warrior and was often heard saying that "he'd rather kill [the] English than any other people." But once again the Seneca community was prepared to hand him over to the British, causing Sherlock to abscond.[73] Under pressure from imperial authorities and increasingly suspicious of whether genuine, long-lasting ties of kinship could be forged with non-Indians, a growing number of Senecas preferred to exchange deserters for economic rewards. Thus, in 1762, the Senecas were "greatly pleased" after receiving a sum of money, ammunition, and provisions for delivering up fourteen deserters to the fort commander at Niagara.[74]

As attitudes toward the value of non-Indian captives shifted in the late eighteenth century, the subject of interracial unions became more contentious on both sides of the frontier. Historically, Iroquois women in their role as wives and consorts to European men provided an invaluable service as facilitators between cultures. But in the postwar period, the western Iroquois came to view this form of imperial entanglement with growing distaste. Part of the problem was the altered context in which these unions occurred.[75] An influx of British and provincial troops to western posts since the war had created enlarged opportunities for sexual unions to occur. But these were not, for the most part, local men accustomed to the practices and mores of Iroquois Indians. Nor did they hold long-term interests in the region. Temporarily assigned to posts, soldiers exhibited intensely casual attitudes in their relations with native women. Iroquois headmen complained to Johnson of "their frequent acts of violence offered . . . to our Women" at forts. Jeffrey Amherst, during his encampment at Oswego, personally observed the mistreatment of one native woman who "had entertained herself so often with the Soldiers that she was almost dying." In the late 1760s, soldiers at Fort Niagara were in the practice of applying for passes "when he finds the spirit move[s] him for a Squaw." On the late colonial frontier, in western New York, casual sexual relations rather than genuine long-term unions tended to be the norm.[76]

Even if marriages occurred, a growing racial divide in British North America altered the meaning and evolution of these partnerships. In November 1769, an anonymous Seneca woman married James Stevenson, the Albany-born fort commander at Niagara. The Seneca wife, described by her English husband as an "*Amiable*" and "*accomplish'd young lady*," had much to gain through this union. Stevenson's military ranking made him an attractive partner. As the Iroquois confronted abusive traders and settlers it made sense to integrate Anglo-American men of influence into kinship networks. Stevenson earned a reputation of being sympathetic to Indians: he instructed soldiers to behave civilly and dispensed medals and passes. His frequently mentioned friendship with Johnson made a positive impression on his wife and her family, and she made sure to send her regards to the superintendent via her husband. There were other advantages to be had. Her British husband enhanced her social status by providing her with goods to distribute among her village. But Stevenson too had much to gain, perhaps more, through this marriage. Rather than demonstrating genuine affection for his wife or a heartfelt desire to bridge two cultures, Stevenson used his marriage to promote imperial interests over indigenous well-being. He employed his wife to improve British standing among the Senecas. "In order to keep up the good name of the English," he informed Johnson, "I will load her with presents." Thus, he boasted, "even in my *amours* I have still the good of the *publick* in view." His marital connection to the Iroquois granted him important influence, which he was prepared to use against the Senecas. Upon hearing about tensions between the Senecas and other Indian nations, Stevenson coolly remarked that his familial ties would make it "an easy matter to stir up some mischief amongst them." Like his wife, Stevenson had much to gain from this union, but unlike her, he had far less to lose when the relationship dissolved.[77]

Soon after celebrating the birth of their "fine Boy" the Seneca wife faced
a dilemma in March 1771 when her husband began efforts to remove their
son from her family. About to be transferred to another post, Stevenson was
troubled by the prospect of leaving his son to be raised in a culture that he believed was alien and inferior. "If the Child is brought up a Savage," Stevenson
noted, "it will be impossible to leave him any thing . . . [as] he would not know
how to make use of it." As part of his tactics of persuasion Stevenson paid a
substantial monetary gift to his wife's family. Revealing his cavalier attitude
toward the marriage, Stevenson grumbled to Johnson, "I can assure you that
the family have cost me £250, 'tho she was with me but one year." He further
complained that he was still "oblig'd to shew" his wife his "usual affection" but
hoped that it would "not be attended with any fruitfull consequences meerly
from the difficulty of getting Children from them."[78]

Other soldiers who had children with Indian women also sought to have
them removed, such as a "Mr. Francis" of the 44th regiment who persuaded
his Seneca consort, the sister of Silverheels, to relinquish their child. Many
British officials believed that it was preferable that such children be raised in
colonial society. Following the Anglo-Indian War, Colonel Bouquet was authorized to retrieve English captives and their mixed offspring, a policy fully
endorsed by Johnson. As he told Bouquet, "I cannot but think your compelling them to give up the Children born of White Women was highly Judicious, for that mixed Race forgetting their Ancestry on one side are found to
be the most Inveterate of any, and would greatly Augment their numbers."[79]

Some Iroquois also began to express suspicion and unease over the presence of biracial children. Seneca chief Cornplanter, the son of a Seneca woman
and Dutch trader, recalled how other Indian boys treated him as an object of
curiosity during his youth: "They took notice of my skin being a different
color from theirs and spoke about it." Similarly, Jemison's métis children were
looked upon differently because of their fair complexion.[80] This shift in attitude may explain why the sister of Silverheels and consort to Mr. Francis felt
compelled to give up her infant. In a period of imperial aggrandizement she
may have believed her child would be better-off living in Anglo-American
society. That she came from a pro-British family—Silverheels was a staunch
ally of Johnson—made the decision easier. During the Anglo-Indian War she
actually sought refuge at Fort Niagara because she feared political tensions
within her own community. As anti-British feeling swelled in many Seneca
villages throughout the 1760s, she had reason to fear for the safety of her
infant. For unspecified reasons Mr. Francis abandoned his child among the

French Iroquois. In 1771, distressed and relatively powerless, this despairing mother appealed to the new commanding officer at Fort Niagara to assist her in redeeming her child.[81]

While Silverheels's sister petitioned an Englishman to retrieve her infant, the nameless Seneca wife confronted the meddling efforts of a Mohawk woman who attempted to procure her son. Stevenson enlisted the help of Molly Brant in his custody battle. She may have negotiated with the wife's family on Stevenson's behalf or perhaps simply offered Stevenson advice. Either way she provided valuable aid. In March 1774, Stevenson wrote, "I beg my Comp[lemen]ts to Molly and thank her for the pains she has taken relative to the Child." As an Iroquois, and as a woman, she was the most appropriate person to arbitrate the conflict between the Seneca wife and Stevenson. That she chose to use her knowledge and skills to serve the interests of the latter demonstrates the level of her political loyalty to the British and degree of her acculturation to European norms.[82] But it seems that even her efforts failed. The unnamed Seneca wife managed to hold onto her son but only until the outbreak of the Revolutionary War, when, according to one source, she was "constrained by her fierce and jealous relatives to abandon the hated offspring in the woods, near Cayuga Lake." The young child was taken in by another Indian family and eventually reunited with his mother after the war. Captain James Stevenson, as he came to be called, lived among the Seneca community at Buffalo for the remainder of his life. Although his father left him money when he died, there is little evidence that Stevenson Jr. had much contact with his non-Indian relatives. Ultimately, the marriage of a nameless Seneca woman to an Anglo-American reveals much about the limits of forging familial ties over an increasingly racialized frontier.[83]

As the language of kinship ceased to make sense of Indian-colonial relations, western Iroquois communities began to embrace a nativist ideology. Since the 1740s, Indian nativism had flourished in the refugee communities of the Ohio Valley as a series of prophets encouraged Indians to revitalize "traditional" rituals. By rejecting European ways, including trade and alcohol use, and reverting to indigenous practices, nativist proponents held that it was possible for Indian society to be reinvigorated. In the early 1760s, a Delaware prophet named Neolin powerfully articulated this message. His promise of Indian revitalization spread among the Indians of the Ohio and Great Lakes regions and provided the ideological underpinnings of the Anglo-Indian War.[84] Increasingly, the western Iroquois were attracted to this nativist doctrine. In numerous villages, Indians renewed the religious observance of age-old rituals. Jemison recalled the active religious life of the Senecas in the postwar decade as they "pertinaciously observed the religious rites of the progenitors, by attending with the most scrupulous exactness and a great deal of enthusiasm to . . . sacrifices."[85]

More than simply encouraging a return to an older way of life, the nativist movement helped foster a pan-Indian identity rooted in a belief of separate origins. For at least two decades, segments of the Iroquois had been developing a discourse on difference, which asserted that distinctions between Indians and Europeans were preordained by the Great Spirit and were therefore both natural and necessary. This ideological precept became more pronounced in the 1760s. A year before the outbreak of the Anglo-Indian War, an Onondaga had a vision in which the Creator outlined to him the distinct destinies he intended for Indians and Europeans. The Great Spirit told him "that when He first made the World, He gave this large Island to the Indians for their Use; at the same time He gave other Parts of the World beyond the great Waters to the rest of his creation, and gave them different languages: That He now saw the white People squabbling, and fighting for these Lands which He gave the Indians . . . This He said, was so contrary to his Intention."[86]

From the 1760s onward, the Iroquois more readily articulated a belief that their way of life was divinely sanctioned by the Great Spirit, sometimes implying a biological basis to such differences: "they say that it appears to them to have been ordained from the beginning that the White People should Cultivate the Arts, and themselves pursue hunting, that no other Way of Life is agreable to them, or consistent with their Maxims of policy and the frame of their Constitution." Men believed that their "Liberty and Happiness" depended on the pursuit of war and hunting and that any other activity was "unworthy the dignity of man." The dangers of cultural conversion were confirmed to them by the example of the New England Indians, who, having abandoned their older way of life, appeared impoverished and demoralized. In Iroquois eyes these Indians had adopted European flaws "without retaining their former Abilities for gaining a Subsistence in the only way they conceive that Nature intended they should." Johnson noted how this belief that Indians were supposed to live differently from colonists was "constantly instilled into the Minds of [their] Youth by often bringing before them the State of those poor-beings-Indians whom they call Women."[87]

When Kirkland attempted to establish a mission at the Seneca town of Kanadesaga in 1765, he experienced firsthand the evolution of a racialized

Indian identity. Although Kirkland had been welcomed by a segment of the community, even symbolically adopted into his host's family, many resented his presence. Located on the northern tip of Lake Seneca, Kanadesaga was the easternmost Seneca village established during the Seven Years' War. One of its leading headmen, Sayenqueraghta, was a professed ally of the British, as were many others in the community. But a growing cohort in Kanadesaga had begun to espouse a new doctrine of racial exclusivity. Among them was Captain Onoingwadekha. He abhorred Kirkland's mission, viewing it as a further assault on his people. He blamed him for his men's refusal to go on the warpath against the Cherokees, claiming that the missionary had "*poisoned their minds* by white people's notions." Rejecting Kirkland's adopted status, Onoingwadekha and others believed that racial difference outstripped fictive kinship ties.[88]

The tense situation was exacerbated when Kirkland's Indian host, a noted elder chief, mysteriously died. Onoingwadekha and others used the situation to arouse anti-white sentiment to have Kirkland removed. In a passionate debate that took place among headmen over Kirkland's fate, Onoingwadekha spoke vehemently on the dangers of racial contamination. He warned that Kirkland was not a benign individual but a foreign agent, a "white man" carrying a "dark design." The chief danger lay in the "white people's book," the Bible, that Kirkland brought with him. The speaker admonished that "this book was never made for *Indians*"; rather, the "*Upholder of the Skies*" gave Indians their own set of instructions: "He wrote it in our heads and in our minds and gave us rules about worshipping him." By performing these ancient rites, earlier generations had enjoyed success in hunting and warfare, but now, overfamiliarity with "*White people and their manners*" endangered Indian society. As Indians neglected to enact customary religious rites they placed their community in peril. The death of the elder headman, who had foolishly welcomed Kirkland into his home, was an omen of "approaching evils." For the survival of their people it was necessary to maintain a policy of racial separatism: "if we Senecas . . . receive this *white man* and attend to the Book which was made solely for White people, we shall become a *miserable abject people*."[89]

Not content with simply pursuing a doctrine of separatism, the western Senecas desired to remove or at least diminish British power in North America. Increasingly they embraced a hostile stance and growing contempt for *whites*. Throughout the 1760s, the Chenussio Senecas engaged in a series of aggressive acts. After the Anglo-Indian War, they continued in their efforts to form a pan-Indian movement. Forging a union with other Indians was a pragmatic political strategy made possible by a developing sense of shared grievances and common identity. During a council meeting between Seneca and Canadian Indians, a colonial trader observed how each side declared "to Each Other that when One was hurt they would feel it Equally so." A year before the Fort Stanwix Treaty, the Chenussio galvanized anti-British feeling in the west by sending war belts among the Ohio villages. They warned of British intentions to rob them of their lands, encouraged violent resistance, and attempted to organize a conference for the purpose of uniting Indians to "become One People." Following the treaty they frequently clashed with frontier settlers, whom they denounced as "*Hogs*." Indian agent Alexander McKee reported how they created havoc around Fort Pitt, "Killing Cattle, Stealing Horses, and in short plundering every House and Field they come to." They also refused to attend British-Iroquois conferences. In the late 1760s, the Chenussio leader Gaustarax again sent war belts to western Indians and by the early 1770s lent support to the Shawnees, who emerged as leaders of a new pan-Indian confederacy in the Ohio country. For some Iroquois by the late colonial period, peaceful coexistence with those of European descent was no longer deemed possible or even desirable. Instead these Indians envisioned a world strikingly similar to many colonists in which British North America was carefully demarcated between *Indian* and *white*.[90]

Iroquois efforts to construct gender, ethnic, and racial identities spanned an entire spectrum. From Canajoharie in the Mohawk Valley to Oquaga in the upper Susquehanna and Kanadesaga in western New York and beyond, Indians resisted, embraced, modified, and applied new ways of thinking about cultural roles and group identity. All across Iroquoia, Indians adjusted their gender system, even as they managed to maintain remarkable continuity to past practices. As they fended off accusations of racial inferiority by pointing to the savagery of "whites," or as they utilized discourses of divinely sanctioned differences to assert their own superiority, the Iroquois demonstrated their resilience. But acts of Indian agency need not be overstated. Shifting socioeconomic conditions in the late colonial period undermined the significance of Indian articulations of group identity. Most colonists largely ignored the efforts made by many eastern Iroquois to cast off their Indianness, preferring instead to focus on points of disparity, and while Indian nativism may have provided a source of empowerment for the western Iroquois, it only affirmed colonists' suspicions of Indian inherent savagery. Indian acts of self-definition proved to have diminishing import in determining the nature of their existence in the modern Atlantic world. Increasingly, their experience was taken up by having to deal with how more powerful groups in British North America defined them.

Conclusion

"'Westward, the Star of Empire takes its way,' and whenever that Empire is held by the white man, nothing is safe or unmolested or enduring against his avidity for gain." When Seneca Indian Maris B. Pierce spoke these words at a public meeting in 1839 in Buffalo, New York, he was referring specifically to the rising American empire. Just over fifty years old, this empire was in the throes of rapid territorial expansion aided in part by the 1830 passage of the Indian Removal Act. Unlike a century earlier, when their westerly position had protected them from colonial incursions, the Senecas in 1839 faced real and immediate threats to their lands. Dartmouth-educated Pierce mounted an articulate defense against removal, asserting the civilized status of his people. Foremost the Senecas had demonstrated a right to their lands by their successful adaptation to a market economy. "In business there is much greater diligence and industry," Pierce assured his middle-class Anglo-American audience. In agriculture "men labor more, comparatively, and the women less." Private landownership was commonplace, and men who chose not to farm were "willing to hire out their services to others, either by the year or by shares." Removing the Senecas to the "western wilds," Pierce warned, would only result in deadening the "spirit of enterprise" that now pervaded their communities, forcing them to live as earlier generations had through subsistence farming and hunting. But as Pierce affirmed, "we desire to renounce those habits of mind and body."[1]

In the 1830s, Pierce and his community found their economic security threatened by the self-aggrandizing efforts of a burgeoning empire. Their struggle was not an isolated or novel event but a continuation of a much longer struggle the Haudenosaunee had been engaged in as a consequence of the advent of colonization. At root, this was a struggle over economic resources. In the eighteenth century, it was the eastern Iroquois nations who were at the forefront of external pressures as they confronted the aggressive attempts of an ascending British mercantile capitalist empire, intent on securing their land, labor, and resources. Political, military, and cultural battles ensued as a consequence, but fundamentally it was the commodification and absorption of their economic resources that caused the Iroquois to be dislodged from their position of relative influence in the eighteenth-century colonial world.

Refusing to be stuck in a historical past, the eighteenth-century Iroquois reoriented economic pursuits to the rhythms of a flourishing market economy: they became land sellers and landlords, developing a commercial understanding of private property; they modified preexisting hunting and horticultural practices to meet the demands of local and foreign marketplaces; they demonstrated an ability to engage in new forms of wage labor; and they moved away from a barter economy to one that relied heavily on foreign currencies. Through this form of adaptation, the Iroquois found ways to exist, and in some cases even prosper, in the new colonial-imperial landscape.

However, absorption of Iroquois land, labor, and resources was not a pain-free process. Internally, the restructuring of Iroquois village economies by the late eighteenth century wore down older values centered on sharing and redistribution among some Indians and created new inequalities among the Mohawks and Oneidas. For the Iroquois as a whole, reliance on external markets and cash marked a loss of autonomy, which equated into a diminishing political importance on the colonial landscape. Whereas the Iroquois had assumed a potent and powerful role at the beginning of the eighteenth century, by the late 1760s, the colonial world viewed them as increasingly irrelevant. The problem was that the Iroquois were becoming more and more dependent on external trade networks and foreign currencies at the same time that colonists were becoming less and less dependent on them for martial labor, furs, or land. With the New York fur trade virtually eclipsed by the more western Great Lakes trade, the French counterweight removed, and having signed away thousands of acres of hunting grounds in the Fort Stanwix Treaty, the Iroquois had lost valuable resources in their bargaining position with the British. Economic negotiations still took place on the frontier, but power relations had begun to shift. The Iroquois had not become a colonized people, but they were no longer truly sovereign either. They still held onto their villages and cornfields and other economic assets but not to the extent that they had done so less than a century earlier. Ultimately economic dislocation, hastened by the Seven Years' War, undermined Iroquois ability to maintain their parity with the larger colonial world.

The Iroquois responded to new material realities by drawing on rich cultural resources. Carefully and creatively they incorporated new practices and forms into preexisting cultural frameworks; hence Mohawk men turned to animal husbandry as an extension of their role as hunters, while women combined their traditional role as farmers with new commercial pursuits. At the same time, however, structural material changes transformed their cultural world. In this dialectic between the material and the cultural, new gendered, ethnic, and racial identities evolved that were partially self-created but also partially imposed. Despite modifications to their gendered practices there remained tremendous continuity. The Mohawks in particular maintained gender parity even as they revised roles. Not prepared to allow new racial definitions to beat them down and stigmatize them, the Iroquois formulated their own racial discourses. Some identified themselves as members of the British Atlantic community, while for others the nativist movement provided a source of cultural and psychological empowerment. As they recrafted cultural roles and identities, they did not become any less Iroquois; they simply reconstituted the meaning of that term. The Iroquois persisted as a people because of their ability to change.

By formulating diverse and oftentimes contending identities, however, the Iroquois created new sources of social division and discord within their communities and the Confederacy at large. Tensions mounted between an older hierarchy of chiefs and clan matrons who held onto traditional sources of authority and a new social elite who brandished their material wealth as a basis for their power. There was friction between Indians who had begun to advocate racial separatism and a community of métis offspring, adopted captives, and their families who maintained a more fluid concept of kinship. Finally, there was also growing division between disciples of Christianity and those who upheld older native religious practices, and between those who championed their alliance with the British and those who saw their interests better aligned with other Indian groups. By the 1770s, many western Senecas had dissolved sociopolitical ties with the Confederacy as they looked westward, identifying more with the native peoples of the Ohio country. They scorned the eastern Iroquois, whom they viewed as mere pawns of the British. Ill feeling between different sectors of a diverse "Iroquois" people found violent expression during the Revolution when unable to unite together under a policy of neutrality, the Iroquois fought on opposing sides.

Furthermore, Iroquois acts of self-determination need to be considered in the context of the larger colonial-imperial landscape they inhabited. Despite clear examples of Indian agency in the numerous ways they formulated cultural responses to material changes, the Iroquois proved largely powerless to stem the rising tide of Euro-American racism. Efforts by some Iroquois to (re)present themselves as culturally akin to *whites* through their shared religion and lifestyle proved futile as most colonists simply ignored or discounted such claims. Attempts by others to construct an empowering pan-Indian identity paled in comparison to the success of colonists in asserting their own racial superiority and commandeering Indian land and resources. As the eighteenth century progressed, Euro-Americans became more strident in their determination to impose racial categories on former Indian neighbors in order to naturalize new relations of domination and expropriation. For colonists intent on securing Indian lands and keen to employ racial models to justify their acts of theft and murder, Native American self-definitions mattered little.

But if the Iroquois were not wholly triumphant in the period of imperial entanglement, neither were they totally vanquished. By the late colonial period, colonists may have envisioned a North America devoid of Native Americans, but in reality they met with an Iroquois nation that remained a viable—albeit weakened—force. Although the eastern nations lived virtually intermixed with colonial settlements, the western nations still occupied a largely settler-free homeland. Iroquois political importance may have ebbed during the 1760s, but it would peak again during the Revolutionary War and then again in the War of 1812, when both the British and Americans would solicit their support. Thus, Iroquois history did not begin or end with the rise of the British Empire in North America. Centuries before Europeans arrived in the New World, the Iroquois faced tremendous challenges and transformations. Furthermore, they would continue to endure and overcome difficulties in the decades that followed the 1770s as they engaged with a new American empire.

"It has been said and reiterated so frequently as to have obtained the familiarity of household words, that it is the doom of the Indian to disappear. . . . But whence and why are we thus doomed?" so Pierce inquired of his audience in 1839. Pierce was disturbed by the readiness with which Anglo-Americans pronounced Indians as racially inferior and susceptible to extinction. But he and his generation, and generations to follow, continued to challenge and undermine this pronouncement through their resilience and ongoing presence in New York. The struggles of the 1830s, just like the struggle of the mideighteenth century, represent a series of colonial encounters that both tested and demonstrated the mettle of the Haudenosaunee people.

Abbreviations

AIQ	*American Indian Quarterly*
Clinton Papers	George Clinton Papers, WLCL
CO	Colonial Office Papers, PRO
DCB	*Dictionary of Canadian Biography*, 14 vols., ed. George W. Brown et al. (Toronto: University of Toronto Press, 1966–)
DHNY	*Documentary History of the State of New York*, 4 vols., ed. E. B. O'Callaghan (Albany, N.Y.: Weed, Parsons, and Company, 1850–51)
DRCHNY	*Documents Relative to the Colonial History of the State of New York*, 15 vols., ed. E. B. O'Callaghan and Bethold Fernow (Albany, N.Y.: Weed, Parsons and Company, 1856–87)
Gage Papers	Thomas Gage Papers: American Series, WLCL
Gage Warrants	Thomas Gage Warrants, WLCL
HNAI	*Handbook of North American Indians*, vol. 15, *Northeast*, ed. Bruce Trigger (Washington, D.C.: Smithsonian Institution, 1978)
IMC	*In Mohawk Country: Early Narratives about a Native People*, ed. Dean R. Snow et al. (Syracuse, N.Y.: Syracuse University Press, 1996)
JAH	*Journal of American History*
MPCP	*Minutes of the Provincial Council of Pennsylvania*, 16 vols., ed. Samuel Hazard (Harrisburg, Pa.: Theophilius Fenn, 1838–53)
NAHC	Native American History Collection, WLCL
NYH	*New York History*
NYHSC	*New-York Historical Society, Collections*
OHBE	*The Oxford History of the British Empire*, 5 vols. (Oxford: Oxford University Press, 1998–)
PMHB	*Pennsylvania Magazine of History and Biography*
PRO	Public Records Office, Kew, London
SWJM	Sir William Johnson's Minutes, 3 vols., Public Archives of Canada,

photostats deposited at the Manuscript Division, Library of Congress, Washington, D.C.

SWJP	*The Papers of Sir William Johnson*, 14 vols., ed. James Sullivan et al. (Albany, N.Y.: University of the State of New York, 1921–65).
WLCL	William L. Clements Library, Ann Arbor, Mich.
WMQ	*William and Mary Quarterly*, 3rd ser.
WO	War Office Papers: Jeffrey Amherst Collection, PRO

Notes

Introduction

1. John Lang, *Voyages and Travels of an Indian Interpreter, describing the Manners and Customs of the North American Indians* . . . (London, 1791), 88–89; Colin G. Calloway, *New Worlds for All: Indians, Europeans and the Remaking of Early America* (Baltimore: Johns Hopkins University Press, 1997), 195–96. For an alternative version of this story, see Dean R. Snow, "Theyanoguin," in *Native Northeastern Lives, 1632–1816*, ed. Robert S. Grumet (Amherst: University of Massachusetts Press, 1996), 217. In the following study, to maintain the spirit of eighteenth-century prose, I have attempted to leave the grammar as close to the original as possible. For the purpose of clarity, however, I have occasionally corrected spelling and inserted punctuation. To make quotations easier to read I have also expanded commonly used abbreviations; hence "ye" becomes "the," "Inds." becomes "Indians," "wch" becomes "which," "&ca." becomes "etc.," and so on.

2. Eric Hinderaker articulates this position exceptionally well in *Elusive Empires: Constructing Colonialism in the Ohio Valley, 1673–1800* (New York: Cambridge University Press, 1997), xi. Other works that have informed my understanding of how Indians shaped empires include Richard White, *The Middle Ground: Indians, Empires, and Republics in the Great Lakes Regions, 1650–1815* (New York: Cambridge University Press, 1991); Martin Daunton and Rick Halpern, eds., *Empire and Others: British Encounters with Indigenous Peoples, 1600–1850* (Philadelphia: University of Pennsylvania Press, 1998); Timothy J. Shannon, *Indians and Colonists at the Crossroads of Empire: The Albany Congress of 1754* (Ithaca, N.Y.: Cornell University Press, 2000); Gregory Evans Dowd, *War Under Heaven: Pontiac, the Indian Nations and the British Empire* (Baltimore: Johns Hopkins University Press, 2002). New Imperial History has started to take note of this research. See, e.g., Peter C. Mancall, "Native Americans and Europeans in English America, 1500–1700" in *OHBE*, vol. 1, *Origins of Empire*, ed. Nicholas Canny (Oxford: Oxford University Press, 1998), 328–50; and Daniel K. Richter, "Native Peoples of North America and the Eighteenth-Century British Empire," in *OHBE*, vol. 2, *Eighteenth Century*, ed. P. J. Marshall (Oxford: Oxford University Press, 1998), 347–71.

3. By placing Native Americans in the foreground of an imperial-colonial landscape and depicting them as actors in their own right, this study builds on a rich body of New Indian History. Recent examples of this scholarship that have influenced my understanding include Jane T. Merritt, *At the Crossroads: Indians and Empires on a Mid-Atlantic Frontier* (Chapel Hill: University of North Carolina Press, 2003); Virginia DeJohn

Anderson, *Creatures of Empire: How Domestic Animals Transformed Early America* (New York: Oxford University Press, 2004); Nancy Shoemaker, *A Strange Likeness: Becoming Red and White in Eighteenth-Century North America* (New York: Oxford University Press, 2004); David J. Silverman, *Faith and Boundaries: Colonists, Christianity, and Community Among the Wampanoag Indians of Martha's Vineyard, 1600–1871* (New York: Cambridge University Press, 2005); and Kathleen Duval, *The Native Ground: Indians and Colonists in the Heart of the Continent* (Philadelphia: University of Pennsylvania Press, 2006).

4. George T. Hunt, *The Wars of the Iroquois: A Study in Intertribal Trade Relations* (Madison: University of Wisconsin Press, 1940); Allen W. Trelease, *Indian Affairs in Colonial New York: The Seventeenth Century* (Ithaca, N.Y.: Cornell University Press, 1960); Richard Aquila, *The Iroquois Restoration: Iroquois Diplomacy on the Colonial Frontier, 1701–1754* (Detroit: Wayne State University Press, 1983); Francis Jennings, *The Ambiguous Iroquois Empire: The Covenant Chain Confederation of Indian Tribes with English Colonies* (New York: W. W. Norton, 1984); James H. Merrell and Daniel K. Richter, eds., *Beyond the Covenant Chain: The Iroquois and Their Neighbors in North America, 1600–1800* (Syracuse, N.Y.: Syracuse University Press, 1987); Daniel K. Richter, *The Ordeal of the Longhouse: The Peoples of the Iroquois League in the Era of European Colonization* (Chapel Hill: University of North Carolina Press, 1992); Matthew J. Dennis, *Cultivating a Landscape of Peace: Iroquois-European Encounters in Seventeenth-Century America* (Ithaca, N.Y.: Cornell University Press, 1993); José A. Brandão, *"Your Fyre Will Burn No More": Iroquois Policy Toward New France and Its Native Allies to 1701* (Lincoln: University of Nebraska Press, 1997); William N. Fenton, *The Great Law of the Longhouse: A Political History of the Iroquois Confederacy* (Norman: University of Oklahoma Press, 1998).

5. On Iroquois political structures and practices, see Elizabeth Tooker, "The League of the Iroquois: Its History, Politics, and Ritual," in *HNAI*, 418–41; Francis Jennings et al., eds., *The History and Culture of Iroquois Diplomacy: An Interdisciplinary Guide to the Treaties of the Six Nations and Their League* (Syracuse, N.Y.: Syracuse University Press, 1985); Michael M. Pomedli, "Eighteenth-Century Treaties: Amended Iroquois Condolence Rituals," *AIQ* 19:3 (1995): 319–39. Interest in Iroquois political forms has ignited debate over whether the Iroquois Confederacy influenced the drafting of the U.S. Constitution. See Elizabeth Tooker, "The United States Constitution and the Iroquois League," *Ethnohistory* 35:4 (1988): 305–36; Bruce E. Johansen, "Native American Societies and the Evolution of Democracy in America, 1600–1800: A Commentary on the Iroquois and the U.S. Constitution," *Ethnohistory* 37:3 (1990): 79–90; Donald A. Grinde and Bruce E. Johansen, *Exemplar of Liberty: Native America and the Evolution of Democracy* (Los Angeles: American Indian Studies Center, 1991); William A. Starna and George R. Hamell, "History and the Burden of Proof: The Case of the Iroquois Influence on the U.S. Constitution," *NYH* 77:4 (1996): 427–52; and Donald A. Grinde, Jr., et al., "Forum: The 'Iroquois Influence' Thesis—Pro & Con," *WMQ* 53:3 (1996): 587–636.

6. The few works that detail Iroquois economic history focus on land issues; see

Georgiana C. Nammack, *Fraud, Politics and the Dispossession of the Indians: The Iroquois Land Frontier in the Colonial Period* (Norman: University of Oklahoma Press, 1969); and Wyllys Terry, "Negotiating the Frontier: Land Patenting in Colonial New York" (Ph.D. diss., Boston University, 1997). David B. Guldenzopf produced an insightful discussion on Mohawk economic inequality in "The Colonial Transformation of Mohawk Iroquois Society" (Ph.D. diss., State University of New York at Albany, 1987).

7. Recent scholarship has provided nuanced interpretations of the impact of a market economy on indigenous societies. Key examples include Daniel H. Usner Jr., *Indians, Settlers, and Slaves in a Frontier Exchange Economy: The Lower Mississippi Valley Before 1783* (Chapel Hill: University of North Carolina Press, 1992); James T. Carson, "Native Americans, the Market Revolution, and Cultural Change: The Choctaw Cattle Economy, 1690–1830," *Agricultural History* 71:1 (1997): 1–18; and Claudio Saunt, *A New Order of Things: Property, Power, and the Transformation of the Creek Indians, 1733–1816* (New York: Cambridge University Press, 1999).

8. On the problematic use of the terms "modern" and "traditional," which are generally used in opposition to one another and not in conjunction, see Colleen O'Neill, "Rethinking Modernity and the Discourse of Development in American Indian History: An Introduction," in *Native Pathways: American Indian Culture and Economic Development in the Twentieth Century*, ed. Brian Hosmer and Colleen O'Neill (Boulder: University of Colorado Press, 2004), 1–24. New research, which explores the economic history of native cultures, demonstrates Indian involvement in capitalism without lamenting their loss of an "authentic" identity. See, e.g., John H. Moore, ed., *The Political Economy of North American Indians* (Norman: University of Oklahoma Press, 1993); Linda Barrington, ed., *The Other Side of the Frontier: Economic Explorations into Native American History* (Boulder, Colo.: Westview Press, 1999); Alice Littlefield and Martha C. Knacks, eds., *Native Americans and Wage Labor: Ethnohistorical Perspectives* (Norman: University of Oklahoma Press, 1996); Brian C. Hosmer, *American Indians in the Marketplace: Persistence and Innovation Among the Menominees and Metlakatlans, 1870–1928* (Lawrence: University Press of Kansas, 1999); and the essays in Hosmer and O'Neill, *Native Pathways*. For an insightful discussion of how Indians have co-opted definitions of "authenticity" for their own ends, even as they engage in market-oriented behavior, see Paige Raibmon, *Authentic Indians: Episodes of Encounter from the Late-Nineteenth-Century Northwest Coast* (Durham, N.C.: Duke University Press, 2005).

9. There has yet to be a comprehensive study of the rise of a market economy in the Mohawk Valley, but for this phenomenon in the neighboring Hudson River Valley, see Thomas S. Wermuth, *Rip Van Winkle's Neighbors: The Transformation of Rural Society in the Hudson River Valley, 1720–1850* (Albany: State University of New York Press, 2001); and Martin Bruegel, *Farm, Shop, Landing: The Rise of a Market Society in the Hudson Valley, 1780–1860* (Durham, N.C.: Duke University Press, 2002).

10. Eric Hinderaker, "The 'Four Indian Kings' and the Imaginative Construction of the First British Empire," *WMQ* 53:3 (1996): 487; Kathleen Wilson, "Introduction: Histories, Empires, Modernities," in *A New Imperial History: Culture, Identity, Modernity,*

1660–1840, ed. Kathleen Wilson (Cambridge: Cambridge University Press, 2003), 1–22. A vast literature examines the ideological dimensions of empire. For a helpful summation, see Dane Kennedy, "Imperial History and Post-Colonial Theory," *Journal of Imperial and Commonwealth History* [hereafter *JICH*] 24:3 (1996): 345–63.

11. Philip D. Morgan, "Encounters Between British and 'Indigenous' Peoples, c. 1500—c. 1800," in *Empire and Others*, ed. Dauton and Halpern, 45. On the fluid and contingent nature of Indian identity, see Jonathan D. Hill, "Introduction: Ethnogenesis in the Americas, 1492–1992," in *History, Power, and Identity: Ethnogenesis in the Americas, 1492–1992*, ed. Jonathan D. Hill (Iowa City: University of Iowa Press, 1996), 1–19; and Alexandra Harmon, "Wanted: More Histories of Indian Identity," in *Blackwell Companion to American Indian History*, ed. Philip J. Deloria and Neal Salisbury (Oxford: Blackwell, 2002), 248–65.

12. The concept of a "gender frontier" belongs to Kathleen M. Brown, who contends that it was central to the colonial experience. "Gender roles and identities," she has argued, "played an important role in shaping English and Indian interactions." "The Anglo-Algonquian Gender Frontier," in *Negotiators of Change: Historical Perspectives on Native American Women*, ed. Nancy Shoemaker (New York: Routledge, 1995), 26–48. For two recent examples of scholarship that explore how ideas about gender shaped colonial encounters, see Kirsten Fischer, "The Imperial Gaze: Native American, African American, and Colonial Women in European Eyes," in *Companion to American Women's History*, ed. Nancy A. Hewitt (Oxford: Blackwell, 2002), 4–9; and Juliana Barr, *Peace Came in the Form of a Woman: Indians and Spaniards in the Texas Borderlands* (Chapel Hill: University of North Carolina Press, 2007).

13. Joan Scott aptly reminds us that "gender is a primary way of signifying relationships of power" in her influential article, "Gender: A Useful Category of Historical Analysis," *American Historical Review* 91:5 (1986): 1067. For a general discussion of gender as a cultural construct, see Nancy Bonvillain, *Women and Men: Cultural Constructions of Gender* (Englewood Cliffs, N.J.: Prentice Hall, 1995), 1–11.

14. For works that explore the gendered dimensions of imperialism, see Philippa Levine, ed., *Gender and Empire*, Oxford History of the British Empire Companion Series (New York: Oxford University Press, 2004). See, in particular, the essay by Kathleen Wilson, "Empire, Gender and Modernity in the Eighteenth Century," 14–43.

15. Literature on Iroquois women is sparse. With the exception of an edited collection of essays (W. G. Spittal, ed., *Iroquois Women: An Anthology* [Ohsweken, Ontario: Iroqrafts, 1990]), the only monograph devoted entirely to them is Barbara A. Mann, *Iroquoian Women: Gantowisas of the Haudenosaunee League* (New York: Peter Lang, 2000). On the neglect of Iroquois women, see Martha H. Foster, "Lost Women of the Matriarchy: Iroquois Women in Historical Literature," *American Indian Culture and Research Journal* 19:3 (1995): 121–40. On the marginalization of native women in mainstream historical literature more generally and suggestions for their inclusion, see Gail D. MacLeitch, " 'Your Women Are of No Small Consequence': Native American Women, Gender, and Early American History," in *The Practice of U.S. Women's History: Narra-*

tives, Intersections, and Dialogues, ed. Jay Kleinberg, Eileen Boris, and Vicki Ruiz (New Brunswick, N.J.: Rutgers University Press, 2007), 30–49.

16. The quintessential text on race as a cultural construct is Barbara Fields, "Ideology and Race in American History," in *Region, Race and Reconstruction: Essays in Honor of C. Vann Woodward*, ed. J. Morgan Kousser and James M. McPherson (New York: Oxford University Press, 1982), 143–78. See also Audrey Smedley, *Race in North America: Origin and Evolution of a World View* (Boulder, Colo.: Westview Press, 1993); and David B. Davis, "Constructing Race: A Reflection," *WMQ* 54:1 (1997): 7–18.

17. Joyce E. Chaplin, *Subject Matter: Technology, the Body, and Science on the Anglo-American Frontier, 1500–1676* (Cambridge, Mass.: Harvard University Press, 2001), 160; idem, "Race," in *The British Atlantic World, 1500–1800*, ed. David Armitage and Michael J. Braddick (New York: Palgrave Macmillan, 2002), 154. The origins of racism debate in the context of American slavery is lengthy. For an overview, see Alden T. Vaughan, "The Origins of Slavery Debates: Slavery and Racism in Seventeenth Century Virginia," *Virginia Magazine of History and Biography* 97 (1989): 311–54.

18. Werner Sollors is one of a number of scholars who have demonstrated that ethnicity "is not a thing but a process." See his "Introduction: The Invention of Ethnicity," in *The Invention of Ethnicity*, ed. Werner Sollors (Oxford: Oxford University Press, 1989), ix–xx. See also Kathleen Neils Conzen et al., "The Invention of Ethnicity: A Perspective from the USA," *Journal of American Ethnic History* 12:1 (1992): 3–6.

19. Most Iroquois studies focus on the seventeenth century (see n. 4 above) or the Revolutionary War period. See Barbara Graymont, *The Iroquois in the American Revolution* (Syracuse, N.Y.: Syracuse University Press, 1972); Joseph R. Fisher, *A Well-Executed Failure: The Sullivan Campaign Against the Iroquois, July–September 1779* (Columbia: University of South Carolina Press, 1997); Max Mintz, *Seeds of Empire: The American Revolutionary Conquest of the Iroquois* (New York: New York University Press, 1999); and Alan Taylor, *The Divided Ground: Indians, Settlers, and the Northern Borderland of the American Revolution* (New York: Alfred A. Knopf, 2006).

20. American colonial historians have rightfully rescued the Seven Years' War from the shadows of the American Revolution; see, in particular, Fred Anderson, *Crucible of War: The Seven Years' War and the Fate of Empire in British North America, 1754–1766* (New York: Alfred A. Knopf, 2000); and Colin Calloway, *The Scratch of a Pen: 1763 and the Transformation of North America* (New York: Oxford University Press, 2006). Scholars of British imperial history have posited the Seven Years' War as a watershed in the British construction of empire. H. V. Bowen explores the changing meaning of the term "empire" in the 1760s as it came to be understood principally in terms of land. See his "British Conceptions of Global Empire, 1756–83," *JICH* 26:3 (1998): 5–6. P. J. Marshall contends that the war gave rise to "a new kind of empire" that revealed new attitudes on the part of the British toward issues of "military power, expansion and dominion over alien peoples." See his "Empire and Authority in the Later Eighteenth Century," *JICH* 15:2 (1987): 106–7. See also his introduction in *OHBE*, 2:4–8.

21. Daniel A. Baugh, "Maritime Strength and Atlantic Commerce: The Uses of 'A

Grand Marine Empire,'" in *An Imperial State at War: Britain from 1689 to 1815*, ed. Lawrence Stone (London: Routledge, 1994), 185–223.

22. While scholars are in general agreement that Britain developed a new interest in territorial empire by midcentury, they differ in emphasis over the principal cause of this reorientation. Many highlight Britain's developing market economy; others emphasize political factors. See, e.g., John Brewer, *The Sinews of Power: War, Money, and the English State, 1688–1783* (London: Unwin Hyman, 1989), chap. 6; and Marie Peters, "The Myth of William Pitt, Earl of Chatham, Great Imperialist, Part I: Pitt and Imperial Expansion, 1738–1763," *JICH* 21 (1993): 55.

23. Kathleen Wilson, "Empire of Virtue: The Imperial Project and Hanoverian Culture, c. 1720–1785," in *An Imperial State at War*, ed. Stone, 148; David Hancock, *Citizens of the World: London Merchants and the Integration of the British Atlantic Community, 1735–1785* (New York: Cambridge University Press, 1995), 80–81; P. J. Marshall, "Empire and Opportunity in Britain, 1763–75," *Transactions of the Royal Historical Society*, 6th ser., 5 (1995): 111–28.

24. Examples of this literature include Margaret C. Szasz, ed., *Between Indian and White Worlds: The Cultural Broker* (Norman: University of Oklahoma Press, 1994); and James H. Merrell, *Into the American Woods: Negotiators on the Pennsylvania Frontier* (New York: W. W. Norton, 1999). For scholarship on Johnson, see Chapter 2, n. 1.

25. My use of the middle ground metaphor is a direct reference to Richard White's important work, *The Middle Ground*. In this study White contends that because neither Europeans nor Algonquians in the Great Lakes region could exert control over the other, "they constructed a common, mutually comprehensible world" in their "search for accommodation" (ix–x).

Chapter 1

1. Tejonihokarawa, also known as Hendrick Peters, has long been confused with another famous Mohawk Indian, Theyanoguin, also known by the English as Hendrick Peters. See Chapter 2 for Theyanoguin. On the distinct histories of these two men, see Dean R. Snow, "Searching for Hendrick: Correction of a Historic Conflation," *NYH* 88:3 (2007): 229–53; and Eric Hinderaker, *The Two Hendricks: Unraveling a Mohawk Mystery* (Cambridge, Mass.: Harvard University Press, 2010). None of these delegates was an actual king. Tejonihokarawa was a League chief, although he may not have been in 1710. The others, two Mohawks and one Mahican, were men of relatively little power or standing.

2. Richmond P. Bond, *Queen Anne's American Kings* (Oxford: Clarendon Press, 1952); John G. Garratt, *The Four Indian Kings/Les Quatre Rois Indiens* (Ottawa: Canada Public Archives, 1985); Hinderaker, "The 'Four Indian Kings,'" 487–526. Contemporary commentaries of this trip include *The Four Kings of Canada . . .* (London, 1710) and *The History and Progress of the Four Indian Kings . . .* (London, 1710).

3. The United Kingdom of Great Britain became a political entity in 1708. For the remainder of this chapter, which is concerned with the period up until the 1710s, I will therefore refer to the *English* Empire.

4. The following discussion has been informed by William N. Fenton, "Northern Iroquois Culture Patterns," in *HNAI*, 306–14; Tooker, "The League of the Iroquois"; idem, "Women in Iroquois Society," in *Extending the Rafters: Interdisciplinary Approaches to Iroquoian Studies*, ed. Michael K. Foster et al. (Albany: State University of New York Press, 1984), 110–12; Dean R. Snow, *The Iroquois* (London: Blackwell, 1994), chaps. 1–4; idem, "The Architecture of Iroquois Longhouses," *Northern Anthropology* 53 (1997): 61–84; and Richter, *Ordeal of the Longhouse*, 19–22.

5. Sara H. Stites, *Economics of the Iroquois* (Lancaster, Pa.: New Era Printing Company, 1905), chap. 2; Arthur C. Parker, "Iroquois Uses of Maize and Other Food Plants," *New York State Museum Bulletin 144* (Albany: University of the State of New York, 1912); Fenton, "Northern Iroquois Culture Patterns," 296–302; Michael Recht, "The Role of Fishing in the Iroquois Economy, 1600–1792," *NYH* 76:1 (1995): 5–30.

6. George S. Synderman, "Concepts of Land Ownership Among the Iroquois and Their Neighbors," in *Symposium on Local Diversity in Iroquois Culture*, ed. William N. Fenton (Washington, D.C.: Smithsonian Institute, 1951), 15–33; Tooker, "Women in Iroquois Society," 114–17; Richter, *Ordeal of the Longhouse*, 21–22. On their distinct hunting and fishing grounds, see Stites, *Economics of the Iroquois*, 21; Lewis Henry Morgan, *League of the Iroquois* (1851; New York: Citadel Press, 1993), 346–47; and Recht, "Role of Fishing in the Iroquois Economy."

7. Joseph François Lafitau, *Customs of the American Indians Compared with the Customs of Primitive Times*, 2 vols., ed. and trans. William N. Fenton and Elizabeth L. Moore (1724; Toronto: Champlain Society, 1974–77), 2:184; Kurt Jordan, "The Archaeology of the Iroquois Restoration: Settlement, Housing and Economy at a Dispersed Seneca Community ca. A.D. 1715–1754" (Ph.D. diss., Columbia University, 2002), 517–28; *The Jesuit Relations and Allied Documents: Travels and Explorations of the Jesuit Missionaries in New France, 1610–1791* [hereafter *JR*], 73 vols., ed. Reuben Gold Thwaites (Cleveland, Ohio, 1896–1901), 58:185–87; Stites, *Economics of the Iroquois*, 79–83. On the social and cultural meaning of gift-giving, see Bruce White, "'Give Us a Little Milk': The Social and Cultural Meanings of Gift Giving in the Lake Superior Fur Trade," *Minnesota History* 48 (1982): 60–71. On the tributary system, see Jennings, *Ambiguous Iroquois Empire*, 8.

8. Stites, *Economics of the Iroquois*, 79–80, 82; Richter, *Ordeal of the Longhouse*, 13–14, 28–29; Jordan, "Archaeology of the Iroquois Restoration," 517–28; James Bradley, *Evolution of the Onondaga Iroquois: Accommodating Change, 1500–1655* (Syracuse, N.Y.: Syracuse University Press, 1987), 178–79; Snow, *Iroquois*, 66–67.

9. Nancy Bonvillain, *Women and Men: Cultural Constructions of Gender* (Englewood Cliffs, N.J.: Prentice Hall, 1995), 66–67; Nurit Bird-David, "Beyond 'The Original Affluent Society': A Culturalist Reformulation," *Current Anthropology* 33:1 (1992): 30. Eric R. Wolf notes that in kinship-based cultures, kinship provides "a way of committing social labor to the transformation of nature through appeals to filiation and marriage, and to consanguinity and affinity." *Europe and the People Without a History* (Berkeley: University of California Press, 1982), 91.

10. Lafitau noted that "The *Agoïanders* are subordinated to the chief one who is their leader and is called *Roïander Gôa.*" *Roïander Gôa*, which meant "noble par excellence," was derived from *gaïander*, "the usual word meaning nobility." *Customs of the American Indians*, 1:293, 290. The Mohawks referred to the hereditary chief as *royáner*. Fenton, "Northern Iroquois Culture Patterns," 312.

11. *JR*, 26:307, 54:93 (mistress here), 281, 55:261 (noble birth), 265, 58:185, 64:77, 79, 81 (managed the affairs); Lafitau, *Customs of the American Indians*, 1:291; William A. Starna and Ralph Watkins, "Northern Iroquoian Slavery," *Ethnohistory* 38:1 (1991): 34–57. I am indebted to Dan Richter, who encouraged me to rethink my ideas regarding reciprocity and equality in Iroquois culture. This discussion was further informed by Kathleen J. Bragdon, *Native People of Southern New England, 1500–1650* (Norman: University of Oklahoma Press, 1996), 43–45; Annette B. Weiner, *Inalienable Possessions: The Paradox of Keeping While Giving* (Berkeley: University of California Press, 1992), 7–9; and Daniel K. Richter, "Stratification and Class in Eastern Native America," in *Class Matters: Early North America and the Atlantic World*, ed. Simon Middleton and Billy G. Smith (Philadelphia: University of Pennsylvania Press, 2007), 35–48.

12. Johannes Megapolensis Jr., "A Short Account of the Mohawk Indians, 1644," in *IMC*, 46; Lafitau, *Customs of the American Indians*, 1:293; Richter, "Stratification and Class in Eastern Native America," 39–42; idem, *Ordeal of the Longhouse*, 22. Bragdon found in her study of the New England Ninnimissinuok that "Economic stratification can also exist alongside an ideology of reciprocity." *Native People of Southern New England*, 44. On forms of asymmetrical reciprocity, see Henry Orenstein, "Asymmetrical Reciprocity: A Contribution to the Theory of Political Legitimacy," *Current Anthropology* 21:1 (1980): 69–91. Orenstein explains, "The leader may be conceived as giving more in goods and/or services than he receives—or, if you will, as giving by grace and receiving as of right; hence, the leader is a 'creditor' and must be obeyed by his constituency, his 'debtors'" (70). Inequality has been documented in other pre-contact native societies, e.g., Alex Barker and Timothy R. Pauketat, eds., *Lords of the Southeast: Social Inequality and the Native Elites of Southeastern North America* (Washington, D.C.: American Anthropological Association, 1992). By contrast, Bruce G. Trigger emphasizes economic equality in pre-contact Iroquoia in "Maintaining Economic Equality in Opposition to Complexity: An Iroquois Case Study," in *The Evolution of Political Systems: Sociopolitics in Small-Scale Sedentary Societies*, ed. Steadman Upham (Cambridge: Cambridge University Press, 1990), 119–45.

13. Megapolensis, "Account of the Mohawk Indians," 45. For another contemporary version, see Adriaen Cornelissen van der Donck, "Description of New Netherland, 1653," in *IMC*, 129. For later versions, see the Jeremiah Curtin and J.N.B. Hewitt rendition in *Tales of the North American Indians*, selected and annotated by Stith Thompson (Cambridge, Mass.: Harvard University Press, 1929), 14–17; Curtin and Hewitt, "Seneca Fiction, Legends, and Myths," in *Bureau of American Ethnology, Annual Report, 1910–1911* (Washington, D.C.: GPO, 1918), 409–15; Hewitt, "Iroquoian Cosmology," in *Bureau of American Ethnology, Annual Report, 1925–1926* (Washington, D.C.: GPO,

1928), 464–66; and William N. Fenton, "This Island, the World on the Turtle's Back," *Journal of American Folklore* 75 (1962): 283–300. Most versions of the Iroquois creation story focus on the third epoch, which concerns the role of the male twins in creating and naming plant and animal life. Barbara A. Mann has sought to reemphasize the second and often ignored epoch of the origins myth, which focuses on the important relationship between Sky Woman and her daughter. See "The Lynx in Time: Haudenosaunee Women's Traditions and History," *AIQ* 21:3 (1997): 423–49.

14. Megapolensis, "Account of the Mohawk Indians," 46, 42; *JR*, 28:51–55; Gabriel Theodat Sagard, *Long Journey to the Country of the Huron*, ed. George Wrong (1632; Toronto: Champlain Society, 1939), 124; Lafitau, *Customs of the American Indians*, 1:352. According to missionaries, Iroquoian Indians "rejoice[d] more in the birth of a daughter than of a son, for the sake of the multiplication of the country's inhabitants." The exalted value attached to girls is also borne out by the fact that reparations for female murder victims were higher. See *JR*, 15:181–83, 33:243–45; and Nancy Bonvillain, "Iroquois Women," in *Studies on Iroquois Culture*, ed. Nancy Bonvillain (Rindge, N.H.: Department of Anthropology, Franklin Pierce College, 1980), 51–53.

15. Parker, "Iroquois Uses of Maize and Other Food Plants," 36–37; Curtin and Hewitt, "Seneca Fiction, Legends, and Myths," 412; Joan M. Jensen, "Native American Women and Agriculture: A Seneca Case Study," in *Women and Power in American History*, vol. 1, ed. Kathryn Kish Sklar and Thomas Dublin (Englewood Cliffs, N.J.: Prentice Hall, 1991), 9–10; Mann, "The Lynx in Time," 443n44.

16. Lafitau, *Customs of the American Indians*, 2:54–55; *JR*, 14:235; Martha C. Randle, "Iroquois Women: Then and Now," [1951], in *Iroquois Women*, ed. Spittal, 136; Judith K. Brown, "Iroquois Women: An Ethnohistoric Note," in *Toward an Anthropology of Women*, ed. Rayna Reiter (New York: Monthly Review Press, 1975), 243–51; Fenton, "Northern Iroquois Culture Patterns," 299–300. For a description of the key ceremonies related to the agricultural cycle, see Snow, *Iroquois*, 70, 124, 134, 162.

17. Lafitau, *Customs of the American Indians*, 1:349, 2:187 (quote); *JR*, 15:155, 43:265; Sagard, *Long Journey to the Country of the Huron*, 123, 132; Pierre de Charlevoix, *Journal of a Voyage to North America* (1721; London: R. and J. Dodsley, 1761), 2:54; J. Brown, "Iroquois Women," 248.

18. Lafitau, *Customs of the American Indians*, vol. 2, chap. 3; Nathaniel Knowles, "The Torture of Captives by the Indians of Eastern America," *American Philosophical Society, Proceedings* 82 (1940): 210–11; George S. Synderman, *Behind the Tree of Peace* (Philadelphia: University of Pennsylvania Press, 1948); Richter, *Ordeal of the Longhouse*, chap. 2.

19. Charlevoix, *Journal of a Voyage to North America*, 1:317, 2:25; Lafitau, *Customs of the American Indians*, 1:69, 2:100; *JR*, 39:75–77, 42:177–79; "Voyages of Pierre Esprit Radisson, 1651–1654," in *IMC*, 69ff; *Letters from North America by Father Antoine Silvy, S.J.*, trans. Ivy Alice Dickson (Belleville, Ontario: Mika Publishing Company, 1980), 199; Synderman, *Behind the Tree of Peace*, 15–20; Cara Richards, "Matriarchy or Mistake: The Role of Iroquois Women Through Time," in *Iroquois Women*, ed. Spittal, 149–51.

20. Lafitau, *Customs of the American Indians*, 1:292–95, 298–99; *Letters from North America by Father Antoine Silvy*, 197–98; Charlevoix, *Journal of a Voyage to North America*, 2:24, 26; *JR*, 54:281, 55:265.

21. Lafitau, *Customs of the American Indians*, 1:294–97; *JR*, 10:231–33; William N. Fenton, "Structure, Continuity, and Change in the Process of Iroquois Treaty Making," in *History and Culture of Iroquois Diplomacy*, ed. Jennings et al., 13.

22. Tooker demonstrates how scholars have exaggerated the political power of Iroquois women in "Women in Iroquois Society," 109–23. Jane Merritt found that, similar to the situation of the Iroquois, "the balance of power in native communities [in Pennsylvania] most likely rested on subtle tensions between female clan lineages and male political needs." *At the Crossroads*, 55. Scholars have tended to stress reciprocal, harmonious, and egalitarian relations between the sexes at the expense of downplaying sources of tension and conflict; see, e.g., Laura F. Klein and Lillian A. Ackerman, eds., *Women and Power in Native North America* (Norman: University of Oklahoma Press, 1995), introduction.

23. David Zeisberger quoted in William N. Fenton, "Iroquoian Culture History: A General Evaluation," in *Symposium on Cherokee and Iroquois Culture*, Bureau of American Ethnology, Bulletin 180, ed. William Fenton and John Gulick (Washington, D.C.: Smithsonian Institution, 1961), 271. On the Hiawatha tradition, see Paul A. W. Wallace, *The White Roots of Peace* (Philadelphia: University of Pennsylvania Press, 1946).

24. *JR*, 39:199 (quote), 40:137–39; James Lynch, "The Iroquois Confederacy, and the Adoption and Administration of Non-Iroquoian Individuals and Groups Prior to 1756," *Man in the Northeast* [hereafter *MIN*] 30 (1985): 83–99; Daniel K. Richter, "War and Culture: The Iroquois Experience," *WMQ* 40:4 (1983): 528–59.

25. Other scholars have already highlighted these resources. See, e.g., Richter, *Ordeal of the Longhouse*, 2–3; and Taylor, *The Divided Ground*, 4–6.

26. Jack P. Greene, "The Origins of the New Colonial Policy, 1748–1763," in *The Blackwell Encyclopedia of the American Revolution*, ed. Jack P. Greene and J. R. Pole (Oxford: Basil Blackwell, 1991), 97; Ian K. Steele, *Politics of Colonial Policy: The Board of Trade in Colonial Administration, 1696–1720* (Oxford: Clarendon Press, 1968), chap. 1. On the early British Empire, see *OHBE*, vol. 1.

27. Iroquois relations with English New York governors are well documented in Richter, *Ordeal of the Longhouse*, chaps. 6–9. On diplomatic neglect, see p. 216. On English reluctance to lend military support, see pp. 156, 174–75, 187, 191.

28. Governors Benjamin Fletcher (1692–98) and Lord Cornbury (1702–8) enhanced their personal wealth by awarding generous land grants without obtaining consent from the Mohawk owners. Ruth L. Higgins, *Expansion in New York, with Especial Reference to the Eighteenth Century* (Columbus: Ohio State University, 1931), 23, 26–28, 29; Nammack, *Fraud, Politics and the Dispossession of the Indians*, 13–15.

29. On the significance of local figures in the conduct of early Iroquois-European relations, see Daniel K. Richter, "Cultural Brokers and Intercultural Politics: New York–Iroquois Relations, 1664–1701," *JAH* 75:1 (1988): 40–67; Thomas E. Burke Jr., *Mohawk*

Frontier: The Dutch Community of Schenectady, New York, 1610–1710 (Ithaca, N.Y.: Cornell University Press, 1991), 143–44.

30. Helen Broshar, "The First Push Westward of the Albany Traders," *Mississippi Valley Historical Review* 7 (1920–21): 228–41; Arthur H. Buffinton, "The Policy of Albany and English Westward Expansion," *Mississippi Valley Historical Review* 8 (1921–22): 327–66; Henry Allain St. Paul, "Governor Thomas Dongan's Expansion Policy," *Mid-America* 17 (1935): 172–84, 236–72.

31. Ian K. Steele, *Warpaths: Invasions of North America* (New York: Oxford University Press, 1994) 158. Steele argues that prior to 1748, "to . . . European powers, the North American theater was an insignificant sideshow to a much more vital and expensive European main event" (132). On England's lackluster response to King William's War (1689–97) and Queen Anne's War, see 140–46, 151–59.

32. Snow, *Iroquois*, 88, 110. Statistics on Iroquois demography are of course highly speculative. Snow's estimates coincide with others. See Richter, *Ordeal of the Longhouse*, 17, 293n16; and Guntha Michelson, "Iroquois Population Statistics," *MIN* 14 (1977): 3–17. For estimates specifically on the Mohawk population, see William A. Starna, "Mohawk Iroquois Populations: A Revision," *Ethnohistory* 27:4 (1980): 371–82; and Dean R. Snow and William A. Starna, "Sixteenth-Century Depopulation: A View from the Mohawk Valley," *American Anthropologist* 91 (1989): 142–49.

33. Aquila, *Iroquois Restoration*, 39, 43–45; Jennings, *Ambiguous Iroquois Empire*, 189–90; Richter, *Ordeal of the Longhouse*, 102–4, 156–58, 174, 186; Snow, *Iroquois*, 131.

34. Richter, *Ordeal of the Longhouse*, 256–60.

35. *JR*, 43:265 (second quote), 45:243 (first quote), 51:123, 187; Lynch, "The Iroquois Confederacy," 90–97; Richter, *Ordeal of the Longhouse*, 65–74, 136, 145–48, 238–39; Aquila, *Iroquois Restoration*, 38–39; Peter C. Mancall, *Valley of Opportunity: Economic Culture Along the Upper Susquehanna, 1700–1800* (Ithaca, N.Y.: Cornell University Press, 1991), 32–36. Seneca population numbers are from Snow, *Iroquois*, 131.

36. William N. Fenton, "Problems Arising from the Historic Northeastern Position of the Iroquois," in *Essays on Historical Anthropology of North America Published in Honor of John R. Swanton* (Washington, D.C.: Smithsonian Institution, 1940), 216, 219–31; Bradley, *Evolution of the Onondaga Iroquois*, 206–7; Jack Campisi, "Oneida," in *HNAI*, 481; Robert Grumet, *Historic Contact: Indian People and Colonists in Today's Northeastern U.S. in the Sixteenth Through Eighteenth Centuries* (Norman: University of Oklahoma Press, 1996), 413; Richter, *Ordeal of the Longhouse*, 257.

37. J. W. Lydekker, *The Faithful Mohawks* (New York: Macmillan, 1938), 37, 40; William N. Fenton and Elizabeth Tooker, "Mohawk," in *HNAI*, 474–75; Fenton, "Problems Arising," 213; Grumet, *Historic Contact*, 370; David L. Preston, "The Texture of Contact: European and Indian Settler Communities on the Iroquoian Borderlands, 1720–1780s" (Ph.D. diss., College of William and Mary, 2002), 29–31, 47.

38. Allan Kulikoff, *From British Peasants to Colonial American Farmers* (Chapel Hill: University of North Carolina Press, 2000), 156–57; Sung Bok Kim, *Landlord and Tenant in Colonial New York: Manorial Society, 1664–1775* (Chapel Hill: University of

North Carolina Press, 1978); Patricia U. Bonomi, *A Factious People: Politics and Society in Colonial New York* (New York: Columbia University Press, 1971), chap. 6.

39. Christopher Hunter and Stephanie Przybylek, "Schenectady," in *Encyclopedia of New York State*, ed. Peter Eisenstadt (Syracuse, N.Y.: Syracuse University Press, 2005), 1362; Burke, *Mohawk Frontier*, 118–19; Philip Otterness, *Becoming German: The 1709 Palatine Migration to New York* (Ithaca, N.Y.: Cornell University Press, 2004), chaps. 5, 6; Preston, "Texture of Contact," 31–36; Lydekker, *Faithful Mohawks*, 32–34.

40. Peter Wraxall, *An Abridgment of the Indian Affairs Contained in Four Folio Volumes, Transacted in the Colony of New York, from the Year 1678 to the Year 1751*, ed. Charles H. McIlwain (1754; New York: Benjamin Blom, 1968), 94; Fenton and Tooker, "Mohawk," 475; Richter, *Ordeal of the Longhouse*, 229–30; Grumet, *Historic Contact*, 370; Preston, "Texture of Contact," 49–50.

41. Meeting Relating to Indian Lands, March 23, 1763, *SWJP*, 4:65; Burke, *Mohawk Frontier*, 118–19, 145–51; Hunter and Przybylek, "Schenectady," 1362.

42. Council held in the City of Albany, July 2, 1754, p. 5, vol. 1199, ser. 16, CO (hereafter in form CO 16/1199/5); Preston, "Texture of Contact," 37–39; Otterness, *Becoming German*, 115–22.

43. "Deed from the Five Nations to the King of their Beaver Hunting Ground, 1701," *DRCHNY*, 4:908–10; Proposition of the Onondaga and Cayuga Indians, August 2, 1684, *DRCHNY*, 3:417; Michael N. McConnell, "People 'In Between': The Iroquois and the Ohio Indians, 1720–1768," in *Beyond the Covenant Chain*, ed. Merrell and Richter, 95–96; Francis Jennings, " 'Pennsylvania Indians' and the Iroquois," in *Beyond the Covenant Chain*, ed. Merrell and Richter, 76–80; Richter, *Ordeal of the Longhouse*, 136. Jennings credits British colonists, more so than the Iroquois, for developing this myth; see *Ambiguous Iroquois Empire*, esp. chap. 2.

44. Abstract of Proposals submitted by two Iroquois Nations, August 2, 1684, *DRCHNY*, 3:347; Proposition of the Onondaga and Cayuga Indians, August 2, 1684, *DRCHNY*, 3:417–18; Conference of Lt. Gov. Nanfan with the Indians, July 19, 1701, *DRCHNY*, 4:904–6; "Deed from the Five Nations . . . 1701," *DRCHNY*, 4:908. The Senecas, Cayugas, and Onondagas reaffirmed this treaty in 1726. "Deed in Trust from three of the Five Nations of Indians to the King," September 14, 1726, *DRCHNY*, 5:800–801. For background on the 1701 treaty, see Trelease, *Indian Affairs in Colonial New York*, 361–62; Jennings, *Ambiguous Iroquois Empire*, 212–13; Richter, *Ordeal of the Longhouse*, 211–12; and J. A. Brandão and William A. Starna, "The Treaties of 1701: A Triumph of Iroquois Diplomacy," *Ethnohistory* 43:2 (1996): 209–44.

45. Older works include Wolf, *Europe and the People Without History*, chap. 6; and Denys Delage, *Bitter Feast: Amerindians and Europeans in Northeastern North America, 1600–1664*, trans. Jane Brierley (1985; Vancouver: University of British Columbia Press, 1993), chaps. 3–4.

46. Recent historiography posits the fur trade as a cross-cultural creation. See, e.g., Jo-Anne Fiske et al., eds., *New Faces of the Fur Trade: Selected Papers on the Seventh North American Fur Trade Conference, Halifax, Nova Scotia, 1995* (East Lansing: Michi-

gan State University Press, 1998); Susan Sleeper-Smith, ed., *Rethinking the Fur Trade: Cultures of Exchange in an Atlantic World* (Lincoln; University of Nebraska Press, 2009). This newer literature also demonstrates that the so-called Beaver Wars contained a tangled mixture of causes (e.g., mourning-war complex, longstanding ethnic tensions) and were not solely attributable to the fur trade. See Richter, "War and Culture"; and William A. Starna and José A. Brandão, "From the Mohawk-Mahican War to the Beaver Wars: Questioning the Pattern," *Ethnohistory* 51:4 (2004): 725–49.

47. Richard Aquila, "The Iroquois as 'Geographic' Middle Men: A Research Note," *Indiana Magazine of History* 80:81 (1984): 51–60.

48. Lafitau, *Customs of the American Indians*, 2:30–31; Van der Donck, "Description of New Netherland," 121–22; Stites, *Economics of the Iroquois*, 20–21; Thomas E. Norton, *The Fur Trade in Colonial New York, 1686–1776* (Madison: University of Wisconsin Press, 1974), 27–28; Richter, *Ordeal of the Longhouse*, 76. For a descriptive account of how northeastern Indians procured, prepared, and transported furs to European trading posts, see Carolyn Gilman, *Where Two Worlds Meet: The Great Lakes Fur Trade* (St. Paul: Minnesota Historical Society, 1982).

49. Bradley, *Evolution of the Onondaga Iroquois*, 130. See also Wayne Lenig, "Patterns of Material Culture During the Early Years of New Netherland Trade," *Northeast Anthropology* 53 (1997): 61–84; and Gilbert W. Hagerty, *Wampum, War and Trade Goods West of the Hudson* (New York: Heart of the Lake Publishing, 1985).

50. Van der Donck, "Description of New Netherland," 109 (first quote); Megapolensis, "Account of the Mohawk Indians," 42; Norton, *Fur Trade in Colonial New York*, 31 (second quote), 126; Gilman, *Where Two Worlds Meet*, 33; William M. Beauchamp, "Metallic Ornaments of the New York Indians," *New York State Museum Bulletin 73* (Albany: University of the State of New York, 1903).

51. Beauchamp, "Metallic Ornaments," 49–50; Bradley, *Evolution of the Onondaga Iroquois*, chap. 5; Richter, *Ordeal of the Longhouse*, 79–86. For a broader discussion of how Indians initially made sense of foreign goods within their own cultural framework, see Christopher L. Miller and George R. Hamell, "A New Perspective on Indian-White Contact: Cultural Symbols and the Colonial Trade," *JAH* 73 (1986): 311–28; George R. Hamell, "The Iroquois and the World's Rim: Speculations on Color, Culture and Contact," *AIQ* 16:4 (1992): 451–69; and James Axtell, *Beyond 1492: Encounters in Colonial America* (New York: Cambridge University Press, 1992), 125–51.

52. Jasper Danckaerts, "Journal of a Voyage to New York and a Tour in Several American Colonies in 1679–1680," in *IMC*, 215; *JR*, 51:123–25, 217. This discussion is informed by Maia Conrad, "Disorderly Drinking: Reconsidering Seventeenth-Century Iroquois Alcohol Use," *AIQ* 23:3–4 (1999): 1–11.

53. See n. 54.

54. Van der Donck, "Description of New Netherland," 119, 109; Megapolensis, "Account of the Mohawk Indians," 44; William M. Beauchamp, "Wampum Used in Council and Currency," *American Antiquarian* 20:1 (1898): 1–13; idem, "Wampum and Shell Articles Used by the New York Indians," *New York State Museum Bulletin 41* (Albany:

University of the State of New York, 1901); Lynn Ceci, "The Value of Wampum Among the New York Iroquois: A Case Study in Artifact Analysis," *Journal of Anthropological Research* 38 (1982): 97–107; Michael K. Foster, "Another Look at the Function of Wampum in Iroquois-White Councils," in *History and Culture of Iroquois Diplomacy*, ed. Jennings et al., 99–114; Bradley, *Evolution of the Onondaga Iroquois*, 178–80; Snow, *Iroquois*, 91–92, 111–12. On the development of a bicultural "forest diplomacy," see Nancy L. Hagedorn, "Brokers of Understanding: Interpreters as Agents of Cultural Exchange in Colonial New York," *NYH* 76:4 (1995): 394–404.

55. Megapolensis, "Account of the Mohawk Indians," 41; Charles T. Gehring, ed. and trans., *Fort Orange Court Minutes, 1652–1660* (Syracuse, N.Y.: Syracuse University Press, 1990), 453, 463–64; Trelease, *Indian Affairs*, 115, 124–37.

56. Evert Wendell, Indian Account Book, 1695–1726, New-York Historical Society (hereafter NYHS), New York City, N.Y.; David A. Armour, *The Merchants of Albany, New York, 1686–1760* (New York: Garland, 1986), 66; Trelease, *Indian Affairs*, 204–27; Norton, *Fur Trade in Colonial New York*, 43–47.

57. Burke, *Mohawk Frontier*, 145–46.

58. Richter, *Ordeal of the Longhouse*, 268–69. According to economic theorists, "dependency" occurs when economies of the periphery are absorbed into a core capitalist economy. Through this process the peripheral economy is no longer able to function independently: its growth is stunted as it begins to operate purely to service the needs of the core. For further elaboration, see the special issue of *International Organization* 32 (1978), titled *Dependence and Dependency in the Global System*, ed. James A. Caporasco.

59. Memoir of M. de Denoville on the State of Canada, November 12, 1685, *DRCHNY*, 9:281; Van der Donck, "Description of New Netherland," 122; Megapolensis, "Account of the Mohawk Indians," 44; Fenton and Tooker, "Mohawk," 468, 478.

60. Van der Donck, "Description of New Netherland," 122; Daniel K. Richter, "Ordeals of the Longhouse: The Five Nations in Early American History," in *Beyond the Covenant Chain*, ed. Merrell and Richter, 11–27; Gretchen Green, "Gender and the Longhouse: Iroquois Women in a Changing Culture," in *Women and Freedom in Early America*, ed. Larry D. Elridge (New York: New York University Press, 1997), 15–16; Richter, "Stratification and Class in Eastern Native America," 43.

61. "Sachem" is an Algonquian term for chief. Megapolensis, "Account of the Mohawk Indians," 43 (first quote); Van der Donck, "Description of New Netherland," 121; Harmen Meyndertsz van den Bogaert, "A Journey into Mohawk and Oneida Country, 1634–1635," in *IMC*, 4; Danckaerts, "Voyage to New York," 196 (second quote); Wendell Indian Account Book; Norton, *Fur Trade in Colonial New York*, 28, 35; Armour, *Merchants of Albany*, 67.

62. Iroquois women were not alone in seeking out European husbands. David Peterson-del Mar notes that the Chinookan Indians of Northwest America were a status-conscious society, which encouraged women of noble birth to seek alliances, if not marriage, with European traders as a means to enhance their wealth and social stand-

ing. See his "Intermarriage and Agency: A Chinookan Case Study," *Ethnohistory* 42:1 (1995): 1–30. See also Susan Sleeper-Smith, *Indian Women and French Men: Rethinking Cultural Encounters in the Western Great Lakes* (Amherst: University of Massachusetts Press, 2001).

63. Megapolensis, "Account of the Mohawk Indians," 43; Cadwallader Colden, *The History of the Five Indian Nations of Canada* (London: Printed for T. Osborne, 1747), 11. Van der Donck also observed how some chiefs "readily accommodate a visiting friend with one of their wives for a night" in "Description of New Netherland," 115. This practice was also evident among the southern Indians; see John Lawson, *A New Voyage to Carolina*, ed. Hugh T. Lefler (Chapel Hill: University of North Carolina Press, 1967), 46–47.

64. It is not known exactly *when* the Delaware first began to be called women, but it is generally thought to be sometime after contact during the seventeenth century. See David Zeisberger, "History of the Northern American Indians," ed. Archer Butler and William N. Schwarze, *Ohio Archaeological and Historical Quarterly* 19:1–2 (1910): 34–35; John Heckewelder, *History, Manners, and Customs of the Indian Nations, Who Once Inhabited Pennsylvania and the Neighbouring States*, ed. William C. Reichel (1876; facsimile reprint, Bowie, Md., 1990), 56–58; and Jay Miller, "The Delaware as Women: A Symbolic Solution," *American Ethnologist* 1 (1974): 507–14. On the use of kinship terms in diplomacy, see Robert A. Williams Jr., *Linking Arms Together: American Indian Treaty Visions of Law and Peace, 1600–1800* (New York: Oxford University Press, 1997), chap. 3, esp. 71–73.

65. Kathleen M. Brown explores the "gendering" of relations between Englishmen and Algonquians in the colonial South. Distinct from the situation in New York, Virginian settlers sought to assert their warrior masculinity by feminizing the male Algonquian population. See her *Good Wives, Nasty Wenches and Anxious Patriarchs: Gender, Race, and Power in Colonial Virginia* (Chapel Hill: University of North Carolina Press, 1996), chap. 2.

66. Proceedings Between Governor Andros and the Five Nations of Indians, September 18–21, 1688, *DRCHNY*, 3:558–59; Baron de Louis Armand de Lom d'Arce Lahontan, *New Voyages to North America . . .* (London, 1703), 41; Colden, *History of the Five Indian Nations of Canada*, 64–65. Seneca chief quoted in Jennings, *Ambiguous Iroquois Empire*, 194.

67. Megapolensis, "Account of the Mohawk Indians," 45; Lawrence W. Leder, ed., *The Livingston Indian Records, 1666–1723* (Gettysburg: Pennsylvania Historical Association, 1756), 115; William M. Beauchamp, ed., *Moravian Journals Relating to Central New York, 1745–66* (1916; New York: AMS Press, 1976), 91, 111n30. On their willingness to incorporate European adoptees into lineages, see "Voyages of Pierre Esprit Radisson," esp. 69–70. For works that examine how northeastern Indians incorporated outsiders into their cultural worlds, see James Axtell, *After Columbus: Essays in the Ethnohistory of Colonial North America* (New York: Oxford University Press, 1988), 125–43; and Bruce Trigger, "Early Native North American Responses to European Contact: Romanticism vs. Rationalistic Interpretations," *JAH* 77 (1991): 1195–1215.

68. On the impact of Catholicism, see Daniel K. Richter, "Iroquois vs. Iroquois: Jesuit Missions and Christianity in Village Politics, 1642–1686," *Ethnohistory* 32:1 (1985): 1–16; Nancy Bonvillain, "The Iroquois and the Jesuits: Strategies of Influence and Resistance," *American Indian Culture and Research Journal* 10:1 (1986): 29–42; Nancy Shoemaker, "Kateri Tekakwitha's Tortuous Path to Sainthood," in *Negotiators of Change*, ed. Shoemaker, 49–71; and Allan Greer, *Mohawk Saint: Catherine Tekakwitha and the Jesuits* (New York: Oxford University Press, 2004). On the impact of Protestantism, see Richter, " 'Some of Them . . . Would Always Have a Minister with Them': Mohawk Protestantism, 1683–1719," *AIQ* 16:4 (1992): 471–84; and Burke, *Mohawk Frontier*, 151–54. On the Kahnawake Mohawks, see Fenton and Tooker, "Mohawk," 469–71.

69. Horatio Hale, ed., *The Iroquois Book of Rites* (1883; Toronto: Coles Publishing Company, 1972), 53–58.

70. Proposition of the Onondaga and Cayuga Indians, August 2, 1684, *DRCHNY*, 3:417; "Deed from the Five Nations . . . 1701," *DRCHNY*, 4:905; Colden, *History of the Five Indian Nations of Canada*, 3.

71. Hinderaker, "The 'Four Indian Kings,' " 488; Colden, *History of the Five Indian Nations of Canada*, 1, 2. The English readily embraced a view of the Iroquois empire. Mirroring the claims of headmen, the Board of Trade asserted in 1709, "From the first settlement of the Colony of New York (which we take to have been about the year 1610)," they found "the five Nations of Indians . . . possessing the Lands to the Westward, and North West of that Plantation. . . . The said five Nations being the most warlike in those parts of the world, held all their neighbouring Indians in a manner of Tributary subjection, they went sometimes as far as the South Sea, the North West Passage and Florida, to war, and extended also their conquests over that part of the Country now called Canada." Memorial of the Right of the British Crown over the New-York Indians, June 2, 1709, *DRCHNY*, 5:75.

72. Danckaerts, "Voyage to New York," 195–98; Burke, *Mohawk Frontier*, 147–50; Richter, "Cultural Brokers and Intercultural Politics"; Hagedorn, "Brokers of Understanding," 381–82; Barbara J. Sivertsen, *Turtles, Wolves and Bears: A Mohawk Family Tree* (Bowie, Md.: Heritage Books, 1996), chap. 1.

Chapter 2

1. The literature on Johnson is vast. Older works depict him as a benign paternalistic father figure or feudalistic overlord: William Stone, *The Life and Times of Sir William Johnson, Bart.*, 2 vols. (Albany, N.Y.: J. Munsell, 1865); Augustus C. Buell, *Sir William Johnson* (New York: D. Appleton and Company, 1903); Arthur Pound, *Johnson of the Mohawks: A Biography of Sir William Johnson* (New York: Macmillan, 1930); James T. Flexner, *Mohawk Baronet: A Biography of Sir William Johnson* (1959; Syracuse, N.Y.: Syracuse University Press, 1989); John C. Guzzardo, "Sir William Johnson's Official Family: Patrons and Clients in an Anglo-American Empire, 1742–1777" (Ph.D. diss., Syracuse University, 1975); Milton W. Hamilton, *Sir William Johnson: Colonial American, 1715–1763* (Port Washington, N.Y.: Kennikat Press, 1976). Michael J. Mullin de-

scribed him as an impartial policy-maker in "Sir William Johnson, Indian Relations and British Policy, 1744–1774" (Ph.D. diss., University of California, Santa Barbara, 1989). More recently he has been depicted as an innocuous facilitator of intercultural mixing and a promoter of Indian interests: Kirk Davis Swinehart, "This Wild Place: Sir William Johnson Among the Mohawks, 1715–1783" (Ph.D. diss., Yale University Press, 2002); Fintan O'Toole, *White Savage: William Johnson and the Invention of America* (London: Faber and Faber, 2005).

2. Guzzardo, "Sir William Johnson's Official Family," esp. chaps. 2, 4, 5; Hamilton, *William Johnson*, 34, 37–38, and chap. 25.

3. For a background on Johnson's marriage partners, see Milton W. Hamilton, "Sir William Johnson's Wives," *NYH* 38:1 (1957): 18–28.

4. On Johnson as a cultural broker, see Timothy J. Shannon, "Dressing for Success on the Mohawk Frontier: Hendrick, William Johnson, and the Indian Fashion," *WMQ* 53:1 (1996): 13–42; Calloway, *New Worlds for All*, 131; and William B. Hart, "Black 'Go-Betweens' and the Mutability of 'Race,' Status, and Identity on New York's Pre-Revolutionary Frontier," in *Contact Points: American Frontiers from the Mohawk Valley to the Mississippi, 1750–1830*, ed. Andrew R. L. Cayton and Fredrika J. Teute (Chapel Hill: University of North Carolina Press, 1998), 101–2.

5. Johnson to George Clinton, May 24, 1750, Clinton Papers, vol. 10 (hereafter Clinton Papers: 10); Transactions with the Six Nations, September 8, 1753, *SWJP*, 9:119. For a background on the Iroquois condolence ritual, see Fenton, *Great Law of the Longhouse*, chaps. 9, 12. On Johnson's self-conscious use of metaphoric devices, see *SWJP*, 1:522. On Johnson's Indian name, see "Journal of Warren Johnson, 1760–1761," in *IMC*, 258. On Johnson's adoption by the Mohawks, see Chapter 5, n. 33.

6. Johnson to Peter Warren, July 24, 1749, *SWJP*, 1:239; Johnson to Clinton, May 30, 1747, *SWJP*, 1:95.

7. Johnson to Clinton, July 30, 1753, *SWJP*, 9:109. Johnson also instructed fort commanders to engage in the condolence ceremony and appoint new chiefs in his name. See John Lindesay to Johnson, September 20, 1750, *SWJP*, 1:300.

8. Indian Proceedings, May 16, 1755, *SWJP*, 1:630; Speeches to Indians and Replies, May 17, 1755, *SWJP*, 9:178–79; Johnson to Arent Stevens, May 1755, *SWJP*, 9:185.

9. Colden, *History of the Five Indian Nations of Canada*, 164; Johnson to William Shirley, December 17, 1754, *SWJP*, 1:430; Johnson to John Catherwood, April 9, 1748, *SWJP*, 1:153.

10. Johnson to Clinton, December 20, 1750, *SWJP*, 1:315; Tench Tilghman Papers, 1775–86, p. 9, Manuscript Division, Library of Congress, Washington, D.C.

11. Clinton to Johnson, February 27, 1756, *SWJP*, 9:386; Isabel T. Kelsay, "Tekawiroñte," *DCB* 4 (1979): 731; Will of Sir William Johnson, *SWJP*, 12:1064–65. For suggestions of other illegitimate offspring, see Donald H. Kent and Merle H. Deardorff, eds., "John Adlum on the Allegheny: Memoirs for the Year 1794," *PMHB* 84:3 (1960): 311n101.

12. Joseph Chew to Johnson, January 1, 1749, *SWJP*, 1:205; John Levine to Johnson,

October 23, 1768, *SWJP*, 6:448; Johnson to Goldsbrow Banyar, April 2, 1762, *SWJP*, 13:277.

13. Johnson to Charles Inglis, April 26, 1770, *SWJP*, 7:599.

14. Ibid.; Frank J. Klingberg, "Sir William Johnson and the Society for the Propagation of the Gospel (1749–1774)," *Historical Magazine of the Protestant Episcopal Church* 8:1 (1939): 4–37.

15. Peter Johnson to William Johnson, December 13, 1773, *SWJP*, 8:945; Francis Wade to William Johnson, December 13, 1773, *SWJP*, 8:946–48; Wade to Johnson, February 1, 1774, *SWJP*, 8:1019–21; Wade to Johnson, March 6, 1774, *SWJP*, 8:1062–63; Peter Johnson to Johnson, April 30, 1774, *SWJP*, 8:1139–40; Guzzardo, "Sir William Johnson's Official Family," 285–89; "Claim of Brant Johnson late of New York Prov. August 30, 1787," included in the appendix of Guldenzopf, "Colonial Transformation," 208.

16. Clinton to Johnson, August 28, 1746, *SWJP*, 1:60–61. For background on the war, see Steele, *Warpaths*, 170–74.

17. Johnson to John Henry Lydius, January 26, 1747, *SWJP*, 1:73–74 (first quote); Johnson to Clinton, August 19 and 28, 1747, *DRCHNY*, 6:389, 390. On Britain's limited war aims, see Steele, *Warpaths*, 170; and Bruce P. Lenman, "Colonial Wars and Imperial Instability, 1688–1793," in *OHBE*, 2:158.

18. Clinton to Johnson, August 28, 1746, *SWJP*, 1:60; Johnson to Clinton, May 30 and 31, 1747, *SWJP*, 1:94–95, 96–97; Johnson to Clinton, May 7, 1747, *DRCHNY*, 6:360–61. On Iroquois neutrality during this war, see Aquila, *Iroquois Restoration*, 92–100; and Jon William Parmenter, "At the Wood's Edge: Iroquois Foreign Relations, 1727–1768" (Ph.D. diss., University of Michigan, 1999), chap. 3.

19. For standard works on Theyanoguin that have misidentified him with Tejonihokarawa, see William L. Stone, "King Hendrick," *New York State Historical Association, Proceedings* 1 (1901): 28–39; W. E. Smith, "Hendrick," *Dictionary of American Biography* (New York: Charles Scribner's Sons, 1960), 4:532–33; Milton W. Hamilton, "Hendrick," *DCB* 3 (1974): 622–24; and Snow, "Theyanoguin," 208–26. For more recent works that have not included this confusion, see Sivertsen, *Turtles, Wolves and Bears*, 136–37ff; and Shannon, *Crossroads of Empire*, 30–31n40. See also Chapter 1, n. 1.

20. On Theyanoguin presenting Canajoharie grievances to colonial authorities, see for e.g. *DRCHNY*, 6:293–95, 781–88, 866–83.

21. Peter Wraxall, "Some Thoughts upon the British Indian Interests in North America," *DRCHNY*, 7:22; Johnson to Clinton, March 18, 1747, *SWJP*, 1:81; Account of Indian Expenses, *SWJP*, 2:573, 621, 9:15–31; Speech of Hendrick, February 2, 1750, *DRCHNY*, 6:548–49; Johnson to Clinton, August 18, 1750, Clinton Papers:

22. Following Theyanoguin's death, Johnson continued to support his widow; see *SWJP*, 2:614, 624, 12:897, 945, 999, 1019. On the Johnson-Theyanoguin relationship, see Shannon, "Dressing for Success on the Mohawk Frontier," 26–35; and Michael J. Mullin, " 'Personal Politics': William Johnson and the Mohawks," *AIQ* 17:3 (1993): 352–53.

22. Arent Stevens to Johnson, May 8, 1751, *SWJP*, 1:330–31; Deed of Land, August 24, 1751, *SWJP*, 13:15; Account of Indian Expenses, June 11, 1755, *SWJP*, 2:573.

23. A Memorial [by Johnson], 1750, *SWJP*, 9:74; Johnson to Catherwood, April 9, 1748, *SWJP*, 1:153; Johnson to Clinton, June 28, 1749, *SWJP*, 9:39.

24. Johnson to Clinton, August 18, 1750, Clinton Papers: 22; Reports of the Council of Commissioners of Indian Affairs of Albany, December 18, 1753, fol. 17, NAHC. Theyanoguin later denounced the commissioners; see Conference between Clinton and the Indians, June 16, 1753, *DRCHNY*, 6:788. Shannon provides the best account of Theyanoguin's ability to wield his colonial and imperial connections in the interests of his community in *Crossroads of Empire*, 30–36, 46–47, and "Dressing for Success on the Mohawk Frontier," 26–35.

25. Johnson to Clinton, May 4, 1750, *SWJP*, 1:278; Johnson to Clinton, August 18, 1750, Clinton Papers: 22; Council held at Philadelphia, January 17, 1755, *MPCP*, 6:281–83; Robert Hunter Morris to Johnson, January 23, 1755, *SWJP*, 9:153; Conference between Clinton and the Indians, June 1753, *DRCHNY*, 6:781–88.

26. Alison G. Olson, "The Changing Socio-Economic and Strategic Importance of the Colonies to the Empire," in *Blackwell Encyclopedia of the American Revolution*, ed. Greene and Pole, esp. 19–21; Greene, "Origins of the New Colonial Policy," 95–96; Patrick O'Brien, "Inseparable Connections: Trade, Economy, Fiscal State, and the Expansion of Empire, 1688–1815," in *OHBE*, 2:53–77; Jacob M. Price, "The Imperial Economy, 1700–1776," in *OHBE*, 2:78–104; T. H. Breen, "An Empire of Goods: The Anglicization of Colonial America, 1690–1776," *Journal of British Studies* 25 (1986): 485–96.

27. For background on French activities in the Ohio country, see Hinderaker, *Elusive Empires*, 134–40; and Michael N. McConnell, *A Country Between: The Upper Ohio Valley and Its Peoples, 1724–1774* (Lincoln: University of Nebraska Press, 1992), chaps. 4–5. "Possession" of this region became a highly contested issue in midcentury. As Steele notes, the Ohio country was "claimed by the Six Nations by conquest, the British colonies by charter, the French crown by discovery, and various Amerindian tribes by occupancy." *Warpaths*, 179.

28. Shannon, *Crossroads of Empire*, 65–72; Alison G. Olson, *Making the Empire Work: London and American Interest Groups, 1690–1790* (New York: Cambridge University Press, 1992).

29. T. R. Clayton, "The Duke of Newcastle, the Earl of Halifax, and the American Origins of the Seven Years' War," *Historical Journal* 24 (1981): 571–603; Steven G. Greiert, "The Board of Trade and Defense of the Ohio Valley, 1748–1753," *Western Pennsylvania Historical Magazine* [hereafter *WPHM*] 64:1 (1981): 1–32; Francis Jennings, *Empire of Fortune: Crown, Colonies and Tribes in the Seven Years' War in America* (New York: W. W. Norton, 1988), 116–18.

30. Archibald Kennedy, *The Importance of Gaining and Preserving the Friendship of the Indians to the British Interest Considered* (London: E. Cave, 1752), 5; Cadwallader Colden to William Shirley, July 25, 1749, *SWJP*, 9:43; Shannon, *Crossroads of Empire*, 72–76.

31. Johnson to Shirley, September 9, 1755, *SWJP*, 9:228–32; *Daniel Claus' Narrative of His Relations with Sir William Johnson and Experiences in the Lake George Fight* (New York: Society of Colonial Wars in the State of New York, 1904); Ian K. Steele, *Betrayals: Fort William Henry and the "Massacre"* (New York: Oxford University Press, 1990), chap. 2.

32. Boleyn Whitney to Johnson, January 31, 1756, *SWJP*, 2:425; Hamilton, *William Johnson*, 187–88; Troy Bickham, *Savages Within the Empire: Representations of American Indians in Eighteenth-Century Britain* (Oxford: Oxford University Press, 2005), 106–7n155. Published colonial accounts include the following: Samuel Blodget, *A Prospective Plan of the Battle Near Lake George . . . With an Explanation Thereof* (Boston, 1755); and Charles Chauncy, *A Second Letter to a Friend, Giving a More Particular Narrative of the Defeat of the French Army at Lake George* (Boston, 1755). Published London accounts include *Gentleman's Magazine*, October 1755, vol. 25, pp. 473–74 (hereafter in form 25:473–74) and November 1755, 25:519–20. For an illuminating discussion of how the British public experienced and celebrated overseas military victories during the Seven Years' War, see Kathleen Wilson, *A Sense of the People: Politics, Culture and Imperialism in England, 1715–1785* (Cambridge, Mass.: Harvard University Press, 1995), chap. 3, esp. 185–205; Bowen, "British Conceptions of Global Empire," 1–5.

33. Steele, *Warpaths*, 188–96; F. Anderson, *Crucible of War*, chap. 6.

34. In North America in 1755, there were only three British regiments in Nova Scotia and seven independent companies stationed in New York and South Carolina. By 1758, there were up to 45,000 British regulars and American provincials in place. The army expanded to 100,000 men in 115 regiments by the end of the war. See F. Anderson, *Crucible of War*, 70, 560. Expenditures also reached novel proportions, with the British government spending in the region of £7.5 million, including £5.5 million on the army. See Lenman, "Colonial Wars and Imperial Instability," 2:161; Julian Gwyn, "British Government Spending and the North American Colonies, 1740–1775," in *The British Atlantic Empire Before the American Revolution*, ed. Peter Marshall and Glyn Williams (London: Routledge, 1980), 77.

35. Minutes of the Council at Alexandria, April 14, 1755, CO 5/46; Braddock's Instructions, 1755, CO 5/6; Commission from Edward Braddock, April 15, 1755, *SWJP*, 1:465–66. For a summation of the conference, see Hamilton, *William Johnson*, 116–18.

36. The minutes of this conference are detailed in *DRCHNY*, 6:964–89 (quote from p. 965). Preliminary meetings for this conference began in May. See Indian Proceedings, May 15–June 21, 1755, *SWJP*, 1:625–42; Johnson to Edward Braddock, June 27, 1755, *SWJP*, 1:663–64.

37. Commission from George Second, February 17, 1756, *SWJP*, 2:434–35. The reputation of the Dutch commissioners is a source of controversy. Contemporaries censured the commissioners for their neglect of Indian affairs and overriding concern with private profit. See Cadwallader Colden, "Memorial concerning the Fur Trade of the Province of New York, presented to His Excellency William Burnet," [November 10, 1724], *DRCHNY*, 5:726–33; and Wraxall, *Abridgment of the Indian Affairs*, 4–5 ff. More

recently, historians have portrayed the commissioners in a sympathetic light. See especially Norton, *Fur Trade in Colonial New York*, 74–82; and Parmenter, "At the Wood's Edge," chap. 3.

38. On recommendations for a Crown-appointed officer, see Clinton to Newcastle, December 9, 1746, *DRCHNY*, 6:313–14; Clinton and Shirley to the Board of Trade, August 18, 1748, *DRCHNY*, 6:438–39; Kennedy, *Importance of Gaining and Preserving*, 4; and Colden to Clinton, August 8, 1751, Clinton Papers: 11. Kennedy's text was printed with an accompanying letter of support penned anonymously by Benjamin Franklin. On Halifax's growing support for a single officer, see Board of Trade to the Privy Council Committee [incorrectly titled "Report of the Privy Council upon the State of New York"], April 2, 1751, *DRCHNY*, 6:635–39; More recommendations for an Indian superintendent were forthcoming at the Albany Congress of 1754. See "Mr. Pownall's Considerations towards a General Plan of Measures for the Colonies," July 11, 1754, *DRCHNY*, 6:896–97; Representation to the King on the Proceedings of the Congress at Albany, October 29, 1754, *DRCHNY*, 6:916–20; and John R. Alden, "The Albany Congress and Creation of the Indian Superintendencies," *Mississippi Valley Historical Review* 27 (1940–41): 193–210.

39. Secretary [John] Pownall to Johnson, March 5, 1756, *DRCHNY*, 7:40–41. For historians who have considered the movement toward Crown control of Indian affairs as indicative of rising British imperialism, see Stephen H. Cutcliffe, "Colonial Indian Policy as a Measure of Rising Imperialism: New York and Pennsylvania, 1700–1755," *WPHM* 64 (1981): 237–68; and Shannon, *Crossroads of Empire*, 220–23. On Johnson's southern counterpart, see J. Russell Snapp, *John Stuart and the Struggle for Empire on the Southern Frontier* (Baton Rouge: Louisiana State University Press, 1996).

40. Johnson had many supporters who advocated his appointment. On Clinton's recommendation to Newcastle, Bedford, and the Board of Trade from 1746 to 1748, see *DRCHNY*, 6:314, 379, 396, 419, 432. As early as 1751, the Board of Trade acknowledged Johnson as "a very diligent, honest, and able Officer." See Board of Trade to the Privy Council Committee, April 2, 1751, *DRCHNY*, 6:638; and Representation to the King on the Proceedings of the Congress at Albany, October 29, 1754, *DRCHNY*, 6:916–20. In support of Johnson, and most likely at his request, Secretary of Indian Affairs Peter Wraxall produced a weighty document for the Board of Trade, upholding the need for a royal officer and stressing Johnson's suitability: "Some Thoughts upon the British Indian Interests in North America, more particularly as it relates to the Northern Confederacy Commonly called the Six Nations [1756]," *DRCHNY*, 7:15–31.

41. For a list of formal conferences that took place during the war, see Jennings et al., *History and Culture of Iroquois Diplomacy*, 188–92; and *SWJP*, 1:xx–xxvi. For Johnson's initial instructions to his Indian officers, see *SWJP*, 9:582–85.

42. Account of Indian Expenses, May–June 1755, *SWJP*, 2:570–71, 572, 573. On the significance of gift-giving in British-Indian relations, see Wilbur R. Jacobs, *Wilderness Politics and Indian Gifts: The Northern Colonial Frontier, 1748–1763* (Lincoln: University of Nebraska Press, 1966).

43. Shirley to Johnson, January 13, 1756, *SWJP*, 2:412; Account of Indian Expenses, March 1755–October 1756, CO 5/1067; Account of Indian Expenses, November 1758–December 1759, CO 5/57 (both accounts are reprinted in *SWJP*, 2:566–645, 3:149–81); Account of Indian Expenses, November 1756–March 1757, *SWJP*, 9:644–58; Johnson to Lord Loudoun, April 15, 1757, *SWJP*, 9:679. See also Board of Trade to Clinton, September 18, 1753, *DRCHNY*, 6:854.

44. Indian Conference, February 7, 1757, *SWJP*, 9:601 (ungrateful). On Johnson's use and misuse of private councils, see *SWJP*, 9:588–89, 595–96, 937–38, 10:76 (folly); and Guzzardo, "Sir William Johnson's Official Family," 261. On installing chiefs, see *DRCHNY*, 8:243; and *SWJP*, 1:634, 1:641, 9:963, 10:75, 237.

45. Jacobs, *Wilderness Politics and Indian Gifts*, chap. 5; Mullin, "'Personal Politics,'" 351–52; Shannon, "Dressing for Success on the Mohawk Frontier."

46. Journal of Indian Proceedings, February–March 1757, *SWJP*, 9:618–19, 621, 623; Journal of Indian Affairs, December 12, 1758, *SWJP*, 10:75.

47. On the Bunt, whose Indian name was Hotsinoñhyahta, see *SWJP*, 2:695, 701; and Arthur Einhorn et al., "Hotsinoñhyahta," *DCB* 4 (1979): 368. On Ottrowana and the Englishman, see *DRCHNY*, 7:239; Johnson to Abercromby, October 3, 1758, ser. 34, vol. 39, p. 59, WO (hereafter in form WO 34/39/59); and (collaborate authors) "Ottrowana," *DCB* 4 (1979): 595–96. On Thomas King, see *SWJP*, 2:632, 3:168. On the Belt and Seneca George, see *DRCHNY*, 7:113, 115. On Sayenqueraghta, also known to the English as Old Smoke, Old King, and the Seneca King, see Thomas S. Abler, "Kaien'kwaahtoñ," *DCB* 4 (1979): 404–6. The quote is from Johnson to the Earl of Shelburne, August 14, 1767, *DRCHNY*, 7:946–47. Fenton explores Johnson's efforts to "remake the . . . confederacy" (p. 493) in *Great Law of the Longhouse*, chap. 31.

48. Journal of Sir William, November 19, 1756, *DRCHNY*, 7:232.

49. Journal of Indian Affairs, April 5, 1757, *SWJP*, 9:670; Journal of Sir William, March 5 and July 21, 1756, *DRCHNY*, 7:91–92, 172 (quote), 10:499–510; Einhorn et al., "Hotsinoñhyahta," 368–69.

50. Shannon has outlined the disadvantages Johnson's new office had specifically for the Mohawks in *Crossroads of Empire*, 223–24.

51. Shirley to Johnson, March 26, June 15, and July 17, 1755, *SWJP*, 1:462 (first quote), 600, 734–35; Johnson to Thomas Pownall, July 31, 1755, *SWJP*, 1:805 (second quote); Account of Indian Expenses, July–September 1755, *SWJP*, 2:583–85, 593; Milton W. Hamilton, ed., "Documents: The Papers of Sir William Johnson: Addenda," *NYH* 60:1 (1979): 86.

52. Johnson to Shirley, December 17, 1754, *SWJP*, 1:430; Kennedy, *Importance of Gaining and Preserving*, 43 (Franklin quote), 6–7; Shirley to Johnson, April 10, 1756, *SWJP*, 9:427; Johnson to Peter Warren, July 24, 1749, *SWJP*, 1:239. See also "Measures Proposed by William Shirley . . . [December 1755]," in *Correspondence of William Shirley, Governor of Massachusetts and Military Commander in America, 1731–1760*, 2 vols., ed. Charles H. Lincoln (New York: Macmillan, 1912), 2:366.

53. On previous efforts by the New York colony to enlist Iroquois martial labor, see

Richter, *Ordeal of the Longhouse*, 166–67, 225–29. On other colonial efforts, see Richard R. Johnson, "The Search for a Usable Indian: An Aspect of the Defense of Colonial New England," *JAH* 64:3 (1977): 623–51. On the Iroquois' longstanding policy of neutrality, see Anthony F. C. Wallace, "Origins of Iroquois Neutrality: The Grand Settlement of 1701," *Pennsylvania History* 24 (1957): 223–35; Aquila, *Iroquois Restoration*, chap. 4; and Richter, *Ordeal of the Longhouse*, chaps. 9–10.

54. Patrick Frazier, *The Mohicans of Stockbridge* (Lincoln: University of Nebraska Press, 1992), 111–12, 113; Banyar to Johnson, September 25, 1754, *SWJP*, 1:415.

55. Loudoun to Johnson, March 11, 1756, *SWJP*, 9:399 (first quote); Shirley to Johnson, April 17 and May 16, 1756, *SWJP*, 9:434, 453; John Appy to Robert Wood, July 2, 1758, *SWJP*, 2:867; James Abercromby to Johnson, July 4, 1758, *SWJP*, 9:940. On the expense of maintaining Indians, see Johnson to Abercromby, September 30, 1758, *WJP*, 10:17 (second quote); and Jeffrey Amherst to Johnson, October 2, 1759, WO 34/38/84.

56. On Johnson's use of Mohawk adoption, see Johnson to Shirley, April 9 and 22, 1756, *SWJP*, 9:425, 9:440 (quote); Journal of Sir William, March 23 and May 22, 1756, *DRCHNY*, 7:94, 113; Laurence M. Hauptman, "Refugee Havens: The Iroquois Villages of the Eighteenth Century," in *American Indian Environments: Ecological Issues in Native American History*, ed. Christopher Vecsey and Robert W. Venables (Syracuse, N.Y.: Syracuse University Press, 1980), 131–32; and Guldenzopf, "Colonial Transformation," 65–67.

57. On Iroquois participation in the Fort Ticonderoga campaign, see Johnson to Abercromby, November 10, 1758, *SWJP*, 10:54; Flexner, *Mohawk Baronet*, 191–93; and Hamilton, *William Johnson*, 232–33, 235. On Fort Frontenac, see John Bradstreet, *An Impartial Account of Lieut. Col. Bradstreet's Expedition to Fort Frontenac . . .* (London, 1759; Toronto: Rous and Mann, 1940), 8–9; and F. Anderson, *Crucible of War*, 260–61. On Iroquois participation at Fort Niagara, see Johnson to William Pitt, October 24, 1760, *SWJP*, 3:271; Johnson to Board of Trade, June 5, 1760, *DRCHNY*, 7:432; Flexner, *Mohawk Baronet*, chap. 15; Hamilton, *William Johnson*, chap. 21; Parmenter, "At the Wood's Edge," 398–99; and F. Anderson, *Crucible of War*, chap. 34. On Iroquois participation at Montreal, see Johnson to Pitt, October 24, 1760, *SWJP*, 3:272; "Return of such Indians as proceeded with the Army . . . to Montreal," September 13, 1760, WO 34/39/159; Hamilton, *William Johnson*, chap. 22; and D. Peter MacLeod, *The Canadian Iroquois in the Seven Years' War* (Toronto: Dundurn Press, 1996), chap. 9. The activities of Iroquois scouting parties are well documented in Johnson's journal, e.g., *SWJP*, 9:720, 726, 780, 782, 788–89, 792, 794, 795.

58. The British army was a truly multiethnic army. Roughly three hundred Cherokee warriors joined Colonel Byrd of Virginia in the 1758 campaign. General Forbes to William Pitt, May 19, 1758, in *Correspondence of William Pitt*, 2 vols., ed. Gertrude Selwyn Kimball (1906; New York 1969), 1:245–46; Tom Hatley, *The Dividing Paths: Cherokees and South Carolinians Through the Revolutionary Era* (New York: Oxford University Press, 1995), 99–103; Gregory Evans Dowd, "'Insidious Friends': Gift Giving and the Cherokee-British Alliance in the Seven Years' War," in *Contact Points*, ed. Cayton and

Teute, 114–50. On the employment of New England Indians, see Frazier, *Mohicans of Stockbridge*, chaps. 9–10; and Peter Way, "The Cutting Edge of Culture: British Soldiers Encounter Native Americans in the French and Indian War," in *Empire and Others*, ed. Daunton and Halpern, 136–38. See also David L. Preston, " 'Make Indians of Our White Men': British Soldiers and Indian Warriors from Braddock's to Forbes's Campaigns, 1755–1758," *Pennsylvania History* 74:3 (2007): 280–306. On the use of African American soldiers, see Larry G. Bowman, "Virginia's Use of Blacks in the French and Indian War," *WPHM* 53:1 (1970): 57–63; and Scott A. Padeni, "The Role of Blacks in New York's Northern Campaigns of the Seven Years' War," *Bulletin of Fort Ticonderoga Museum* [hereafter *BFTM*] 16:2 (1999): 153–69.

59. Return of Killed, Wounded, and Missing in Battle of Lake George, *SWJP*, 9:238; Milton W. Hamilton, ed., "The Diary of the Reverend John Ogilvie, 1750–1759," *BFTM* 10:5 (1961): 381; "Journal of Warren Johnson," 254, 259, 262; Journal of Indian Proceedings, February 28, 1757, *SWJP*, 9:622–23; Account of Indian Expenses, February 20, 1759, *SWJP*, 3:160; Journal of Indian Affairs, January 29, 1764, *SWJP*, 11:34; Guldenzopf, "Colonial Transformation," 67–69. The Mohawks were also exposed to smallpox when they visited Philadelphia for a treaty in 1757. See John Pemberton to Samuel Fothergill, July 4, 1757, p. 57, vol. 34, Pemberton Papers, Historical Society of Pennsylvania, Philadelphia.

60. Colden, *History of the Five Indian Nations of Canada*, 164; Johnson to Braddock, June 27, 1755, *SWJP*, 1:664; Speeches to Indians and Replies, May 17, 1755, *SWJP*, 9:178.

61. Banyar to Johnson, September 24, 1755, *SWJP*, 2:86; Louis Antoine de Bougainville, "Journal of Bougainville's Campaigns in Canada," *BFTM* 11:1 (1962): 5; M. de Vaudreuil to M. de Machault, February 2, 1756, *DRCHNY*, 10:392.

62. Indian Intelligence, February 18, 1757, *SWJP*, 9:612–13; Indian Congress, April 29, 1757, *SWJP*, 9:706; Thomas Butler to Johnson, April 7, 1757, *SWJP*, 2:699–700.

63. George S. Conover, *Sayenqueraghta, King of the Senecas* (Geneva, N.Y.: Observer Steam Job Printing House, 1885), 14; Walter Pilkington, ed., *The Journals of Samuel Kirkland: 18th Century Missionary to the Iroquois, Government Agent, Father of Hamilton College* (Clinton, N.Y.: Hamilton College, 1980), 45nn26, 29; Fenton, "Problems Arising," 216; Jack Campisi, "Oneida," in *HNAI*, 481; Graymont, *The Iroquois in the American Revolution*, 33.

64. Johnson to Shirley, Braddock, and Sir William Pepperrell, March 17, 1755, *SWJP*, 1:457; Steele, *Betrayals*, chap. 2.

65. For an alternative view that stresses that the building of this fort, along with French Fort Niagara, had more serious consequences for the Iroquois, marking their new status as a colonized people, see Richter, *Ordeal of the Longhouse*, 249–54. .

66. *State of the British and French Colonies in North America . . . in Two Letters to a Friend* (London, 1755), 105, quoted in Shannon, *Crossroads of Empire*, 67. Halifax quoted in L. H. Gipson, "A French Project for Victory Short of a Declaration of War, 1755," *Canadian Historical Review* 26 (1945): 362.

67. Johnson to Clinton, second of two letters dated March 12, 1754, Clinton Papers: 13. This fictive legal argument of British right to Iroquois lands was broadly disseminated and unquestioningly accepted. It was reaffirmed at the Albany Conference in 1754 (see *DRCHNY*, 6:886) and encased in political pamphlets of the day, e.g., [John Huske], *The Present State of North America, etc. Part I* (London, 1755). See also Jennings, *Empire of Fortune*, 118, 126, 132–33.

68. Kennedy, *Importance of Gaining and Preserving*, 6–11; Colonel Johnson's Suggestions for defeating the designs of the French, July 1754, *DRCHNY*, 6:897–99; Johnson to Clinton, second of two letters dated March 12, 1754, Clinton Papers: 13.

69. Johnson to Amherst, August 9, 1759, *SWJP*, 3:121; Johnson to William Baker, September 28, 1759, *SWJP*, 3:140.

70. Indian Conference, February 20, 1756, *SWJP*, 9:365; Johnson to Board of Trade, September 10, 1756, *DRCHNY*, 7:129; Colonel Johnson's Suggestions, *SWJP*, 6:897; Secret Conference held at Montreal with the Indians, October 23, 1754, *DRCHNY*, 10:269.

71. Conference between Major General Johnson and the Indians, June 24, 1755, *DRCHNY*, 6:970.

72. John Burk Diary, July–October 1755, Peter Force Papers, ser. 8D, entry no. 16, reel 31, Library of Congress, Manuscripts Division, Washington, D.C.; Chauncy, *Second Letter to a Friend*, 16; James Brown to Johnson, October 23, 1755, *SWJP*, 9:278; George Muirson to Johnson, November 2, 1755, *SWJP*, 9:294. See also James Gilbert, "A Copy of a Journal Kept by James Gilbert of Morton, Mass., in the Year 1755," *Magazine of New England History* 3 (1893): 191, 193; and James Hill, "The Diary of a Private on the First Expedition to Crown Point," ed. Edna V. Moffat, *New England Quarterly* [hereafter *NEQ*] 36:3 (1963): 607.

73. Hinderaker, "The 'Four Indian Kings'"; David Milobar, "Aboriginal Peoples and the British Press, 1720–1763," in *Hanoverian Britain and Empire: Essays in Memory of Philip Lawson*, ed. Stephen Taylor et al. (Woodbridge, Eng.: Boydell Press, 1998), 65–81.

74. On Londoners' keen interest in Theyanoguin, see Hinderaker, "The 'Four Indian Kings,'" 523–24. A print of Theyanoguin was advertised in *Gentleman's Magazine*, November 1755, 25:527. For his speech, see *Gentleman's Magazine*, June 1755, 25:252–56. For suggestions of his hybrid identity, see Shannon, *Crossroads of Empire*, 224–26. Despite historical accounts to the contrary, Theyanoguin never visited London; see Alden T. Vaughan, "American Indians Abroad: The Mythical Travels of Mrs. Penobscot and King Hendrick," *NEQ* 80:2 (2007): 299–316.

75. William Hervey, *The Journals of the Hon. William Hervey, in North America and Europe, from 1755 to 1814*, Suffolk Green Books no. 14 (Bury St. Edmunds: Paul and Mathew, 1906), 6; Blodget, *Prospective Plan of the Battle Near Lake George*, 1. For other works that consider the importance of dress in Indian-colonial relations, see Shannon, "Dressing for Success on the Mohawk Frontier"; Ann M. Little, "Shoot That Rogue, for He Hath an Englishman's Coat On!: Cultural Cross-Dressing on the New England Frontier, 1620–1760," *NEQ* 74:2 (2001): 238–73.

76. For a broader discussion of the cultural imagining of Indians and their place in the visual imagery of the empire and Atlantic world, see Beth Fowkes Tobin, *Picturing Imperial Power: Colonial Subjects in Eighteenth-Century British Painting* (Durham, N.C.: Duke University Press, 1999), chap. 3; Bickham, *Savages Within the Empire*; and Stephanie Pratt, *American Indians in British Art* (Norman: University of Oklahoma Press, 2005).

77. For examples of Johnson providing Indian character references, see *SWJP*, 2:500, 550, 9:439 (quote), 515.

Chapter 3

1. "Journal of Warren Johnson, 1760–1761," in *IMC*, 250–73, quotes from 255, 259–60.

2. Other scholars have noted "the deepening thrust of commercial relations" between the British and other native groups at midcentury (quote here from Richard White, *The Roots of Dependency: Subsistence, Environment, and Social Change Among the Choctaws, Pawnees, and Navajos* [Lincoln: University of Nebraska Press, 1983], p. 34). See White, *The Roots of Dependency*, chap. 4; James H. Merrell, *The Indians' New World: Catawbas and Their European Neighbors from European Contact Through the Era of Removal* (New York: W. W. Norton, 1989), chap. 2; Merritt, *At the Crossroads*, 83.

3. This economic order can best be described as transitional, "not yet fully capitalistic, but located in an increasingly capitalist world." Allan Kulikoff, "The Transition to Capitalism in Rural America," *WMQ* 44:1 (1989): 140.

4. John Bartram, "Observations on . . . His Travels from Pensilvania to Onondago" [London, 1751], in *A Journey from Pennsylvania to Onondaga in 1743 by John Bartram, Lewis Evans and Conrad Weiser*, ed. Whitefield J. Bell (Barre, Mass.: Imprint Society, 1973), 65–66; John B. Van Eps to Johnson, May 6, 1746, *SWJP*, 1:50; Frederick W. Barnes, "The Fur Traders of Early Oswego," *New York Historical Association, Proceedings* 13 (1914): 130–33. Albany still operated as an important center of commerce, but Albany merchants were heavily involved in an illegal traffic with Canada. See Jean Lunn, "The Illegal Fur Trade out of New France, 1713–60," *Canadian Historical Association, Papers* (1939): 61–76; and Jon Parmenter, "The Significance of the 'Illegal' Fur Trade to the Eighteenth Century Iroquois," in *Aboriginal People and the Fur Trade: Proceedings of the 8th North American Fur Trade Conference, Akwesasne*, ed. Louise Johnston (Ontario: Akwesasne Notes Publishing, 2001), 40–47.

5. Guzzardo, "Sir William Johnson's Official Family," 108–11; Hagedorn, "Brokers of Understanding," 388. On trade with German neighbors, see accounts of George Weaver, Lodowick Crane, and John Dygert [Sygant] in Unidentified Account Book, Schenectady, April 7, 1756–July 23, 1764, box 18, Campbell Family Papers, New York State Library (hereafter NYSL), Albany, N.Y.; and Indian Proceedings, September 15, 1757, *SWJP*, 9:832. On the presence of traders in Iroquois country, see *SWJP*, 1:291; Beauchamp, *Moravian Journals*, 129, 142; Arthur C. Parker, "Notes on the Ancestry of Cornplanter," *New York State Archaeological Association, Researches and Transactions* 5:2 (1927): 4–7;

William Ketchum, *An Authentic and Comprehensive history of Buffalo, with some account of its early inhabitants both savage and civilized . . .* , 2 vols. (Buffalo, N.Y.: Rockwell, Baker and Hill, 1864), 2:122–24.

6. Governor Hunter's Answer to the Five Nations, August 29, 1715, *DRCHNY*, 5:442; Council held at Philadelphia, July 12, 1742, *MPCP*, 4:581.

7. Council held at Philadelphia, July 5, 1727, *MPCP*, 3:275; Conference between Lt. Gov. Clarke and the Six Nations, August 12, 1740, *DRCHNY*, 6:177.

8. Biographical Sketch of the Rev. Abbe Picquet, *DHNY*, 1:285; Reports of the Council of Commissioners of Indian Affairs of Albany, September 13–14, 1754, fols. 71, 73–74, NAHC. On Indians as active consumers, see Arthur J. Ray, "Indians as Consumers in the Eighteenth Century," in *Old Trails, New Directions: Papers of the Third North American Fur Trade Conference*, ed. Carol M. Judd and Arthur J. Ray (Toronto: University of Toronto Press, 1980), 255–71; Dean L. Anderson, "The Flow of European Trade Goods into the Western Great Lakes Region, 1715–1760," in *The Fur Trade Revisited: Selected Papers on the Seventh North American Fur Trade Conference, Mackinac Island, Michigan, 1991*, ed. Jennifer S. H. Brown et al. (East Lansing: Michigan State University Press, 1994), 93–115; and Ann M. Carlos and Frank D. Lewis, "Trade, Consumption, and the Native Economy: Lessons from York Factory, Hudson Bay," *Journal of Economic History* 61:4 (2001): 1037–63.

9. Arent Stevens to Johnson, July 11, 1750, *SWJP*, 1:288. The Joncaire brothers were Philip Thomas and Daniel, Sieur de Chabert et de Clausonne. See Wraxall, *Abridgment of the Indian Affairs*, 238, 243; Johnson to Clinton, August 18, 1750, Clinton Papers: 22; Jacobs, *Wilderness Politics and Indian Gifts*, 29–35; Donald H. Kent, *Iroquois Indians II: Historical Report on the Niagara River and the Niagara River Strip to 1759* (New York: Garland, 1974), 109–34.

10. Cadwallader Colden to Clinton, August 8, 1751, Clinton Papers: 11; Johnson to Clinton, September 14, 1750, Clinton Papers: 22; Butler to Johnson, May 29, 1751, *SWJP*, 1:338; W. J. Eccles, "The Fur Trade and Eighteenth-Century Imperialism," *WMQ* 40:3 (1983): 355. Johnson frequently complained that the British were "far outbid by the French in the purchase of . . . [Iroquois] Freindship." Johnson to Clinton, second letter dated March 12, 1754, Clinton Papers: 13.

11. The fort commander, commissary, interpreter, and traders all participated in these activities; see Teady McGinn to Johnson, June 2, 1747, *SWJP*, 1:97; Van Eps to Johnson, December 15, 1747, *SWJP*, 1:123–25; Arent Stevens to Johnson, July 11, 1750, *SWJP*, 1:287–88; and John Lindesay to Johnson, September 7, 1750, *SWJP*, 1:296–97 and September 20, 1750, *SWJP*, 1:300. On British dispersal of gifts, see Wraxall, *Abridgment of the Indian Affairs*, 221 (food provision); 95, 192, 194, 220 (presents); 175, 196, 225, 229 (smiths). Richard Aquila explores the economic boons the Iroquois enjoyed, positioned between two imperial powers, in *Iroquois Restoration*, 112–28. See also Jacobs, *Wilderness Politics and Indian Gifts*, chap. 2.

12. Lieut. [John] Lindesay's Report, February 5–July 27, 1751, pp. 11–12, Clinton Papers: 11; Mary Black-Rogers, "Varieties of 'Starving': Semantics and Survival in the

Subarctic Fur Trade, 1750–1850," *Ethnohistory* 33:4 (1986): 353–83; White, "Give Us a Little Milk."

13. Extracts from the Journal of Conrad Weiser, [June 1745], item 20, fol. 84, Daniel Horsmanden Papers, NYHS.

14. Council held at Lancaster, June 26, 1744, *MPCP*, 4:707–8.

15. Norton, *Fur Trade in Colonial New York*, 149, 221; Richter, *Ordeal of the Longhouse*, 270–71; Cathy Matson, *Merchants and Empire: Trading in Colonial New York* (Baltimore: Johns Hopkins University Press, 1998), 222–27.

16. "Conrad Weiser's Journal of Journey to Onondaga in 1737," reprinted in William M. Beauchamp, *The Life of Conrad Weiser* (Syracuse, N.Y.: Onondaga Historical Association, 1925), 25; Anne Grant, *Memoirs of an American Lady: With Sketches of Manners and Scenery in America* (1808; New York: D. Appleton & Company, 1846), 65, 69.

17. Daniel Claus to Conrad Weiser, August 23, 1752, in Paul A. Wallace, *Conrad Weiser, 1696–1760: Friend of Colonist and Mohawk* (Philadelphia: University of Pennsylvania Press, 1945), 338; Johnson to Samuel and William Baker, September 12, 1751, *SWJP*, 1:347 (quote); Johnson to John G. Libenrood, August 4, 1752, *SWJP*, 1:372; Beauchamp, *Moravian Journals*, 113 (quote), 120, 122, 123, 134; Gideon Hawley, "A Letter from Rev. Gideon Hawley of Marshpee, Containing an Account of his Services Among the Indians of Massachusetts and New-York, and a Narrative of his Journey to Onohoghgwage," *Massachusetts Historical Society, Collections* [hereafter *MHSC*], 1st ser., 4 (1795): 53.

18. Journal of William Johnson's Mission to the Iroquois, April 24–26, 1748, Clinton Papers: 7; Johnson to Clinton, July 30, 1753, *SWJP*, 9:109; Clinton to Johnson, January 6, 1749, *SWJP*, 1:207; Johnson to Clinton, January 22, 1750, Clinton Papers: 10; Robert Sanders to Johnson, May 8, 1751, *SWJP*, 1:330; A. H. Young, ed., "Letters from and concerning the Reverend John Ogilvie . . . Written to the Society for the Propagation of the Gospel in Foreign Parts," *Ontario Historical Society* 22 (1925): 314. "To leave their Castles" quoted in Shannon, *Crossroads of Empire*, 48. On the issue of credit and debt in the Indian trade, see Wilbur J. Jacobs, "Unsavory Sidelights on the Colonial Fur Trade," *NYH* 34:2 (1953): 135–48; and James C. King, "Indian Credit as a Source of Friction in the Colonial Fur Trade," *Mississippi Valley Historical Review* 49:1 (1966): 57–65.

19. Report on the Affairs of Canada, May 7, 1726, *DRCHNY*, 9:952–53. Older studies emphasize Iroquois victimhood at the hands of land-hungry colonists; see Nammack, *Fraud, Politics and the Dispossession of the Indians*. More recent work has emphasized Iroquois control over this process. See Terry, "Negotiating the Frontier"; and Preston, "Texture of Contact," chap. 1.

20. Council held at Lancaster, June 28, 1744, *MPCP*, 4:716; "Witham Marshe's Journal of the Treaty Held with the Six Nations by the Commissioners of Maryland, and other Provinces, at Lancaster, in Pennsylvania, June, 1744," *MHSC*, 1st ser., 7 (1801): 188–89; Council held at Philadelphia, August 16–21, 1749, *MPCP*, 5:398–410, quote from p. 400; Council held at Philadelphia, July 7, 1742, *MPCP*, 4:570. The political benefits the Iroquois stood to gain from these land treaties are detailed in Aquila, *Iroquois Restora-*

tion, chap. 6, and Jennings, *Ambiguous Iroquois Empire*. Canassatego was a critical figure in these land negotiations. For a sense of his motivations and agenda, see William A. Starna, "The Diplomatic Career of Canasatego," *Friends and Enemies in Penn's Woods: Colonists, Indians, and Racial Construction of Pennsylvania*, ed. William A. Pencak and Daniel K. Richter (University Park: Penn State University Press, 2004), 144–63.

21. Conference between Major-General Johnson and the Indians, July 4, 1755, *DRCHNY*, 6:985; Johnson to Colden, March 19, 1761, *NYHSC* 65 (1932): 18, see also pp. 87–88; *SWJP*, 3:619, 4:115, 116, 10:216, 367, 487–88. Other native groups also became landlords in this period. See Thomas J. Humphrey, " 'Extravagant Claims' and 'Hard Labour': Perceptions of Property in the Hudson Valley, 1751–1801," *Explorations in Early American Culture* 65 (1998): 141–66, esp. 143; Frazier, *Mohicans of Stockbridge*, 156–59; and Merrell, *The Indians' New World*, 209–11, 230–33.

22. Indian Deed, 1735, New York, Ayer Mss 404, n. 17, Newberry Library, Chicago; Conference between Governor Clinton and the Indians, June 12, 1753, *DRCHNY*, 6:783.

23. Johnson to William Smith, May 11, 1763, *SWJP*, 4:116; Wraxall, *Abridgment of the Indian Affairs*, 185. The background to these claims is documented in Higgins, *Expansion in New York* and Nammack, *Fraud, Politics and the Dispossession of the Indians*.

24. Conference between Clinton and Indians, June 12, 1753, *DRCHNY*, 6:781–88; Council held at Lancaster, June 30, 1744, *MPCP*, 4:720. See also *DRCHNY*, 6:985.

25. Conference between Clinton and Indians, June 12, 1753, *DRCHNY*, 6:783. The Pennsylvania government also used the occasion of the Albany Conference to press the Iroquois to sell seven million acres of land in western Pennsylvania for £400. Merritt, *At the Crossroads*, 172–73; Shannon, *Crossroads of Empire*, 108–9, 169–71.

26. Bartram, "Observations," 61, 62; Beauchamp, *Moravian Journals*, 85. By contrast, New England Indians, having experienced greater land loss, were far more familiar with wage labor by the early eighteenth century. See John A. Sainsbury, "Indian Labor in Early Rhode Island," *New England Quarterly* 48:3 (1975): 378–93; Daniel Vickers, "The First Whalemen of Nantucket," *WMQ* 40:4 (1983): 560–83; and Daniel R. Mandell, *Behind the Frontier: Indians in Eighteenth-Century Eastern Massachusetts* (Lincoln: University of Nebraska Press, 1996), 197–98. Wage labor had also developed among southern Indians. See Usner, *Indians, Settlers, and Slaves in a Frontier Exchange Economy*, 232–34; Kathryn E. Holland Braund, *Deerskins and Duffels: The Creek Indian Trade with Anglo-America, 1685–1815* (Lincoln: University of Nebraska Press, 1993), 73–74; and Helen C. Rountree and Thomas E. Davidson, *Eastern Shore Indians of Virginia and Maryland* (Charlottesville: University Press of Virginia, 1997), 76.

27. *Letters from North America by Father Antoine Silvy*, 193; Johnson to Thomas Gage, January 27, 1764, vol. 13, Gage Papers (hereafter in form Gage Papers: 13); *DRCHNY*, 9:885, 1057, 1112; "A Letter from Mr. [Peter] Kalm, a Swedish Gentleman, late on his travels in America, to his friends in Philadelphia; containing a particular account of the Great Fall of Niagara [Albany, September 2, 1750]," in *The Annual Register, or a View of the History, Politicks, and Literature of the Year 1759* (London: R. and J. Dodsley, 1760), 390. See also Kent, *Iroquois Indians II*, 110–13, 151.

28. Bartram, "Observations," 64; Proceedings of the Colonial Congress held at Albany, June 18, 1754, *DRCHNY*, 6:857–58; Reports of the Council of Commissioners, June 18, 1754, fol. 37, NAHC; Armour, *Merchants of Albany*, 196.

29. "Item 863: Receipt for Wolves Heads," in *The Old Stone Church and Fortress: Catalogue and Historical Notes*, ed. Chauncey Rickard (New York: Schoharie Historical Society, 1933), 67; William B. Hart, "'For the Good of Our Souls': Mohawk Authority, Accommodation, and Resistance to Protestant Evangelicalism, 1700–1780" (Ph.D. diss., Brown University, 1998), 216, 226–46.

30. Johnson to Clinton, August 13, 1747, *SWJP*, 1:108; Clinton to Johnson, August 28, 1746, *SWJP*, 1:60–61n1; Receipt, July 2, 1747, *SWJP*, 9:8; Account of Expenses with Receipt, December 13, 1746–July 28, 1747, *SWJP*, 9:15–31; Johnson to John Stoddard, March 24, 1747, *SWJP*, 1:82.

31. Extract from the Rev. H. Barclay's Journal of a Visit to the Mohawks, March 1745, item 22, fol. 67, addenda to the Daniel Horsmanden Papers, NYHS; Johnson to Clinton, May 30 and 31, 1747, *SWJP*, 1:94–95, 97. Evan Haefeli and Kevin Sweeney note that "like furs and scalps, captives had become commercialized commodities by 1704, and Montreal was the center of this trade"; see their *Captors and Captives: The 1704 French and Indian Raid on Deerfield* (Amherst: University of Massachusetts Press, 2003), 147 (quote), 149–51. See also Brett Rushforth, "'A Little Flesh We Offer You': The Origins of Indian Slavery in New France," *WMQ* 60:4 (2003): 808.

32. Conference between M. de Vaudreuil and the Indians, December 13, 1756, *DRCHNY*, 10:503; Journal of Sir William, August 7, 1756, *DRCHNY*, 7:179. On reports of French emissaries among the Iroquois, see *SWJP*, 2:665, 668, 671.

33. Journal of Sir William, March–April 1759, *DRCHNY*, 7:390 (quote), 383, 384; Report of Charles Thomson and Christian Frederick Post to William Denny, June 1, 1758, in *Iroquois Indians: A Documentary History of the Diplomacy of the Six Nations and Their League*, ed. Francis Jennings et al., 50 microfilm reels (Woodbridge, Conn.: Research Publications, 1985), reel 22. On Britain's early war policy of cheap trade, see *SWJP*, 2:410, 9:371.

34. Abstract of Dispatches from America, August 30, 1756, *DRCHNY*, 10:479; Indian Proceedings, December 8, 1756, *DRCHNY*, 9:568–69. For scholars who argue that the Iroquois welcomed the loss of Fort Oswego, see Parmenter, "At the Wood's Edge," 371–73, and Jennings, *Empire of Fortune*, 293–94.

35. "Sir Will. Johnson's Speech to the 5 Nations," [May 1758], *SWJP*, 9:911. On the removal of traders, see various reports from Thomas Butler to Johnson, *SWJP*, 2:665–72. On Iroquois requests for trade to be resumed, see *SWJP*, 2:770, 9:689; and *DRCHNY*, 7:258.

36. Indian Proceedings, December 8, 1756, *SWJP*, 9:568–69; Journal of Sir William, August 10, 1756, *DRCHNY*, 7:183. On warfare and the presence of soldiers disrupting agriculture, see *SWJP*, 3:218, 9:546–47, 591, 688, 965 (quote).

37. Butler to Johnson, April 28 and May 25, 1757, *SWJP*, 9:702–3, 777; Journal of Indian Affairs, January 4, 1757–February 3, 1759, *SWJP*, 9:591, 10:68, 97; Johnson

to Amherst, March 7, 1760, *SWJP*, 3:197; Johnson to Amherst, March 24, 1760, WO 34/39/125; Johnson to Gage, April 8, 1760, *SWJP*, 3:218; Gage to Johnson, April 13, 1760, *SWJP*, 3:219; Johnson to Amherst, May 26, 1760, WO 34/39/139. Johnson provisioned both the Canajoharie and Fort Hunter communities during the war. See, e.g., *SWJP*, 9:798, 802–3.

38. The new commander in chief, James Abercromby, welcomed their economic plight as "not a less lucky incident." Still, in formulating an appropriate response to Iroquois demands, Johnson warned that "a Blunt refusal would be fatal." He urged a policy of "Conditional Promises" rather than "unrestrained Trade." Abercromby to Johnson, April 6, 1758, WO 34/38/32; Johnson to Abercromby, second letter dated April 28, 1758, CO 5/50/147–49.

39. Johnson to Board of Trade, June 25, 1757, *DRCHNY*, 7:228; Journal of Sir William, June 14–16, 1757, *DRCHNY*, 7:258, 262.

40. Indian Congress, June 16–18, 1758, *SWJP*, 9:926–29. See also "Sir Will. Johnson's Speech to the 5 Nations," [May 1758], *SWJP*, 9:911.

41. Journal of Indian Affairs, December 9–12, 1758, *SWJP*, 10:65–73.

42. Ibid., 10:67, 71; Speech of Abercromby to the Six Nations, July 8, 1758, *SWJP*, 9:941. Johnson dispatched a string of officers to regulate trade at Fort Stanwix; see *SWJP*, 2:892–93, 10:62. On Indian attitudes toward this trading post, see Journal of Sir William, April 18, 1759, *DRCHNY*, 7:390.

43. Johnson to John Stanwix, December 16, 1758, WO 34/39/68–69; Journal of Indian Affairs, February 3, 1759, *SWJP*, 10:97; Account of Indian Expenses, 1758–59, *SWJP*, 3:149, 150ff; Butler to Johnson, January 30, 1759, *SWJP*, 10:93.

44. Report of Thomson and Post, June 1, 1758, in *Iroquois Indians*, reel 22; Report of Jellas Fonda, June 12, 1758, *SWJP*, 9:925; Johnson to Lord Loudoun, September 3, 1757, *SWJP*, 9:825–26; Hervey, *Journals*, 10.

45. On the installation of garrisoned forts in Iroquoia, see *SWJP*, 1:603–5, 2:297–98, 9:384, 416, 438–41, 468, 509–10, 527, 568. For instructions to carpenters, see *DRCHNY*, 7:101–2. On building forts at the Oneida Carrying Place, see *SWJP*, 9:191–92. On the series of fortifications built around Oswego, see Douglas J. Pippin, "Fort Ontario," in *Encyclopedia of New York State*, ed. Peter Eisenstadt (Syracuse, N.Y.: Syracuse University Press, 2005), 591.

46. Journal of Sir William, May 23 and 21, 1756, *DRCHNY*, 7:114, 110–11; Johnson to Edward Braddock, May 17, 1755, *SWJP*, 1:512–13; Johnson to Goldsbrow Banyar, May 20, 1755, *SWJP*, 1:524; Thomas Butler to Johnson, May 14, 1755, *SWJP*, 1:495; Williams to Johnson, July 4, 1755, *SWJP*, 9:192. The Fort Bull assault is detailed in MacLeod, *The Canadian Iroquois in the Seven Years' War*, 22–34.

47. Journal of Indian Affairs, November 19, 1758, *SWJP*, 10:59; Johnson to William Baker, December 4, 1762, *SWJP*, 3:954; Johnson to Daniel Claus, June 11, 1761, *SWJP*, 10:282; "By the Honourable James De Lancey . . . A Proclamation," March 7, 1759, *NYHSC* (1892): 516; Proclamation for the Settlement of Land between Fort Edward and Lake George, September 21, 1759, *DHNY*, 4:345–46.

48. Jeffrey Amherst to William Pitt, December 16, 1759, in *Correspondence of William Pitt*, ed. Kimball, 1:199; John Pell, "Philip Skene of Skenesborough," *New York State Historical Association, Proceedings* (1928): 27–44; Higgins, *Expansion in New York*, 88. Johnson, too, was keen to settle former officers and soldiers at Kingsborough. See Guzzardo, "Sir William Johnson's Official Family," 176–82. A large number of Highlander officers and soldiers emigrated to the region at the close of the war; see Colin G. Calloway, "Sir William Johnson, Highland Scots, and American Indians," *NYH* 89:2 (2008): 164–65.

49. On Silverheels, see *SWJP*, 3:175, 177, 9:612, 614, 645, 653 (quote), 10:21, 24, 13:138, 143, 149; and Abercromby to Johnson, September 19, 1758, WO 34/38/48. On Gawèhe, see *SWJP*, 2:626, 3:176, 13:137; *DRCHNY*, 7:151–52; and Arthur Einhorn, "Gawèhe," *DCB* 3 (1974): 255–56. On David, see *SWJP*, 2:593, 594, 626, 639, 640 (quote), 3:153. On Thomas King, see *SWJP*, 2:632, 3:168. On Daniel, see *SWJP*, 2:626, 3:166, 175, 177, 9:792, 13:143, 149. On Aaron, see *SWJP*, 2:576, 3:160, 165. On Captain Dick, see *SWJP*, 9:722; and *DRCHNY*, 7:93.

50. Evidence of payment to Indians is well documented in Johnson's Indian accounts in *SWJP*, 2:566–45, 3:149–81, 9:644–58. See, e.g.: carrying messengers and letters, 1:765, 3:153, 166, 168, 170, 9:593; serving as escorts, 2:600, 3:178, 9:798; carrying baggage, 2:668; transporting provisions and cattle to forts, 2:627, 3:176, 7:503, 9:401; manning whaleboats, 3:175; and capturing deserters, 2:635, 3:176. On payments for military services, see *SWJP*, 2:635, 3:165, 168, 173, 174, 9:533–34, 619, 702. For specific examples cited, see 3:173, 165, 174. On women's involvement in a cash economy, see Chapter 4.

51. Indian Proceedings, July 27, 1755, *SWJP*, 9:212–19, 213 (quote); Shirley to Thomas Robinson, December 20, 1755, in *Correspondence of William Shirley*, ed. Lincoln, 2:355–56; Johnson to James De Lancey, August 8, 1755, *SWJP*, 1:841; Disputes between Shirley and Johnson, September 3–October 5, 1755, *SWJP*, 2:2. Scholars have documented the Shirley-Johnson dispute as a political, not economic, conflict. See, e.g., Jennings, *Empire of Fortune*, 153, 162–63; and Hamilton, *William Johnson*, 177, 180–81, 190–98.

52. Journal of Sir William, August 13, 1756, *DRCHNY*, 7:185.

53. Johnson to Loudoun, March 17, 1757, *SWJP*, 9:641; Johnson to De Lancey, August 8, 1755, *SWJP*, 1:841; Account of Indian Expenses, February 11, 1757, *SWJP*, 2:646; Journal of Sir William, August 13, 1756, *DRCHNY*, 7:184–85. Indian agent Thomas Butler provided a similar rationale for Indian inclinations for cash: "I acquainted him [Col. Bradstreet] how redy the Indians were to serve formerly without money but the expedition last year to Oswego spolt them by giving them great wages. So that they now all expect to have the same." Butler to Johnson, May 4, 1756, *SWJP*, 9:449. Indians oftentimes purchased goods from traders with nothing but cash. See Unidentified Account Book, Schenectady, April 7, 1756–July 23, 1764, fols. 40, 52, 221, and *SWJP*, 10:93.

54. Johnson to Board of Trade, September 10, 1756, *DRCHNY*, 7:129; Johnson to Loudoun, March 17, 1757, *SWJP*, 9:641; Expense of an Indian Regiment, March 15, 1757, *SWJP*, 9:639.

55. Mercer to Williams, April 7, 1756, *SWJP*, 9:423; Bradstreet to Johnson, April 9, 1756, *SWJP*, 9:423–24; John Butler's Receipt, May 20, 1756, *SWJP*, 7:503. See also John St. Clair to Johnson, March 12, 1756, *SWJP*, 9:401–2.

56. Thomas Butler to Johnson, May 3, 1756, *SWJP*, 9:446; George Croghan to Johnson, March 12, 1758, *SWJP*, 2:780; Account of Indian Expenses, *SWJP*, 2:626; Hamilton, "Documents: The Papers of Sir William Johnson," 86; Johnson to Amherst, May 29, 1760, WO 34/39/149; "By the Honourable James De Lancey . . . A Proclamation," 513; *Extract of an Act of the General Assembly of the Colony of New-York published the 22nd of March, 1760* (New York: W. Weuman, 1760), 3; Edward H. Knoblauch, "Mobilizing Provincials for War: The Social Composition of New York Forces in 1760," *NYH* 78:2 (1997): 156–58.

57. Account of Indian Expenses, July 30, 1756, *SWJP*, 2:626; Johnson to Amherst, May 29, 1760, WO 34/39/149; Butler to Johnson, August 29, 1756, *SWJP*, 2:553. For the varied prices of captives, see *SWJP*, 2:749, 3:257; and Johnson to Abercromby, April 13, 1758, WO 34/39/18.

58. Johnson to Board of Trade, September 28, 1757, *DRCHNY*, 7:278; Journal of Sir William, August 13, 1756, *DRCHNY*, 7:184.

Chapter 4

1. Proceedings of the Colonial Congress held at Albany, July 2, 1754, *DRCHNY*, 6:870; Journal of Sir William, November 20, 1756, *DRCHNY*, 7:235; Indian Proceedings, April 25, 1762, *SWJP*, 3:707–8; Johnson to George Clinton, December 20, 1750, *SWJP*, 1:315.

2. Conference between Governor Clinton and the Indians, August 19, 1746, *DRCHNY*, 6:318–20, emphasis added.

3. Bartram, "Observations," 91; Colden, *History of the Five Indian Nations of Canada*, vii (quote), v–vi, 4. On the heroization of military men in English culture, see Gerald Jordan and Nicolas Rogers, "Admirals as Heroes: Patriotism and Liberty in Hanoverian England," *Journal of British Studies* 28 (1989): 201–24; Nicholas Rogers, "Brave Wolfe: The Making of a Hero," in *A New Imperial History*, ed. Wilson, 239–59.

4. On Iroquois modes of warfare, see Knowles, "The Torture of Captives by the Indians of Eastern America," 151–225; Thomas S. Abler, "Iroquois Cannibalism: Fact Not Fiction," *Ethnohistory* 27:4 (1980): 309–16; Richter, "War and Culture," 528–59; Lynch, "The Iroquois Confederacy"; Thomas S. Abler and Michael H. Logan, "The Florescence and Demise of Iroquoian Cannibalism: Human Sacrifice and Malinowski's Hypothesis," *MIN* 35 (1988): 1–17; Starna and Watkins, "Northern Iroquoian Slavery"; and Craig S. Keener, "An Ethnohistorical Analysis of Iroquois Assault Tactics Used against Fortified Settlements of the Northeast in the Seventeenth Century," *Ethnohistory* 46:4 (1999): 777–807. Ironically, this mode of hit-and-run warfare was relatively new. Indians, like Europeans, traditionally fought in open battle clothed in wooden armor. The introduction of European firearms rendered this old-style warfare too deadly, encouraging Indians to develop guerrilla-style tactics. Richter, *Ordeal of the Longhouse*, 54–55; Calloway,

New Worlds for All, 92–93. See also Patrick M. Malone, *The Skulking Way of War: Technology and Tactics Among the New England Indians* (Baltimore: Johns Hopkins University Press, 1993).

5. H. Worthington, *A Letter Adapted to the Present Critical Juncture Addressed to All Military Gentlemen by Sea and Land; Pointing out the True Soldier as Animated by Religion, and the Love of His Country* (London, 1758), 7.

6. Colden, *History of the Five Indian Nations of Canada*, 163 (quote); Johnson to Clinton, May 31, 1747, *SWJP*, 1:97; Contingencies, 1746, Clinton Papers: 15; Shannon, "Dressing for Success on the Mohawk Frontier," 22, 36–41; Guzzardo, "Sir William Johnson's Official Family," 267–68.

7. Johnson to Clinton, May 7 and August 9, 1747, *DRCHNY*, 6:360, 389; Johnson to Clinton, March 15, 1748, *SWJP*, 1:146–48.

8. Conference between Major General Johnson and the Indians, June 24, 1755, *DRCHNY*, 6:971–73.

9. Chauncy, *Second Letter to a Friend*, 16; Indian Conference, February 23, 1756, *SWJP*, 9:372; Journal of Sir William, November 20, 1756, *DRCHNY*, 7:235. For another example of Johnson's use of virile language, see *SWJP*, 9:938–39. Likewise, Richard R. Johnson argues that Algonquian men assisted the English during King Philip's War (1675–76) because "it allowed young men to earn their manhood in the traditional ways frowned upon by a surrounding white society." "The Search for a Usable Indian," 644.

10. Johnson to Earl of Hillsborough, August 21, 1769, *DRCHNY*, 8:181; Johnson to Jeffrey Amherst, January 19, 1759, WO 34/39/74; Colden, *History of the Five Indian Nations of Canada*, 10; Johnson to William Shirley, June 19, 1755, *SWJP*, 1:615. Orderly troops were the ideal and by no means the reality as William Johnson, serving as major general at the Battle of Lake George, quickly discovered; e.g., see his letter to James De Lancey, September 4, 1755, *SWJP*, 2:6–8.

11. Johnson to Thomas Butler et al., March 13, 1757, *SWJP*, 9:635; Orders to Butler and Jellas Fonda, December 20, 1756, *SWJP*, 9:583. On gifts to war chiefs and warriors, see Account of Indian Expenses, 1755–56, *SWJP*, 2:572, 574, 575, 577, 582, 593ff.

12. Colden, *History of the Five Indian Nations of Canada*, 6–7; Journal of Indian Affairs, June 25, 1757, *SWJP*, 9:787. On the Mohawks' stipulating conditions, see *SWJP*, 1:516, 524, 603–4, 9:468, 498; and *DRCHNY*, 7:105. On keeping French prisoners, see *SWJP*, 2:80, 388, 9:300, 357, 13:115; Hamilton, "Diary of the Reverend John Ogilvie," 370. On Johnson's encouragement, see *SWJP*, 9:586, 726, 767, 780.

13. Johnson to Benjamin Stoddert, May 23, 1755, *SWJP*, 1:535; Journal of Indian Proceedings, January 19, 1757, *SWJP*, 9:586–87.

14. Gilbert, "A Copy of a Journal Kept by James Gilbert," 191; Charles Lee to Sidney Lee, June 18, 1756, *NYHSC* 6 (1872): 4.

15. Londa Schiebinger, "The Anatomy of Difference: Race and Sex in Eighteenth-Century Science," *Eighteenth Century Studies* 23:4 (1990): 391–92; "Guy Johnson's Opinions on the American Indian," *PMHB* 77 (1953): 316. See also "Opinions of George Croghan on the American Indian," *PMHB* 71 (1946): 154.

16. Paul E. Kopperman, "The British Command and Soldiers' Wives in America, 1755–1783," *Journal of the Society for Army Historical Research* 60 (1982): 14–34. Johnson was keen to curtail the presence of Anglo-American women who joined the encampment at the Battle of Lake George. He was adamant that "bad Women" be sent away but agreed to permit the wives of soldiers "while they behave Decently" because they were "thought necessary to Wash and mend." Johnson to Phineas Lyman, July 27, 1755, *SWJP*, 1:783.

17. Thomas S. Abler, "Scalping, Torture, Cannibalism, and Rape: An Ethnohistorical Analysis of Conflicting Cultural Values in War," *Anthropologica* 34 (1992): 13–15; "Opinions of George Croghan," 154; "Guy Johnson's Opinions," 317.

18. De Lancey to Johnson, August 3, 1755, *SWJP*, 1:826–27; "Journal of Warren Johnson, 1760–1761," in *IMC*, 255–56, 259. The only other group of European men who wore tattoos in this period was seafarers. Although European males had acquired tattoos for centuries as a result of foreign travel and contact, Simon P. Newman hypothesizes that "the relative popularity of tattooing among late eighteenth-century mariners" might be explained by their "exposure to the ornate tattooing of the South Sea Islanders in the wake of Captain Cook's voyages of the 1770s." *Embodied History: The Lives of the Poor in Early Philadelphia* (Philadelphia: University of Pennsylvania Press, 2003), 113–23, 168–69nn9–11.

19. "Guy Johnson's Opinions," 316. The very fact that some provincial soldiers scalped French enemies after they killed them suggests their appreciation for scalping as a war custom. See Robert Rogers and others to Johnson, October 22, 1755, *SWJP*, 2:226; James Axtell and William C. Sturtevant, "The Unkindest Cut, or Who Invented Scalping?" *WMQ* 37:3 (1980): 451–72; and Abler, "Scalping, Torture, Cannibalism, and Rape," 6–8.

20. Michèle Cohen, *Fashioning Masculinity: National Identity and Language in the Eighteenth Century* (London: Routledge, 1996), 7; Worthington, *Letter Adapted to the Present Critical Juncture*, 23; James Brown, *An Estimate on the Manners and Principles of the Time* (London, 1757), 51; Mary Peace and Vincent Quinn, eds., "Luxurious Sexualities: Effeminacy, Consumption, and the Body Politic in Eighteenth-Century Representation," *Textual Practice* 11 (1997): esp. 429–43; Wilson, *A Sense of the People*, 185–205.

21. Johnson to Amherst, August 20, 1763, *DRCHNY*, 7:541; Loudoun to Duke of Cumberland, November 22–December 26, 1756, in *Military Affairs in North America, 1748–1765: Selected Documents from the Cumberland Papers in Windsor Castle*, ed. Stanley Pargellis (New York: Archon Books, 1969), 269; Thomas Butler to Johnson, August 29, 1756, *SWJP*, 2:554; James Mercer to Johnson, April 16, 1756, *SWJP*, 9:432; Bradstreet, *An Impartial Account*, 21. For a general discussion of European attitudes toward native warriors, see John E. Ferling, *A Wilderness of Miseries: War and Warriors in Early America* (Westport, Conn.: Greenwood Press, 1980), 33–36.

22. Hamilton, "Diary of the Reverend John Ogilvie," 361; Johnson to Robert Orme, September 18, 1755, *SWJP*, 2:52–53; Conference between M. de Vaudreuil and the Five Nations, August 12, 1756, *DRCHNY*, 10:449. Similarly, the Cherokees expressed dislike at the gendered power relations among the army. See Hatley, *The Dividing Paths*, 103.

23. Journal of Sir William, June 14, 1757, *SWJP*, 7:259.

24. Council held at Philadelphia, July 12, 1742, *MPCP*, 4:579–80; Council held at Philadelphia, October 24, 1756, *MPCP*, 7:297. For two insightful discussions on the Indian use and manipulation of gender metaphors in Indian diplomacy, see Nancy Shoemaker, "An Alliance Between Men: Gender Metaphors in Eighteenth-Century American Indian Diplomacy East of the Mississippi," *Ethnohistory* 46:2 (1999): 239–64; and Jane T. Merritt, "Metaphor, Meaning, and Misunderstanding: Language and Power on the Pennsylvania Frontier," in *Contact Points*, ed. Cayton and Teute, 60–87.

25. Council held at Philadelphia, July 12, 1742, *MPCP*, 4:579–80; Council held at Easton, July 31, 1756, *MPCP*, 7:218. On English attitudes toward female sexuality, see Anthony Fletcher, *Gender, Sex, and Subordination in England, 1500–1800* (New Haven, Conn.: Yale University Press, 1995), 74–76, 109–13.

26. Council held at Lancaster, June 30, 1744, *MPCP*, 4:721; Treaty at Lancaster, 1757, in *Indian Treaties Printed by Benjamin Franklin, 1736–1762*, ed. Carl Van Doren and Julian P. Boyd (Philadelphia: Historical Society of Pennsylvania, 1938), 178; Ludovick Grant to Governor Glen, April 29, 1755, *Documents Relating to Indian Affairs*, 2 vols., ed. William L. McDowell Jr. (Columbia: South Carolina Archives Department, 1970), 2:52–53.

27. Johnson to Clinton, December 20, 1750, *SWJP*, 1:315; Wraxall, "Some Thoughts upon the British Indian Interest in North America," *DRCHNY*, 7:19. William Shirley also observed that during King George's War "the opinion which they [the Iroquois] had entertained of the English Courage and Strength was lessened almost to a Degree of Contempt." In *Correspondence of William Shirley*, ed. Lincoln, 1:449–50. See also Kennedy, *Importance of Gaining and Preserving*, 25.

28. Johnson to Robert Orme, May 19, 1755, *SWJP*, 1:523; Goldsbrow Banyar to Johnson, July 25, 1755, *SWJP*, 1:768.

29. Report of Conrad Weiser to Pennsylvania Council, June 13, 1748, Clinton Papers: 8; Journal of Sir William, April 29, 1756, *DRCHNY*, 7:100; Johnson to Lords of Trade, May 28, 1756, *DRCHNY*, 7:89–90.

30. Journal of Sir William, June 14, 1756, *DRCHNY*, 7:132. The Iroquois made repeated requests to the French not to attack the Mohawk Valley; see *SWJP*, 9:446, 832, 964–65.

31. Indian Proceedings, June 27, 1758, *SWJP*, 9:937; Reply of Indian Messengers, October 1, 1755, *SWJP*, 2:127. On Iroquois war rituals, see Lafitau, *Customs of the American Indians*, 2:111–13; Knowles, "The Torture of Captives by the Indians," 214; Synderman, *Behind the Tree of Peace*, 49–55; and Harold Blau, "The Iroquois White Dog Sacrifice: Its Evolution and Symbolism," *Ethnohistory* 11:2 (1964): 97–119. Elizabeth Tooker contends that the white dog sacrifice "among the Mohawks and Oneidas, at least . . . had lapsed in the latter part of the 18th century," though it was later revived in the early nineteenth century. "The Iroquois White Dog Sacrifice in the Latter Part of the Eighteenth Century," *Ethnohistory* 12:2 (1965): 136. Cherokee warriors faced similar challenges to their gendered war practices; see Theda Perdue, *Cherokee Women: Gender and Culture Change, 1700–1835* (Lincoln: University of Nebraska Press, 1998), 90.

32. Thomas Butler to Johnson, May 3 and 4, 1756, *SWJP*, 9:446, 448; Hamilton, "Diary of the Reverend John Ogilvie," 372–73. Complaints about the disruptive behavior of drunken warriors are numerous. See James Abercromby to Johnson, September 19 and 26, 1758, WO 34/38/48–49; and Johnson to Board of Trade, June 25, 1757, *DRCHNY*, 7:228–29. On Iroquois purification rites, see Synderman, *Behind the Tree of Peace*, 49–55.

33. "Guy Johnson's Opinions," 317; Michael Cardy, "The Iroquois in the Eighteenth Century: A Neglected Source," *MIN* 38 (1989): 10; "Journal of Warren Johnson," 268, emphasis added.

34. Henry Barclay to Colden, December 7, 1741, *NYHSC* 67 (1934): 279, 280; Journal of Sir William, June 16, 1757, *DRCHNY*, 7:260; Account of Indian Expenses, August 1, 1756, September 17, 1759, *SWJP*, 2:631, 3:176; Indian Proceedings, September 16, 1757, *SWJP*, 9:834–35; Journal of Niagara Campaign, September 5–23, 1759, *SWJP*, 13:125, 136, 148; (collaborate authors), "Teyohaqueande," *DCB* 4 (1979): 734. For a background on the southern wars, see Richard Aquila, "Down the Warrior's Path: The Causes of the Southern Wars of the Iroquois," *AIQ* 4:3 (1978): 211–21; James H. Merrell, "'Their Very Bones Shall Fight': The Catawba-Iroquois Wars," in *Beyond the Covenant Chain*, ed. Merrell and Richter, 115–34; and Ute Ferrier, "All That Is Past Is Buried in Oblivion: The Iroquois-Catawba Wars," *European Review of Native American Studies* 12:2 (1998): 41–50.

35. Johnson to Shirley, September 22, 1755, *SWJP*, 2:74; Baron De Dieskau to Count d'Argenson, June 22, 1756, *DRCHNY*, 10:422–23; Journal of Indian Affairs, March 8, 1761, *SWJP*, 10:238; Amherst to Johnson, April 17, 1761, *SWJP*, 3:378; George Croghan to Johnson, July 25, 1761, *SWJP*, 10:317; Bradstreet, *An Impartial Account*, 21–22; Journal of the Niagara Campaign, July 27, 1759, *SWJP*, 13:115.

36. This trend was already well established in British culture. The evolution of a market economy provided Englishmen with new arenas in which to demonstrate their manliness, which was no longer determined solely by how orderly they kept their households but ever more by their ability to accumulate wealth. Toby Ditz, "Shipwrecked; or, Masculinity Imperiled: Mercantile Representations of Failure and the Gendered Self in Eighteenth-Century Philadelphia," *JAH* 81:1 (1994): 51–80; Alexandra Shepard, *Meanings of Manhood in Early Modern England* (Oxford: Oxford University Press, 2003), chap. 7.

37. "Letters from and Concerning the Reverend John Ogilvie," 314, 318, 319; Croghan to Johnson, March 12, 1758, *SWJP*, 2:780; Account of Indian Expenses, August 1, 1755, July 30, 1756, *SWJP*, 2:589, 624; Gus Richardson, "Sahonwagy," *DCB* 4 (1979): 691–92; Hart, "'For the Good of Our Souls,'" 226, 229–30, 244.

38. Journal of Conrad Weiser at the Albany Treaty of 1745, in *Indian Treaties*, ed. Van Doren and Boyd, 310; Hamilton, "Diary of the Reverend John Ogilvie," 362–63; Banyar to Johnson, September 24, 1755, *SWJP*, 2:85–86; Message to the Indians, September 24, 1755, *SWJP*, 2:92–93; Journal of Indian Proceedings, March 4, 1757, *SWJP*, 9:631–32. During a conference in November 1756, Johnson ignored Iroquois protocol

by appealing directly to warriors to take up the hatchet, though afterward he was compelled to reassure the attending chiefs that he had not meant to exclude them. *DRCHNY*, 7:139–40.

39. William Smith, *Some Account of the North-American Indians their genius, characters, customs, and dispositions, toward the French and English nations; To which are added, Indian miscellanies* (London: R. Griffiths, 1754), 26.

40. Colden, *History of the Five Indian Nations of Canada*, 13; Bartram, "Observations," 90. The view of Indian male laziness and Indian female degradation persisted throughout the century. See "Opinions of George Croghan," 153; "Guy Johnson's Opinions," 320; and Joseph Bloomfield, *Citizen Soldier: The Revolutionary Journal of Joseph Bloomfield*, ed. Mark E. Lender and James Kirby Martin (Newark: New Jersey Historical Society, 1982), 66. David Smits demonstrates how this view permeated Euro-American thought from earliest encounters up until the mid-nineteenth century in "The 'Squaw Drudge': A Prime Index of Savagism," *Ethnohistory* 29:4 (1982): 281–306.

41. "Journal of Warren Johnson," 258; Banyar to Johnson, September 23, 1755, *SWJP*, 2:80.

42. Beauchamp, *Moravian Journals*, 146, 147, 199; "Letters from and Concerning the Reverend John Ogilvie," 313; "Guy Johnson's Opinions," 320. For a broader discussion of native women's role in the liquor trade, see Peter C. Mancall, *Deadly Medicine: Indians and Alcohol in Early America* (Ithaca, N.Y.: Cornell University Press, 1995), 60.

43. Thomas Butler to Johnson, April 22, 1757, *SWJP*, 9:688; Journal of Indian Affairs, August 2, 1758, *SWJP*, 9:965; Complaint of the Canajoharie Indians, September 27, 1756, *SWJP*, 9:546–47. See also Journal of Indian Proceedings, January 24, 1757, *SWJP*, 9:591; and Johnson to Thomas Gage, April 8, 1760, *SWJP*, 3:218. A decline in village numbers can probably account for the growing assistance of men in farming during the eighteenth century. When a Moravian missionary visited the Onondagas in 1753 he noted how the entire community was engaged in hoeing the land. Johnson also acknowledged the presence of men "planting their corn." Beauchamp, *Moravian Journals*, 165, 169; Johnson to Arent Stevens, May 1755, *SWJP*, 9:185.

44. Journal of Sir William, March 5, 1756, *DRCHNY*, 7:92; Indian Proceedings, April 23, 1757, *SWJP*, 9:689; *Correspondence of William Shirley*, ed. Lincoln, 2:357; Account of Indian Expenses, 1755–59, *SWJP*, 2:569, 572, 625, 640, 3:167; Indian Conference, February 27, 1756, *SWJP*, 9:392–93; Journal of Sir William, May 12 and 15, 1756, *DRCHNY*, 7:105, 109.

45. Croghan to Lord Loudoun, November 20, 1757, *SWJP*, 9:856; Indian Congress, June 16, 1758, *SWJP*, 9:927; Journal of Sir William, June 19, 1757, *DRCHNY*, 7:264. As traders, native women's activities were similar to those of women of Dutch descent who, from the beginning of colonial times, participated in trading networks. See Jean P. Jordan, "Women Merchants in Colonial New York," *NYH* 58:4 (1977): 412–39; Martha Dickinson Shattuck, "Women and Trade in New Netherland," *Itinerario* 18 (1994): 2, 40–49; and Aileen B. Agnew, "Silent Partners: The Economic Life of Women on the Frontier of Colonial New York" (Ph.D. diss., University of New Hampshire, 1998). Iro-

quois women residing in New France and Pennsylvania were also active in the fur trade. See E. P. H., "Unrest at Caughnawaga or the Lady Fur Traders of Sault St. Louis," *BFTM* 11 (1963): 155–60; Alison Duncan Hirsch, "Women and the Fur Trade in Eighteenth-Century Pennsylvania," in *Aboriginal People and the Fur Trade*, ed. Johnston, 200–207; and Green, "Gender and the Longhouse," 12.

46. Johnson to Abercromby, March 17, 1758, WO 9/34/39; Johnson to Loudoun, September 27, 1756, *SWJP*, 9:545; Johnson to Abercromby, July 5, 1758, *SWJP*, 2:871. Ironically Johnson himself provided women with alcohol so that they could exchange it for food staples from colonial neighbors. See *SWJP*, 9:630. A law was passed in July 1755 forbidding the sale of rum to Indians anywhere except Oswego. It was only loosely enforced until it expired in July 1757. See *Colonial Laws of New York from the Year 1664 to the Revolution*, 5 vols. (Albany, N.Y.: James B. Lyon State Printers, 1894–96), 3:1096–98, 4:93.

47. Account of Indian Expenses, 1755–59, *SWJP*, 2:636, 3:157, 158, 161, 164–67. Johnson paid an Onondaga woman eight shillings for preparing eight animal skins; *SWJP*, 3:162. See also *SWJP*, 2:579, 3:158; and *MPCP*, 7:216. On Seneca women selling corn, see Report of Charles Thomson and Christian Frederick Post to William Denny, June 1, 1758, in *Iroquois Indians*, ed. Jennings et al., reel 22.

48. Indian Conference, February 27, 1756, *SWJP*, 9:393, 389; Indian Congress, June 16, 1758, *SWJP*, 9:927; Indian Proceedings, March 14, 1757, *SWJP*, 9:638; Account of Indian Expenses, July 30 and September 10, 1756, *SWJP*, 2:625, 639. See also Journal of Indian Proceedings, March 4, 1757, *SWJP*, 9:629; Thomas Butler to Johnson, May 23, 1757, *SWJP*, 9:769; and Journal of Indian Affairs, December 12, 1758, *SWJP*, 10:72.

49. Indian Congress, June 16, 1758, *SWJP*, 9:927; Account of Indian Expenses, February 5 and June 29, 1759, *SWJP*, 3:157, 175.

50. Butler to James Clephane, April 9, 1759, *SWJP*, 3:25; Indian Proceedings, March 14, 1757, *SWJP*, 9:638; Butler to Johnson, September 18, 1756, *SWJP*, 9:533; Journal of Indian Affairs, July 9, 1757, *SWJP*, 9:797; Journal of Indian Proceedings, March 5, 1757, *SWJP*, 9:634. For additional references to women providing intelligence, see *SWJP*, 1:124, 9:675. For women's roles as messengers, see *SWJP*, 2:687, 688, 9:461, 610, 10:57, 61, 13:134.

51. Beauchamp, *Moravian Journals*, 205; Thomas Butler and Jellas Fonda to Johnson, January 1757, *SWJP*, 2:670.

52. Mohawks to Johnson, February 7, 1755, *SWJP*, 1:453; Journal of Sir William, May 10 and 26, 1756, *DRCHNY*, 7:103, 116; Journal of Indian Affairs, January 19, 1759, *SWJP*, 10:87; Journal of Indian Affairs, May 5, 1758, *SWJP*, 13:111–12. References to women attending conferences and informal meetings are numerous. See *SWJP*, 1:663, 9:626, 943, 946, 10:38, 65; *DRCHNY*, 7:254, 255.

53. Shirley to Johnson, March 26, 1755, *SWJP*, 1:462; Conference between Major General Johnson and the Indians, June 21, 1755, *DRCHNY*, 6:966, emphasis added; John Henry Lydius to Shirley, [1755], *SWJP*, 1:738; Journal of Sir William, May 10, 1756, *DRCHNY*, 7:103; Journal of Indian Affairs, October 12, 1758, *SWJP*, 10:38. For back-

ground on Nicholas and Sarah, see Isabel T. Kelsay, *Joseph Brant, 1743–1807: Man of Two Worlds* (Syracuse, N.Y.: Syracuse University Press, 1984), 50–51.

54. Hamilton, "Diary of the Reverend John Ogilvie," 352; Journal of Sir William, May 26, 1756, *DRCHNY*, 7:116; Account of Indian Expenses, September 16, 1756, November 17, 1758, *SWJP*, 2:641, 3:150; June Namias, ed., *Narrative of the Life of Mrs. Mary Jemison by James Seaver* (Norman: University of Oklahoma Press, 1992), 74–77; Myndert Wempel to Johnson, November 22, 1755, *SWJP*, 2:325. Mohawk women had similarly turned to Johnson for physical protection during King George's War. See Johnson to Clinton, May 14, 1748, *DHNY*, 2:361; and Johnson to Clinton, May 4, 1750, Clinton Papers: 22.

55. "Some Hints for a Commanding Officer," May 24, 1755, *SWJP*, 1:539. On the distribution of goods, see Journal of Indian Proceedings, January 21 and March 3, 1757, *SWJP*, 9:589, 627; Account of Indian Expenses, 1755–59, *SWJP*, 2:589, 590, 607, 3:173, 9:655; and Journal of Indian Affairs, May 7, 1758, *SWJP*, 13:112.

56. On Molly Brant's parentage, see Barbara Graymont, "Koñwatsi'tsiaiéñne," *DCB* 4 (1979): 416; Kelsay, *Joseph Brant*, chap. 2; and Sivertsen, *Turtles, Wolves and Bears*, 165–66. The standard biographies on Brant include Gretchen Green, "Molly Brant, Catherine Brant, and Their Daughters: A Study in Colonial Acculturation," *Ontario History* 81:3 (1989): 235–50; Thomas Earle, *The Three Faces of Molly Brant: A Biography* (Kingston, Ontario: Quarry Press, 1996); Lois M. Feister and Bonnie Pulis, "Molly Brant: Her Domestic and Political Roles in Eighteenth-Century New York," in *Northeastern Indian Lives, 1632–1816*, ed. Robert S. Grumet (Amherst: University of Massachusetts Press, 1996), 295–320; Lois M. Huey and Bonnie Pulis, *Molly Brant: A Legacy of Her Own* (Youngstown, N.Y.: Old Fort Niagara Association, 1997); and Dean R. Snow, "Molly Brant," in *Sifters: Native American Women's Lives*, ed. Theda Perdue (New York: Oxford University Press, 2001), 48–59.

57. Kelsay, *Joseph Brant*, 51–54; Feister and Pulis, "Molly Brant," 298–301; Earle, *Three Faces of Molly Brant*, chap. 1; Huey and Pulis, *Molly Brant*, chap. 1; Snow, "Molly Brant," 51. On Johnson's use of Brant's home, see *SWJP*, 3:164, 10:87; *DRCHNY*, 7:378; and "Journal of Warren Johnson," 258.

58. Feister and Pulis, "Molly Brant," 301–6; Earle, *Three Faces of Molly Brant*, chaps. 2–3; Huey and Pulis, *Molly Brant*, chap. 2; Tench Tilghman Papers, 1775–86, p. 12, Manuscript Division, Library of Congress, Washington, D.C. For an article that stresses Brant's influential status among the Mohawks, see Snow, "Molly Brant." For Brant's personal accounts, see Extracts from Account Book of John Butler, 1761–1771, *SWJP*, 508, 509, 515; and the numerous entries in Items from Day Book of Robert Adems, 1768–1773, *SWJP*, 13:532–616.

59. Johnson to Board of Trade, November 13, 1763, *DRCHNY*, 7:580; Tench Tilghman Papers, 1775–86, p. 9. The last quote is taken from Feister and Pulis, "Molly Brant," 302. Gifts to Nickus are listed in Johnson's Indian accounts, e.g., *SWJP*, 2:604, 643ff.

60. Indian Conference, February 23, 1756, *SWJP*, 9:372–73, emphasis added.

61. Johnson to Benjamin Stoddert, May 23, 1755, *SWJP*, 1:536; Banyar to Johnson,

September 23, 1755, *SWJP*, 2:80; Indian Council, July 21–24, 1758, *SWJP*, 9:950, 958. Johnson's journal is replete with entries that describe the outfitting and provisioning of warriors; e.g., *SWJP*, 9:626, 780, 782, 792, 794. Cherokee women provisioned their warriors and neighboring British forts during the war. See Hatley, *The Dividing Paths*, 96–97.

62. Journal of Niagara Campaign, August 21, 1759, *SWJP*, 13:125. According to one estimate, out of the 1,358 Indians who collected at Oswego during the Montreal campaign, only 585 were warriors. "Journal of Warren Johnson," 256. See also J. Clarence Webster, ed., *The Journal of Jeffrey Amherst* (Toronto: Ryerson Press, 1931), 225.

63. Hamilton, "Diary of the Reverend John Ogilvie," 358–59; Blodget, *Prospective Plan of the Battle Near Lake George*, 3. French Iroquois women were also present at the Battle of Lake George and may have participated in the killing of Theyanoguin when he stumbled into their camp after being shot. *Daniel Claus' Narrative*, 14; MacLeod, *The Canadian Iroquois in the Seven Years' War*, 6–7, 74.

64. Instructions for Croghan, May 29, 1758, *SWJP*, 9:909; Instructions to John Butler, May 29, 1758, *SWJP*, 9:912; Journal of Indian Affairs, July 3 and September 23, 1758, *SWJP*, 9:942, 10:12–13; Journal of Niagara Campaign, September 2, 1759, *SWJP*, 13:134.

65. Indian Proceedings, April 21–26, 1762, *SWJP*, 3:707–8, 711–12; Proceedings of Sir William, May 10, 1756, *DRCHNY*, 7:103.

Chapter 5

1. Johnson to Earl of Loudoun, September 3, 1757, *SWJP*, 9:828; Johnson to Peter and Elizabeth Wraxall, July 17, 1757, *SWJP*, 9:799; Johnson to Jeffrey Amherst, June 21, 1761, WO 34/39/190; Journal of Sir William, April 12–13, 1759, *DRCHNY*, 7:380–81.

2. Journal of Indian Affairs, July 8–9, 1757, *SWJP*, 9:796–98.

3. Recent literature has stressed the idea of the frontier as a porous zone of cultural exchange and synthesis. See White, *The Middle Ground*; and Andrew R. L. Cayton and Fredrika J. Teute, "Introduction: On the Connection of Frontiers," in *Contact Points*, ed. Cayton and Teute, 1–15. For the definitive and older view of the frontier as a dividing line between "civilization" and "savagery," see Frederick J. Turner, *The Frontier in American History* (1893; New York: Holt, 1920).

4. Grant, *Memoirs of an American Lady*, 67; Mark E. Lender and James Kirby Martin, eds., *Citizen Soldier: The Revolutionary Journal of Joseph Bloomfield* (Newark: New Jersey Historical Society, 1982), 62.

5. Accounts of George Weaver and Lodowick Crane in Unidentified Account Book, Schenectady, April 7, 1756–July 23, 1764, box 18, Campbell Family Papers, NYSL; Indian Proceedings, September 15, 1757, *SWJP*, 9:832; Helga Doblin and William A. Starna, trans. and eds., *The Journals of Christian Daniel Claus and Conrad Weiser: A Journey to Onondaga, 1750* (Philadelphia: American Philosophical Society, 1994), 38–39; Beauchamp, *Moravian Journals*, 113, 114, 152; "Journal of Warren Johnson," 260. These economic connections are explored in Chapter 3.

6. On multiethnic scouting parties, see *SWJP*, 1:64, 80 (quote), 146; Doblin and Starna, eds., *Journals of Claus and Weiser*, 33, emphasis added; and "Letters from and Concerning the Reverend John Ogilvie," 312. In 1709, 150 Mohawks, 105 Oneidas, 88 Onondagas, and 100 Cayugas enlisted to serve in an English invasion of Canada. See Wraxall, *Abridgment of the Indian Affairs*, 68–69.

7. Through his analysis of church records, David L. Preston found that out of the 251 Iroquois baptisms and marriages that took place at the Dutch Reformed Congregation at Schoharie between 1731 and 1778, the majority had European sponsors or witnesses. See his "Texture of Contact," 196–97; "Letters from and Concerning the Reverend John Ogilvie," 319–20, 311n1; Grant, *Memoirs of an American Lady*, 68–69.

8. "Journal of Warren Johnson," 257; Jeremy Belknap and Jedidiah Morse, *Report on the Oneida, Stockbridge and Brotherton Indians, 1796* (New York: Museum of the American Indian, Heye Foundation, 1955), 8. Similarly, Friedrich Rohde in 1802 came across an Oneida chief who "was bred by a white, a German to boot, and a Negro in Canada; and is consequently a mulatto"; see "Journal of a Trip from New Jersey to Oneida Lake," in *IMC*, 380–81. See also Burke, *Mohawk Frontier*, 147–50; and Hagedorn, "Brokers of Understanding," 381–82. On the prevalence of interracial sex in early America, see Gary B. Nash, "The Hidden History of Mestizo America," *JAH* 82:3 (1995): 941–64.

9. Brant Kaghneghtago was also called Brant Johnson. See Kelsay, *Joseph Brant*, 68, 110, 121; Sivertsen, *Turtles, Wolves and Bears*, 131–33, 135, 165, 302n12; Will of Sir William Johnson, *SWJP*, 12:1064–65; and "Claim of Brant Johnson late of New York Prov. August 30, 1787," reproduced in Guldenzopf, "Colonial Transformation," 208.

10. Kelsay, *Joseph Brant*, 110. Other North American frontiers demonstrated a similar métis character. There were exceptionally high rates of intermarriage in the Great Lakes region, where the actual term "métis" originated. See Sleeper-Smith, *Indian Women and French Men*. James F. Brooks examines complex cross-cultural ties in the Southwest in *Captives and Cousins: Slavery, Kinship, and Community in the Southwest Borderlands* (Chapel Hill: University of North Carolina Press, 2002).

11. Council held at Philadelphia, July 12, 1742, *MPCP*, 4:581; Council held at Easton, August 3, 1761, *MPCP*, 8:631–32; P. Wallace, *Conrad Weiser*, 17–18, 25–26; Hagedorn, "Brokers of Understanding," 385–86; Sivertsen, *Turtles, Wolves and Bears*, 163–64. On Lydius, see E. P. H., "John Henry Lydius, Fur Trader at Fort Edward," *BFTM* 2:5 (1964): 270–79; and Sivertsen, *Turtles, Wolves and Bears*, 53–56, 169–70. Like Conrad Weiser, James Dean was also escorted as a child by his missionary step-uncle to reside among the Iroquois at Oquaga to be trained as an interpreter. See Sidney Norton Deane, "A New England Pioneer Among the Oneida Indians: The Life of James Dean of Westmoreland, New York" (paper read before the Northampton Historical Society, January 28, 1926), film 1101, American Philosophical Society, Philadelphia; and Karim M. Tiro, "James Dean in Iroquoia," *NYH* 80:4 (1999): 391–422.

12. "Letters from and Concerning the Reverend John Ogilvie," 313.

13. Colden, *History of the Five Indian Nations of Canada*, vi, 4; Smith, *Some Account of the North-American Indians*, 26.

14. Franklin to James Parker, March 20, 1751, in *The Writings of Benjamin Franklin*, 21 vols., ed. Albert H. Smyth (New York: MacMillan, 1907), 3:42; Smith, *Some Account of the North-American Indians*, 28; Bartram, "Observations," 90; "Journal of Warren Johnson," 258.

15. Henry Barclay to Colden, December 7, 1741, *NYHSC* 67 (1934): 279; Lee to Sidney Lee, June 18, 1756, *NYHSC* 5 (1872): 4; Beauchamp, *Moravian Journals*, 51, 52, 34, 33, 42. See also Colden, *History of the Five Indian Nations of Canada*, 11–12.

16. On Lydius and Montour, see Sivertsen, *Turtles, Wolves and Bears*, 56, chap. 8; Jon Parmenter, "Isabel Montour: Cultural Broker on the Frontiers of New York and Pennsylvania," in *The Human Tradition in Colonial America*, ed. Ian K. Steele and Nancy L. Rhoden (Wilmington, Del.: Scholarly Resources, 1999), 141–59; and Alison Duncan Hirsch, "The Celebrated Madame Montour: Interpretess Across Early American Frontiers," *Explorations in Early American Culture* 4 (2000): 81–112. On Spelman, see *SWJP*, 9:779. On Lee, see Lee to Sidney Lee, June 18, 1756, *NYHSC* 5 (1872): 5. On Croghan, see Nicolas B. Wainwright, *George Croghan: Wilderness Diplomat* (Chapel Hill: University of North Carolina Press, 1959), 138, 140, 151; Green, "Molly Brant, Catherine Brant, and Their Daughters," 243; and Sivertsen, *Turtles, Wolves and Bears*, 24, 172–74. For a study that explores how perceptions of Indians were filtered through a class lens, see Karen Kupperman, *Settling with the Indians: The Meeting of English and Indian Cultures in America, 1580–1640* (London: Rowman and Littlefield, 1980).

17. Report of Board of Trade Respecting the Palatines, August 30, 1709, *DRCHNY*, 5:88; Wraxall, "Some Thoughts upon the British Indian Interest in North America," *DRCHNY*, 7:27; John Bartram to Peter Collinson, February 4, 1756, p. 44, vol. 1, Bartram Papers, Historical Society of Pennsylvania, Philadelphia. For nineteenth-century views of interracial mixing, see David D. Smits, "'Squaw-Men,' 'Half Breeds,' and Amalgamators: Late Nineteenth-Century Anglo-American Attitudes Toward Indian-White Race Mixing," *American Indian Cultural Research Journal* 15:3 (1991): 29–61. For an account that stresses the more varied and liberal attitudes of the colonial era, see Richard Goodbeer, "Eroticizing the Middle Ground: Anglo-Indian Sexual Relations Along the Eighteenth-Century Frontier," in *Sex, Love, Race: Crossing Boundaries in North American History*, ed. Martha Hodes (New York: New York University Press, 1999), 91–111.

18. Smedley, *Race in North America*, 52–61; Johnson to Horatio Gates, August 10, 1756, *SWJP*, 2:539; Goldsbrow Banyar to Johnson, March 9, 1757, *SWJP*, 2:683; Journal of Indian Affairs, July 5, 1757, *SWJP*, 9:795; Butler to Johnson, March 17, 1757, *SWJP*, 9:643. Hans Croyn (also spelled Kryn and Crine) was the brother-in-law of Brant Canagaraduncka and a close friend to Johnson. His full Indian name was Johannes Aneqwendahonji, but his light complexion meant he was also referred to as White Hans. See Sivertsen, *Turtles, Wolves and Bears*, 178, 87. On the changing use of color metaphors, see Alden T. Vaughan, "From White Man to Redskin: Changing Anglo-American Perspectives of the American Indian," *American Historical Review* [hereafter *AHR*] 87:4 (1982): 931–32; Nancy A. Shoemaker, "How Indians Got to Be Red," *AHR* 102:3 (1997): 625–44.

19. Bartram, "Observations," 88–90. For a general discussion of European speculation on Indian origins, see Lee E. Huddleston, *Origins of the American Indians: European Concepts, 1492–1729* (Austin: University of Texas Press, 1967).

20. Beauchamp, *Moravian Journals*, 178.

21. John Lindesay to Johnson, September 7, 1750, *SWJP*, 1:297; Johnson to William Shirley, December 17, 1754, *SWJP*, 1:431. Johnson's complaints about the detrimental influence of the French are numerous. See, e.g., Johnson to Clinton, August 18, 1750, Clinton Papers: 22; Johnson to Banyar, January 21, 1755, *SWJP*, 1:442; and "Letters from and Concerning the Reverend John Ogilvie," 310.

22. Barclay to Colden, December 7, 1741, *NYHSC* 67 (1934): 283, 285; "Letters from and Concerning the Reverend John Ogilvie," 313–14ff; Johnson to Loudoun, September 17, 1756, *SWJP*, 9:531.

23. "Letters from and Concerning the Reverend John Ogilvie," 310, 313; Bartram, "Observations," 73; Kennedy, *Importance of Gaining and Preserving*, 25. Barclay observed of the Mohawks: "As to their Morals I am very apt to think they have been much Corrupted since their conversing with Europeans." Barclay to Colden, December 7, 1741, *NYHSC* 67 (1934): 283. See also Colden, *History of the Five Indian Nations of Canada*, 13–14.

24. Bartram, "Observations," 91; Conrad Weiser, "Notes on the Iroquois and Delaware Indians," [1746–49], *PMHB* 1 (1877): 167, 319; Barclay to Colden, December 7, 1741, *NYHSC* 67 (1934): 279; "Letters from and Concerning the Reverend John Ogilvie," 311. For British efforts at propagation, see Lydekker, *Faithful Mohawks*; Frank J. Klingberg, *Anglican Humanitarianism in Colonial New York* (Philadelphia: Church Historical Society, 1940); and Richter, "'Some of Them . . . Would Always Have a Minister with Them.'"

25. Colden, *History of the Five Indian Nations of Canada*, v, 6; Lee to Sidney Lee, June 18, 1756, *NYHSC* 5 (1872): 3–4; Smith, *Some Account of the North-American Indians*, 24, 41–42; Klingberg, "Sir William Johnson," 4–37.

26. McConnell, *A Country Between*, 15–20.

27. Douglas W. Boyce, "'As the Wind Scatters the Smoke': The Tuscaroras in the Eighteenth Century," in *Beyond the Covenant Chain*, ed. Merrell and Richter, 151–63. There are numerous variations to the spelling of Oquaga. See Colin G. Calloway, *The American Revolution in Indian Country: Crisis and Diversity in the Native American Communities* (Cambridge: Cambridge University Press, 1995), 108n2; Mancall, *Valley of Opportunity*, 37; Franklin J. Hesse, "The Egli and Lord Sites: The Historic Component—'Unadilla,' 1753–1778," *Bulletin of the New York Society Archaeological Association* 66 (1975): 14–31; and Dolores Elliot, "Otsiningo, an Example of an Eighteenth Century Settlement Pattern," in *Current Perspectives in Northeastern Archaeology: Essays in Honor of William A. Ritchie*, ed. Robert E. Funk and Charles F. Hayes, *New York State Archaeological Association, Researches and Transactions* 17:1 (1977): 93–105.

28. For a broader discussion about how Native Americans developed new ways of thinking about human difference in the eighteenth century, including but not specific

to the Iroquois, see Shoemaker, *A Strange Likeness*, chap. 6 and her earlier article, "How Indians Got to Be Red."

29. This version is recounted in W. N. Fenton, "This Island, the World on the Turtle's Back," *Journal of American Folklore* 75 (1962): 283–300; Curtin and Hewitt, "Seneca Fiction, Legends, and Myths," 411; J.N.B. Hewitt, "Iroquoian Cosmology," *Bureau of American Ethnology, Annual Report, 1925–1926* (Washington, D.C.: GPO, 1928), 466.

30. Council held at Lancaster, June 26 and 30, 1744, *MPCP*, 4:706–7, 720.

31. Council held at Philadelphia, July 12, 1742, *MPCP*, 4:581; Council held at Lancaster, June 30, 1744, *MPCP*, 4:720; Thomas Butler to Johnson, March 11, 1757, *SWJP*, 2:685. The "Hott blood" quote is taken from Parmenter, "At the Wood's Edge," 200.

32. Beauchamp, *Moravian Journals*, 10–11. On the political implications of renaming, see Williams, *Linking Arms Together*, 73–74; Merritt, *At the Crossroads*, 57–59.

33. Colden, *History of the Five Indian Nations of Canada*, 10–11; Wraxall, *Abridgment of the Indian Affairs*, 248n1; Six Nations and Johnson, July 3, 1751, *SWJP*, 1:342; "Journal of Warren Johnson," 266–67; Lee to Sidney Lee, June 18, 1756, *NYHSC* 5 (1872): 4–5. At one conference the Mohawks claimed that Johnson was "*one of the Five Nations*" (July 5, 1754, Colonial Congress held at Albany, *DRCHNY*, 6:876). At another they told Johnson "we look upon [you] as one of our selves" (Indian Proceedings, June 15, 1755, *SWJP*, 1:638).

34. On French captives, see Clinton to Indians, October 11, 1748, Clinton Papers: 8; and Colden to Clinton, February 26, 1749, Clinton Papers: 9. On Indianization, see A. Irving Hallowell, "American Indians, White and Black: The Phenomenon of Transculturation," *Current Anthropology* 4 (1963): 519–31; Norman J. Heard, *White into Red: A Study of the Assimilation of White Persons Captured by Indians* (Metuchen, N.J.: Scarecrow Press, 1973); and James Axtell, "The White Indians of Colonial America," *WMQ* 32:4 (1975): 55–88. On the obstacles to Indianization, see Alden Vaughan and Daniel K. Richter, "Crossing the Cultural Divide: Indians and New Englanders, 1605–1765," in Alden T. Vaughan, *Roots of American Racism: Essays on the Colonial Experience* (New York: Oxford University Press, 1995), 213–52. For an account of the adoption process, see Axtell, "White Indians of Colonial America," and Colin G. Calloway, "An Uncertain Destiny: Indian Captivities on the Upper Connecticut River," *Journal of American Studies* 17:2 (1983): 189–210.

35. Beauchamp, *Moravian Journals*, 7.

36. "Letters from and Concerning the Reverend John Ogilvie," 315. Benjamin Franklin, who was present at the conference, recorded this verbal exchange between the Iroquois and Virginian commissioners from memory in "Remarks Concerning the Savages of North America," in *Writings of Benjamin Franklin*, 10:98–99. The official minutes of the conference contain a similar sentiment expressed by the Iroquois: "We must let you know we love our Children too well to send them so great a way, and the Indians are not inclined to give their Children learning. We allow it to be good, and we thank you for your Invitation; but our Customs differing from yours, you will be so good to excuse us." *MPCP*, 4:733. For parental opposition to missionaries, see James Axtell, "Dr.

Wheelock and the Iroquois," in *Extending the Rafters: Interdisciplinary Approaches to Iroquoian Studies,* ed. Michael K. Foster et al. (Albany: State University of New York Press, 1984), 51–64.

37. Jonnhaty is quoted in Merrell, *Into the American Woods,* 170; Extracts from the Journal of Conrad Weiser, [June 1745], item 20, fols. 85–88, Daniel Horsmanden Papers, NYHS.

38. The presence of African Americans in the Mohawk Valley is well documented. See "Letters from and Concerning the Reverend John Ogilvie," 309, 316; "Diary of the Reverend John Ogilvie," 345; *SWJP,* 1:43, 230, 2:670, 9:3, 69; and "Journal of Warren Johnson," 263. See also Burke, *Mohawk Frontier,* chap. 4; "Blacks in New Netherland and Colonial New York," papers from the 6th Annual Rensselaerswijck Seminar in *Journal of the Afro-American Historical and Genealogical Society* 5:3 (1984); and Paul W. Herring, "Selected Aspects on the History of the Afro-American in the Mohawk and Upper Hudson Valley, 1633–1940" (Ph.D. diss., Binghamton State University of New York, 1992).

39. Johnson to Clinton, January 22, 1750, Clinton Papers: 10; Grant, *Memoirs of an American Lady,* 66; Reports of the Council of Commissioners of Indian Affairs of Albany, May 26, 1754, fol. 33, NAHC; Beauchamp, *Moravian Journals,* 163–64. An Iroquois chief named Black Prince, because of his dark complexion, may have been of African parentage. See *SWJP,* 13:23; and "Witham Marshe's Journal of the Treaty Held with the Six Nations by the Commissioners of Maryland, and Other Provinces, at Lancaster, in Pennsylvania, June, 1744," *MHSC,* 1st ser., 7 (1801): 179–80. A Cayuga chief called "the Negro" may also have been of non-Iroquoian or mixed ancestry; see *SWJP,* 9:955.

40. Conference at Onondaga, April 26, 1748, *SWJP,* 1:164.

41. Israel Williams to William Pitkin, July 5, 1755, NAHC; Wheelock to Johnson, July 12, 1756, *SWJP,* 9:481. A number of scholars argue that the lines of racial division became firmly entrenched *during* the Seven Years' War and largely as a consequence of warfare. These studies, however, are concerned with Pennsylvania and the Ohio country. See Merrell, *Into the American Woods;* Merritt, *At the Crossroads,* chap. 5; Preston, "Texture of Contact," chap. 3; and Peter Silver, *Our Savage Neighbors: How Indian War Transformed Early America* (New York: W. W. Norton, 2007).

42. For another work that stresses cross-cultural cooperation during the war, see David L. Preston, "'We intend to live our lifetime together as brothers': Palatine and Iroquois Communities in the Mohawk Valley," *NYH* 89:2 (2008): 179–90.

43. Indian Proceedings, May 1, 1757, *SWJP,* 9:713. For other similar incidences, see *SWJP,* 2:545, 9:435, 553.

44. Johnson to Loudoun, September 27, 1756, *SWJP,* 9:544–45; Complaint of the Canajoharie Indians, September 27, 1756, *SWJP,* 9:546–48; Indian Conference, February 7, 1757, *SWJP,* 9:600 (quote); Johnson to James Abercromby, January 14, 1758, *SWJP,* 2:773; Journal of Indian Affairs, January 13, 1758, *SWJP,* 13:104–7.

45. Johnson to Shirley, April 22, 1756, *SWJP,* 9:439 and June 27, 1756, *SWJP,* 2:495. See also Henry I. Wendell to Johnson, May 3, 1756, *SWJP,* 9:447–48; Arent Stevens

to Johnson, July 26, 1756, *SWJP*, 2:517; Johnson to Loudoun, August 15, 1756, *SWJP*, 9:503; and Journal of Sir William, July 27, 1756, *DRCHNY*, 7:172–73.

46. Journal of Indian Proceedings, February 20, 1757, *SWJP*, 9:617; Indian Congress, April 29, 1757, *SWJP*, 9:704–5.

47. In his transatlantic study of the Jacobite Rising of 1745, Geoffrey Plank contends that British army personnel applied their derogative view of Highland Scots to other subaltern groups in the British Empire, including Native Americans. Suggesting the limits of racial ideology, Plank demonstrates that by the mid-eighteenth century the army perceived itself in a missionary role, as an agent of civilization determined to reform these "deviant" communities. See his *Rebellion and Savagery: The Jacobite Rising of 1745 and the British Empire* (Philadelphia: University of Pennsylvania Press, 2005).

48. Orders for Thomas Butler and Jellas Fonda, June 25, 1757, *SWJP*, 9:787–88; Johnson to Charles Hardy, April 21, 1757, *SWJP*, 9:686.

49. Abercromby to Johnson, September 26, 1758, WO 34/38/49; Johnson to Lt. Col. Ellison, June 30, 1755, *SWJP*, 1:669; Johnson to Alexander Turnbull, August 9, 1756 *SWJP*, 2:537–38; Johnson to Phineas Lyman, July 17, 1755, *SWJP*, 1:732. Instructions for conduct were also issued to carpenters employed to build forts in Iroquoia. See *SWJP*, 9:457–58; and *DRCHNY*, 7:101–2.

50. Loudoun to Johnson, August 5, 1756, *SWJP*, 9:495–96; Johnson to Loudoun, August 6, 1756, *SWJP*, 9:496–97; Loudoun to Johnson, August 8, 1756, *SWJP*, 9:499–500. Peter Way uses this murder to exemplify patterns of cultural borrowing and distancing that took place between British soldiers and native allies in "The Cutting Edge of Culture," 123–24.

51. Horatio Gates to Johnson, August 8, 1756, *SWJP*, 2:534; Johnson to Loudoun, September 17, 1756, *SWJP*, 9:531; Journal of Indian Affairs, November 18, 1758, *SWJP*, 10:58. On the widespread presence of alcohol, see Butler to Johnson, January 6, 1757, *SWJP*, 2:664.

52. Journal of Indian Affairs, December 5–9, 16, 1758, *SWJP*, 10:63–64, 80; Instructions to Jellas Fonda, December 9, 1758, *SWJP*, 10:64–65. See also *SWJP*, 9:966, 10:58; and *DRCHNY*, 7:116.

53. The documents reveal that only one other interracial murder was committed on the Mohawk frontier during the war. In 1761, a group of Oneidas went to the German Flats to have their children christened and a marriage ceremony performed when one Oneida shot dead a local official after the latter accused the Indian of killing a hog. See Conrad Frank to Johnson, June 17, 1761, *SWJP*, 3:407; and Johnson to Amherst, July 7, 1761, *SWJP*, 3:504.

54. Journal of Indian Affairs, July 9, 1757, *SWJP*, 9:796–98; Johnson to Peter and Elizabeth Wraxall, July 17, 1757, *SWJP*, 9:799.

55. Thomas Butler to Johnson, December 29, 1758, *SWJP*, 10:82–84; Journal of Sir William, April 12–13, 1759, *DRCHNY*, 7:380–81. There are various spellings of the trader's name: "McMickel," *DRCHNY*, 7:381; "McMicking," *SWJP*, 10:86; "McMichael," *SWJP*, 10:95.

56. Abercromby to Johnson, July 4, 1758, *SWJP*, 9:940. References to Indian-colonial scouting parties are numerous. See, e.g., *SWJP*, 1:525; 2:295, 816, 9:768, 780; *DRCHNY*, 7:93.

57. Fonda to Johnson, December 30, 1756, *SWJP*, 2:660; Thomas Butler to Johnson, January 9, 1757, *SWJP*, 2:665–66; Butler and Fonda to Johnson, January 1757, *SWJP*, 2:667–73 (first quote from p. 669); Johnson to Myndert Wempel, July 22, 1755, *SWJP*, 1:765; Journal of Niagara Campaign, September 9, 1759, *SWJP*, 13:138; Stephen L. Lawton, *The Printup Family in America, 1695–1988* (Baltimore: Gateway Press, 1989), 4–25; Journal of Indian Proceedings, January 15, 1757, and July 6, 1758, *SWJP*, 9:585, 942; Johnson to Clinton, November 6, 1750, *SWJP*, 1:307–8; Journal of Sir William, March 5 and April 29, 1756, *DRCHNY*, 7:92, 100.

58. Journal of Indian Proceedings, January 19, 1757, *SWJP*, 9:586; Johnson to Thomas Butler, April 9, 1757, *SWJP*, 9:674; Journal of Sir William, April 13, 1759, *DRCHNY*, 7:382; Johnson to Daniel Webb, May 16, 1757, *SWJP*, 9:723; Journal of Indian Affairs, January–February 1759, *SWJP*, 10:86, 87, 99.

59. Namias, *Narrative of the Life of Mrs. Mary Jemison.*

60. Thomas Butler to Johnson, April 7, 1757, *SWJP*, 2:700; William Williams to Johnson, March 1756, *SWJP*, 9:413–14; Johnson to Lords of Trade, May 28, 1756, *DRCHNY*, 7:87–88; Journal of Henry Wendell, December 14, 1757, *SWJP*, 9:864.

61. Johnson to Lords of Trade, May 28, 1756, *DRCHNY*, 7:87–88; Journal of Sir William, May 20 and 22, 1756, *DRCHNY*, 7:110, 112.

62. Journal of Sir William, March 5, 1756, *DRCHNY*, 7:92; Johnson to Shirley, May 26, 1756, *SWJP*, 9:461; Indian Conference, February 7, 1757, *SWJP*, 9:600. See also Johnson to Shirley, April 22, 1756, *SWJP*, 9:441.

63. On German men plowing, see *DRCHNY*, 7:92. On German-Iroquois trade relations, see *SWJP*, 9:832. On Dutch traders and smiths, see *DRCHNY*, 7:94–95. On multiethnic scouting parties, see *DRCHNY*, 7:93; and *SWJP*, 9:768, 2:780.

64. Johnson to Thomas Pownall, September 8, 1757, CO 5/888/150; Johnson to Abercromby, September 16, 1757, *SWJP*, 2:739–40; Philip Townsend to Johnson, November 13, 1757, *SWJP*, 2:757; George Croghan to Loudoun, November 20, 1757, *SWJP*, 9:856–57; Croghan to Johnson, December 3, 1757, *SWJP*, 9:860–62.

65. Loudoun to Johnson, June 1757, *SWJP*, 2:723; Butler to Johnson, April 7, 1757, *SWJP*, 2:701–2.

66. Gates to Johnson, August 8, 1756, *SWJP*, 2:534; Indian Intelligence, March 4, 1757, *SWJP*, 2:679; Johnson to Abercromby, April 13, 1757, *SWJP*, 9:676; Orders to John Butler, May 12, 1757, *SWJP*, 9:721; Johnson to Loudoun, September 3, 1757, *SWJP*, 9:825–26; Johnson to Pownall, September 8, 1757, CO 5/888/150; Johnson to Abercromby, September 16, 1757, *SWJP*, 2:739. For further reports of Germans sending messages to the French via Indians, see *SWJP*, 9:699, 919. George Klock was suspected of having "endeavoured by false tales, and artfull insinuating to create differences, and misunderstandings, between the Army Inhabitants and Indians"; *SWJP*, 10:338.

67. Thomas Butler to Johnson, April 7, 1757, *SWJP*, 2:702; Johnson to Abercromby,

April 13, 1757, *SWJP*, 9:676; McAulay to Johnson, December 2, 1758, *SWJP*, 10:56. Johnson offered rewards for information on the "evil low designing People among the Inhabitants" who attempted to "stir up the Indians"; *SWJP*, 10:63. For a history of Anglo-Dutch relations, see Donna Merwick, *Possessing Albany, 1630–1710: The Dutch and English Experiences* (New York: Cambridge University Press, 1990).

68. Journal of Indian Affairs, March 28, 1757, *SWJP*, 9:669; Indian Proceedings, September 15, 1757, *SWJP*, 9:832–33; Council held at Fort Augusta, October 18, 1756, *MPCP*, 7:299. See also Johnson's Proceedings with Deputies, February 13–14, 1760, *SWJP*, 3:189. Indian nativism began to flourish among Indian communities in the Ohio country during the 1740s. See Gregory E. Dowd, *A Spirited Resistance: The North American Indian Struggle for Unity, 1745–1815* (Baltimore: Johns Hopkins University Press, 1992), 23–25; and Jane T. Merritt, "Dreaming of the Savior's Blood: Moravians and the Indian Great Awakening in Pennsylvania," *WMQ* 54:4 (1997): 723–46.

69. "Review of the Trade and Affairs of the Indians . . . 1767," *DRCHNY*, 7:960.

Chapter 6

1. Journal of Indian Affairs, January 27, 1762, *SWJP*, 10:360; Proceedings of Sir William, March 4, 1768, *DRCHNY*, 8:40; William A. Starna, "The Oneida Homeland in the Seventeenth Century," in *The Oneida Indian Experience: Two Perspectives*, ed. Jack Campisi and Lawrence M. Hauptman (Syracuse, N.Y.: Syracuse University Press, 1988), 9–10.

2. On the different meanings "victory" held for colonists, imperialists, and Native Americans, see F. Anderson, *Crucible of War*, parts 7–10.

3. SWJM, May 26, 1763, vol. 6, part 4, p. 416 (hereafter in form 6/4/416); Conference held at Easton, August 8, 1761, *MPCP*, 8:642. See also Johnson to Board of Trade, November 13, 1763, *DRCHNY*, 7:577; and From Indians at Oquaga, August 30, 1762, *SWJP*, 3:871.

4. Amherst's Permit for Settlement at Niagara, April 10, 1761, CO 5/61/part 1/285; Walter Rutherford to Amherst, April 28, 1761, CO 5/61/part 1/289; Amherst to Johnson, May 7, 1761, *SWJP*, 3:387; Rutherford to Johnson, May 12, 1761, *SWJP*, 10:265; Rutherford to Amherst, April 9, 1761, and Amherst to Rutherford, same date, in Louis des Cognets Jr., *Amherst and Canada* (Princeton, N.J.: Privately published, 1962), 310–11; Nicholas B. Wainwright, ed., "George Croghan's Journal, April 3, 1759–April [30], 1763," *PMHB* 71:4 (1974): 410; Milo Milton Quaife, ed., *The Siege of Detroit in 1763: The Journal of Pontiac's Conspiracy and John Rutherfurd's Narrative of a Captivity* (Chicago: R. R. Donnelley and Sons, 1958), xxviii–xxix; F. Anderson, *Crucible of War*, 473–74; Walter S. Dunn Jr., *Frontier Profit and Loss: The British Army and the Fur Traders* (Westport, Conn.: Greenwood Press, 1998), 76.

5. SWJM, May 28, 1763, 6/4/418 (quote); Niagara and Detroit Proceedings, July 21, 1761, *SWJP*, 3:444; Indian Proceedings, April 25, 1762, *SWJP*, 3:707; SWJM, September 9, 1762, 6/3/301–2; Johnson to Alexander Duncan, September 21, 1762, *SWJP*, 3:882; Johnson to Board of Trade, November 13, 1763, *DRCHNY*, 7:577.

6. President Colden to Board of Trade, February 25, 1761, *DRCHNY*, 7:455; Sir William Johnson's Proceedings with the Lower Mohawk Indians, March 20, 1760, *DRCHNY*, 7:435–36; SWJM, March 1, 1761, 6/1/13–14; SWJM, August 10, 1763, 6/5/484 (quote); Johnson to Board of Trade, November 13, 1763, *DRCHNY*, 7:576–77.

7. Johnson to Colden, February 20, 1761, *NYHSC* 65 (1932): 12–13 (second quote). For Indian complaints against Klock, see Address of the Canajoharie Indians to Johnson, February 25, 1760, *DRCHNY*, 7:434; SWJM, February 17, 1761, 6/1/1, March 1, 1761, 6/1/13–14 (first quote), and January 28, 1762, 6/2/155; Meeting with Canajoharies, March 10, 1763, *SWJP*, 4:50–61; and From the Sachems of Canajoharie, July 8, 1763, *SWJP*, 4:165–66. On Klock evicting tenants, see Johnson to Daniel Claus, March 10, 1761, *SWJP*, 3:356; Johnson to William Corry, March 15, 1762, *SWJP*, 3:649; and Johnson to John Tabor Kempe, August 20, 1762, *SWJP*, 10:487..

8. Indian Proceedings, April 24 and 28, 1762, *SWJP*, 3:705 (quote), 714; SWJM, May 12 and 28, 1763, 6/4/407–10, 419–25. On colonial settlement in the upper Susquehanna Valley, see Narrative of Daniel Brodhead's Journey to Wyoming, September 27, 1762, in *Susquehannah Company Papers*, ed. Julian P. Boyd (Ithaca, N.Y.: Cornell University Press, 1962), 2:166–70; Mancall, *Valley of Opportunity*, 76–78, 88–89; and Anthony F. C. Wallace, *King of the Delawares: Teedyuscung, 1700–1763* (Philadelphia: University of Pennsylvania Press, 1949), 47–53ff.

9. Thomas Baugh to Amherst, July 20, 1762, *SWJP*, 3:831 (first quote); Amherst to Baugh, August 1, 1762, *SWJP*, 3:835; Hugh Wallace to Alexander Duncan, August 27, 1762, *SWJP*, 3:869–70 (second quote); Duncan to Johnson, August 29, 1762, *SWJP*, 10:497–98; Johnson to Duncan, September 21, 1762, *SWJP*, 3:882; SWJM, August 11–12, 1762, 6/3/287–88, September 13, 1762, 6/3/306.

10. SWJM, July 9 and 11, 1763, 6/4/449–50, 453; George Croghan to Johnson, July 2, 1763, *SWJP*, 10:727–28; Court of Inquiry, July 6–10, 1763, *SWJP*, 10:732, 734–36; Amherst to Johnson, July 7, 1763, WO 34/38/243; Jean Baptiste De Couagne to Johnson, September 16, 1763, *SWJP*, 10:815; George Etherington to Johnson, September 17, 1763, *SWJP*, 10:817–18; Johnson to Amherst, October 6, 1763, WO 34/39/416; Johnson to Board of Trade, September 25, 1763, *DRCHNY*, 7:562. For an informative account of the war, see Dowd, *War Under Heaven*.

11. Recent interpretations of this war deemphasize economic grievances, highlighting instead how British disregard for Indian protocol or attempts to "assert imperial superiority" incited Indians to war. See, e.g., William R. Nester, *"Haughty Conquerors": Amherst and the Great Indian Uprising of 1763* (Westport, Conn.: Praeger, 2000), 36; and Dowd, *War Under Heaven*, 2.

12. SWJM, July 11, 1763, 6/4/453 (first quote); Johnson to Amherst, July 11, 1763, *DRCHNY*, 7:532; Journal of Indian Congress, September 5 and 6, 1763, *SWJP*, 10:830, 833; Johnson to Thomas Gage, January 27, 1764, Gage Papers: 13 (second quote); Johnson to John Vaughan, April 18, 1765, *SWJP*, 11:701; Minutes of Detroit Indian Conference, July 3, 1761, *SWJP*, 3:451 (third quote). On French-Iroquois relations at Niagara, see Pierre Pouchet, *Memoirs on the Late War in North America Between France and*

England, trans. Michael Cardy (Youngstown, N.Y.: Old Fort Niagara Association, 1994), 108, 116–17, 126–27ff; and Kent, *Iroquois Indians II*, chap. 8.

13. Indian Conference, March 24–April 23, 1764, *SWJP*, 11:134–61; Articles of Peace with the Seneca, April 3, 1764, *DRCHNY*, 7:621–23, 652–53; Johnson to the Earl of Halifax, August 30, 1764, *DRCHNY*, 7:647. Current scholarship downplays British victory, instead emphasizing themes of stalemate and continued Indian agency. Mc-Connell, *A Country Between*, 206–7; White, *The Middle Ground*, chaps. 7–8; Dowd, *A Spirited Resistance*, 36ff.

14. Lord Adam Gordon, "Journal of an Officer who Travelled in America and the West Indies in 1764 and 1765," in *Travels in the American Colonies*, ed. Newton D. Mereness (New York: Macmillan Company, 1916), 420; Colin D. Campbell, "They Beckoned and We Came: The Settlement of Cherry Valley," *NYH* 79:3 (1998): 215–32.

15. Walter Pilkington, ed., *The Journals of Samuel Kirkland: 18th Century Missionary to the Iroquois, Government Agent, Father of Hamilton College* (Clinton, N.Y.: Hamilton College, 1980), 71; Journal of Indian Affairs, June 21 and December 25, 1765, *SWJP*, 11:817, 985.

16. On the 1765 famine, see Johnson to Gage, April 20, 1765, Gage Papers: 34 (first quote); Proceedings of Sir William, May 10, 1765, *DRCHNY*, 7:737; Indian Congress, June 7, 1765, *SWJP*, 11:783; and Journal of Indian Affairs, June 21, 1765, *SWJP*, 11:817. On the 1767 famine, see Laura J. Murray, ed., *To Do Good to My Indian Brethren: The Writings of Joseph Johnson, 1751–1776* (Amherst: University of Massachusetts Press, 1998), 62 (second and third quotes); and SWJM, March 4, 1767, 7/4/436. The 1769 famine is documented in the entry for January 10, 1769, Gage Warrants, box 20, fol. 74 (hereafter in form Gage Warrants 20:74) (fourth quote); Johnson to Gage, May 5, 1769, *SWJP*, 12:717; Johnson to Hillsborough, July 12, 1769, *DRCHNY*, 8:222; and Francis W. Halsey, ed., *A Tour of the Hudson, the Mohawk, the Susquehanna, and the Delaware in 1769: Being the Journal of Richard Smith* (New York: Purple Mountain Press, 1989), 150. See also James P. Ronda, "Reverend Samuel Kirkland and the Oneida Indians," in *Oneida Indian Experience*, ed. Campisi and Hauptman, 26.

17. For the Schoharie land dispute, see Account Against the Crown, *SWJP*, 12:865, 925, 999. On the Mohawk Flats controversy, see Indian Congress, June 14, 1768, *SWJP*, 12:541; Deed of the Mohawks, 1733, *DRCHNY*, 6:16; and Proceedings of Sir William, July 28, 1772, *DRCHNY*, 8:306. On the Canajoharies' troublesome neighbors, see Johnson to Colden, August 23, 1764, *SWJP*, 4:513–14; Johnson to Kempe, September 7, 1765, *SWJP*, 11:926; and SWJM, January 31, 1765, 7/3/259, March 14, 1767, 7/4/436.

18. For Canajoharie complaints against Klock, see SWJM, July 5 and August 13, 1766, 7/4/382 (first quote), 413; and Proceedings of Sir William, July 28, 1772, and July 11, 1774, *DRCHNY*, 8:304–5, 478 (second quote). Johnson also detailed Klock's illegal activities in numerous correspondences right up until 1774; e.g., *SWJP*, 3:647–48, 8:938, 1008–9. On the Canajoharies leaving for Canada, see SWJM, 7/4/382, 413. The Canajoharies also appealed to the Oneidas for land. See *SWJP*, 12:167; and Pilkington, *Kirkland Journals*, 82. Klock's eventual legal claim to Mohawk land is detailed in Nam-

mack, *Fraud, Politics and the Dispossession of the Indians*, 51. See also David L. Preston, "George Klock, the Canajoharie Mohawks, and the Good Ship *Sir William Johnson*: Land, Legitimacy, and Community in the Eighteenth-Century Mohawk Valley," *NYH* 86:4 (2005): 473–99.

19. SWJM, September 20, 1764, 7/2/177, January 31, 1765, 7/3/258 (first and second quotes), and February 25–26, 1765, 7/3/262–63; Johnson to Colden, February 27, 1765, *SWJP*, 4:652–54; Johnson to Kempe, September 7, 1765, *SWJP*, 11:923–26; Johnson to Board of Trade, May 24, 1765, *DRCHNY*, 7:712; SWJM, June 21, 1766, 7/4/381 (third quote); Indian Congress, June 8–9, August 2–4, 1768, *SWJP*, 12:533–38 (fourth quote), 572–78; Moore to Earl of Hillsborough, August 17, 1768, *SWJP*, 8:92. On Little Abraham, see Ralph T. Pastor, "Teiorhéñhsere," *DCB* 4 (1979): 730.

20. SWJM, September 19, 1766, 7/4/415 (first quote), June 9 and August 4, 1767, 7/4/441, 443; John Bradstreet to Johnson, August 10, 1769, *SWJP*, 12:747 (second quote). For additional examples of voluntary land sales, see *SWJP*, 12:538, 899; and *DRCHNY*, 8:308–9.

21. Johnson to Gage, April 17, 1766, Gage Papers: 50; Johnson to Goldsbrow Banyar, September 22, 1766, *SWJP*, 12:192 and April 27, 1767, *SWJP*, 12:302.

22. Barbara Graymont, "The Oneidas and the American Revolution," in *Oneida Indian Experience*, ed. Campisi and Hauptman, 31; Fenton, "Problems Arising," 216–17; Congress at Fort Stanwix, October 30, 1768, *SWJP*, 12:629.

23. SWJM, May 24, 1766, 7/4/378 and June 18, 1766, 7/4/379–80; Johnson to Gage, June 27, 1766, Gage Papers: 53 (first quote); Gage to Johnson, July 12, 1767, Gage Papers: 67 (third quote); Johnson to Gage, August 6, 1767, Gage Papers: 68; SWJM, August 8, 1767, 7/4/449; John Galland to Johnson, August 11, 1767, *SWJP*, 5:613; Gage to Johnson, September 7, 1767, *SWJP*, 5:659; Galland to Johnson, September 9, 1767, *SWJP*, 5:663; Johnson to Gage, September 22, 1767, Gage Papers: 70 (second quote); Francis Grant, "Journal from New York to Canada, 1767," *NYH* 13 (1932): 189, 190. In late 1768, the Oneidas attacked Fort Stanwix, plundering "Three good Cows, and a Mare and Colt," and destroyed the fences and garden. See Huge Wallace to Johnson, December 5, 1768, *SWJP*, 6:517. See also Proceedings of Sir William, May 6, 1765, *DRCHNY*, 7:729.

24. Johnson to Banyar, August 14, 1766, *SWJP*, 12:156; Higgins, *Expansion in New York*, 58–59.

25. Moore to Johnson, June 14, 1766, *SWJP*, 5:266–67; SWJM, September 19, 1766, 7/4/415; Johnson to Gage, October 4, 1766, Gage Papers: 58 (first, second, and third quotes); Johnson to Colden, November 8, 1766, *SWJP*, 5:416 (fourth quote); Johnson to Banyar, April 27, 1767, *SWJP*, 12:301.

26. Johnson to Moore, November 24, 1768, in *Iroquois Indians*, ed. Jennings et al., reel 29. Plans for a new boundary were initially agreed upon in April 1765; see *DRCHNY*, 7:718–38. The Fort Stanwix Treaty minutes are reprinted in *DRCHNY*, 8:111–34. Standard works on this treaty conference include Ray A. Billington, "The Fort Stanwix Treaty of 1768," *NYH* 25:2 (1944): 182–94; Jack M. Sosin, *Whitehall and the Wilderness: The Middle West in British Colonial Policy, 1760–1775* (Lincoln: University

of Nebraska Press, 1961), chap. 7; Peter Marshall, "Sir William Johnson and the Treaty of Fort Stanwix, 1768," *Journal of American Studies* 1 (1967): 149–79; and Dorothy V. Jones, *License for Empire: Colonialism by Treaty in Early America* (Chicago: University of Chicago Press, 1982), 75–92.

27. Johnson, Indian agent George Croghan, and local trader Jellas Fonda, among others, patented lands around Fort Stanwix. See Indian Receipt to Jellas Fonda for Lands Sold, item 22, folder 1, box 4; Lands Sold to Johnson and Croghan, item 129, folder 5, box 4; and List of the Names of those concerned in the Indian Purchase . . . near Fort Stanwix, item 133, folder 5, box 4. All three items are in the Jellas Fonda Family Papers, NYSL. See also Council Minutes, June 19, 1771, *SWJP*, 8:152–53; and Oliver De Lancey to Johnson, August 3, 1772, *SWJP*, 8:557.

28. A. T. Volwiler, "George Croghan and the Development of Central New York, 1763–1800," *New York State Historical Association, Quarterly Journal* 4:1 (1923): 21–40; idem, *George Croghan and the Westward Movement, 1741–1782* (Cleveland: Arthur H. Clark Company, 1926), 248–52; Wainwright, *George Croghan*, 255–57, 261–70; G. William Beardslee, "An Otsego Frontier Experience: The Gatzburg Tract, 1770–1795," *NYH* 79:3 (1998): 233–43; Frances Whiting Halsey, *The Old New York Frontier: Its Wars with Indians and Tories, Its Missionary Schools, Pioneers and Land Titles, 1614–1800* (New York: Charles Scribner's Sons, 1901), part 3; Higgins, *Expansion in New York*, 93–96; Bernard Bailyn, *Voyagers to the West: A Passage in the Peopling of America on the Eve of the American Revolution* (New York: Knopf, 1986), 579–80; Mancall, *Valley of Opportunity*, chap. 5.

29. Johnson's Susquehanna land interests are documented in a series of letters written to his associate Goldsbrow Banyar. See *SWJP*, 12:719, 754, 787–88, 829–30, 875. See also Guzzardo, "Sir William Johnson's Official Family," chaps. 4–5.

30. Proceedings of Colonel Guy Johnson with the Oneidas and Oughquageys, February 11–13, 1775, *DRCHNY*, 8:550–51, 554; Gage to Earl of Hillsborough, October 1, 1771, CO 5/89/170. Adam is quoted in Calloway, *The American Revolution in Indian Country*, 122. See also Proceedings of Sir William, July 28, 1772, *DRCHNY*, 8:305–6; and Johnson to Earl of Dartmouth, June 20, 1774, CO 5/75/139. Studies tend to emphasize Iroquois gains over other Indian groups (e.g., McConnell, *A Country Between*, 252), ignoring the distinct experiences of the individual six nations.

31. George Croghan to Gage, January 1, 1770, CO 5/88/44; Colden to Johnson, June 13, 1765, *SWJP*, 11:786.

32. On Amherst's views of the fur trade, see the following letters from Amherst to Johnson: February 22, 1761, WO 34/38/137–38; July 11, 1761, *SWJP*, 3:507; August 9, 1761, WO 34/38/161 (third quote); December 2, 1761, *SWJP*, 10:347; and January 16, 1762, WO 34/38/174–75 (second quote). On Johnson's more cautious approach, see the following letters from Johnson to Amherst: March 21, 1761, WO 34/39/175–77 (first quote); April 23, 1761, WO 34/39/178; and January 7, 1762, *SWJP*, 3:601 (fourth quote).

33. Johnson to Amherst, February 12, 1761, *SWJP*, 3:331; SWJM, March 8, 1761,

6/1/20. See also Niagara and Detroit Proceedings, July 3–21, 1761, *SWJP*, 3:432–33, 443–45, 451; and SWJM, May 26, 1763, 6/4/416.

34. William Walters to Johnson, November 11, 1761, *SWJP*, 10:332; Indian Proceedings, April 25, 1762, *SWJP*, 3:707. See also SWJM, September 10, 1762, 6/3/299, 301; and George Croghan to Johnson, October 8, 1762, *SWJP*, 10:548–49.

35. Johnson to Amherst, December 6, 1761, *SWJP*, 3:581; SWJM, August 11, 1762, 6/3/290; Eleazar Wheelock to George Whitefield, September 16, 1762, quoted in W. DeLoss Love, *Samson Occom and the Christian Indians of New York* (Boston: Pilgrim Press, 1899), 96; SWJM, April 21, 1763, 6/4/403. On Indian requests for aid, see *SWJP*, 3:445–46, 464, 709; and SWJM, 6/4/383. On the use of bows and arrows, see SWJM, 6/1/11. On the Iroquois stealing livestock, see SWJM, 6/1/22, 6/3/306; and *SWJP*, 10:498.

36. Conference held at Easton, August 7–12, 1761, *MPCP*, 8:641–43, 652.

37. Conference held at Lancaster, August 23–27, 1762, *MPCP*, 8:752–55, 768.

38. SWJM, July 11, 1763, 6/4/453; Johnson to Amherst, July 11, 1763, *DRCHNY*, 7:532; Journal of Indian Congress, September 5, 1763, *SWJP*, 10:830; To the Authorities at German Flats, November 3, 1763, *SWJP*, 10:915–16; Volkert P. Douw to Johnson, November 3, 1763, *SWJP*, 10:916; Colden to Johnson, December 28, 1763, *SWJP*, 10:988; Indian Congress, July 24, 1764, *SWJP*, 11:293.

39. Sosin, *Whitehall and the Wilderness*, chaps. 2–3; Peter Marshall, "Colonial Protest and Imperial Retrenchment: Indian Policy, 1764–1768," *Journal of American Studies* 5 (1971): 1–17; Daniel K. Richter, "Native Americans, the Plan of 1764, and the British Empire That Never Was," in *Cultures and Identities in Colonial British America*, ed. Robert Olwell and Alan Tully (Baltimore: Johns Hopkins University Press, 2006), 269–92.

40. Johnson to Thomas Penn, September 15, 1769, *SWJP*, 7:177; Johnson to Gage, August 9, 1769, *SWJP*, 7:86; Gage to Johnson, August 20, 1769, *SWJP*, 7:107; Ferrell Wade and C. Keiuser to Johnson, June 3, 1772, *SWJP*, 8:508–9.

41. Braund, *Deerskins and Duffels*, 103ff; John R. Alden, *John Stuart and the Southern Colonial Frontier* (Ann Arbor: University of Michigan Press, 1944), 207–9. The proclamation is printed, among other places, in *Canadian Archives: Documents Relating to the Constitutional History of Canada, 1759–1791*, ed. Adam Shortt and Arthur G. Doughty (Ottawa: Canada Archives, 1918), part 1, 163–68.

42. On Indian complaints against the removal of commissaries, see *SWJP*, 7:119; *DRCHNY*, 8:475; and Johnson to Frederick Haldimand, June 30, 1773, fol. 62, ser. 21670, Frederick Haldimand Papers, Additional Manuscripts (hereafter in form Add Mss) 21670, fol. 62, British Library, London. See also Johnson to Hillsborough, April 4, 1772, *DRCHNY*, 8:292.

43. Johnson to Thomas Penn, January 30, 1770, *SWJP*, 7:363; Stevenson to Johnson, January 8, 1772, and December 18, 1770 *SWJP*, 8:363, 7:1040.

44. Indian Congress, October 15, 1766, *SWJP*, 12:210; Proceedings of Sir William, July 9, 1774, *DRCHNY*, 8:475–76; Johnson to Hillsborough, August 14, 1770, CO 5/71/ part 2/93; From sachems of Oquaga, January 22, 1770, *SWJP*, 7:348. On fake silver, see

SWJP, 7:717, 12:860. On watered-down rum, see SWJM, March 4, 1767 7/4/436. On the poor behavior of traders, see SWJM, August 30, 1766, 7/4/414; and *DRCHNY*, 8:46.

45. SWJM, June 25, 1764, 7/1/130 and June 3, 1766, 7/4/378; Michael Byrne to Johnson, October 2, 1767, *SWJP*, 5:719; Allan Grant to Johnson, August 8, 1769, *SWJP*, 12:745.

46. The impact of alcohol among the Choctaws in the same period offers a striking contrast to the situation of the Iroquois; see White, *Roots of Dependency*, 58–59, 83–86.

47. References to the Iroquois purchasing "Indian shoes" are plentiful in the Account Book of unidentified Mohawk Valley Indian Trader, 1762–76, Jellas Fonda Family Papers, NYHS. See fols. 3, 4, 6, 7, 8, 9, 10ff. Wheelock is quoted in Calloway, *New Worlds for All*, 46. The colonial boycott of British goods led to "wants and disappointments" among the Iroquois (Johnson to Hillsborough, August 14, 1770, CO 5/71/part 2/93). In 1770, Johnson had tremendous difficulty locating Indian goods anywhere in the Mohawk Valley. See Johnson to Gage, April 6, May 10, and August 22, 1770, Gage Papers: 91, 92, 95.

48. Normand MacLeod to Johnson, August 25, 1766, *SWJP*, 12:162–63; Journal of Indian Transactions at Niagara, July 2–September 24, 1767, *DHNY*, 2:506–8; Byrne to Johnson, October 2, 1767, *SWJP*, 5:718; MacLeod to Johnson, October 25, 1767, *SWJP*, 5:758; John Brown to Johnson, October 26, 1767, *SWJP*, 5:759; Brown to Johnson, April 25, 1770, *SWJP*, 7:582–83; Account Against the Crown, April 28, 1772, *SWJP*, 12:999. See Byrne to Johnson, September 25, 1767, *SWJP*, 5:699, for theft at Fort Ontario.

49. Byrne to Johnson, September 25, 1767, *SWJP*, 5:699; Brown to Johnson, October 17 and 18, November 4, 1770, *SWJP*, 7:942–44, 986–87; Johnson to Gage, November 8, 1770, *SWJP*, 7:993–94.

50. Guy Johnson to Haldimand, September 9, 1773, *SWJP*, 12:1029 (quote); Hector Theos. Cramahé, October 13, 1773, *SWJP*, 12:1036; Johnson to Haldimand, April 21, 1774, Add Mss 21670, fol. 127; Haldimand to Johnson, April 27, 1774, Add Mss 21670, fol. 129; Johnson to Haldimand, April 29, 1774, Add Mss 21670, fol. 135.

51. Murray G. Lawson, *Fur: A Study in English Mercantilism, 1700–1775* (Toronto: University of Toronto Press, 1943), 71–72. See also Dunn, *Frontier Profit and Loss*, chap. 4, esp. 69.

52. References to the trade in animal furs, corn, peas, and wheat are listed throughout. For specific examples cited, see Account Book of unidentified Mohawk Valley Indian Trader, fols. 52, 61, 88b. A "scipple" is a Dutch measurement of uncertain size.

53. Account Book of unidentified Mohawk Valley Indian Trader, fols. 49, 88b, 98, 111, 117, 118.

54. Ibid., fols. 20, 61, 78b, 80, 100. References to Indians paying "cash in full" and settling their accounts "by cash" are noted throughout. See, e.g., fols. 1, 2, 5, 23, 24, 40, 42, 43, 47, 90, 117. Other examples of "cash lent" to Indians include fols. 61, 76, 118. Payments of cash to Indians are also listed as "to cash." See, e.g., fols. 17, 42, 93, 98b, 113.

55. Johnson to Kempe, October 4, 1769, *SWJP*, 7:201–2; Halsey, *Journal of Richard Smith*, 126, 90, 132–33; H. L. Bourdin and S. T. Williams, eds., "Crèvecoeur on

the Susquehanna, 1774–1776," *Yale Review* 14 (1925): 581; SWJM, March 4, 1767, 7/4/436; Congress at Fort Stanwix, October 18, 1768, *SWJP*, 12:625; Account Book of unidentified Mohawk Valley Indian Trader, fols. 5, 42, 51, 52, 71, 77, 78, 80, 96, 98b, 99, 113, 118; Effects and Possessions Left Behind in 1777 by the Mohawk at La Chine, CO 42/47/238–52; Pilkington, *Kirkland Journals*, 70, 83; Charles Inglis, "Memorial Concerning the Iroquois, 1771," *DHNY*, 4:665; Graymont, *The Iroquois in the American Revolution*, 146–47. See also Thomas R. Wessel, "Agriculture and Iroquois Hegemony in New York, 1610–1779," *Maryland Historian* 1:2 (1970): 93–104; and David Levinson, "An Explanation for the Oneida-Colonist Alliance in the American Revolution," *Ethnohistory* 23:3 (1976): 280–81.

56. Effects and Possessions Left Behind in 1777 by the Mohawk at La Chine, CO 42/47/238–52; "Losses Sustained by the Oneida and Tuscaroras in consequence of their Attachment to the United States," Timothy Pickering Papers, pp. 157–65, reel 62, Massachusetts Historical Society, Boston; Halsey, *Journal of Richard Smith*, 126, 133, 153; Bourdin and Williams, "Crèvecoeur on the Susquehanna," 581; Carl Bridenbaugh, ed., "Patrick M'Robert's Tour Through Part of the North Provinces of America," *PMHB* 59 (1935): 170; Lender and Martin, *Citizen Soldier*, 66, 84–85; Debtor Accounts, July 14, 1770, *SWJP*, 7:39; Account Against the Crown, 1768–72, *SWJP*, 12:666, 667, 1017; Anthony Wonderley, "An Oneida Community in the 1780s: Study of an Inventory of Iroquois Property Losses During the Revolutionary War," *Northeast Anthropology* 56 (1998): 25; Grumet, *Historic Contact*, 414; Jordan, "Archaeology of the Iroquois Restoration," 495–505. For an informative article on the Mohawks' introduction to livestock and the initial problems it raised, see James Homer Williams, "Great Doggs and Mischievous Cattle: Domesticated Animals and Indian-European Relations in New Netherlands and New York," *NYH* 76:3 (1995): 245–64. Virginia DeJohn Anderson has noted that it was common practice among colonists as well to allow cattle to roam freely. See her *Creatures of Empire*.

57. Halsey, *Journal of Richard Smith*, 152, 137; Bridenbaugh, "Patrick M'Robert's Tour," 170. See also "Diary of Eli Forbes . . . 1762," *MHSC*, 2nd ser., 7 (1891–92): 392, 393; "Journal of Warren Johnson," 255; Lender and Martin, *Citizen Soldier*, 77; and Debtor Accounts, June 27, 1769, *SWJP*, 7:31.

58. Halsey, *Journal of Richard Smith*, 138; Account Book of unidentified Mohawk Valley Indian Trader, fols. 5, 47, 84, 86b, 88b; Unidentified Account Book of a General Store, [Albany N.Y.?], 1771–74, NYSL; Hendrick Frey Jr. and John Butler to Johnson, November 6, 1764, *SWJP*, 11:398; Fonda to Johnson, September 24, 1771, *SWJP*, 8:276; Fonda to Stefanes Degora, September 13, 1774, folder 4, Fonda Family Box, Jellas Fonda Family Papers, NYHS. See also *SWJP*, 11:963, 12:150–51, 168, 209.

59. Account of David Schuyler, February 9, 1762, *SWJP*, 3:631–33; Proceedings of the Fort Stanwix Treaty, October 31, 1768, *DRCHNY*, 8:124–25; Debtor Accounts, July 6, 1769, *SWJP*, 7:32; Journal of Wade and Keiuser's Trading Expedition, May–June 1770, *SWJP*, 7:724–25; Benjamin Davis Affidavit, August 8, 1775, box 13, Philip Schuyler Papers, New York Public Library, N.Y.

60. SWJM, December 21, 1764, 7/3/254; Halsey, *Journal of Richard Smith*, 113, 114, 137; Pass of Conrad Franck, July 13, 1766, *SWJP*, 5:331; Account Book of John Butler, October 8, 1767, *SWJP*, 13:517; Account Book of unidentified Mohawk Valley Indian Trader, fols. 49, 88b, 98, 111, 117, 118. Trader account books reveal similar forms of labor and rates of pay among colonial settlers. See Jellas Fonda Account Book, Caughanwaga, 1774–82, box 5, Jellas Fonda Family Papers, NYSL, for payment to local Euro-American men for digging ditches, cutting wood, and transporting goods.

61. Pilkington, *Kirkland Journals*, 70 (quote), 72, 85–86 (quote), 87n10, 88n13, 90nn30, 31; Kirkland to Wheelock, April 25, 1770, Samuel Kirkland Papers, Hamilton College, Clinton, New York (hereafter SKP); Hart, "'For the Good of Our Souls,'" 299–300; Jellas Fonda's Account, September 1769, *SWJP*, 7:981.

62. Amherst to Johnson, December 20, 1761, *SWJP*, 3:594; Richard Shuckburgh to Johnson, April 12, 1762, *SWJP*, 3:682; Johnson to Amherst, August 1, 1762, WO 34/39/278; Amherst to Johnson, August 7, 1762, *SWJP*, 3:857. On tracking down army deserters, see WO 71/71/147–55.

63. SWJM, January 31, 1764, 7/1/63; Johnson to Montour, February 21, 1764, *SWJP*, 4:336–37; Johnson to Gage, December 30, 1763, Gage Papers: 11; Gage Warrants 8:47; Mohawk Indians under Henry Gladwin, Certificate of Services, May 13, 1764, p. 49, Ferdinand J. Dreer Autograph Collection, vol. 1, Officers in America before the Revolution, Historical Society of Pennsylvania, Philadelphia. Stockbridge Indians also sold their martial skills for cash; see *SWJP*, 10:757, 761, 771, 11:68.

64. Extract from John Wilkin's Account, May 5, 1769, *SWJP*, 7:70; Certificate of Charles Edmonstone, July 25, 1769, *SWJP*, 7:70–71; MacLeod to Johnson, March 12, 1770, *SWJP*, 7:484; Account of Myndert M. Wempel, July 29, 1766, *SWJP*, 5:339; George Phyn to Johnson, September 19, 1767, *SWJP*, 5:681; "Jeremy Lister, 10th Regiment," *Journal of the Society for Army Historical Research* 41 (1963): 38; Kelsay, *Joseph Brant*, 113–14. On the parallel development of the commodification of Indian labor in other colonies, see White, *Roots of Dependency*, 76, 80; McConnell, *A Country Between*, 156; Braund, *Deerskins and Duffels*, 73–74; Michael N. McConnell, *Army and Empire: British Soldiers on the American Frontier* (Lincoln: University of Nebraska Press, 2004), 107; and Merritt, *At the Crossroads*, 152–53.

65. Johnson's postwar accounts are detailed in the Gage Warrants, parts of which are reprinted in the *SWJP*, 7:1091–97, 12:644–49, 665–68, 734–39, 758–65, 797–803, 856–58, 863–71, 897–903, 920–27, 944–49, 998–1004, 1015–22. For examples cited, see SWJM, January 30, 1765, 7/3/258; and *SWJP*, 12:762.

66. Receipts of Job Bullingham and Son, Indians, August 27, 1770, *SWJP*, 7:867; Thomas Flood's Account, *SWJP*, 7:918–19; Debtor Accounts, March 16, 1770, *SWJP*, 7:34; Jellas Fonda's Account, March–August 1770, *SWJP*, 7:974, 979, 980. Although he is not directly identified as "Indian," a "Job Bullingham" also appears in the Account Book of unidentified Mohawk Valley Indian Trader (part 2, fols. 15, 23, 28) for receiving wages.

67. Johnson to Gage, April 5, 1771, Gage Papers: 101; Certificate of Charles Edmon-

stone, July 25, 1769, *SWJP*, 7:70–71; Johnson to Gage, November 23, 1769, *SWJP*, 7:264; Gage to Johnson, December 11, 1769, *SWJP*, 7:298–99; Halsey, *Journal of Richard Smith*, 139, 137. See also Johnson to Amherst, August 1, 1762, WO 34/39/278.

68. MacLeod to Johnson, January 4, 1769, *SWJP*, 6:566; Journal of Indian Affairs, February, 2, 1769, *SWJP*, 12:693–94; James Stevenson to Johnson, February 4, 1770, *SWJP*, 7:369–70; MacLeod to Johnson, March 12, 1770, *SWJP*, 7:484–85; John B. Van Eps' Account, June 20, 1769, *SWJP*, 7:441.

69. Account, July 31, 1772, *SWJP*, 8:556; Thomas Wharton to Johnson, April 26, 1770, *SWJP*, 7:591.

70. Beauchamp, "Metallic Ornaments," 49–50; "Witham Marshe's Journal," 189. On the use of wampum as a currency, see Chapter 1. On the use of corn as a currency, see Beauchamp, *Moravian Journals*, 208, 209, 211.

71. Halsey, *Journal of Richard Smith*, 150; Grant to Johnson, August 8, 1769, *SWJP*, 12:745; Account Book of unidentified Mohawk Valley Indian Trader, e.g., fols. 23, 80, 84bff.

72. Halsey, *Journal of Richard Smith*, 134–35; Beauchamp, "Metallic Ornaments," 74–76; Zeisberger, "History of the North American Indians," 86; Lender and Martin, *Citizen Soldier*, 82.

73. William Henry, who was taken captive in 1755 and spent six years and seven months among the Senecas, recorded this story. He mistakenly refers to the Seneca headman as "Old Canassatego," who was in fact a well-known Onondaga headman who died in 1754. *Account of the Captivity of William Henry* (Boston, 1766; New York: Garland Publishing, 1977). Quotes are from pp. 2–3.

74. For another example of an Iroquois narrative of punishments meted out by the Great Spirit, see "Conrad Weiser's Journal," 22.

75. Sachems of Oquaga, January 22, 1770, *SWJP*, 7:348, emphasis added; Proceedings of Sir William, July 9, 1774, *DRCHNY*, 8:476,emphasis added; Zeisberger, "History of the North American Indians," 90, 117–18. Johnson believed that the unscrupulous behavior of colonial traders made a lasting impression on some Iroquois who "begin to act the same part." Johnson to Arthur Lee, November 6, 1771–March 28, 1772, *SWJP*, 12:953.

76. Journal of Indian Affairs, December 15, 1768, *SWJP*, 12:670; "Opinions of George Croghan," 156; Pilkington, *Kirkland Journals*, 14; Murray, *To Do Good to My Indian Brethren*, 62; Account Against the Crown, 1770–73, *SWJP*, 12:801, 897, 898, 1019.

77. "Guy Johnson's Opinions," 321; "Opinions of George Croghan," 156. Zeisberger has observed that "*Formerly* it was the custom to place the pouch, tobacco, pipe, knife, fire material, kettle and hatchet in the grave but this is no longer done." "History of the North American Indians," 89, emphasis added.

78. SWJM, December 21, 1764, 7/3/254.

79. Guldenzopf, "Colonial Transformation," 95; Hendrick Heger et al. to Johnson, May 8, 1772, *SWJP*, 8:466–67; Kelsay, *Joseph Brant*, 116.

80. The Mohawk war loss claims (Effects and Possessions Left Behind in 1777 by the

Mohawk at La Chine) are documented in two attachments sent in a letter by Frederick Haldimand to Secretary of State Lord Sydney, June 21, 1785, CO 42/47/238–52. Guldenzopf has transcribed these documents in the appendix of "Colonial Transformation," 190–207. See chap. 5 for his analysis of these documents. Class stratification developed among other non-Iroquoian Indian communities by the late eighteenth and early nineteenth centuries. Braund, *Deerskins and Duffels*, 130; Claudio Saunt, "Taking Account of Property: Stratification Among the Creek Indians in the Early Nineteenth Century," *WMQ* 57:4 (2000): 733–60; Daniel R. Mandell, "Subaltern Indians, Race and Class in Early America," in *Class Matters*, ed. Middleton and Smith, 49–61. On archaeological evidence regarding the Brant family home and Enders House site, see Guldenzopf, "Colonial Transformation," 104–11; and Jordan, "Archaeology of the Iroquois Restoration," 427–28.

81. "Losses Sustained by the Oneida and Tuscaroras," reel 62:157–65. According to Wonderley, the average Oneida claim was for £30: "By non-native standards of the time, Oneidas were not wealthy." By contrast, the average Mohawk claim (which, unlike those of the Oneidas, also included claims to land) was for £108 and £180 at the Upper and Lower Castles, respectively. "An Oneida Community," 26.

82. Johnson's "private presents" to loyal chiefs and warriors are well documented in the Gage Warrants; see 8:47, 15:32, 17:19, 20:74, 23:129, 24:116, 27:20. For example cited, see *SWJP*, 12:857.

83. Guldenzopf, "Colonial Transformation," chap. 6; Wonderley, "An Oneida Community," 27.

84. Heckewelder quoted in Beauchamp, "Metallic Ornaments," 76; Zeisberger, "History of the Northern American Indians," 86; Halsey, *Journal of Richard Smith*, 149–50; Lender and Martin, *Citizen Soldier*, 90–91.

85. Halsey, *Journal of Richard Smith*, 134, 150.

Chapter 7

1. Samuel Kirkland to Andrew Oliver, November 12, 1770, folder 12, SKP; Pilkington, *Kirkland Journals*, 23. "Silly women" quote taken from John C. Guzzardo, "The Superintendent and the Ministers: The Battle for Oneida Allegiances, 1761–75," *NYH* 7:3 (1976): 282.

2. Johnson to Gage, November 8, 1770, Gage Papers: 97.

3. John Johnston to Johnson, December 1, 1762, *SWJP*, 10:582; Pilkington, *Kirkland Journals*, 84–85.

4. Johnson to Board of Trade, November 16, 1765, *DRCHNY*, 7:777–78; John Stuart to Johnson, June 1, 1766, *SWJP*, 12:98–99; Proceedings of Sir William with the Indians, March 1768, *DRCHNY*, 8:38–53; Theda Perdue, "Cherokee Relations with the Iroquois in the Eighteenth Century," in *Beyond the Covenant Chain*, ed. Merrell and Richter, 144–46. Johnson initially supported the Iroquois-Cherokee conflict as a means to deflect Indian aggression away from colonial society. See Johnson to Stuart, September 17, 1765, CO 5/67/10.

5. Gage to Earl of Hillsborough, January 6, 1770, CO 5/88/26; Johnson to Hillsborough, February 10, 1770, CO 5/71/part 1/73; Hillsborough to Johnson, April 14, 1770, CO 5/71/part 1/81; Johnson to Hillsborough, August 14, 1770, CO 5/71/part 2/93; Proceedings of Sir William with the Indians, July 1770, *DRCHNY*, 8:227–44.

6. Proceedings of Sir William with the Indians, July 20, 1770, *DRCHNY*, 8:231, 235; Johnson to Hillsborough, August 14, 1770, CO 5/71/part 2/93; Merrell, "'Their Very Bones Shall Fight,'" 132.

7. Pilkington, *Kirkland Journals*, 37–38, 24, 46n48.

8. Namias, *Narrative of the Life of Mary Jemison*, 96; Lt. Col. John Cadwell quoted in Paul L. Stevens, *A King's Colonel at Niagara, 1774–1776: Lt. Col. John Cadwell and the Beginnings of the American Revolution on the New York Frontier* (Youngstown, N.Y.: Old Fort Niagara Association, 1987), 28.

9. Fowler to Wheelock, June 24, 1765, and May 28, 1767, in *The Letters of Eleazar Wheelock's Indians*, ed. James Dow McCallum (Hanover, N.H.: Dartmouth College Publications, 1932), 96, 110. On the presence of Indian missionaries among the Oneidas, see Love, *Samson Occom and the Christian Indians of New England*, chaps. 5–6; and Murray, *To Do Good to My Indian Brethren*.

10. Pilkington, *Kirkland Journals*, 70, 83, 95; Kirkland to Wheelock, October 9, 1770, SKP; Kirkland to Dr. Rodgers, June 4, 1771, SKP. For a discussion of Kirkland's work among the Oneidas, see Guzzardo, "The Superintendent and the Ministers"; Stephen Valone, "Samuel Kirkland, Iroquois Missions, and the Land, 1764–1774," *American Presbyterian* 65:3 (1987): 187–94; and Ronda, "Reverend Samuel Kirkland and the Oneida Indians," 23–29.

11. Algonquian men of New England made similar adjustments to their masculine identities. See R. Todd Romero, "'Ranging Foresters' and 'Women-Like Men': Physical Accomplishment, Spiritual Power, and Indian Masculinity in Early-Seventeenth-Century New England," *Ethnohistory* 53:2 (2006): 281–329; and David Silverman, "The Impact of Indentured Servitude on the Society and Culture of Southern New England Indians, 1680–1810," *New England Quarterly* 74:4 (2001): 650–51.

12. On the connections between wage employment and Mohawk notions of masculinity in a nineteenth- and early twentieth-century context, see David Blanchard, "High Steel! The Kahnawake Mohawk and the High Construction Trade," *Journal of Ethnic Studies* 11:2 (1983): 41–60; Bruce Katzer, "The Caughnawaga Mohawks: The Other Side of Ironwork," *Journal of Ethnic Studies* 15:4 (1988): 39–55; and Arthur C. Einhorn, "Warriors of the Sky: The Iroquois Iron Workers," *European Review of Native American Studies* 13:1 (1999): 25–34.

13. Effects and Possessions Left Behind in 1777 by the Mohawk at La Chine, CO 42/47/238–52; Account Book of unidentified Mohawk Valley Indian Trader, fols. 28, 59, 60; Wonderley, "An Oneida Community," 25. On Johnson's gifts of livestock to men as well as purchases from them, see *SWJP*, 2:626, 9:647, 648, 12:666, 667. Likewise, New England Indians incorporated livestock in culturally familiar ways. See David J. Silverman, "'We chuse to be bounded': Native American Animal Husbandry in Colonial New

England," *WMQ* 60:3 (2003): 511–48; and Virginia DeJohn Anderson, "King Philip's Herds: Indians, Colonists, and the Problem of Livestock in Early New England," *WMQ* 51:4 (1994): 601–24.

14. Pilkington, *Kirkland Journals*, 83–84, 85; Speech from the chiefs of the Oneidas to Earl of Dunmore, December 31, 1770, in *Iroquois Indians*, ed. Jennings et al., reel 30; Inglis, "Memorial Concerning the Iroquois," 4:665.

15. Hart, "'For the Good of Our Souls,'" 226–35. Kirkland's popularity among the Oneidas was due in part to his ability to dispense goods among the needy; see Pilkington, *Kirkland Journals*, 59, 70, 71, 72.

16. Wheelock to Johnson, July 4, 1766, *DHNY*, 4:231; Johnson to Wheelock, August 8, 1766, *SWJP*, 5:343–44; Isabel T. Kelsay, "Tekawiroñte," *DCB* 4 (1979): 731; Halsey, *Journal of Richard Smith*, 113. On the success and mainly failures of Wheelock's missionary efforts, see Axtell, "Dr. Wheelock and the Iroquois"; and Hart, "For the Good of Our Souls," 275–83.

17. Pilkington, *Kirkland Journals*, 70, 79; Stuart to Rev. Worthy Sir, July 20, 1772, in the *Records of the Society for the Propagation of the Gospel in Foreign Parts* (hereafter *SPG*), *Letter Books*, ser. B, part II, microfilm (London: Micro Methods, 1964), no. 199, fols. 686–87; Minutes of SPG Meeting, April 16, 1773, *S.P.G, The Journals*, 50 vols., microfilm (London: Micro Methods, 1964), 19:407; Hart, "For the Good of Our Souls," 299–300n69.

18. Eleazar Wheelock, *A Plain and Faithful Narrative of the Original Design, Rise, Progress and Present State of the Indian Charity School at Lebanon, in Connecticut* (Boston, 1763), 40; Wheelock to Andrew Gifford, February 24, 1763, in *Letters of Wheelock's Indians*, ed. McCallum, 70; Johnson to Board of Trade, November 13, 1763, *DRCHNY*, 7:580; Hart, "For the Good of Our Souls," 247–50, 279–81. Brant biographies include William L. Stone, *Life of Joseph Brant, Thayendanegea*, 2 vols. (1838; Albany, N.Y.: Munsel, 1865); and Kelsay, *Joseph Brant*.

19. Kelsay, *Joseph Brant*, 113–17; Halsey, *Journal of Richard Smith*, 113ff, 126 (quote); Effects and Possessions Left Behind in 1777 by the Mohawk at La Chine, 206; entries for November 14, 1772, September 3, 1773, and July 26, 1774 in Daniel Campbell [Sr.], Account Book, 1772–99, box 20, Campbell Family Papers, NYSL. Kelsay estimates that between January 1769 and May 1773, Joseph charged nearly £150 worth of goods at Robert Adem's store in Johnstown (p. 116); Guldenzopf, "Colonial Transformation," 95–96, 98, 102–29; Richter, "Stratification and Class in Eastern Native America," 45–47.

20. Namias, *Narrative of the Life of Mary Jemison*, 84.

21. Conference held at Lancaster, August 23 and 27, 1762, *MPCP*, 8:756, 770; SWJM, March 4, 1767, 7/4/436. See also Congress at Fort Stanwix, October 20, 1768, *SWJP*, 12:625.

22. SWJM, March 10, 1763, 6/4/371; Account Book of unidentified Mohawk Valley Indian Trader, fols. 10, 12.

23. SWJM, March 10, 1763, 6/4/372; Halsey, *Journal of Richard Smith*, 137; Lender and Martin, *Citizen Soldier*, 77; "Journal of Warren Johnson," 255; Fowler to Whee-

lock, December 2, 1766, in *Letters of Wheelock's Indians*, ed. McCallum, 105–6. On the increased market value and collectablility of Indian handicrafts in the eighteenth century, see Wanda Burch, "Sir William Johnson's Cabinet of Curiosities," *NYH* 71:3 (1990): 261–82.

24. Sally Ainse was also known as Sarah Monteurs, Montieres, and Montour. Standard works on her include John Clarke, "Ainse, Sarah," *DCB* 6 (1987): 7–9; and Tim Brisco, "Sallee Ainse, 1728–1823," in *Aboriginal People and the Fur Trade*, ed. Johnston, 228–29. See also Agnew, "Silent Partners," chap. 4; Milo M. Quaife, ed., *The John Askin Papers*, 2 vols. (Detroit: Municipal Institutions, Public Library, 1928), 1:194. Regarding Ainse's ancestry, Kirkland described her as "a half sister of skenandoes, one of the Oneida Chiefs." Pilkington, *Kirkland Journals*, 34. Historian James H. Merrell suggests that she was related to the Conoy tribe in "'The Cast of His Countenance': Reading Andrew Montour," in *Through a Glass Darkly: Reflections on Personal Identity in Early America*, ed. Ronald Hoffman et al. (Chapel Hill: University of North Carolina Press, 1997), 25n27.

25. Unidentified Account Book, Schenectady, April 7, 1756–July 23, 1764, box 18, Campbell Family Papers, NYSL; Unidentified Account Book, 1761–65, item 2, box 17, Campbell Family Papers, NYSL. For her traffic in ginseng, see account entry for May 8, 1766, in Campbell and Andrews Cash/Account Book, 1765–66, item 2, box 19, Campbell Family Papers, NYSL. For references to her involvement in the rum trade, see *SWJP*, 3:160, 997, 12:357.

26. Indian Conference, August 12, 1762, *SWJP*, 10:481; Brisco, "Sallee Ainse," 228; Agnew, "Silent Partners," 198–200. On Ainse's struggles to maintain her property in the post-Revolutionary era, see Taylor, *The Divided Ground*, epilogue.

27. Older works that explore the impact of market economy integration on native gender relations stress female subordination. See Mary C. Wright, "Economic Development and Native American Women in the Early Nineteenth Century," *American Quarterly* 33:5 (1981): 525–36; and Carol Devens, *Countering Colonization: Native American Women and the Great Lakes Missions, 1630–1900* (Berkeley: University of California Press, 1992). Recent studies provide a more nuanced reading. See Carson, "Native Americans, the Market Revolution, and Cultural Change"; Saunt, *A New Order of Things*, chap. 6; and James Taylor Carson, "Dollars Never Failed to Melt Their Hearts: Native Women and the Market Revolution," in *Neither Lady Nor Slave: Working Women of the Old South*, ed. Susanna Delfino and Michele Gillespie (Chapel Hill: University of North Carolina Press, 2002), 15–33.

28. Extracts from Account Book of John Butler, September 14, 1765, *SWJP*, 13:511; John Loney's Account, 1770, *SWJP*, 7:1056. At least nine Iroquois women are listed as individual account holders in the Account Book of unidentified Mohawk Valley Indian Trader. See fols. 3, 10, 12, 16, 27, 35, 38, 46, 79, 89, 103, 109b.

29. For works that document the evolution of Iroquois housing structures, see Richter, *Ordeal of the Longhouse*, 260–62; and Jordan, "Archaeology of the Iroquois Restoration," chap. 8.

30. Halsey, *Journal of Richard Smith*, 131–32; Bourdin and Williams, "Crèvecoeur on the Susquehanna," 581; Frederick Cook, ed., *Journals of the Military Expedition of Major General John Sullivan* (Auburn, N.Y.: Knapp, Peck and Thomson, 1887), 23.

31. "Losses Sustained by the Oneida and Tuscaroras in consequence of their Attachment to the United States," reel 62, pp. 157–65, Timothy Pickering Papers, Massachusetts Historical Society, Boston; Wonderley, "An Oneida Community," 22–23; Pilkington, *Kirkland Journals*, 83–84, 85; Lender and Martin, *Citizen Soldier*, 66.

32. Doblin and Starna, *Journals of Claus and Weiser*, 35; Johnson to Gage, April 6, 1773, *SWJP*, 8:753; Gage Warrants, 17:91, 20:74, 27:20; Lender and Martin, *Citizen Soldier*, 84–85; 1780s observer [James Cockburn] quoted in Guldenzopf, "Colonial Transformation," 101, see also 46–47, 71–72; Jordan, "Archaeology of the Iroquois Restoration," 427–28; Dean R. Snow, *Mohawk Valley Archaeology: The Sites*, Occasional Papers in Anthropology, no. 23 (University Park, Pa.: Penn State University Press, 1995), 471–86.

33. Grumet, *Historic Contact*, 414; James H. Tuck, *Onondaga Iroquois Prehistory: A Study in Settlement Archaeology* (Syracuse, N.Y.: Syracuse University Press, 1971), 191–95.

34. Webster, *Journal of Jeffrey Amherst*, 217; Recht, "The Role of Fishing in the Iroquois Economy," 26–30.

35. Hendrick's family accounts are detailed in fols. 3, 69, 86b; Canategarie's family accounts are detailed in fols. 36, 61, 90, 107, 108; and Lydia's family accounts are detailed in fols. 46, 51, 54, 67, 73, 87, 105, all in Account Book of unidentified Mohawk Valley Indian Trader. Spouses with their children also turned up to forts to trade; e.g., *SWJP*, 10:93.

36. Paulus Peter's Indian name was also spelled Sagsanowano; see Sivertsen, *Turtles, Wolves and Bears*, 85. Among the Senecas, Captain Edward Pollard, Captain John Abeel (Abail), also known as Cornplanter, and Captain James Stevenson, sons of Seneca women and European men, carried their father's names. Trader account books also list children with their father's name, e.g., Hanse Crine's sons are recorded as "Abraham Crine" and "John Crine" in Account book of unidentified Mohawk Valley Indian Trader, fols. 71, 120, and index page.

37. Wonderley, "An Oneida Community," 25–26, 30.

38. Halsey, *Journal of Richard Smith*, 132, 151, emphasis added; Kelsay, *Joseph Brant*, 114. William N. Fenton has noted that a mixture of matrilocal and patrilocal residence remained the norm in the twentieth century in "Locality as a Basic Factor in the Development of Iroquois Social Structure," in *Symposium on Local Diversity in Iroquois Culture*, ed. Fenton, 43.

39. Fenton, "Structure, Continuity, and Change in the Process of Iroquois Treaty Making," 10–11; idem, "Locality as a Basic Factor," 43; Jordan, "Archaeology of the Iroquois Restoration," 441–42.

40. On the continued importance of clans, see Pilkington, *Kirkland Journals*, 10; and E. P. Chase, ed., *Our Revolutionary Forefathers: The Letters of Francois, Marquis de Barbe-Marbois* (New York: Duffield and Company, 1929), 209.

41. Johnson to Wheelock, November 23, 1764, *SWJP*, 4:598–99, and September 16, 1766, *SWJP*, 12:183; Pilkington, *Kirkland Journals*, 130.

42. Kelsay, *Joseph Brant*, 114–15. Guldenzopf, "Colonial Transformation," 98. Kelsay notes that references to Brant Canagaranduncka in the *SWJP* cease after 1764 (670n15).

43. SWJM, September 13 and December 5, 1763, 6/5/527, 7/1/17–18. See also SWJM, October 21, 1763, 7/1/3, and February 4, 16, 1764, 7/1/65, 70.

44. SWJM, March 4, 1761, 6/1/15; Meeting with Canajoharies, March 10, 1763, *SWJP*, 4:50. Women demonstrated their continued interest in matters of land by including their signatures on petitions and by continuing to be present at land surveys and land related meetings. See *SWJP*, 8:20–22, 4:233, 6:6; and *DRCHNY*, 7:728, 729.

45. SWJM, July 11, 1763, 6/4/454, and March 8, 1764, 7/1/86; Journal of Indian Transactions at Niagara, July 2–September 24, 1767, *DHNY*, 4:504; Brown to Johnson, September 16, 1771, *SWJP*, 8:255; William H. Egle, ed., *Notes and Queries, Historical and Genealogical, Chiefly Relating to Interior Pennsylvania*, 3rd ser. (Harrisburg, Pa.: Harrisburg Publishing, 1895), 1:126–27.

46. SWJM, February 7, 1764, 7/1/67. On Johnson's knowledge of the principal women, see *SWJP*, 12:96. Johnson demonstrated his respect for women by paying for their burials (see Gage Warrants 17:91, *SWJP*, 12:897, 900) and providing for widows of his allies. See Gage Warrants 23:129, 27:20; and *SWJP*, 12:170, 897, 945, 999, 1019. Johnson continued to make use of Iroquois women, such as when he sent a message to the Mohawks "by Zacharia's Wife." See *SWJP*, 10:799. Head women requested gifts like strouds and chocolate from Johnson. See *SWJP*, 7:379; and *DHNY*, 4:312.

47. SWJM, May 19, 1768, 8/1/49–50; Instructions to John Butler, May 30, 1764, *SWJP*, 13:327; "Guy Johnson's Opinions," 321; Journal of Sir William, June 15, 1756, *DRCHNY*, 7:133.

48. Canajoharie Indians to Sir William Johnson, February 25, 1760, *DRCHNY*, 7:434.

49. Fenton, *Great Law of the Longhouse*, 493–95, 737–42. Guldenzopf persuasively demonstrates the emergence of a new wealthy elite who challenged the traditional power base of hereditary chiefs in "Colonial Transformation," chap. 6. Wonderley suggests that a similar phenomenon may have occurred among the Oneidas in "An Oneida Community," 27.

50. Johnson to Gage, November 8, 1770, Gage Papers: 97; Proceedings of Sir William, July 9, 1774, *DRCHNY*, 8:476; Journal of Indian Affairs, February 18, 1771, *SWJP*, 12:779.

51. Conference held at Lancaster, August 19, 1762, *MPCP*, 8:747; Indian Proceedings, April 23, 1762, *SWJP*, 3:698; Pilkington, *Kirkland Journals*, 67, 57. Other Europeans made similar observations; see Zeisberger, "History of the North American Indians," 76–77; and "Guy Johnson's Opinions," 321.

52. SWJM, February 4, 1764, 7/1/65–66; Proceedings of Sir William, July 18, 1770, *DRCHNY*, 8:230.

53. For works that explore the rise of Indian-hating in these regions during the 1760s and beyond, see Daniel K. Richter, *Facing East from Indian Country: A Native History of Early America* (Cambridge, Mass.: Harvard University Press, 2001), chap. 6; Dowd, *War Under Heaven*, chap. 6; Merritt, *At the Crossroads*, chap. 8; Pencak and Richter, *Friends and Enemies in Penn's Woods*; and Patrick Griffin, *American Leviathan: Empire, Nation, and Revolutionary Frontier* (New York: Hill & Wang, 2007).

54. Johnson to Secretary Conway, June 28, 1766, *DRCHNY*, 7:835; Johnson to Board of Trade, December 26, 1764, *DRCHNY*, 7:689; John Penn to Gage, December 31, 1763, Gage Papers: 11. The classic study on the Paxton Boys is Alden T. Vaughan, "Frontier Banditti and the Indians: The Paxton Boys' Legacy, 1763–1775," *Pennsylvania History* 5 (1984): 1–29. For a more recent interpretation, see Merritt, *At the Crossroads*, 285–94.

55. Roxann Wheeler, *The Complexion of Race: Categories of Difference in Eighteenth-Century British Culture* (Philadelphia: University of Pennsylvania Press, 2000); Alexander O. Bouton, "The American Paradox: Jeffersonian Equality and Racial Science," *American Quarterly* 47:3 (1995): 467–92; Bruce Dain, *A Hideous Monster of the Mind: American Race Theory in the Early Republic* (Cambridge, Mass.: Harvard University Press, 2002).

56. Gage to the Earl of Shelbourne, October 10, 1767, in *The Correspondence of General Thomas Gage with the Secretaries of State and with the War Office and the Treasury, 1763–1775*, 2 vols., ed. Clarence E. Carter (New York: Archon Books, 1969), 1:152; Johnson to Conway, June 28, 1766, *DRCHNY*, 7:836.

57. Vaughan, "Frontier Banditti," 8; Deposition of Lemuel Barrit, March 6, 1766, *SWJP*, 5:52–54; Penn to Johnson, March 11, 1766, *SWJP*, 12:41; Johnson to Croghan, March 28, 1766, *SWJP*, 5:119.

58. SWJM, May 24, 1766, 7/4/377 (first quote); Johnson to Gage, April 17, 1760, Gage Papers: 50 (second quote); Papers Relative to the Murder of an Oneida Indian, April 3–15, 1766, *SWJP*, 5:169–74; William Franklin to Johnson, April 15, 1766, *SWJP*, 12:72–73; Johnson to Henry Moore, April 21, 1766, *SWJP*, 5:194; New Jersey Council Proceedings, December 11, 1766, *SWJP*, 5:418–22.

59. James Tilghman to Johnson, July 20, 1769, *SWJP*, 7:62–64; Gage Warrants, 24:116; Vaughan, "Frontier Banditti," 12; Johnson to Frederick Haldimand, June 9, 1774, Add Mss 21670, fol. 147; Johnson to Dartmouth, June 20, 1774, CO/5/75/139; Johnson to Gage, July 4, 1774, Gage Papers: 119. The Cresap murders and Dunmore's War are discussed in McConnell, *A Country Between*, 268–79; and Hinderaker, *Elusive Empires*, 170–75.

60. Because Indian-hating was so intense on the Pennsylvania frontier, some scholars have offered the New York frontier as a point of contrast, thereby overstating themes of Indian-colonial harmony in this region. See Preston, "Texture of Contact," chap. 4.

61. Declaration of Sachems, November 24, 1762, *SWJP*, 10:571; Journal of Indian Affairs, February 14, 1767, *SWJP*, 12:272–73.

62. SWJM, January 28, 1762, 6/2/154–55; David Van Der Heyden to Johnson, February 8, 1763, *SWJP*, 4:43–44; Johnson to Gage, December 23, 1763, Gage Papers: 11; Johnson to Colden, August 23, 1764, *SWJP*, 4:514.

63. SWJM, March 4, 1767, 7/4/436, and June 28 and July 20, 1767, 7/4/441–42; Johnson's Account with the Crown, December 22, 1773, *SWJP*, 8:1093. On Indians being taken to England, see *SWJP*, 8:935, 938, 970, 1160.

64. Inglis, "Memorial Concerning the Iroquois," 4:671, 672.

65. Calloway, *The American Revolution in Indian Country*, chap. 4; Halsey, *The Old New York Frontier*, 27–29.

66. In a similar vein, Merritt argues that some Indians in Pennsylvania by 1763 "went to great lengths to strip themselves of the remnants of savagism, to take on the external markings of good Indians," but also notes that "giving up the outward trappings of Indianness did not guarantee that native Americans would be widely accepted as 'white People.'" *At the Crossroads*, 280–81.

67. Johnson to Thomas Wharton, September 12, 1769, *SWJP*, 7:167. For works that document how Indians began to racialize Euro-Americans in this period, see Richter, *Facing East From Indian Country*, chap. 6; Kirsten Fischer, *Suspect Relations: Sex, Race, and Resistance in Colonial North Carolina* (Ithaca, N.Y.: Cornell University Press, 2002), 88–90; and Merritt, *At the Crossroads*, chap. 8.

68. Namias, *Narrative of the Life of Mary Jemison*, 160. On efforts to evaluate Jemison's ethnic identity, see Karen Oakes, "'We Planted, Tended and Harvested Our Corn': Gender, Ethnicity and Transculturation in *A Narrative of the Life of Mrs. Mary Jemison*," *Women and Language* 18:1 (1995): 45–51; Hilary E. Wyss, "Captivity and Conversion: William Apess, Mary Jemison and Narratives of Racial Identity," *AIQ* 23:3–4 (1999): 63–82. On the presence of "Indianized" captives among the Senecas, see *SWJP*, 4:500, 581, 10:564, 11:812; and Pilkington, *Kirkland Journals*, 15–17.

69. Johnson to Colden, January 12, 1764, *SWJP*, 4:287; Johnson to Gage, January 12 and 20, 1764, Gage Papers: 12; Gage to Johnson, January 31, 1764, Gage Papers: 13; Johnson to Gage, February 19, 1764, Gage Papers: 14.

70. Information Concerning White Prisoners, [July 1764], *SWJP*, 4:498. On the blacksmithing skills of captives, see *Account of the Captivity of William Henry*, 1. Indians living in the Ohio also made nonfamilial use of captives; see Matthew C. Ward, "Redeeming the Captives: Pennsylvania Captives Among the Ohio Indians, 1755–1765," *PMHB* 125:3 (2001): 162, 176–78.

71. Johnson to Gage, February 19, 1764, Gage Papers: 14.

72. Johnson to Frederick Haldimand, February 7, 1774, Add Mss 21670, fol. 113; Haldimand to Johnson, February 10, 1774, Add Mss 21670, fol. 115; Johnson to Haldimand, May 5, 1774, Add Mss 21670, fol. 139.

73. Jean Baptiste De Couagne, May 26, 1763, *SWJP*, 10:684; News from the Chenussios, July 21, 1764, *SWJP*, 4:492; Information Concerning White Prisoners, [July 1764], *SWJP*, 4:495–96, 498; Johnson to Gage, June 28, 1765, Gage Papers: 38; Gage to Johnson, July 8, 1765, Gage Papers: 39.

74. They received forty shillings per deserter. Jean Baptiste De Couagne to Johnson, December 6, 1762, *SWJP*, 3:957–8.

75. On the presence of interracial marriage and offspring, see *SWJP*, 4:496, 11:817.

For a study that historicizes interracial unions, see Fischer, *Suspect Relations*, chap. 2. The sociopolitical context influenced the nature and meaning of interracial relationships. See Albert L. Hurtado, "When Strangers Met: Sex and Gender on Three Frontiers," in *Writing the Range: Race, Class, and Culture in the Women's West*, ed. Elizabeth Jameson and Susan Armitage (Norman: University of Oklahoma Press, 1997), 122–42.

76. Niagara and Detroit Proceedings, July 21, 1761, *SWJP*, 3:444; Webster, *Journal of Jeffrey Amherst*, 219; James Stevenson to Johnson, first letter dated May 18, 1770, *SWJP*, 7:681.

77. See the following letters from Stevenson to Johnson: October 19, 1769, *SWJP*, 7:223; first letter dated May 18, 1770, *SWJP*, 7:681–82; second letter dated May 18, 1770, *SWJP*, 7:683–84; September 18, 1770, *SWJP*, 7:907–8; and May 8, 1772, *SWJP*, 8:470.

78. Stevenson to Johnson, March 13, 1771, *SWJP*, 8:16, and April 1, 1774, *SWJP*, 8:1108.

79. John Brown to Johnson, August 25, 1771, *SWJP*, 8:235; Bouquet to Johnson, November 15, 1764, *SWJP*, 4:586; Johnson to Bouquet, December 17, 1764, *SWJP*, 4:620. For an account of Bouquet's campaign to redeem English captives and their offspring, see Paul K. Adams, "Colonel Bouquet's Ohio Expedition in 1764," *Pennsylvania History* 40:2 (1973): 139–48.

80. Parker, "Notes on the Ancestry of Cornplanter," 14; Namias, *Narrative of the Life of Mary Jemison*, 160.

81. Brown to Johnson, August 25, 1771, *SWJP*, 8:235; De Couagne to Johnson, November 11, 1763, *SWJP*, 10:922.

82. Stevenson to Johnson, March 31, 1774, *SWJP*, 8:1103; see also Stevenson to Johnson, May 8, 1772 and December 25, 1773, *SWJP*, 8:469, 974. On the acculturation of Brant, see Green, "Molly Brant, Catherine Brant, and Their Daughters."

83. Stevenson Family Genealogy, ca. 1862, Mss A64–214, Buffalo and Erie County Historical Society, New York; "Know all men by these present that whereas James Stevenson late of London . . . May 3, 1796," Ayer MS 832, Newberry Library, Chicago; William C. Bryant, "The Brave's Rest; or, The Old Seneca Missionary Cemetery," *Buffalo Historical Society Publications* 1 (1879): 87.

84. Charles E. Hunter, "The Delaware Nativist Revival of the Mid-Eighteenth Century," *Ethnohistory* 18:1 (1971): 39–49; Duane Champagne, "The Delaware Revitalization Movement of the Early 1760s: A Suggested Reinterpretation," *AIQ* 12:2 (1988): 107–26; Dowd, *A Spirited Resistance*, chap. 2; Alfred A. Cave, "The Delaware Prophet Neolin: A Reappraisal," *Ethnohistory* 46:2 (1999): 265–90.

85. Namias, *Narrative of the Life of Mary Jemison*, 96–97.

86. SWJM, July 1761, January 1762, and September 9, 1762, 6/1/47, 6/2/150, 6/3/299–300.

87. Johnson to Charles Inglis, April 26, 1770, *SWJP*, 7:597; Johnson to Arthur Lee, November 6, 1771–March 28, 1772, *SWJP*, 12:955. See also Zeisberger, "History of the North American Indians," 121–22.

88. Pilkington, *Kirkland Journals*, 37, 45n29; Conover, *Sayenqueraghta*.

89. Pilkington, *Kirkland Journals*, 23–25.

90. Ferrell Wade and C. Keiuser to Johnson, June 3, 1772, *SWJP*, 8:508; Howard Peckham, ed., *George Croghan's Journal* (Ann Arbor: University of Michigan Press, 1939), 23–24; Journal of Indian Affairs, September 10, 1767, *SWJP*, 12:363; Journal of Alexander McKee, [1769], *SWJP*, 7:184–85; Johnson to Gage, July 31, 1770, *SWJP*, 7:817, and August 9, 1771, Gage Papers: 105; Proceedings of Sir William, July 16, 1771, *DRCHNY*, 8:282–83; Johnson to Hillsborough, April 4, 1771, *DRCHNY*, 8:291; Croghan to Johnson, May 10, 1770, *SWJP*, 7:651–53; Johnson to Gage, April 18, 1771, Gage Papers: 102. Shawnee efforts to construct a pan-Indian alliance are detailed in McConnell, *A Country Between*, 264–68; White, *The Middle Ground*, 354–56; and Woody Holton, *Forced Founders: Indians, Debtors, Slaves and the Making of the American Revolution in Virginia* (Chapel Hill: North Carolina Press, 1999), 13–26, 31.

Conclusion

1 M. B. Pierce, *Address on the present Condition and Prospects of the Aboriginal Inhabitants of North America, with particular reference to the Seneca Nation* (Philadelphia: J. Richards Printer, 1839), 15, 11, 16, 17. For background on Pierce, see H. A. Vernon, "Maris Bryant Pierce: The Making of a Seneca Leader," in *Indian Lives: Essays on Nineteenth and Twentieth Century Native American Leaders*, ed. L. G. Moses and Raymond Wilson (Albuquerque: University of New Mexico Press, 1985), 17–42. On Iroquois removal, see Laurence M. Hauptman, *Conspiracy of Interests: Iroquois Dispossession and the Rise of New York State* (Syracuse, N.Y.: Syracuse University Press, 2001).

Index

Acknowledgments

Writing this book felt akin to running a marathon: seemingly unending, utterly exhausting, but ultimately satisfying. Now that the finish line is finally in view, I wish to thank the institutions, colleagues, friends, and family members who through their guidance and support helped keep me and this project on track.

I was fortunate enough to be the recipient of numerous grants and fellowships. The University of Sussex awarded me the Marcus Cunliffe bursary, which, alongside a British Association for American Studies travel grant, allowed me to carry out research at the Library of Congress in Washington, D.C. I also received a Jacob M. Price Visiting Research Fellowship from the William L. Clements Library at the University of Michigan. I wish to give special thanks to the staff at the library for being so amenable during my stay. I benefited enormously from becoming a research fellow at the Newberry Library in Chicago. In addition to giving me access to the library's magnificent collection, the fellowship afforded the time and intellectual space needed to reenvision my work. Substantial research was also conducted at the British Library and Public Records Office in London, and I thank the staff at both places for their assistance. I am also obliged to the School of Humanities at King's College London, which provided travel grants and two sabbaticals, thus enabling me to make significant headway in my work. Through their funding I was able to visit the New-York Historical Society and New York State Archives. I am extremely indebted to the Arts and Humanities Research Board for awarding me a much needed research leave grant. Through their generous assistance I was able to complete my manuscript.

Numerous individuals championed me along the way, greatly enriching my work. I extend my gratitude to Woody Holton, Timothy Shannon, Ann M. Little, Jennifer Spear, Jane T. Merritt, and Billy Smith, all of whom read and commented on parts of my work. George R. Hamell at the New York State Archives patiently answered my many queries. Susan Sleeper-Smith graciously took an interest in my book and gave tremendous advice. I am extremely appreciative of Peter Way, my longtime mentor and friend. He challenged, inspired, and encouraged me, proving to be my most resourceful critic and enduring supporter. I owe a big part of this book to him. I would also like to extend thanks to Dan Richter, who so kindly read this book while it was in its early stages. Over the years he has afforded immeasurable support, supplying references, inviting me to present at the McNeil Center for Early American Studies, and appraising drafts. I am deeply touched by his level of generosity and time.

I wish to thank the staff at the University of Pennsylvania Press for their efficiency and professionalism. I am particularly grateful to Bob Lockhart, who will never know how much I was comforted by his telephone call when he told me that I was almost there. I wish also to acknowledge the various presses that granted permission to publish earlier versions of parts of several chapters. Sections from Chapter 4 draw upon material from Gail D. Danvers, "Gendered Encounters: Warriors, Women, and William Johnson," *Journal of American Studies* 35:2 (2001): 187–202, © Cambridge University Press. Portions from Chapters 3 and 6 first appeared in Gail D. MacLeitch, " 'Red Labor': Iroquois Participation in the Atlantic Economy," *Labor: Studies of Working-Class History of the Americas* 1:4 (2004): 71–92, © Duke University Press. Segments from Chapter 2 are published in Gail D. MacLeitch, "Sir William Johnson (1740s): English Emissary to the Iroquois," in *The Human Tradition in the Atlantic World, 1500–1850*, ed. Karen Racine and Beatriz Gallotti Mamigonian (Wilmington, Del.: Scholarly Resources Press, 2011).

Finally, my thanks go to my family, notably my parents, Ann and Roland, for their love and support and my in-laws, Lucy and Larry, particularly Lucy, who always encouraged me to finish this book and provided critical child care in the summer of 2008. My husband and best friend, Nate, who has been with me since this book's inception, is no doubt more relieved than I am that it is finally written. Thanks for your belief in me and for your patience; William Johnson has left the house! I want also to acknowledge my son Daniel, who in his enthusiasm to climb up on my desk and draw on copies of the manuscript reminded me not to take this all too seriously, and my newest born, Joshua, whose impending birth provided me with the final impetus to get this work done. I hope you guys read this one day.